PURLEY IN OLD IMAGES

Purley on Thames
Berkshire

Edited by
Catherine Sampson

PROJECT PURLEY
Local History Society

Published by Goosecroft Publications

Goosecroft Publications
5 Cecil Aldin Drive
Purley on Thames
Berkshire, RG31 6YP
England

First Published 2010

ISBN 978-0-9566341-0-8

Printed and bound in Great Britain by
CPI Antony Rowe, Chippenham and Eastbourne

Foreword

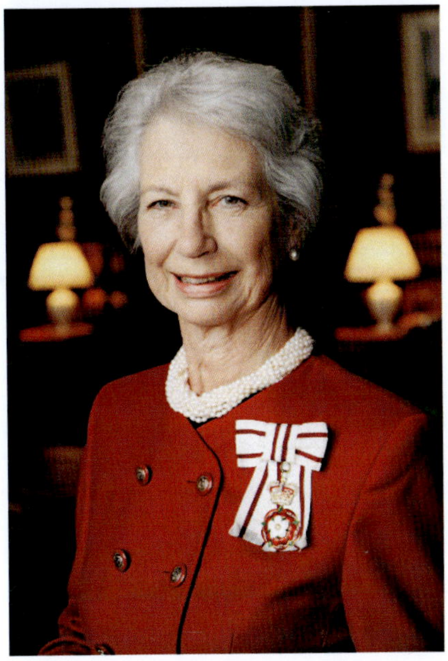

History is not just about dates and major events; it is primarily about people – who they were, what they did and how they lived. One of the privileges of serving as Lord Lieutenant is to meet so many people across Berkshire who appreciate the County's history and who seek to document and preserve the past.

This book has been written and compiled by Project Purley. It draws together a wide range of images from extensive archives in our local museums and libraries and also from the collections and albums of many private individuals. Together these photographs tell a powerful story of how a small and rural Berkshire village has developed over more than 150 years.

Old images are a very powerful medium for establishing community identity and recording history. Their impact is immediate and they can trigger many memories for those who can remember how things used to be. But they can also remind the younger generation of the enormous changes that have occurred and encourage them to preserve our present for future generations before that too vanishes into history.

It is very heartening to see Project Purley collect and describe so many images. They are presented in a way that will appeal to those who know or knew the village and also to people contemplating a move to Purley, helping them to become a vital part of that community.

It gives me great pleasure to introduce this book. 'Purley in Old Images' makes a major contribution towards the store of knowledge of our County and Project Purley is to be congratulated on such a fine effort.

Mary Bayliss.

The Hon. Mrs Bayliss
Lord Lieutenant of the Royal County of Berkshire

About Project Purley

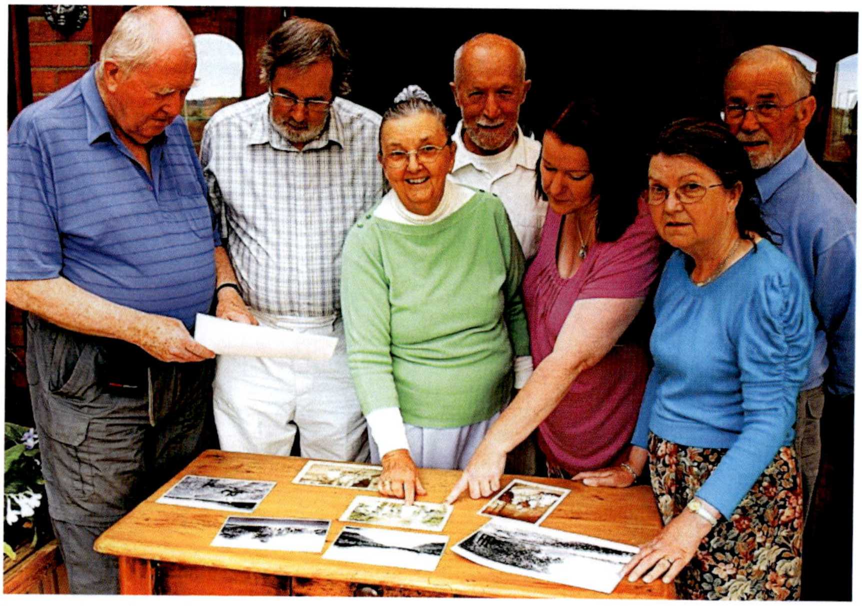

Preparing 'Purley in Old Images'

Project Purley, founded in 1982, is the local history society of Purley on Thames. A regular programme of monthly meetings is held at The Barn in the Goosecroft Recreational Ground, off Beech Road, including a variety of visits and activities.

A number of Project Purley's members are involved in research and regularly contribute articles to their thrice-yearly journal together with other publications including the Purley Parish News. They also raise monies for local charities and each year invite a professional theatre company to perform in The Barn for a local cause.

Since its formation Project Purley has organised or contributed to many exhibitions including: The Opening of The Barn in 1995, A Wilder Celebration Exhibition in 1997, Project Purley Millennium Exhibition in 2000, The Golden Jubilee Celebratory Exhibition in 2002, St Mary the Virgin Church Exhibition in 2006 and Purley on Thames Village Celebration in 2008.

Details of all Project Purley publications can be found on their website www.project-purley.eu.

Preface

Purley has a long association with photographers, both professional and amateur, who have been drawn to the village largely by the majesty of the river and lock. In addition, generations of Purley residents have captured on film events, scenes and people.

We are grateful to the Museum of English Rural Life and Images and Voices, Oxfordshire County Council for permission to use photographs by Phillip Osborne Collier, Eric Guy, the Dann-Lewis Studio and Henry Taunt. We also thank Reading Museum (Reading Borough Council), Judges Postcards Ltd, the Imperial War Museum and The Reading Chronicle for their kind permission to use images.

We are particularly indebted to the following individuals; Peter Fullerton and Henry Scutt for lending the private albums of the Storer and Wilder families respectively, Ian Nash, whose photographs encompass life in the village 1940–1970 and John Chapman and Rita Denman who have shared their personal photograph collections. We also wish to thank the very many current and former residents, who over many years have given us copies of photographs. Unfortunately it has not been possible to trace the owners of all of the photographs and we apologise if we have used any material without permission or due acknowledgement.

The historical introductions within this book, together with many of the captions, have been drawn largely from extensive research carried out by John Chapman, Jean Debney and Rita Denman. The layout of this book and its cover have been designed by Ben Viljoen. I also wish to thank Ann Betts, Martin Bishop, Cliff Debney, David Downs and Peter Perugia for the part they have played in bringing this book together.

Thank you to everyone who has been involved in helping to identify the faces in the pictures. We apologise for any misidentifications or misspelt names in this book and welcome any corrections.

To all of the above and anyone else I may have inadvertently missed, I express my gratitude.

Catherine Sampson
Project Purley

Front cover: *A view of Purley Village from the east probably taken in the 1950s; Ivy Cottage on the right of the image dates from the 1600s. (Also appears as 4.11 in Chapter 4)*

Back Cover: *A photograph of Mapledurham Lock taken in 1885 by the Oxfordshire photographer Henry Taunt. The lock-keeper operating the gates is almost certainly R H Carter who was the keeper at Mapledurham 1882-1887.*

Sweete Themmes! runne softly, till I end my Song.

Prothalamion, Edmund Spencer (c.1522-1599)

F*orget the spreading of the hideous town;*
Think rather of the pack-horse on the down,
The clear Thames bordered by its gardens green.

The Earthly Paradise, William Morris (1834-1896)

Contents

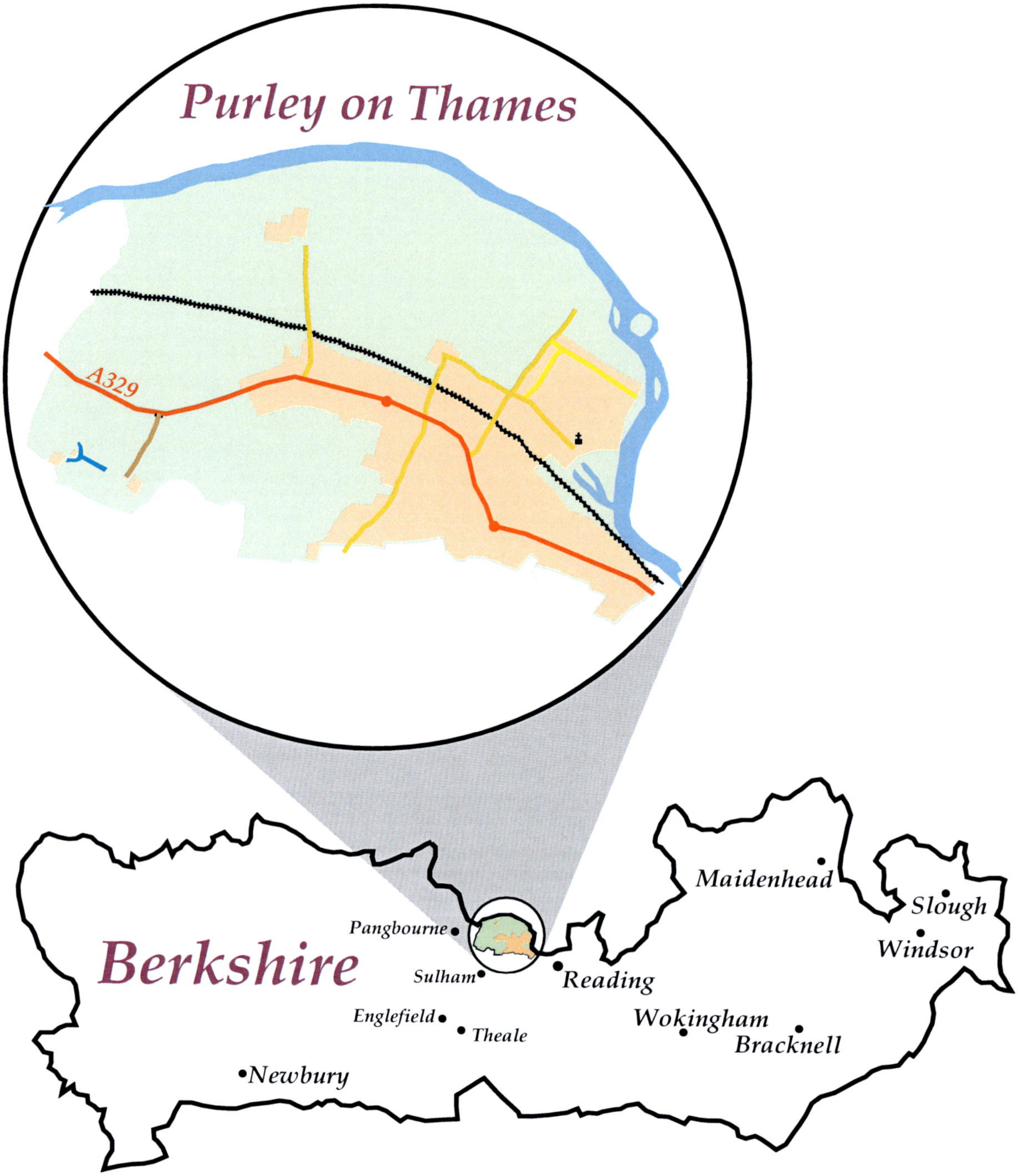
Purley on Thames
A329
Berkshire
Pangbourne
Sulham
Englefield
Theale
Newbury
Reading
Maidenhead
Slough
Windsor
Wokingham
Bracknell

1 A Brief History of Purley

Purley on Thames, in the Royal County of Berkshire, is a small but historic village nestling in a curve of the River Thames, just to the west of Reading. The name 'Purley' is said to derive from Old English words meaning either a 'wood or clearing frequented by snipe or bittern' or a 'wood or clearing with pear trees'. It is most likely that the village has its origins in the Saxon migrations of the fifth or sixth centuries when travellers on the Thames settled on a dry piece of land within the marshes of the flood plain.

There is some evidence from archaeological finds of prehistoric activity in the local area with finds including Palaeolithic hand axes, Neolithic projectile points and Bronze Age spearheads, one with part of its wooden shaft intact. Some of these, however, were discovered on the river bed during dredging of the silt and so are unlikely to have been in situ. Relatively recently a number of burials, typical of the late Saxon period, were unearthed just outside the old north aisle of the church, shortly before its demolition; more on this later in the chapter on The Church and School, along with an overview of the history of our church.

The earliest known written evidence for the village comes from the beginning of the Norman period in William the Conqueror's Domesday Survey of 1086. In it we can recognise Purley as Porlaa and Porlei.

Purley consisted mostly of three mediaeval manors: Purley Magna (Great Purley), Purley Parva (Little Purley) and part of La Hyde; the latter straddling the border with Sulham and detached portions of Whitchurch. Each had a manor house or farm and cottages in agricultural estates. Estimates suggest that the population of Purley in 1086 was around 80.

These manorial estates created the shape of the village that developed and even today their influence can be seen in the layout of the roads and the development of housing, especially in the twentieth century. Our chapters on The Estates and Big Houses, Development of the Village, Farming and Agriculture and The River Estate give more details about the development of these estates and the village around them.

Over the ensuing centuries Purley, like many ancient villages, was rocked by some of the events which shaped our country as a whole. It is possible that our original church was destroyed in the mid twelfth century by Matilda's army based at

Wallingford, in the anarchy and rioting which characterised her fight with King Stephen for the English throne. Further upheaval occurred during the traumatic religious changes of the 1500s, and the dissolution of Reading Abbey brought about the confiscation of its property in Purley. Later still the Catholic family of Hyde, living in Purley Hall or Hyde Hall as it was then known, were taxed out of their estate for continuing to practice their religion.

Nothing survives to tell us what happened in Purley during the English Civil War although the village and church probably suffered at the hands of both the Royalist and Parliamentarian soldiers who each held Reading at varying times. Soldiers from both sides roamed local villages helping themselves to food, horses and anything else that took their fancy and Purley must have been vulnerable. On the opposite bank of the river, Mapledurham House was attacked and ransacked by the Parliamentarians after Sir Charles Blount fought on the side of the King. The St John family, then lords of the manor of Purley Magna, also supported the Royalists and three of their sons were killed in battle.

After the restoration of the monarchy and the established church in 1660, life in the village settled back down to a familiar pattern as one farming season rolled into the next. It was not until the nineteenth century that events happening locally and nationally started to impact upon this essentially rural way of life. The first changes were to alter the shape and layout of the village.

In 1793 Purley Magna was purchased by Anthony Morris Storer the elder, MP, and around 1800, Purley Park mansion was constructed on the brow of the hill replacing the old manorial farmhouse by the church. A rolling parkland estate was created by enclosing land and diverting further south the turnpike road which ran through the village. The chapter on The Estates and Big Houses contains images of the old and new houses and our chapter on The Church and School shows the impact this enclosure had upon our church. One other possible outcome was the demolition of Purley's only known inn, the Red Lyon, which disappeared around this time.

Equally dramatic in its impact upon the village was the arrival of Brunel's railway, which opened through Purley in 1840. Our chapter on Industry, Commerce and Transport covers this in more detail.

The twentieth century brought a multitude of economic, technological and social changes which began to be reflected in the development of the village. In 1920 Purley Park was sold and was gradually broken up allowing new development to take place.

In the 1930s a large field alongside the River was sold and divided into small camping and caravan plots. This development became known as 'The River Estate' and is the subject of Chapter 8. After the Second World War Purley began to become more desirable as a commuter village. Reading, London and Bristol were all accessible by train and motorway, and builders exploited fields felt to be no longer suitable for agriculture and redeveloped some of the larger properties.

The population increased quickly after the Second World War, having previously been relatively static. In 1676 there was a recorded adult population of 80 in Purley, which by 1801 had grown to 153 including children. By 1946 this had risen to 867 and it is now well over 4,000, even after a significant reduction in the parish area in 1991. It is these people who make and have made Purley the strong community that it is today. We capture just a few of their celebrations and social activities in our final chapter but 'Purley people' are quite rightly at the heart of each chapter.

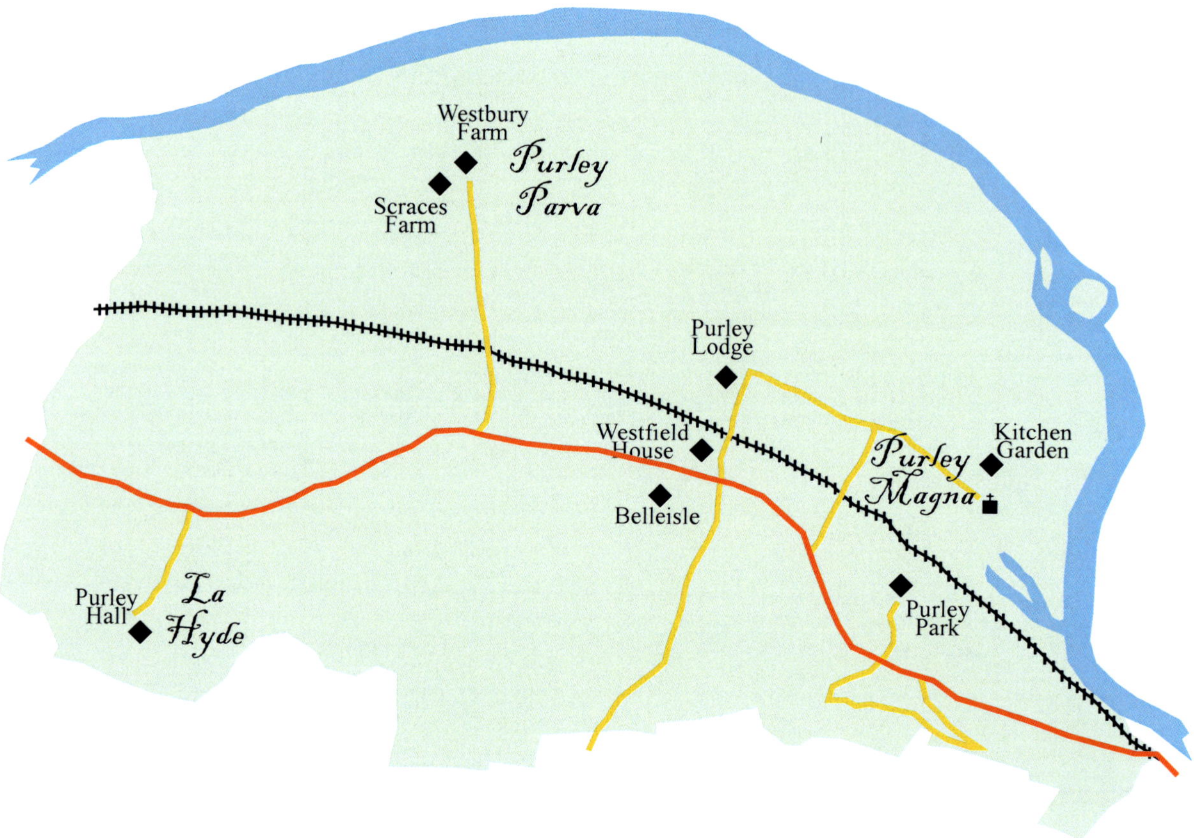
Westbury Farm
Purley Parva
Scraces Farm
Purley Lodge
Westfield House
Kitchen Garden
Purley Magna
Belleisle
Purley Hall
La Hyde
Purley Park

2 *The Estates and Big Houses*

Our first group of pictures relate to the estates of the three former medieval manors of Purley together with other big houses in the village.

Purley Magna mostly formed the eastern part of the parish. We know that in the 1500s a timber-framed house was built near to the church and that this manor house was where Ann Hyde, the first wife of Edward Hyde, 1st Earl of Clarendon, died of smallpox in 1632. This house was replaced by one of brick around 1740 and by the present Palladian mansion, Purley Park, on the brow of the hill in about 1800. We gain a sense of the late eighteenth century estate through the drawings of Humphry Repton which he presented in his Red Book. He was appointed in 1793 by the MP Anthony Morris Storer the elder, then lord of the manor, to design a more palatial estate fitting for a gentleman. A new farmhouse was also built further up the hill, together with three relocated timber-framed barns. Purley Park was broken up and sold in the 1920s.

The second manorial estate, Purley Parva, was centred on Westbury Farm and has remained almost entirely agricultural. The village cottages around the manorial farm were probably deserted in the fourteenth century as a result of the Black Death. In the late twelfth century a piece of land belonging to Purley Parva was given to the newly founded Reading Abbey and this half virgate, roughly fifteen acres, may have run in a strip alongside Purley Lane. Purley Lodge, built c1750, appears to occupy the northern part of this land and Westfield House, constructed in the late nineteenth century by the Sykes family, the southern portion.

We finish our chapter with Purley Hall, the third manorial estate of La Hyde, which was built in the early seventeenth century and originally called Hyde Hall. The Hyde family were staunch Catholics and were forced to sell their estate to meet severe taxation demands. Other occupiers provide connections to the South Sea Bubble, Warren Hastings, the Wilder family of Sulham and Olave Baden-Powell. This estate too has remained largely agricultural.

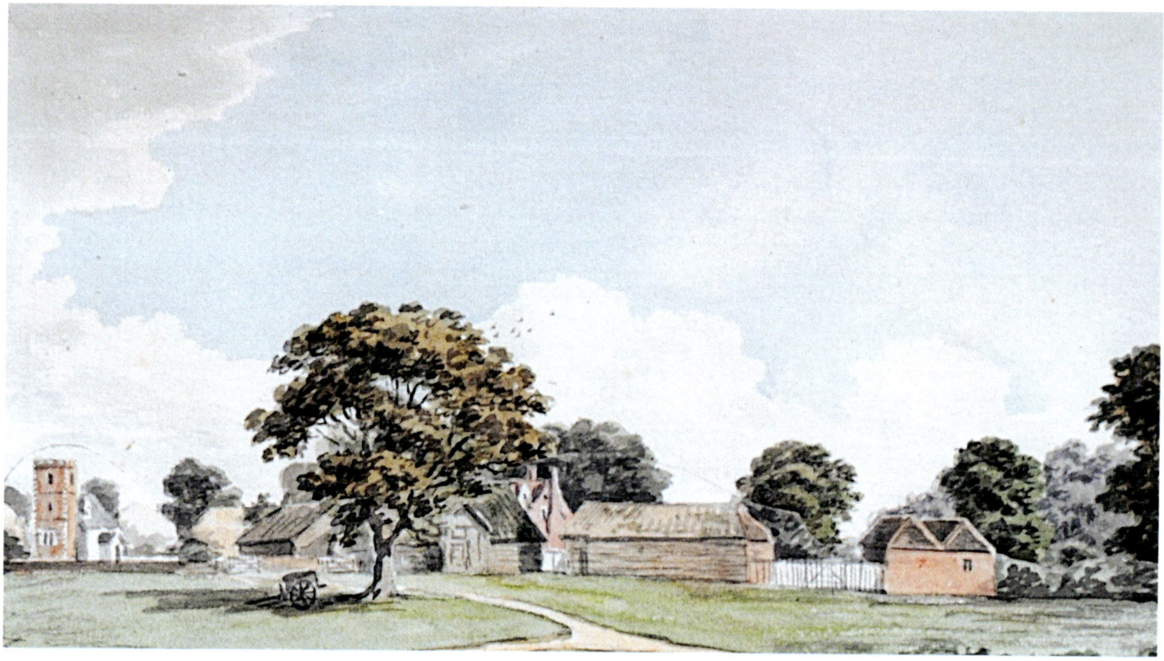

2.1 & 2.2 ***Above and Below:*** Part of the Purley Magna estate of 1793 can be seen in this pair of 'before' drawings from Humphry Repton's Red Book of Purley. The array of barns close to the church is clearly visible, together with the brick manor house of 1740. Three of these barns were dismantled and rebuilt at Belleisle Farm (see image 2.15) as part of the redesign of the estate and one of these, the manorial barn, survives today on a new site in the Goosecroft Recreation Ground off Beech Road.

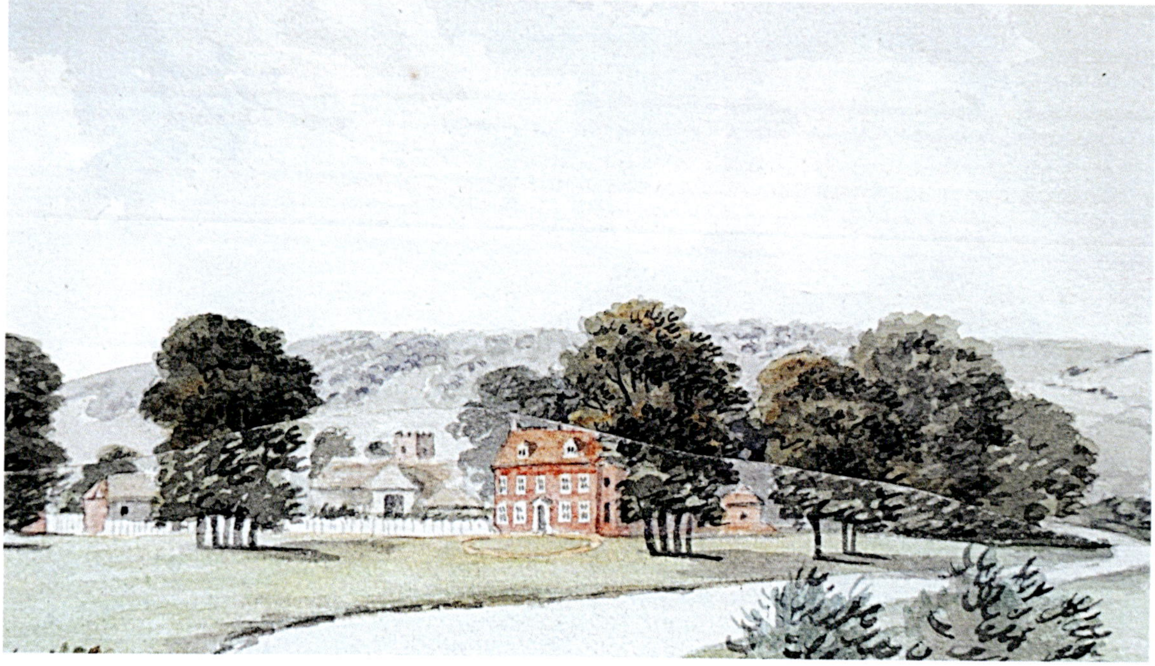

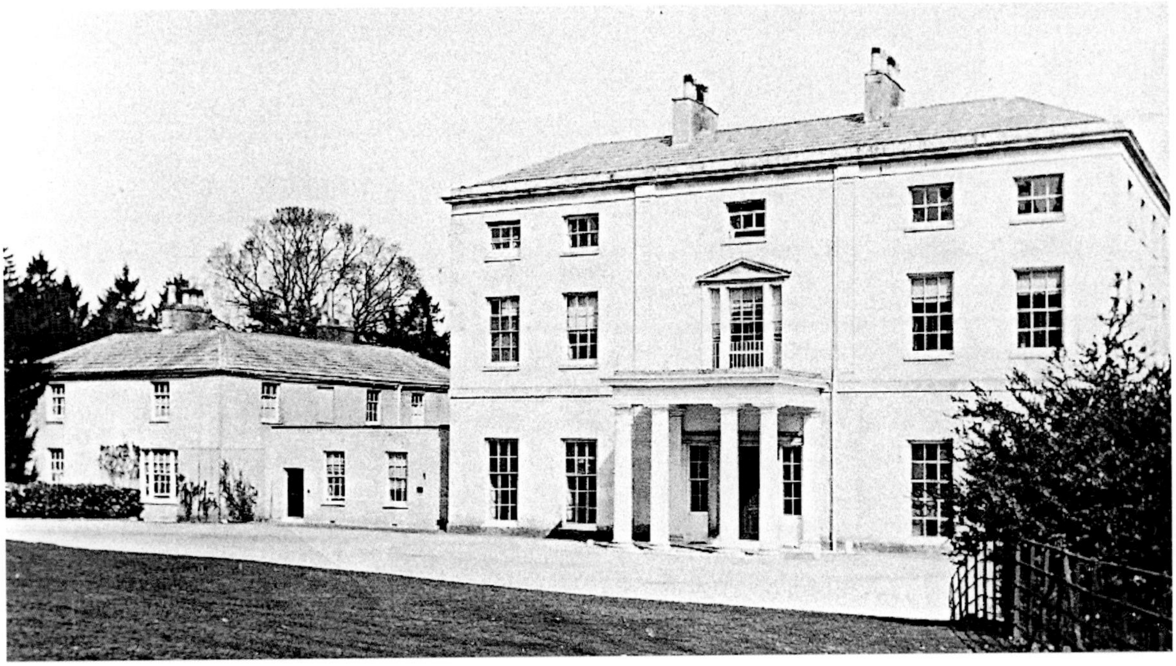

2.3 & 2.4 ***Above and Below:*** The new Purley Magna mansion, seen here in front and rear views, was built around 1800 to a design by James Wyatt and called Purley Park. It was positioned on the brow of the hill well away from any flooding. On the left is the stable block which contained the servants' accommodation.

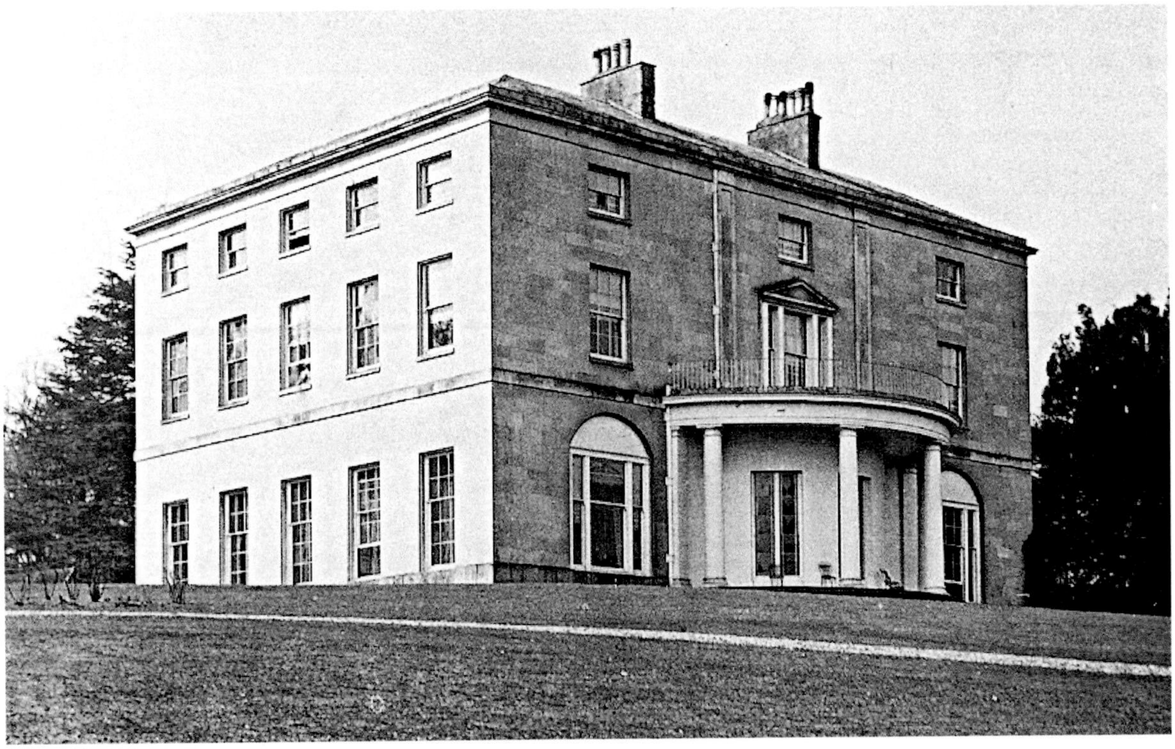

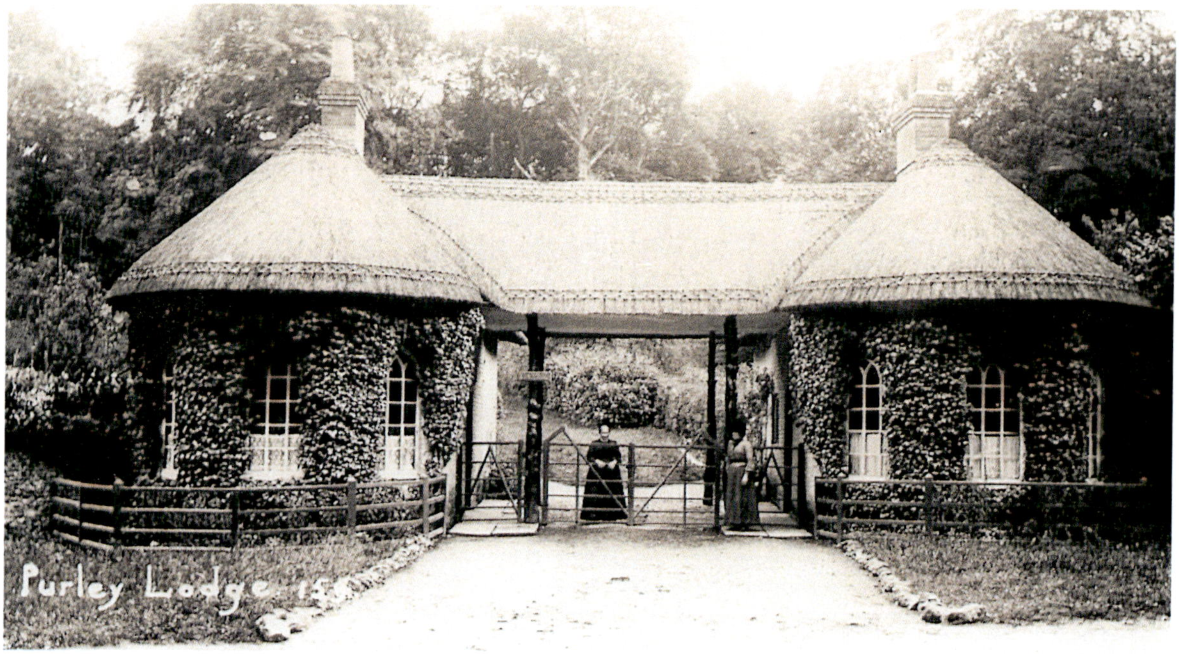

2.5 ***Above:*** The thatched lodge gates to Purley Park were located on the south side of the main Turnpike Road and carriages would clatter round a long and winding entrance drive, created to give an illusion of a sweeping country estate. Pictured here around 1910, they were demolished in the 1970s.

2.6 ***Below:*** Edward, chauffeur to the Fullerton family, poses with Frederick Fullerton's old touring car on his right and the new replacement.

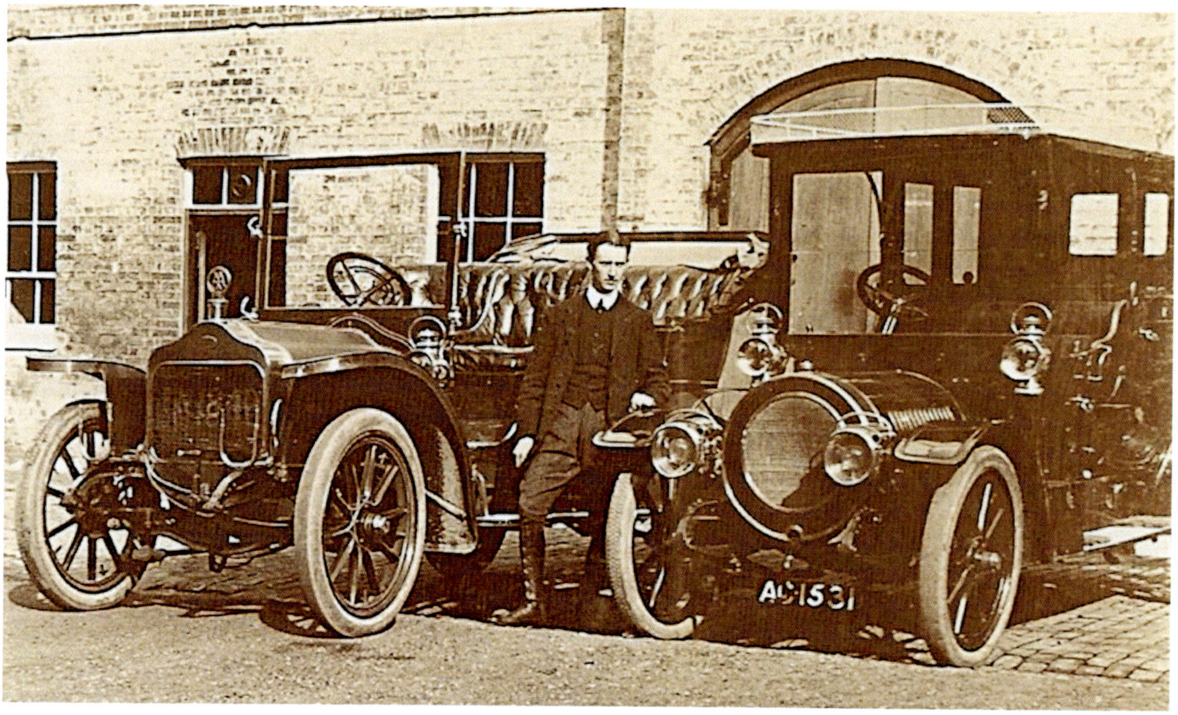

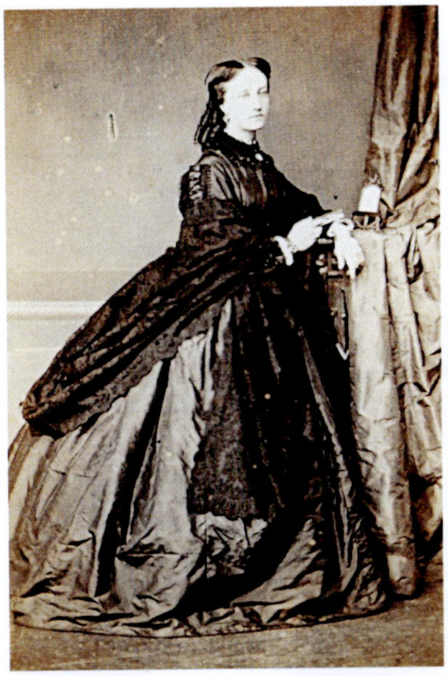

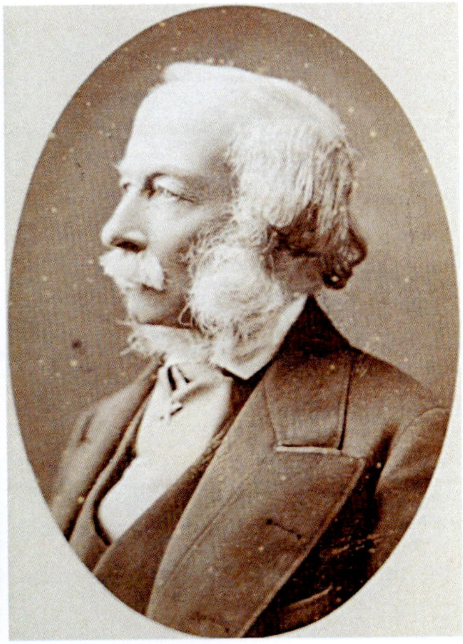

2.7 & 2.8 ***Right:*** For much of the nineteenth century, the lord of the manor of Purley Magna was Major Anthony Morris Storer the younger. In 1860 he brought his new bride, Cicely to live at Purley Park, having inherited it as a five year old boy. Both of these photographs were taken in the 1860s.

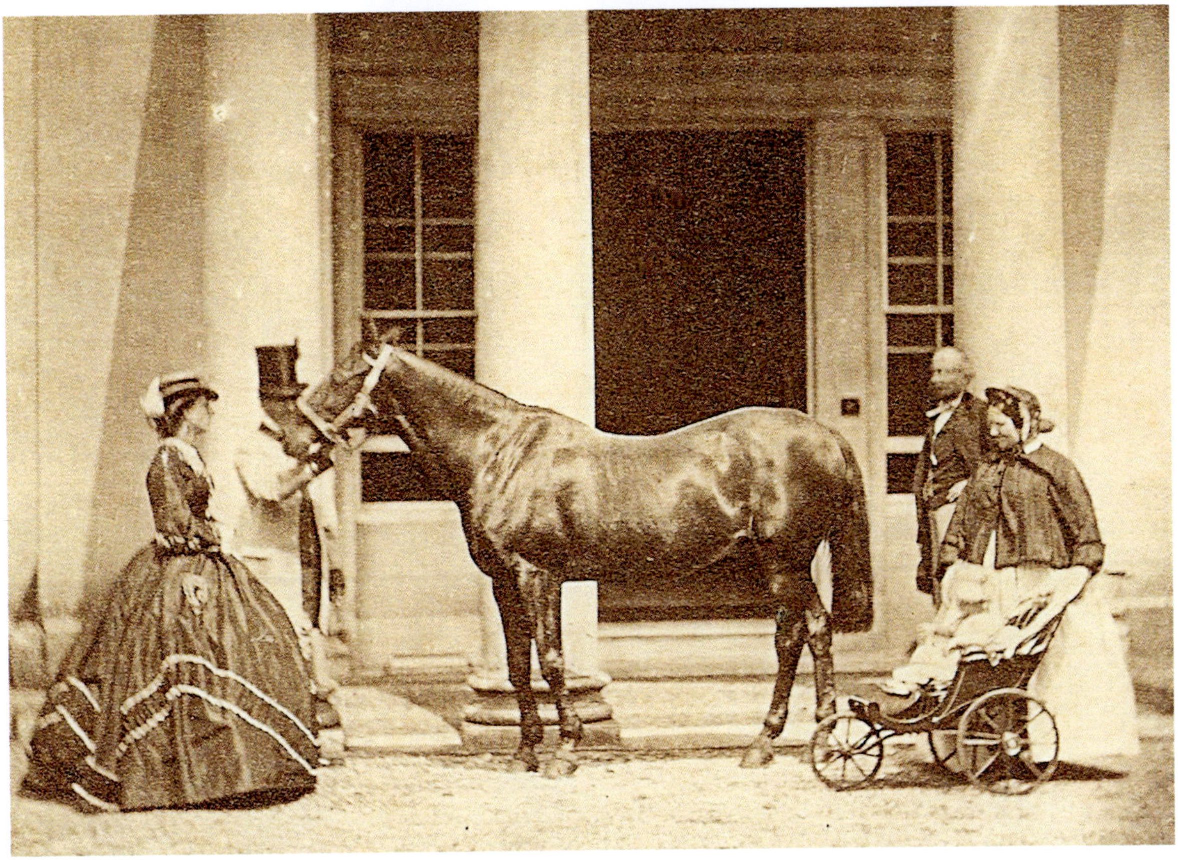

2.9 Major and Mrs Storer pose in front of the house c1864 with their favourite horse Conrad, groom William (most probably William Bazeley), nanny Woods and their young daughter Leila.

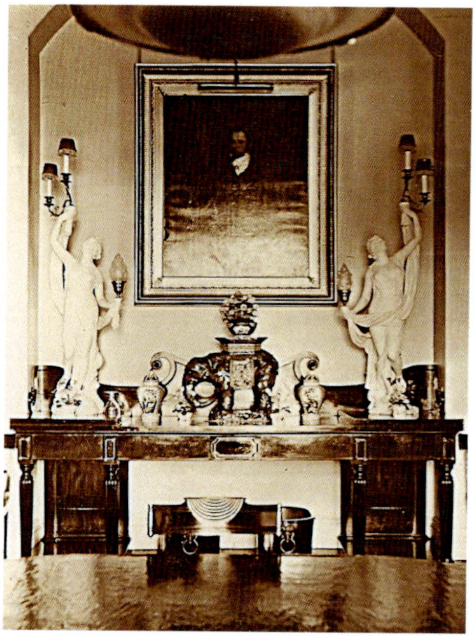

2.10 ***Right:*** Inside, the house reflected the wealth of the Storer family with the fashionable furniture and objets d'art of the day.

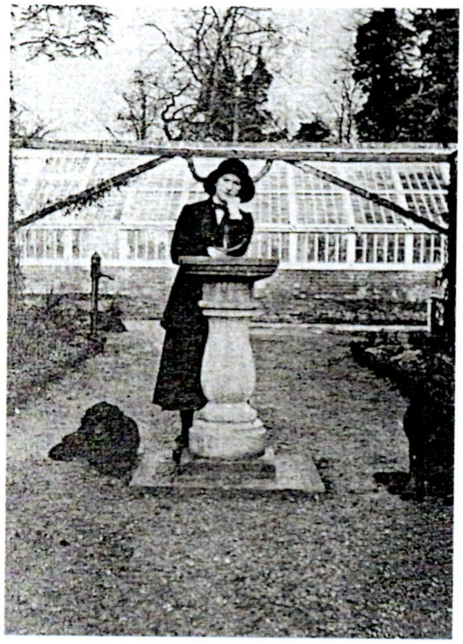

2.11 & 2.12 ***Above right and below:*** Outside, the grounds included glasshouses, here with Major Storer's granddaughter Myra c1912, and a donkey operated press, c1920, possibly a remnant of Purley's only documented inn, the Red Lyon, which may have been sited somewhere in this vicinity.

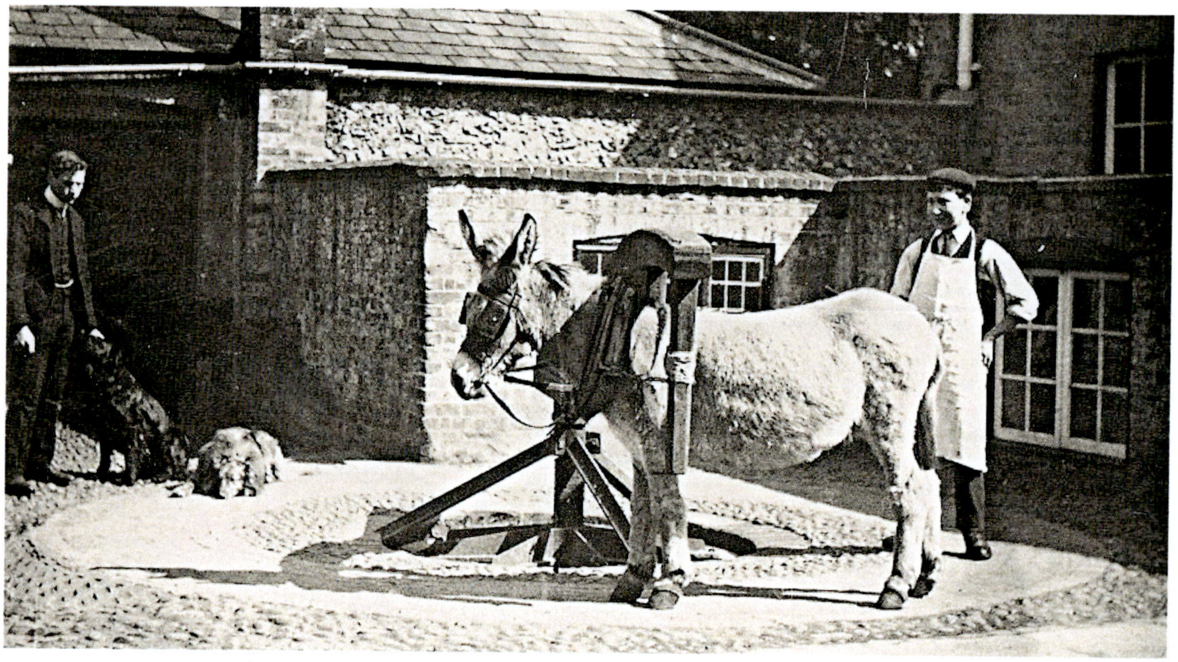

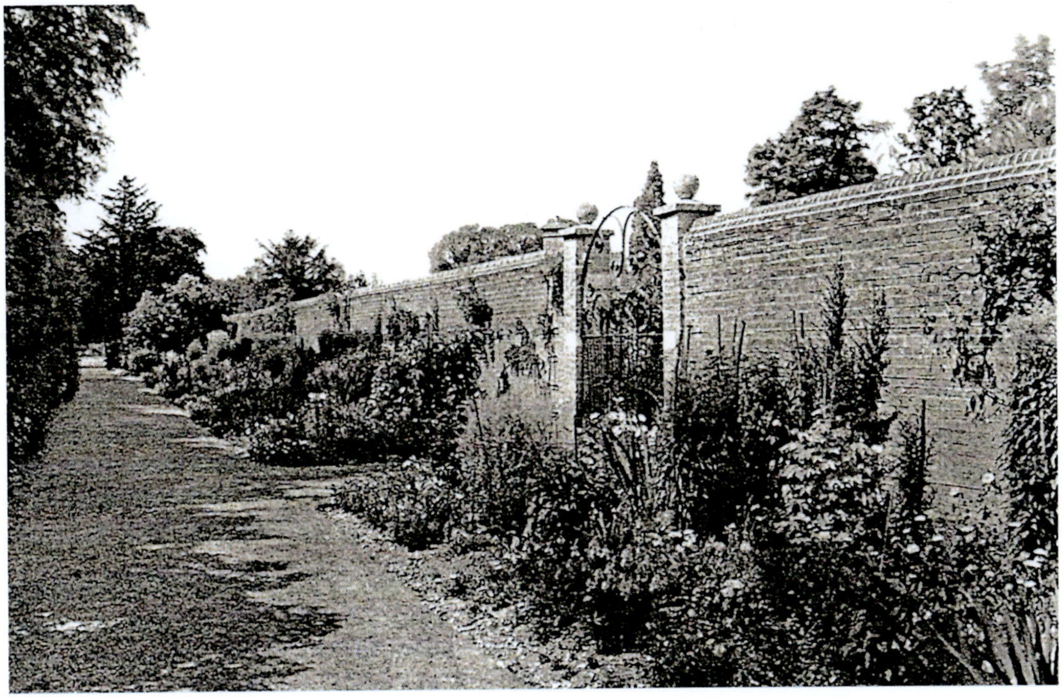

2.13 & 2.14 ***Above and Below:*** Beyond the church, on the land now occupied by Church Mews and Waterside Drive, lay Purley Park's walled kitchen garden, pictured here in the 1920s, and the gardener's cottage, pictured c1863. Designed by the Reading Borough architect, Joseph Morris, the cottage pioneered the use of cavity walls for insulation.

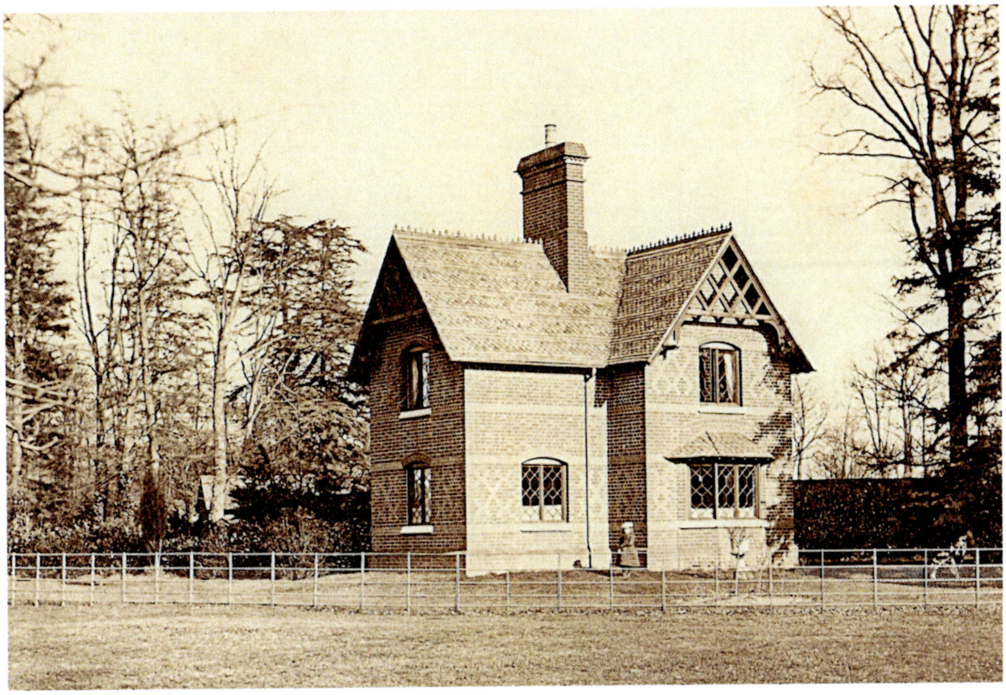

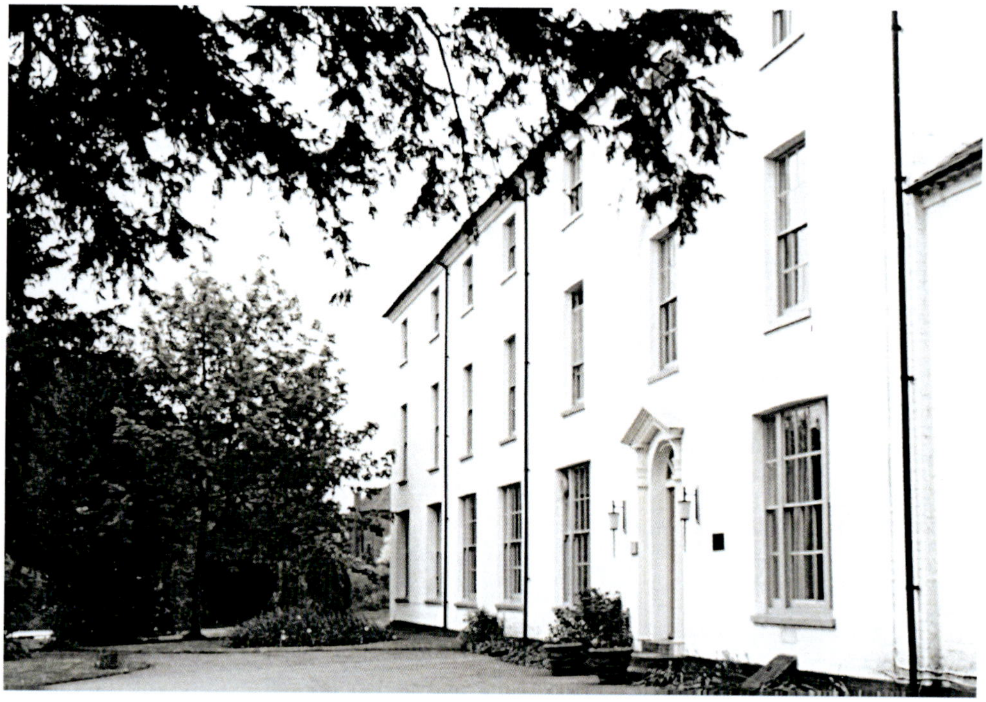

2.15 The Storers constructed Belleisle farmhouse on higher ground to designs from Repton's Red Book of Purley. It was built in a quadrangle with the reassembled timber barns from the church site. Belleisle was the home for many years of the Sherwood family, who by the early 1800s leased most of the farmland in Purley.

2.16 ***Right:*** Edward Purvis Sherwood, here with his family c1896, was the great, great grandson of Edward Sherwood who moved to Purley about 1730.

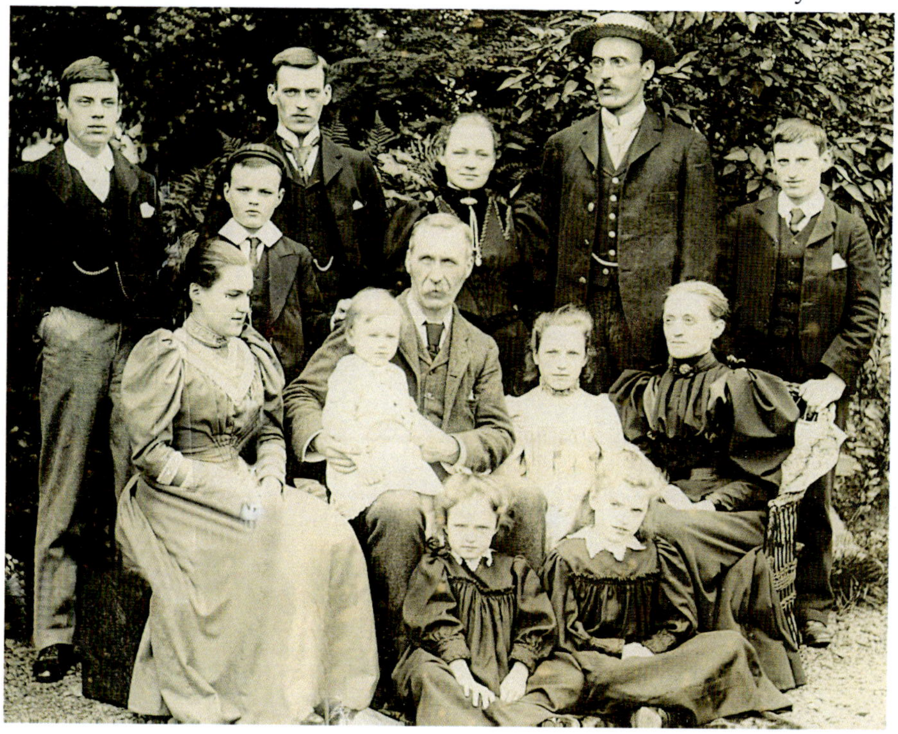

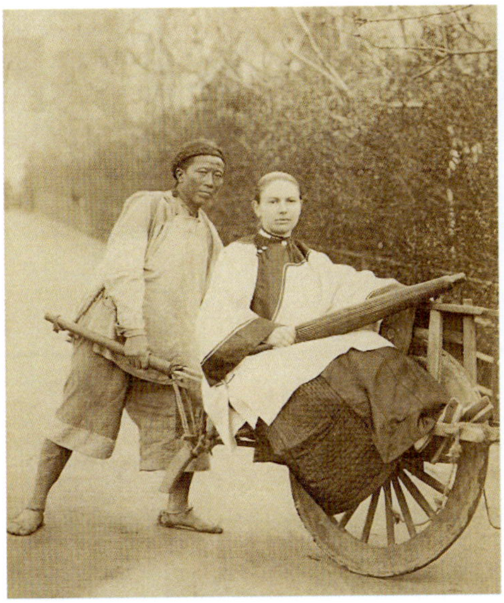

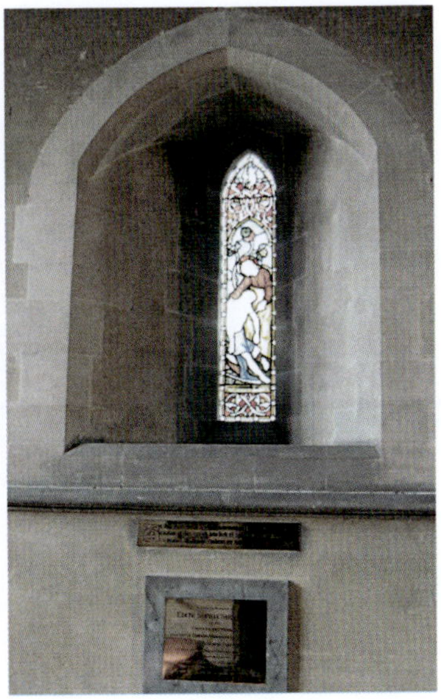

2.17 & 2.18 ***Left:*** Edith Sophia Sherwood is pictured in China where she became a missionary. She was killed in the Boxer Rebellion in July 1900 and there is a memorial to her in St Mary's Church.

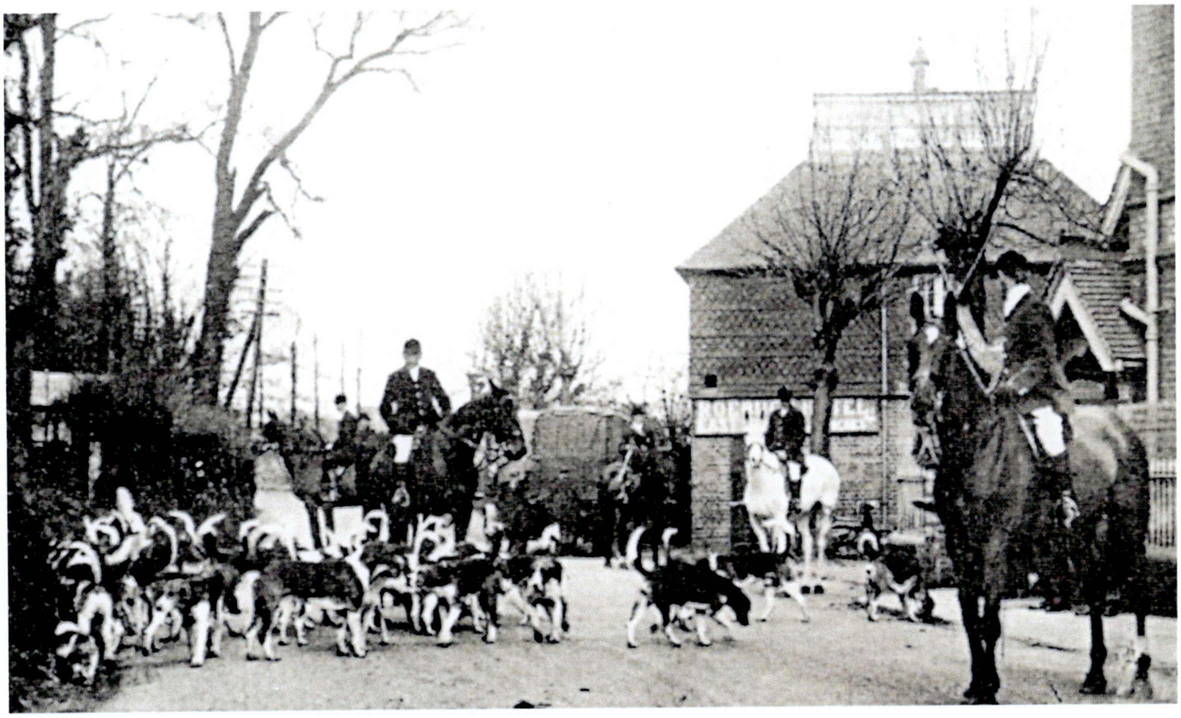

2.19 In 1900 the South Berks Hunt purchased Belleisle and the barn became a stable. Cecil Aldin, a noted artist, became the Master of Foxhounds and lived in the farmhouse. Here is the hunt by the Roebuck in the 1940s.

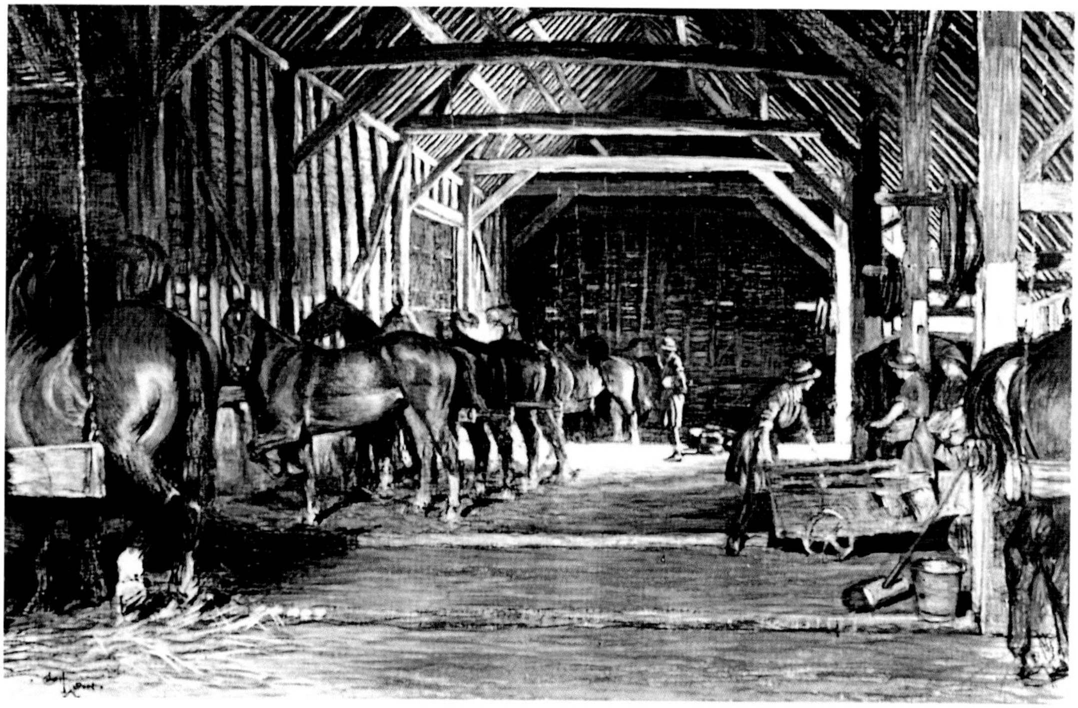

2.20 (IWM ART 1985) During the First World War, Cecil Aldin operated a Remount Depot from the site and painted this interior scene of the manorial barn. His vet was the more famous artist Alfred Munnings, who rode over from Calcot each day. Later Belleisle and the barn became part of the head office complex of Messrs G Percy Trenthams.

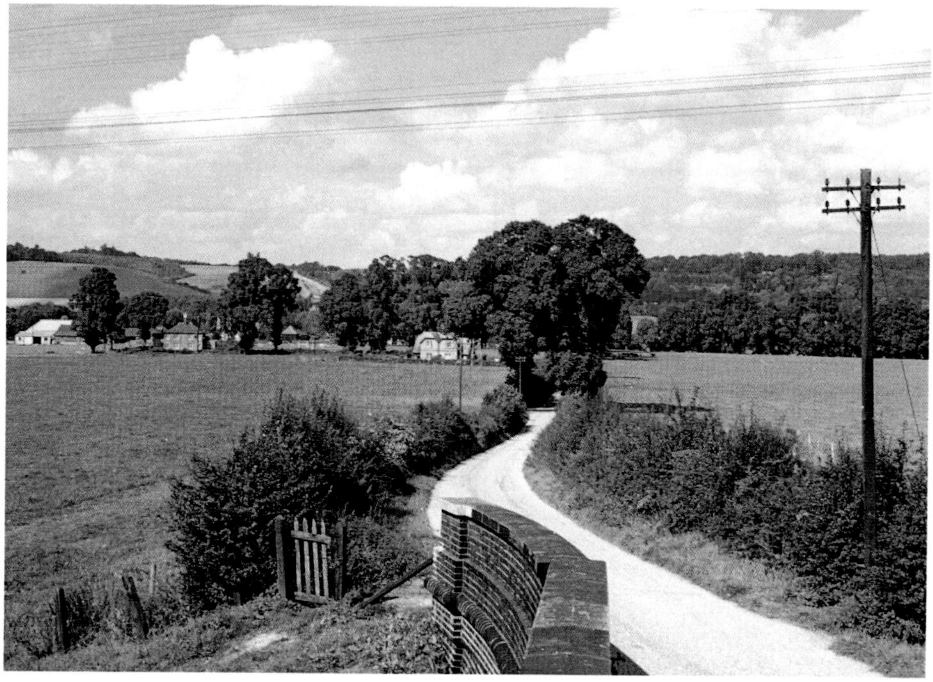

2.21 ***Right:*** The manor of Purley Parva lay to the west of Purley Magna and centred on Westbury Farm, seen here in 1958.

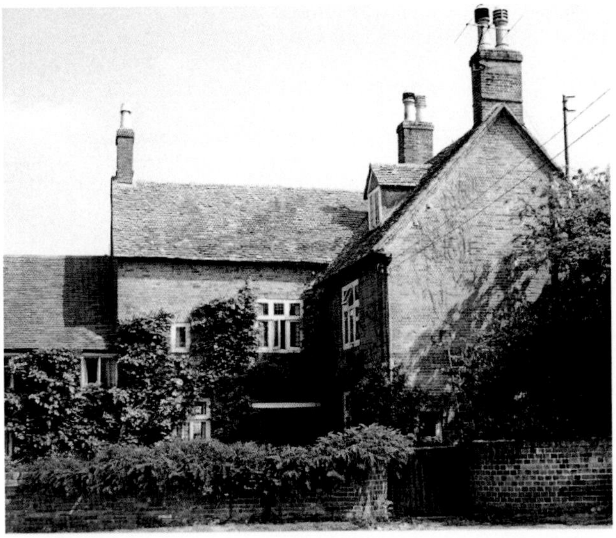

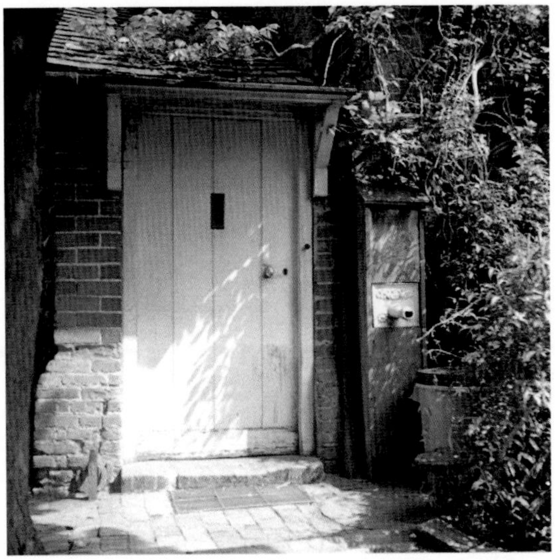

2.22 & 2.23 The current Westbury Farm farmhouse dates from the sixteenth century and has seventeenth and eighteenth century additions. These photographs, taken in the 1950s, show the homestead when it was still principally a dairy farm.

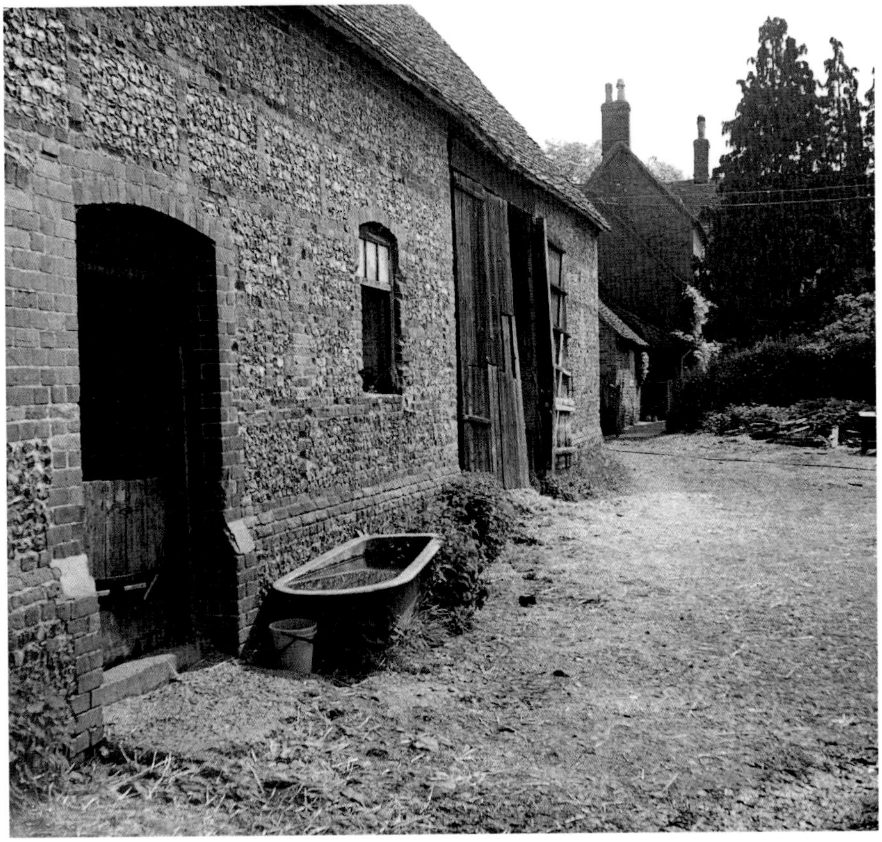

2.24 ***Left:*** The Tudor Barn, typical of its era, and seen here with a trough for the cattle in front of it, later became a demonstration area for Westbury Vineyard.

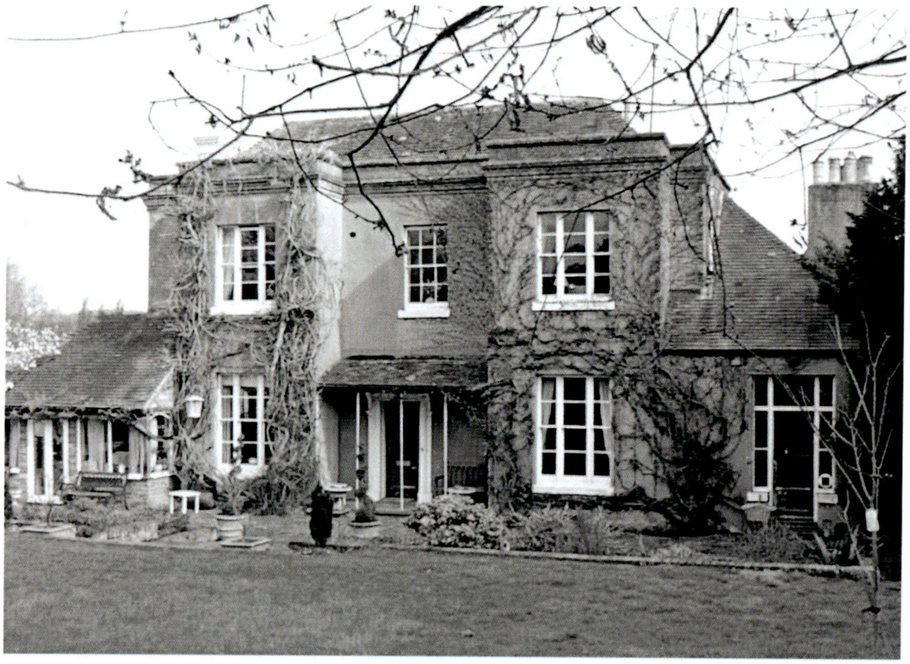

2.25 Purley Lodge, built on land thought to have been granted to Reading Abbey, may have replaced a previous religious building. Occupants included John George Liebenrood, a Dutch merchant, Lieutenant-General Sir James Hope, who served with great distinction in the Peninsular War and Charles Hodgkin who ran Pulsometer Pumps in Norcot.

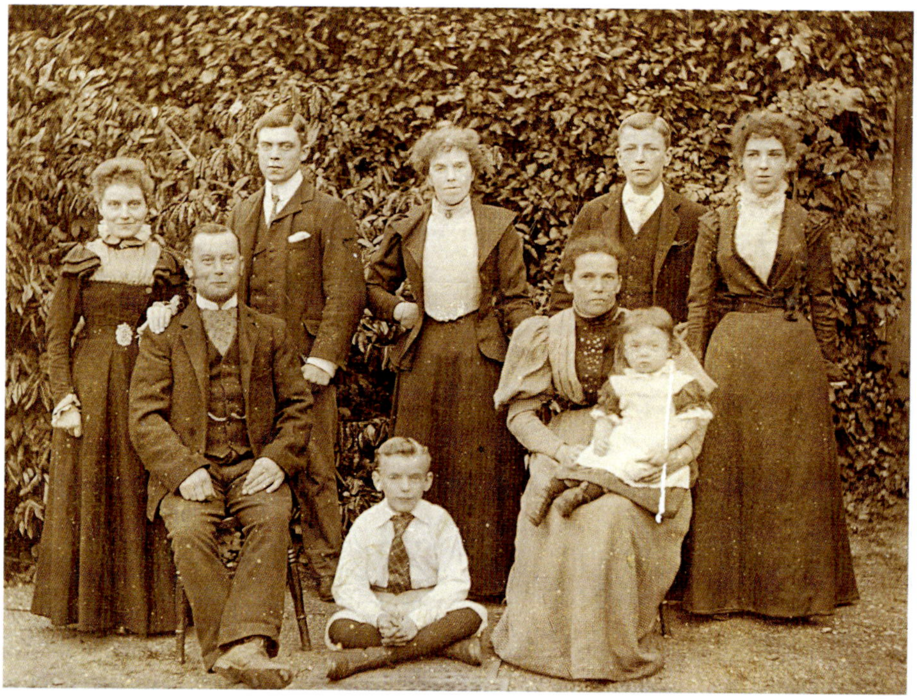

2.26 ***Right:*** The servants of Purley Lodge, c1899, included Henry and Elizabeth Leath (seated).

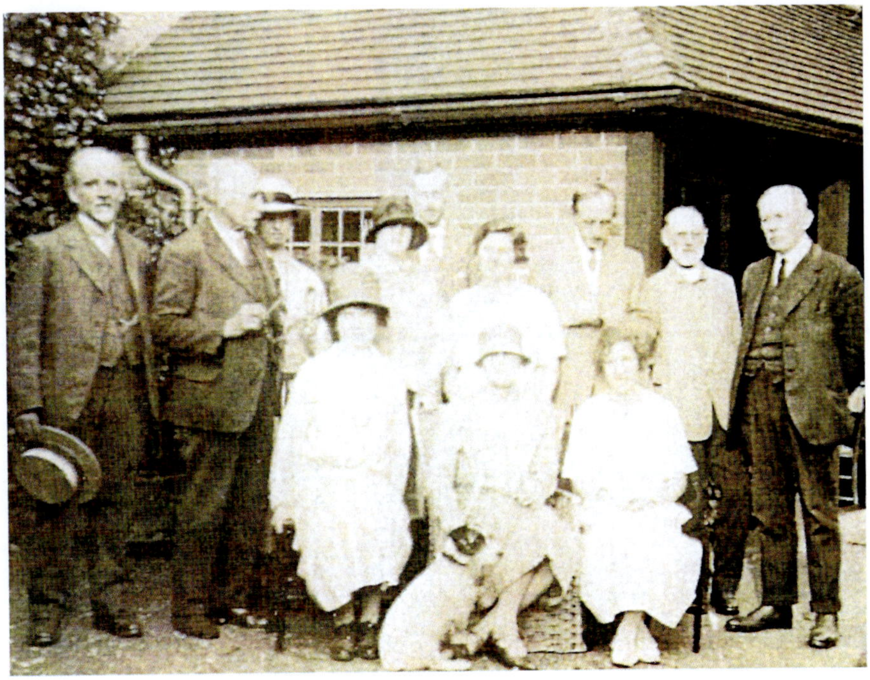

2.27 ***Right:*** Charles Hodgkin, on the far left, and family and friends celebrate the completion of his new summerhouse at Purley Lodge in the late 1920s.

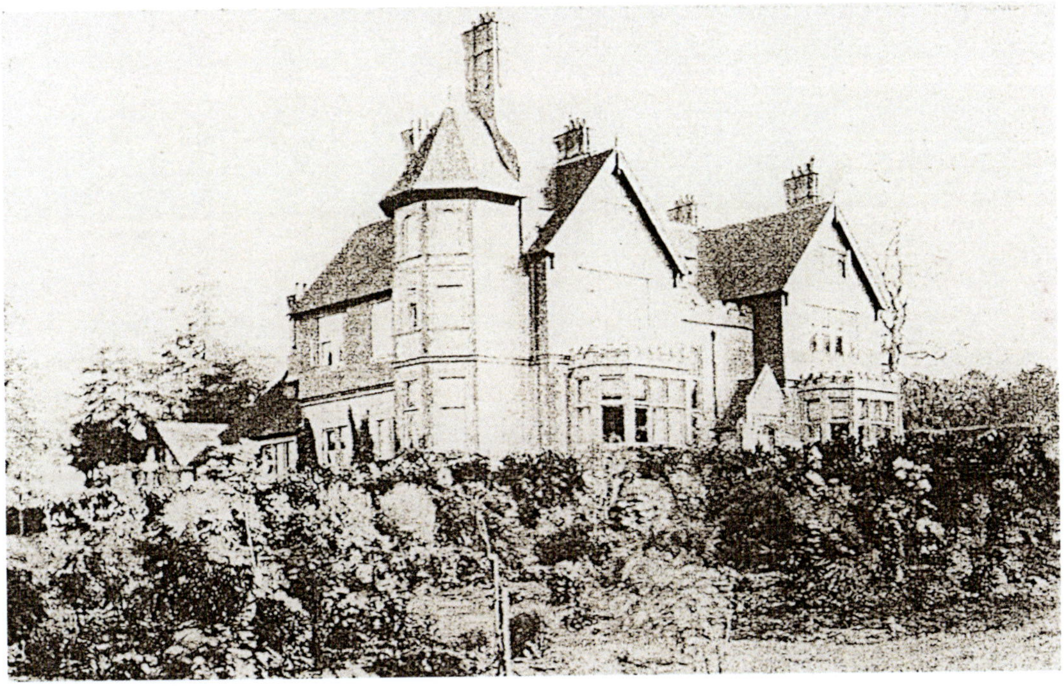

2.28 Westfield House, pictured pre 1940, was built by the Sykes family of Basildon Park and included within its estate a lodge house and stables, still surviving on the corner of Purley Lane and Purley Rise, and a gardener's house on Purley Rise. This is now the site of Nursery Gardens.

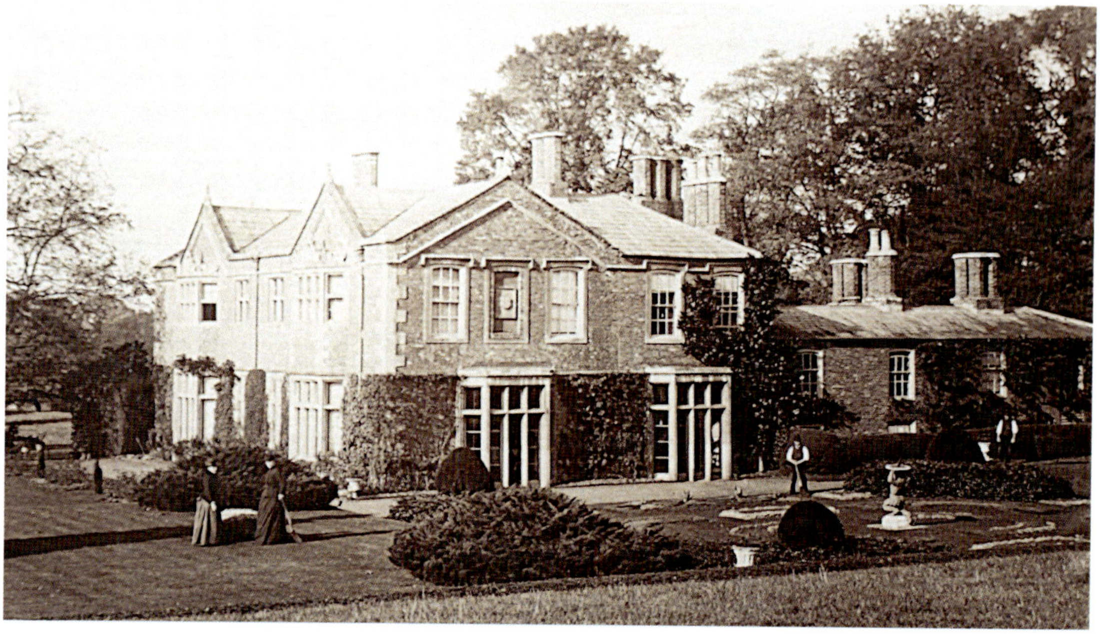

2.29 & 2.30 Purley Hall, pictured in 1885 ***(above)*** and 1895 ***(below)*** was built in the early seventeenth century to replace a previous, less grand house and went through a number of alterations. It was purchased in 1777 by the Wilders of Sulham.

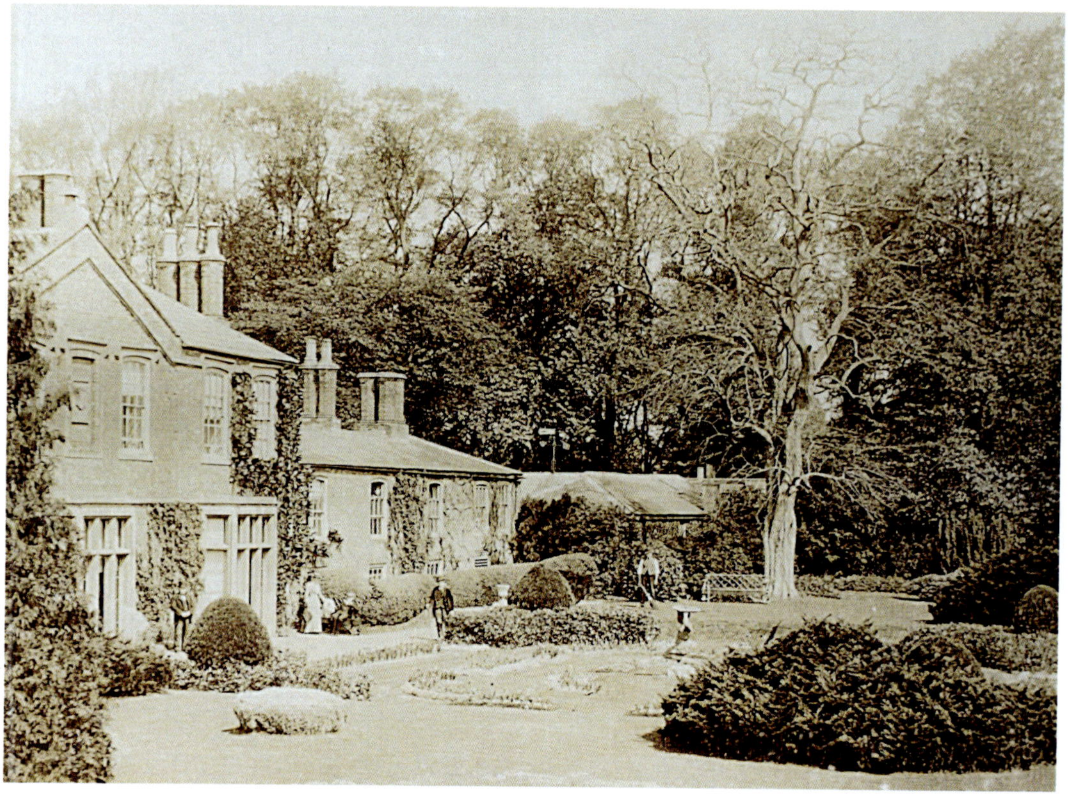

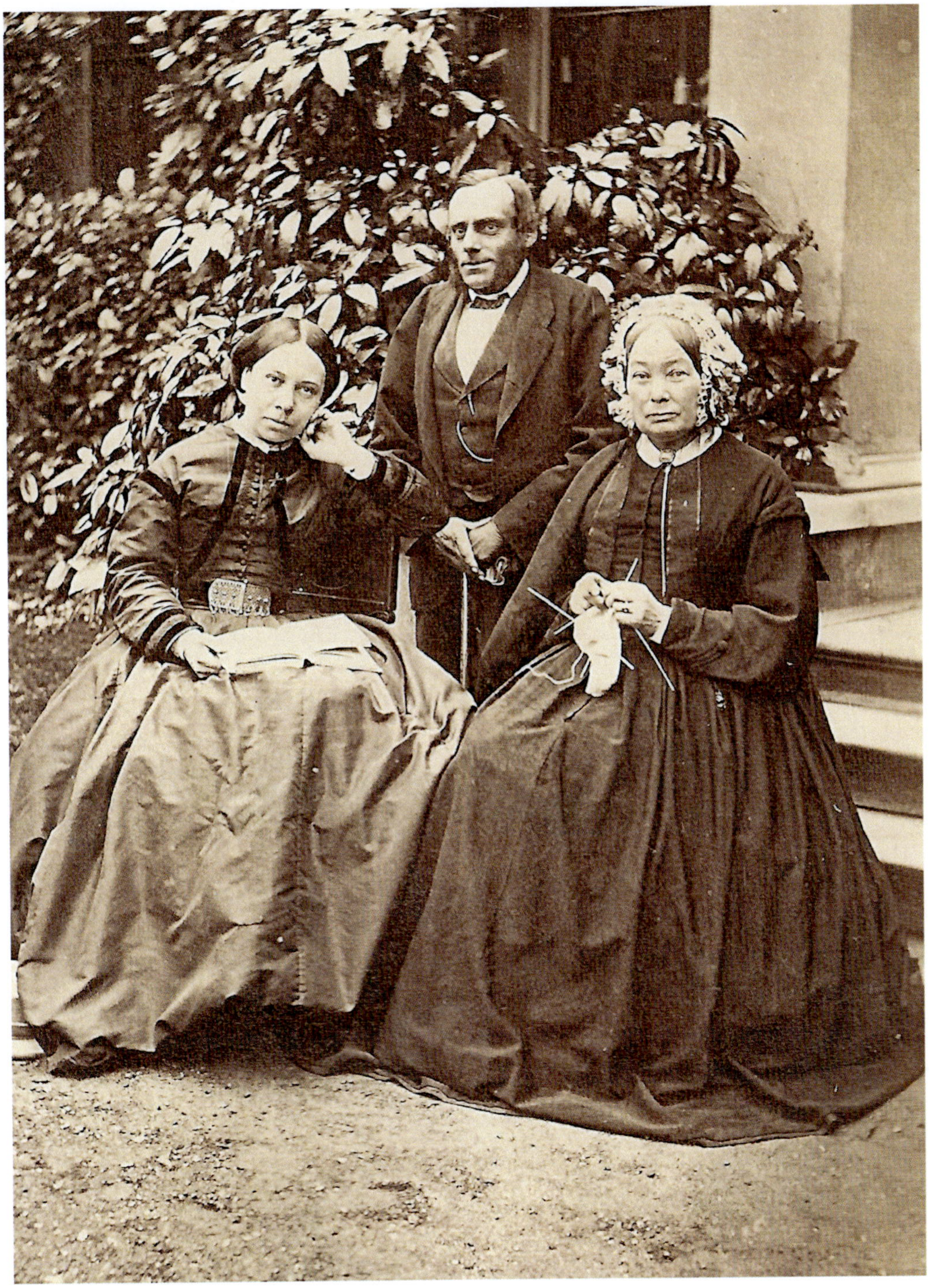

2.31 Frederick Wilder, a JP for Berkshire, inherited the Sulham estate as a boy when his parents died in a boating accident. He lived in Purley Hall for much of his adult life and is seen here c1865 with his first wife Sarah (on his right), and Mrs Antoinette Debes, a German nanny who had looked after him when he was a child.

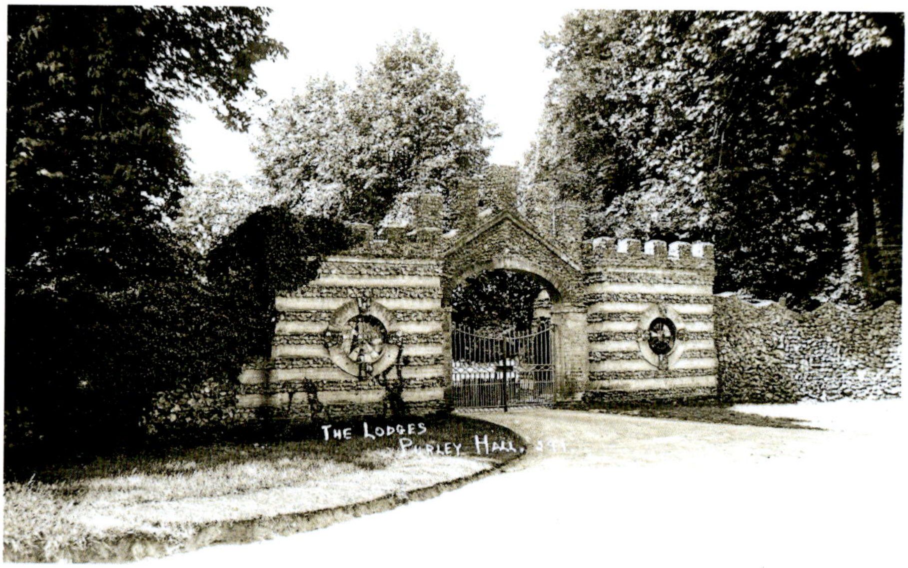

2.32 ***Right:*** The main entrance to Purley Hall, pictured c1950, is on the road between Purley and Pangbourne and has a lodge with two rooms connected by an underground passage.

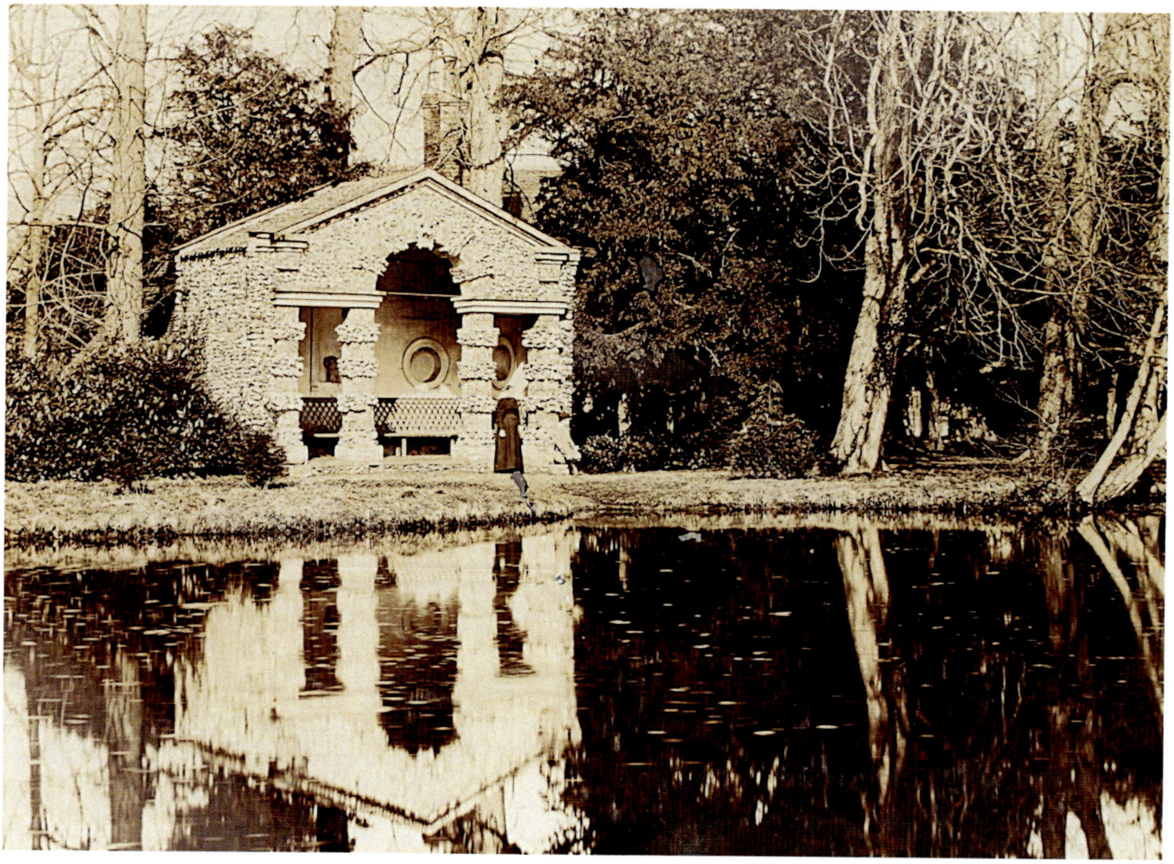

2.33 The ornamental temple, photographed c1895. This was built in the grounds of Purley Hall reputedly to commemorate the Battle of Culloden, 1746.

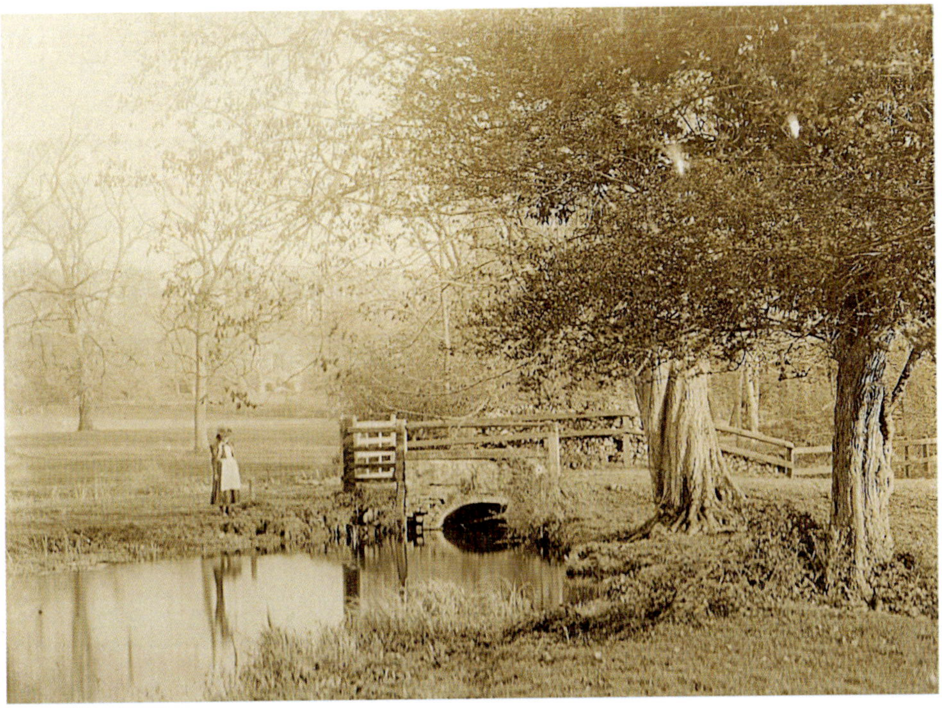

2.34 & 2.35 ***Above and Below:*** Our glimpse into the past of our estates and big houses closes with images of the lower pond at Purley Hall ***(above)*** c1895, and the lake ***(below)*** c1885, with grazing cattle and the front elevation of the Hall clearly visible in the background.

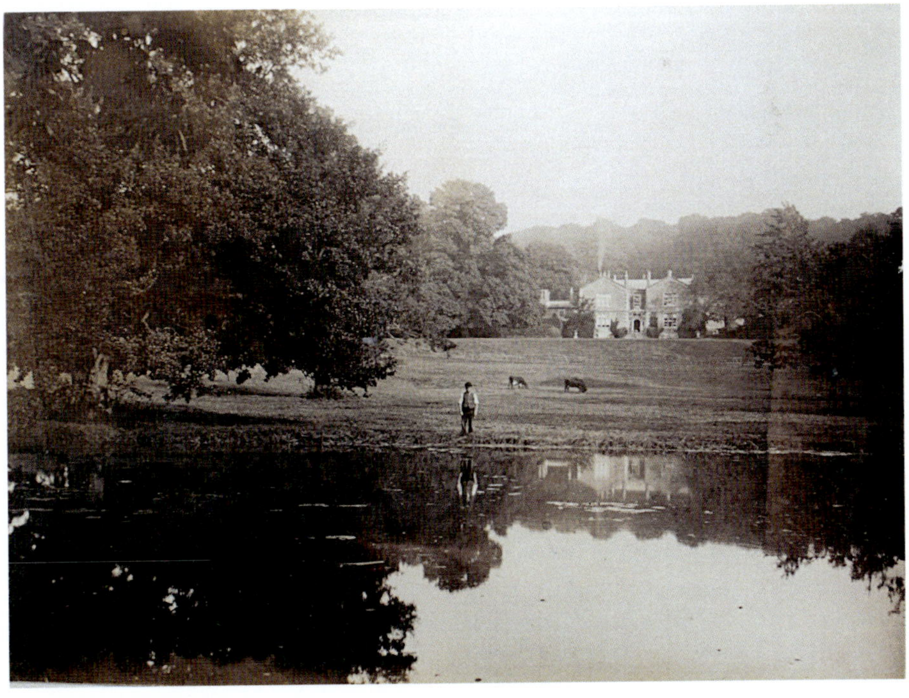

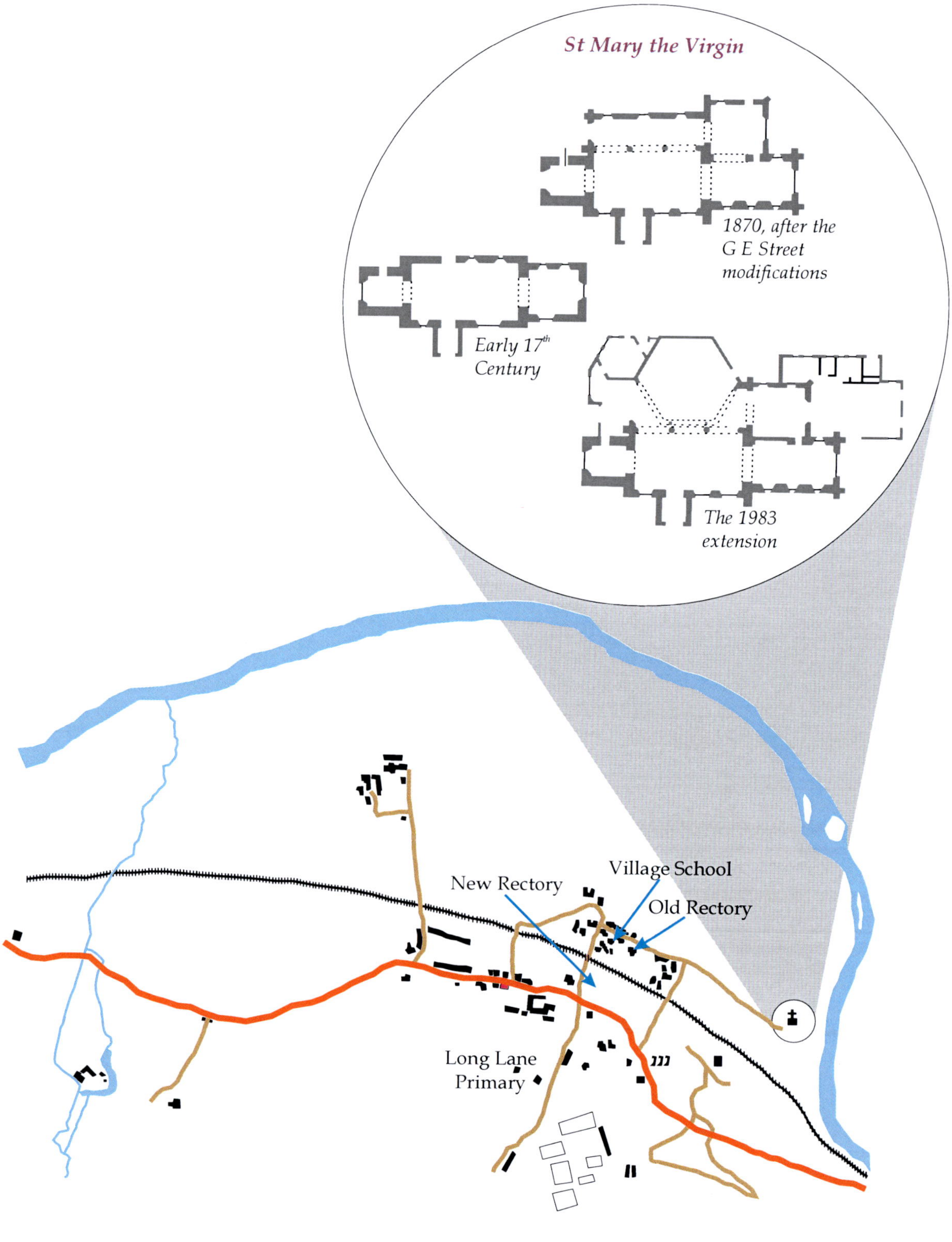
St Mary the Virgin
1870, after the
G E Street
modifications
Early 17th
Century
The 1983
extension
New Rectory
Village School
Old Rectory
Long Lane
Primary

3 The Church and School

Christianity came to Purley relatively early, probably some time in the sixth or seventh centuries and a first church was almost certainly built around 800 AD. When Reading Abbey was built in 1121 the church at Purley was already described as ancient. Curiously though, within just another forty years this early church was destroyed and completely rebuilt, and we can speculate that this was as a consequence of being burnt down in the chaos that surrounded the conflicts between King Stephen and Queen Matilda. The Norman font and the arch on the north side of the choir date from the time of this rebuild.

What followed over the ensuing centuries was a series of modifications and sometimes almost complete rebuilds, the remnants of which survive in some of the stonework, windows and doors. In the early seventeenth century an almost entire rebuild, designed to conform to the ideas of that time, resulted in a new chancel, a tower and a peal of bells. Gothic Revival brought about another virtually complete rebuild in 1870, part of which was subsequently replaced with an extension in 1983.

But the church is more than a building, it is about people. In earlier days we had a vicar and since the Reformation we have had a rector and, together with the churchwardens, the Sunday School teachers, the choir leaders, the organists and everyone else who has led church activities, many of them have made a significant impact upon our community.

In addition the church has been responsible for bringing education to our children. It probably began with the rector running classes at the rectory and developed into the founding of a Church of England School, at least two hundred years ago. The current school building, which was opened in 1875, replaced an earlier one and was designed to provide places for fifty-five children. Nowadays the school caters for the youngest children after which most transfer to Long Lane Primary School, which opened in 1966 to accommodate the increasing number of children in the village.

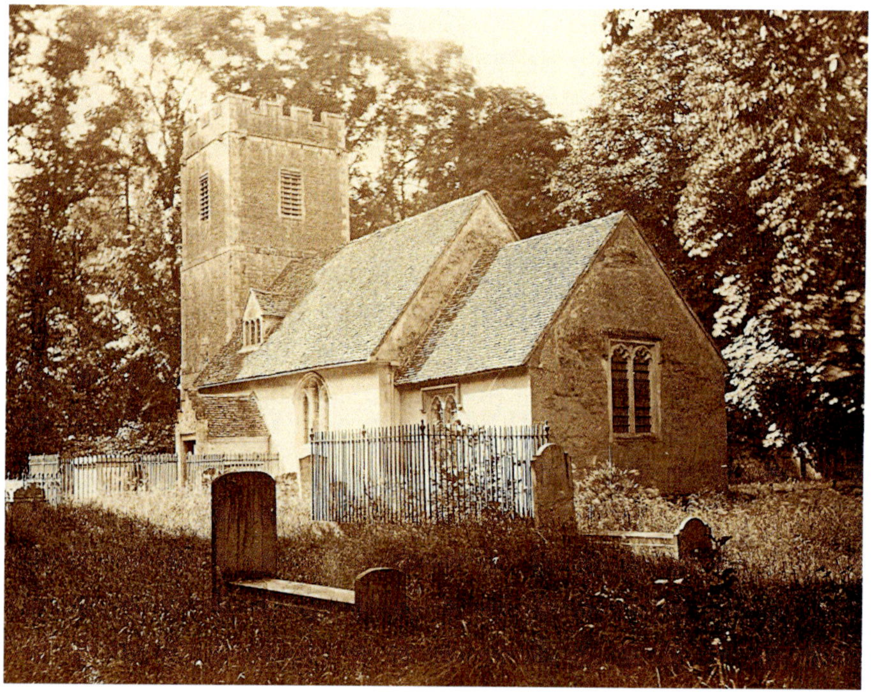

3.1 ***Above:*** The church is dedicated to St Mary the Virgin and has been altered and extended many times over its history. This image shows the building in 1860 before the architect G E Street completed substantial rebuilding works between 1868 and 1870.

3.2 ***Below:*** The south and east facades of the church following Street's rebuild, pictured here by Collier in the 1930s, are still familiar to us today.

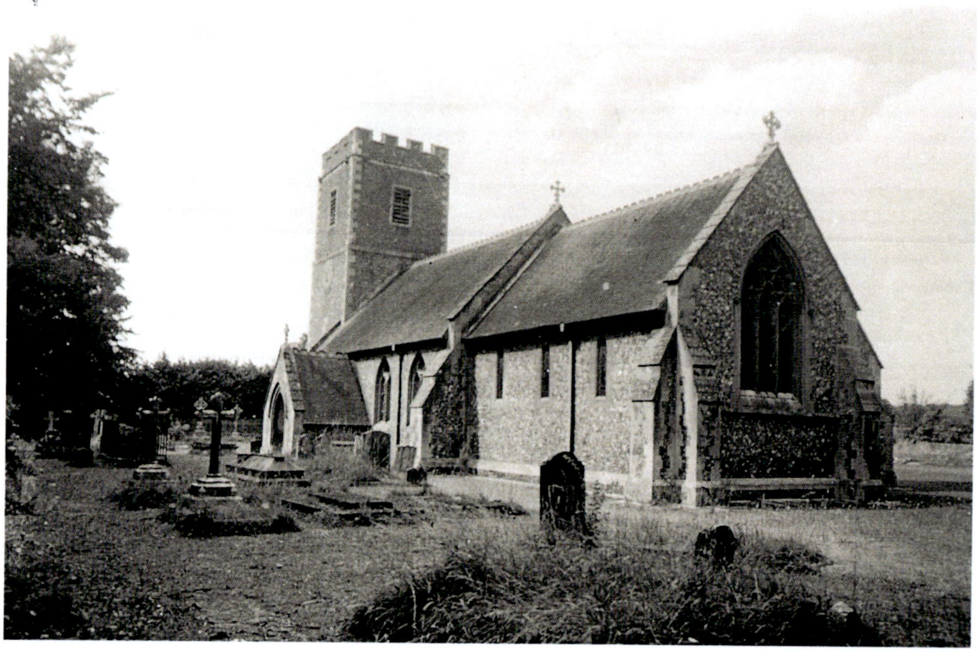

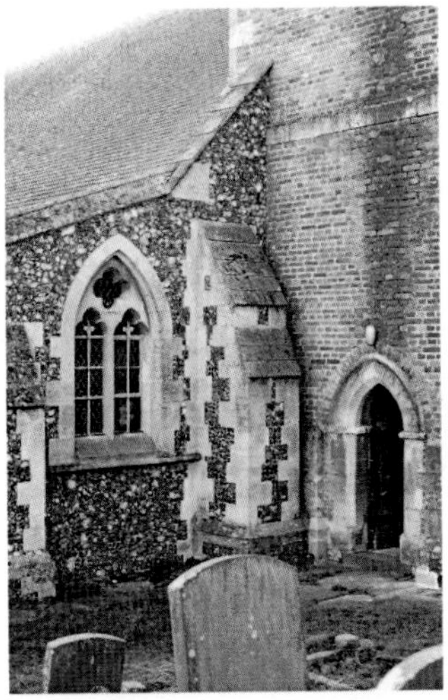

3.3 ***Above:*** The tower door is the oldest door in the church and was probably the original north door of the church.

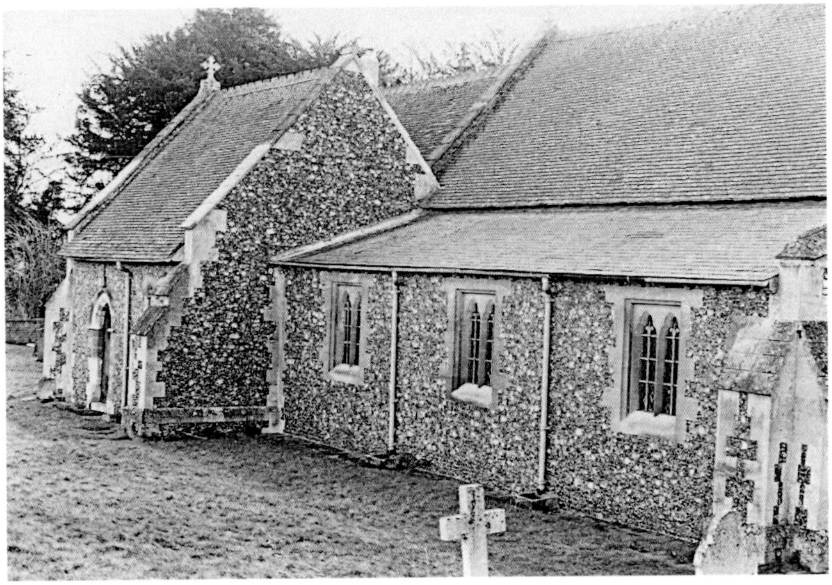

3.4 ***Above:*** G E Street created a new north aisle and vestry, seen here before it was demolished in 1983.

3.5 ***Right:*** Collier also photographed the interior of the church around 1930, when it was still lit by oil lamps. The Norman font, in the front right of the image, includes a depiction of the head of Christ within an arcade. The crack visible in the font dates from before 1800 and was probably caused by one of its very many moves around the church.

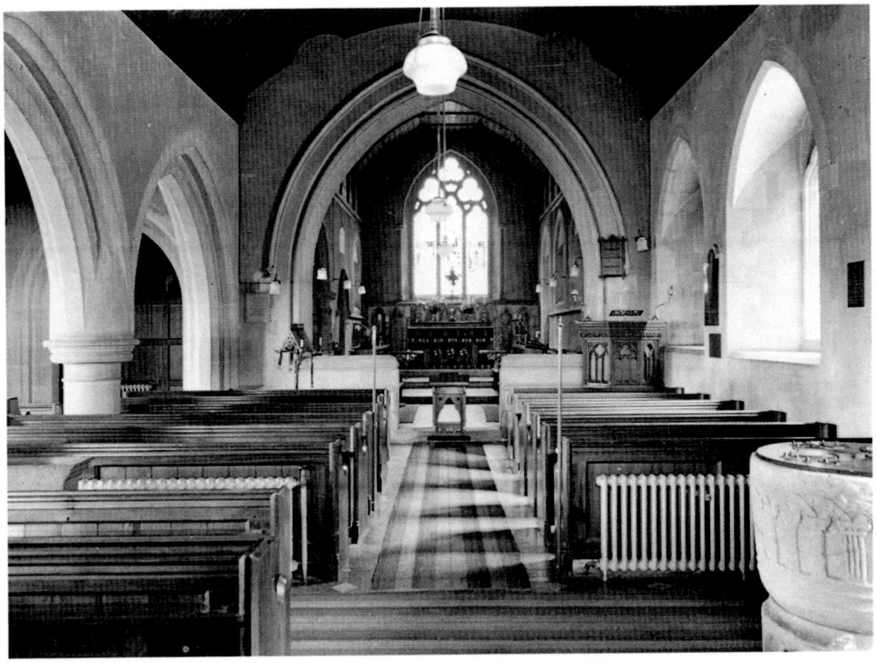

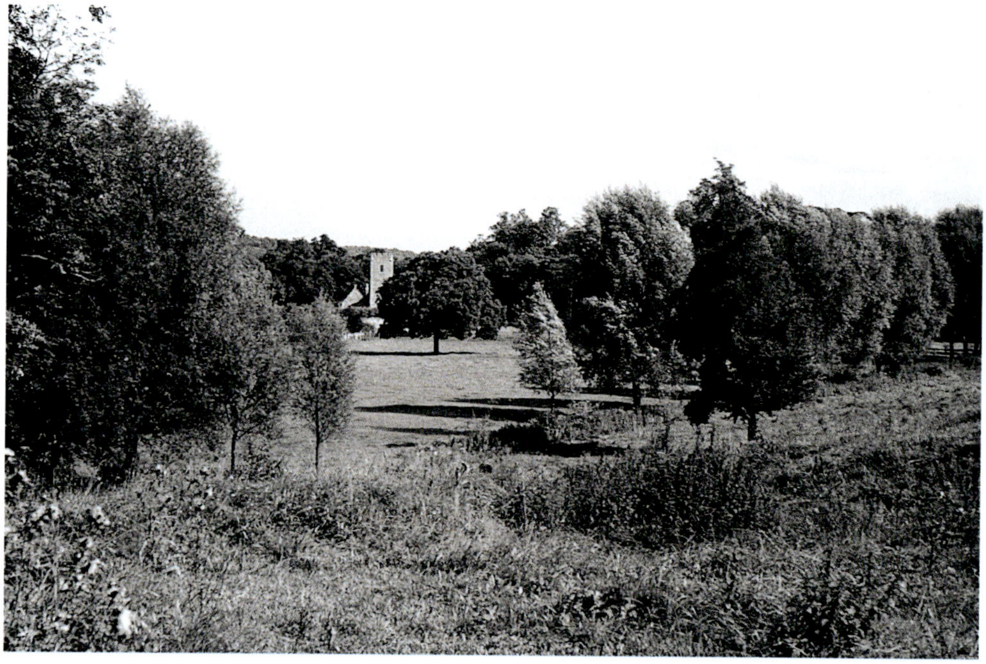

3.6 & 3.7 ***Above and Below:*** With the creation of Purley Park around 1800, the church was left surrounded by undulating parkland and isolated from its parishioners. This landscape remained largely unchanged until the sale and gradual break-up of the park after 1920. The image above shows the view in the early 1960s across the land where Primrose Close, Lilac Close, Chiltern View and Thames Reach now stand. The image below also shows the lych gate which was erected in 1870 to the memory of John and Harriet Sherwood.

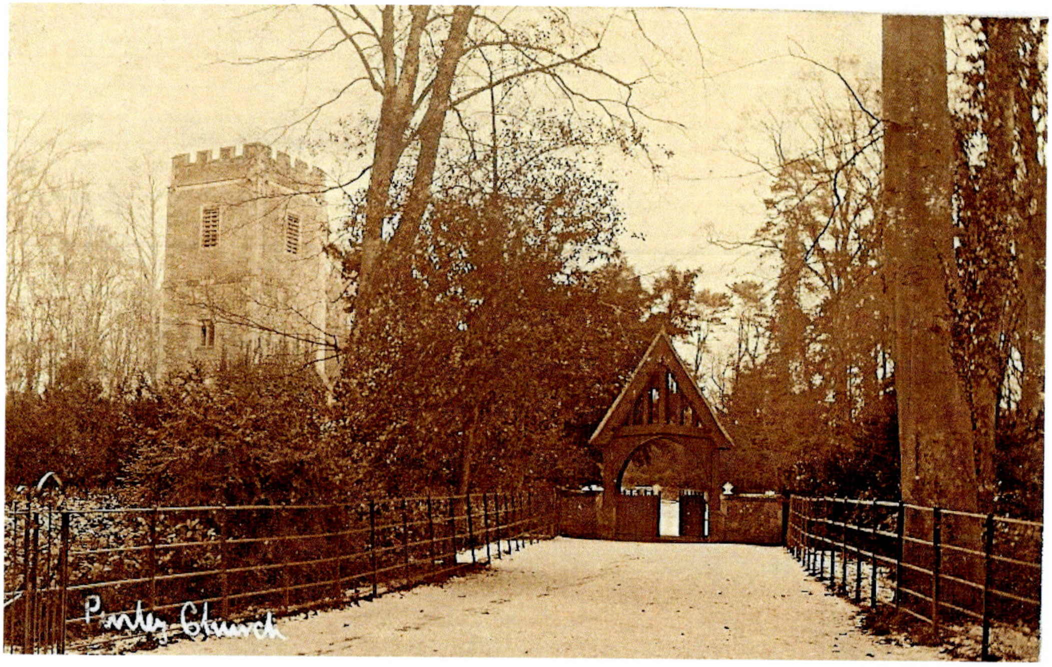

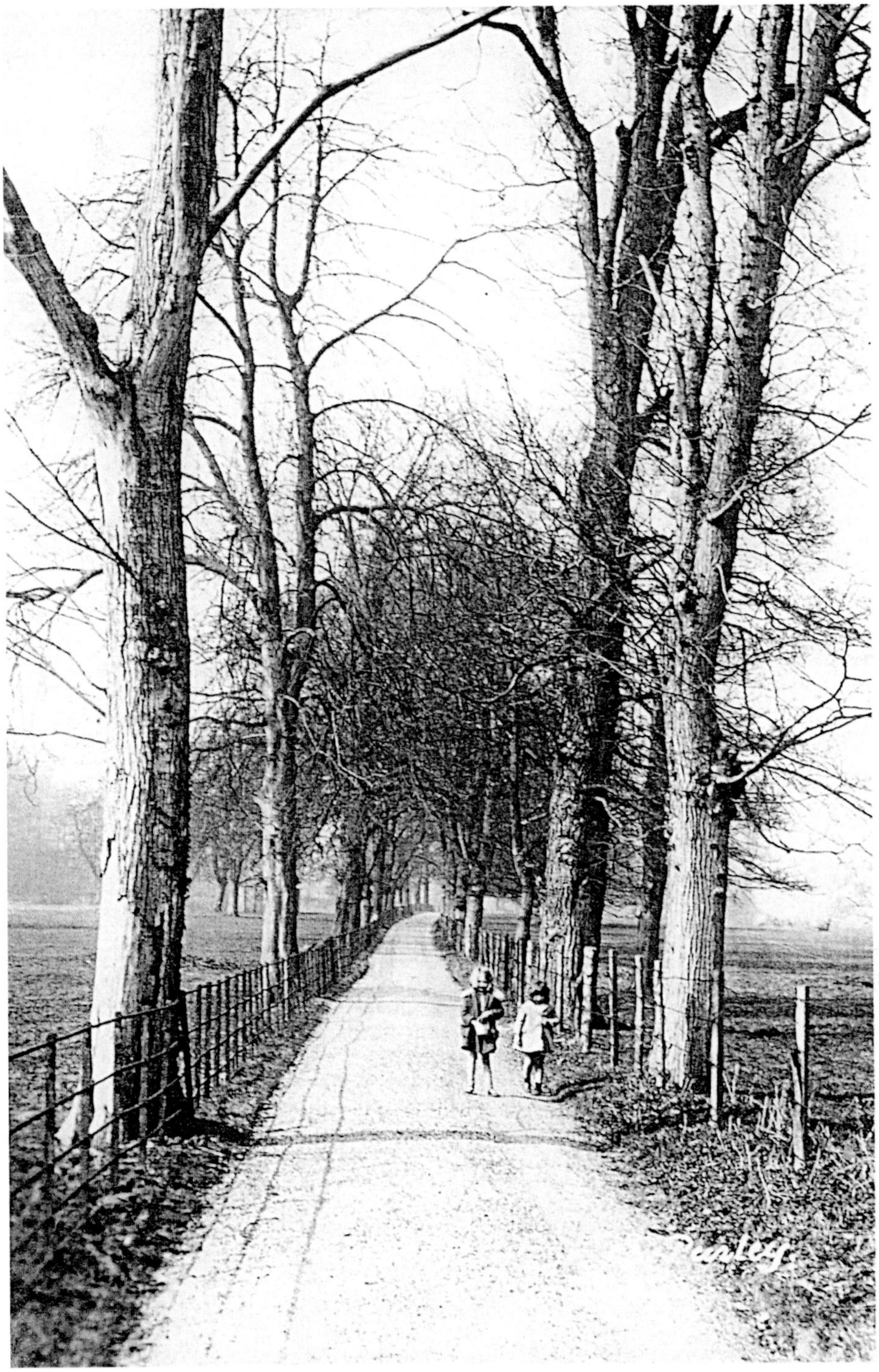

3.8 The villagers were given access to attend church services by way of a fenced-off and gated path called Church Walk, now St Mary's Avenue, seen here in the 1920s. The children are Barbara and Rosemary Rodell.

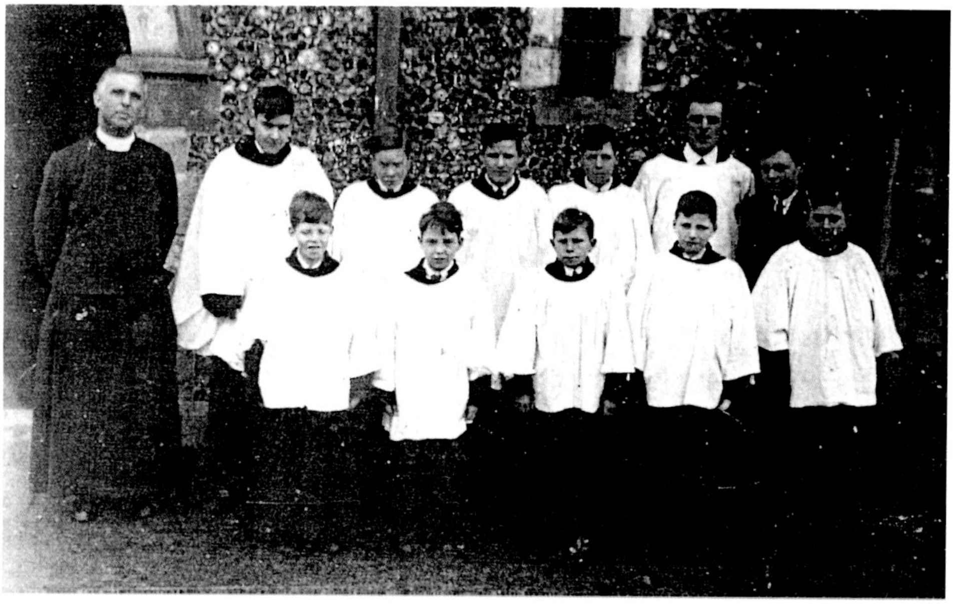

3.9 ***Above:*** The church choir in 1932 with the Revd Ernest Skuse who was rector between 1931 and 1956. From left to right, back row: Revd Skuse, Victor Rawlins, Joe Kirk, Fred Rawlins, Ted Reed, Nelson Cooper (organist and choirmaster), Cecil Tidbury, front row: Bob Reed, Pat Smith, Frank Stubbs, Harry Fox, Pete Griffith.
3.10 ***Below:*** The choir in 1962. From left to right, standing: Teresa Wright, Paul Morris, Janet Collins, Billy Morris, Colin Schofield, Frances Titlow, front row: Martin Corbishley, Bobby Morris, Brian Tappin, Jeremy Simpson, Brinley Nash, Grenville Annetts.

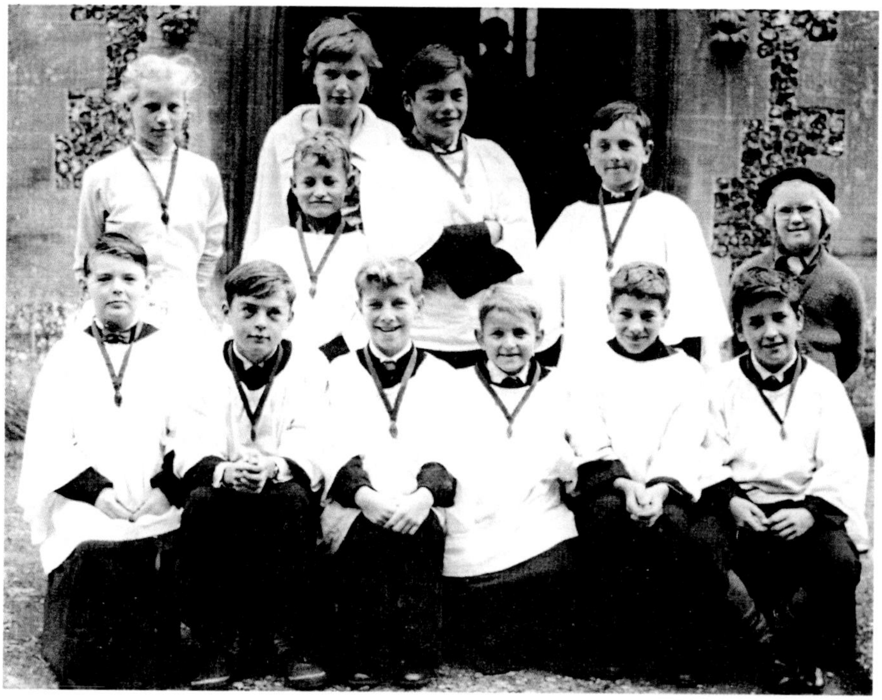

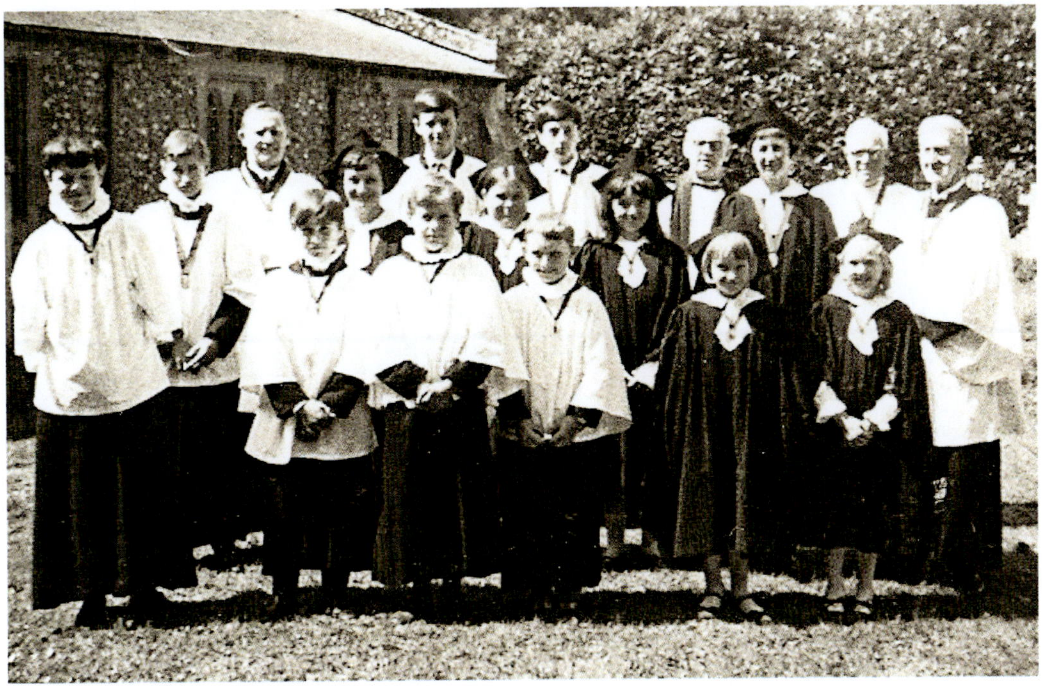

3.11 The choir in 1968. From left to right, back row: Paul Schofield, Paul Morris, Bill Fisher, Alan Winters, Colin Schofield, Revd Harold Hawkins, Lynette Barnes, Nelson Cooper, Ernest Spong, middle row: Gladys Morris, Anne Morris, Sandra Rhodes, front row: Kevin Lamb, Paul Pocock, Stephen Prentice, Anna Hurl, Susan Punter.

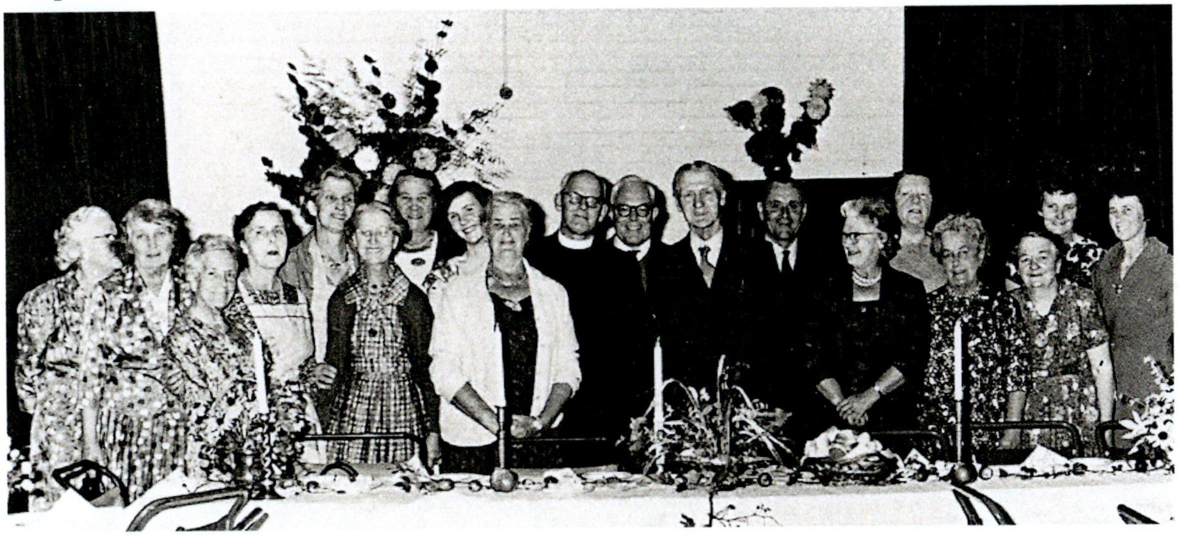

3.12 Harvest Festival in 1964. From left to right: ?, Edith Tidbury, Miss Graman, Phyllis Fothergill, Elizabeth Pryor, Miss Fisher, Mrs Laucher(?), Sally Wilcox, Mrs Smith, Revd Harold Hawkins, Nelson Cooper, Ernest Spong, Arthur (John) Bucknell, Mrs Brown, Mrs Hawkins, Winifred Rabone, Elsie Kirton, Joan Wilcox, Lynette Barnes.

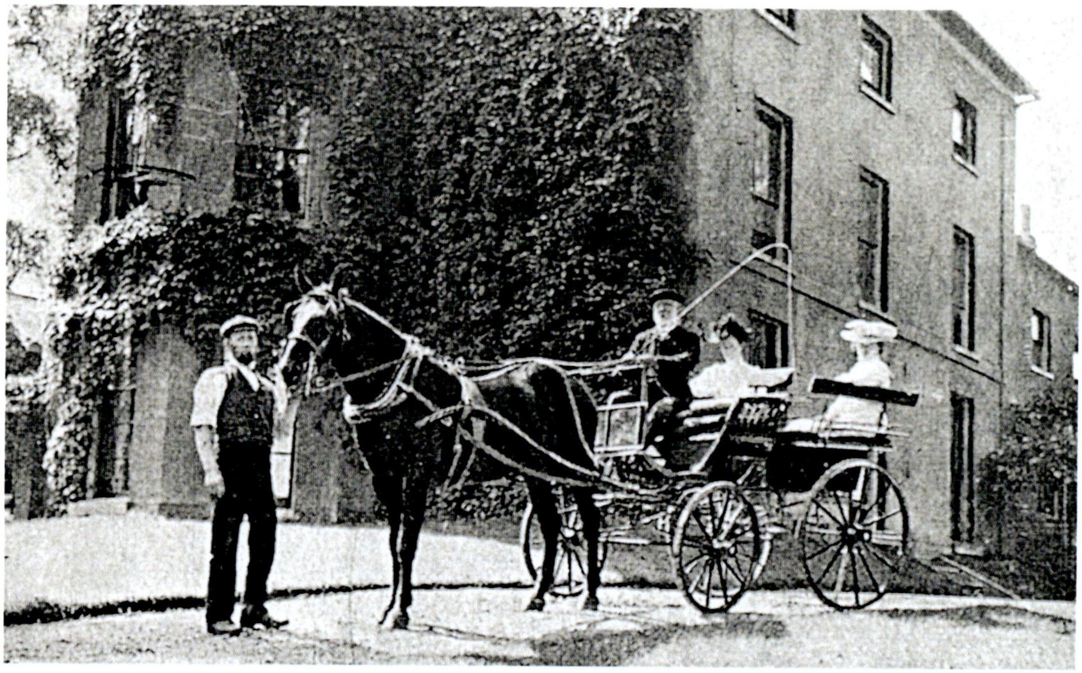

3.13 & 3.14 ***Above and Below:*** The old rectory, on the site of what is now Lister Close, is pictured around 1910 ***(above)*** and in 1964 ***(below)***. The upper image shows Revd John Dudley Matthews, his wife Edith and daughter, Rose, in a carriage in front of their home. Revd Dudley Matthews lost his life in 1914 when his boat capsized as he returned from taking evensong across the river at Mapledurham Church.

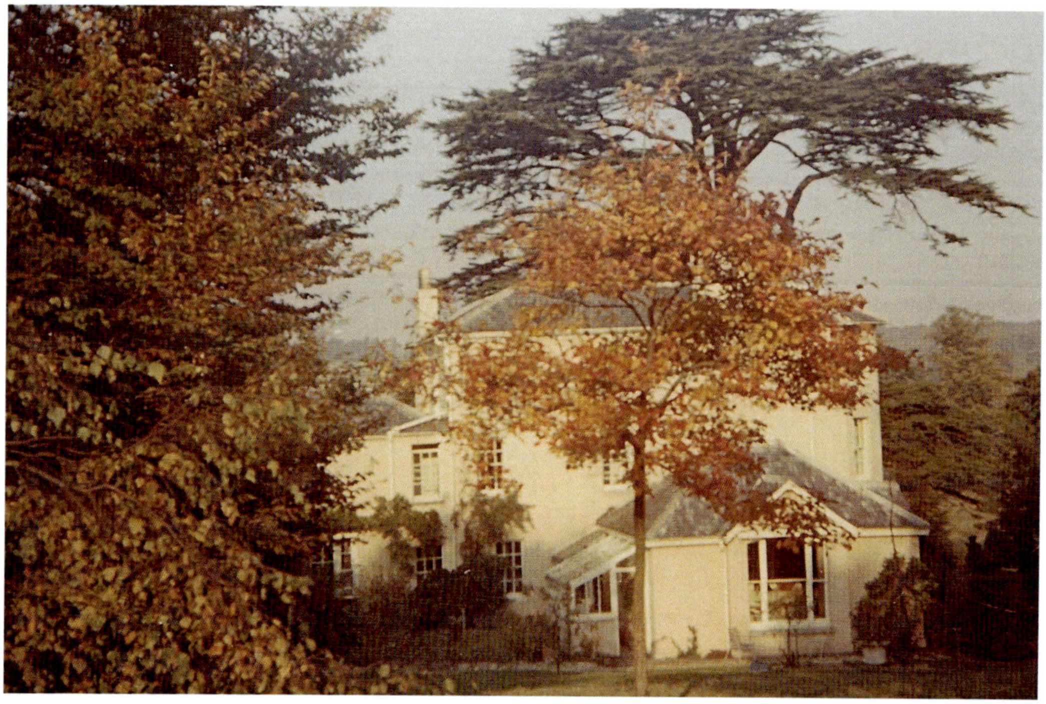

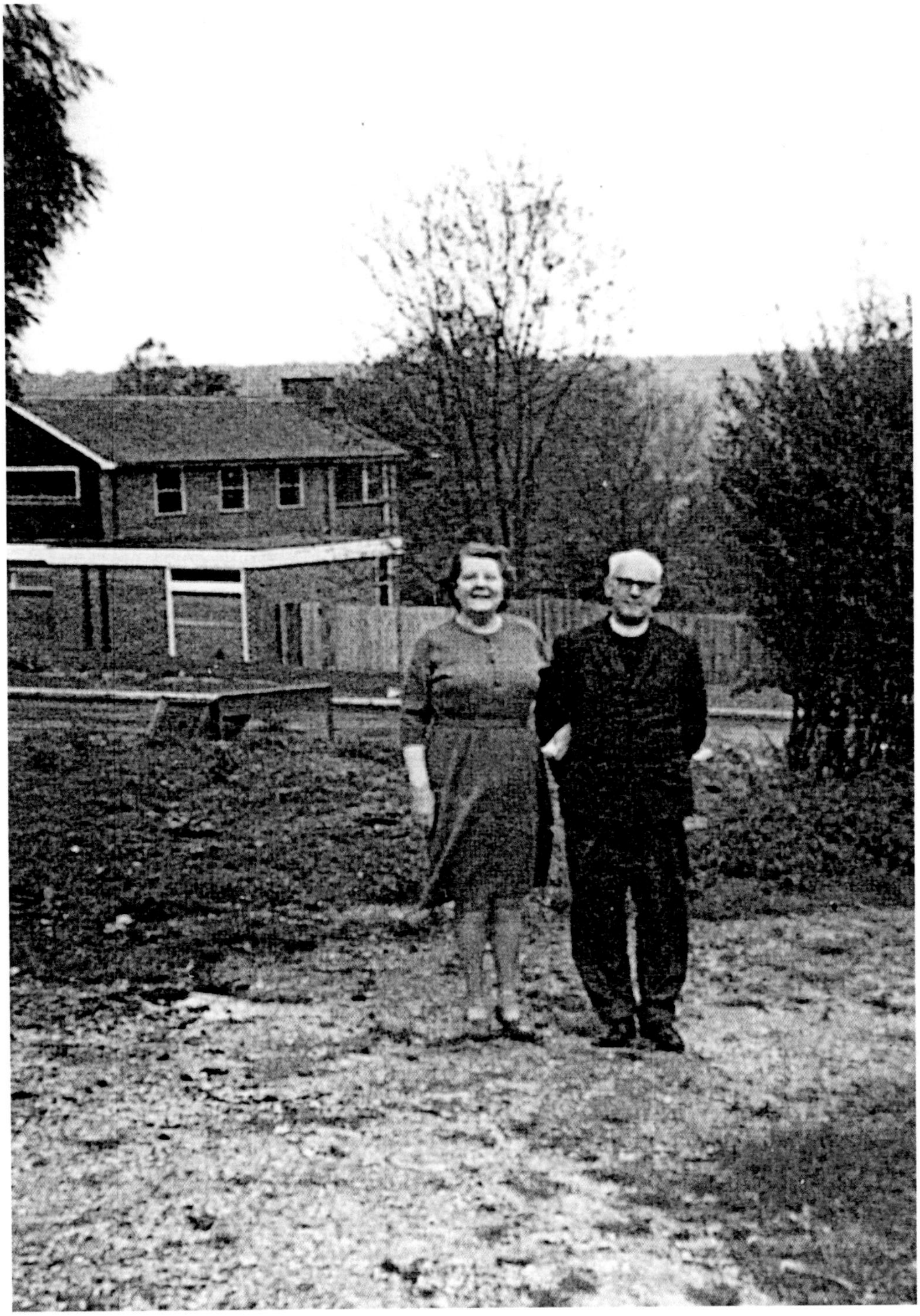

3.15 The Reverend Harold Hawkins and his wife Nellie in 1969 in front of the present rectory then under construction on the corner of Purley Lane and Westridge Avenue.

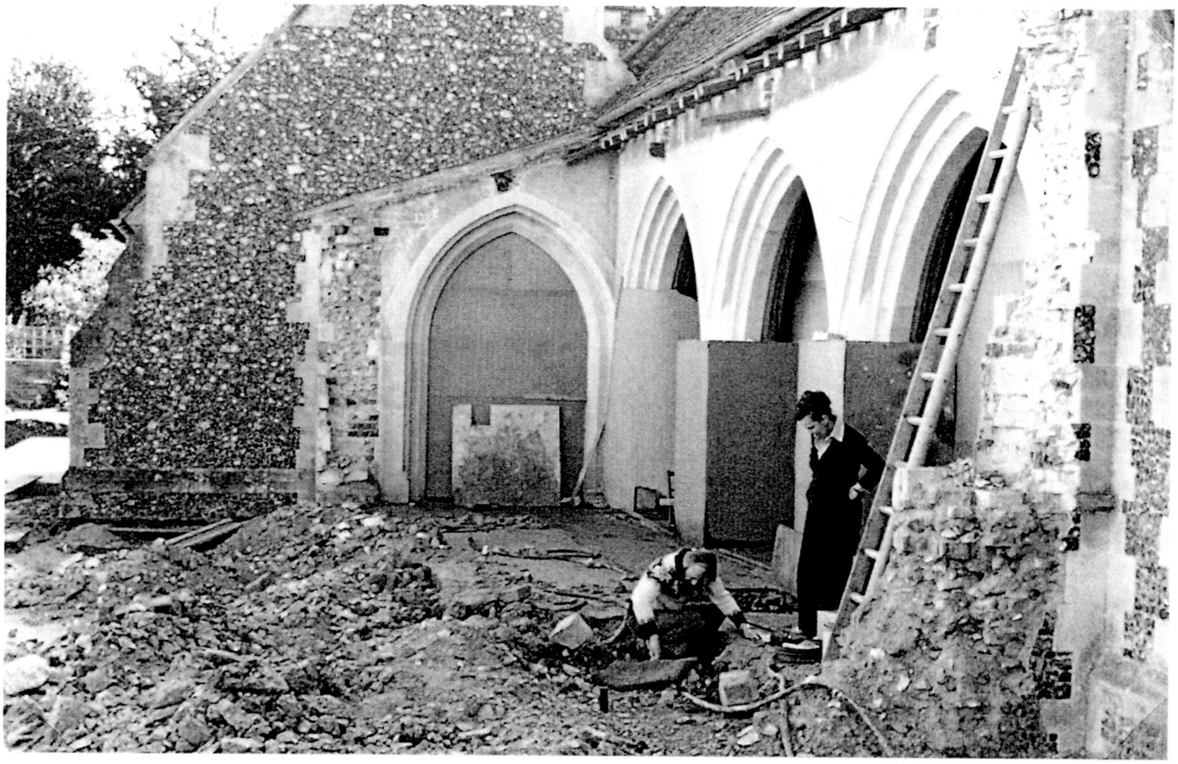

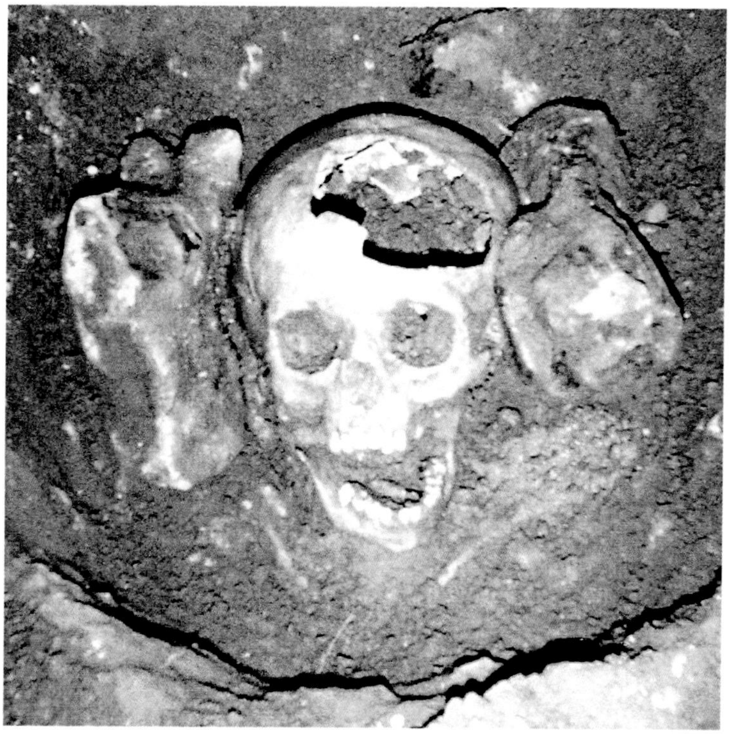

3.16 ***Above:*** In the early 1980s, before the demolition of the north aisle extension, an archaeological excavation by local historians uncovered early graves probably dating to the eleventh or twelfth centuries. Here Cliff Debney, watched by his wife Jean, checks the area exposed after the builders had started work and removed the wooden floor.

3.17 ***Left:*** One of the typical 'pillow' burials unearthed during the excavation. These were so called due to the large flints supporting each side of the head.

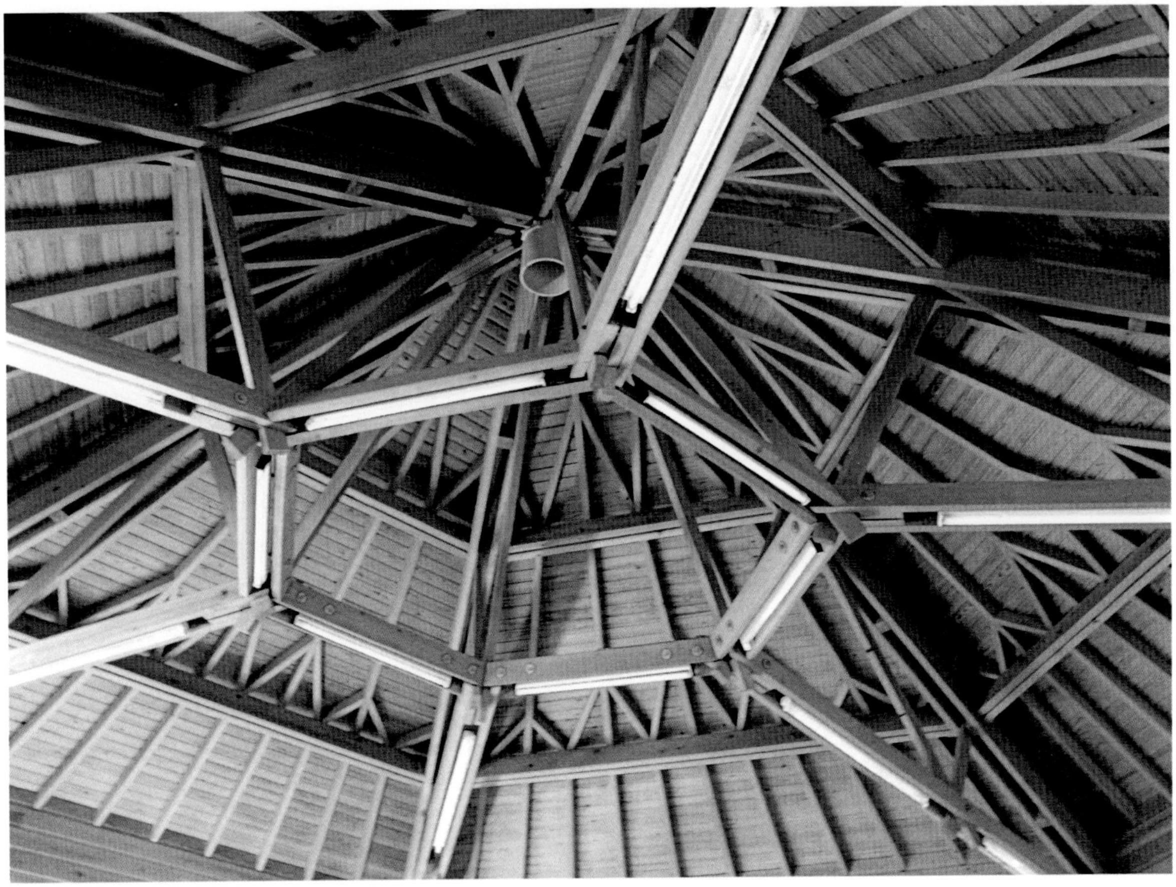

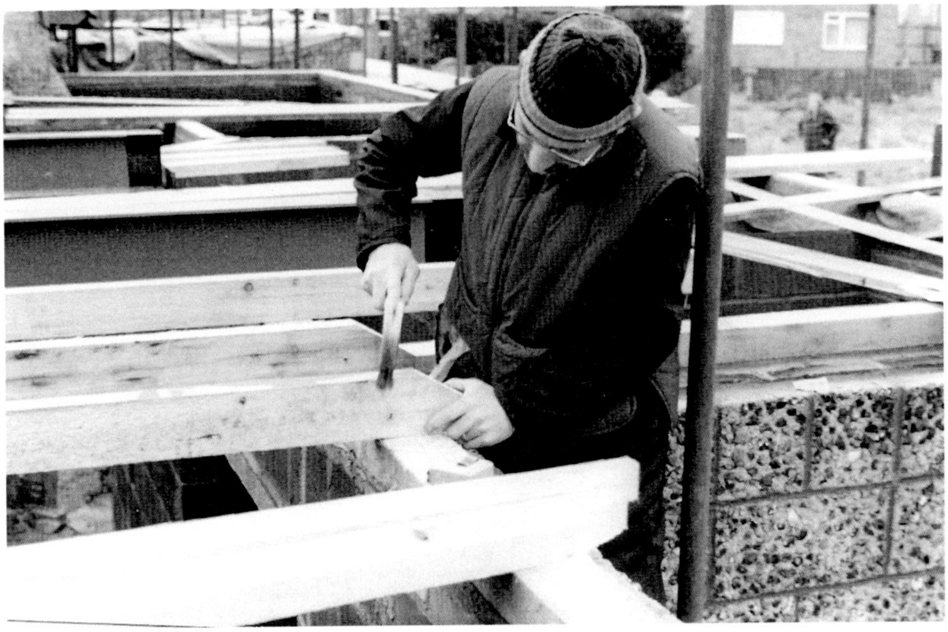

3.19 ***Left:*** Ron Herbert the carpenter works on the 1983 extension to the church.
3.18 ***Above:*** the impressive finished roof.

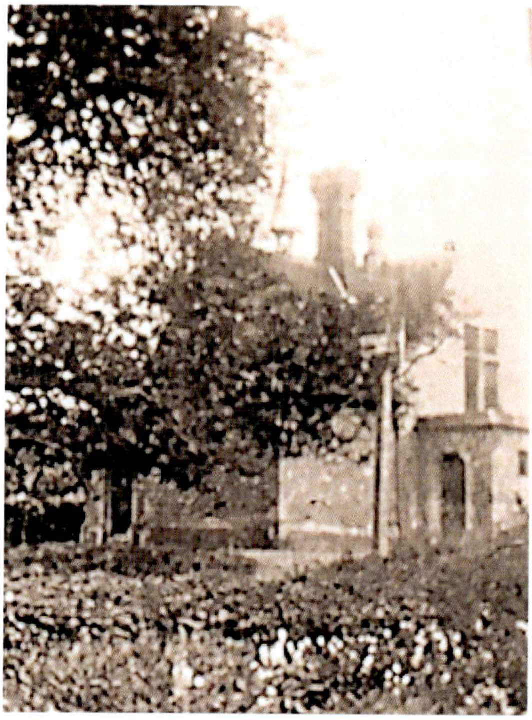

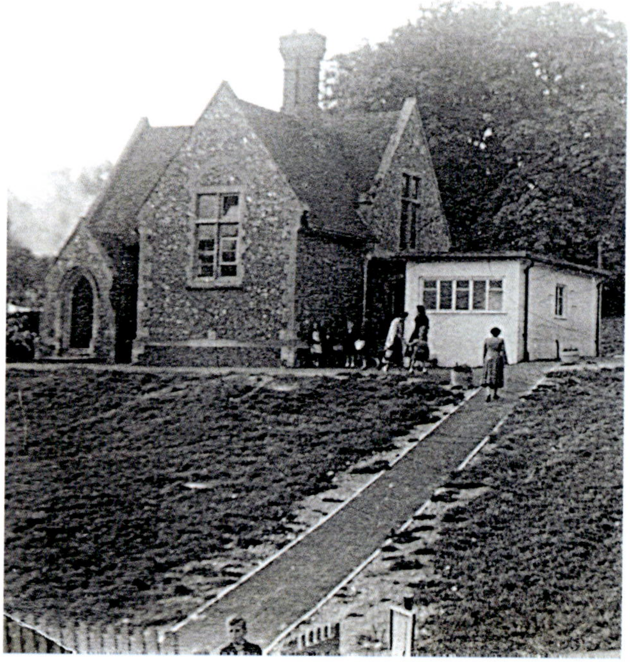

3.20 & 3.21 Purley Church of England School pictured around 1940, left, and in 1958, after completion of the new extension. The earlier photograph shows the separate entrances for boys and girls, still in use at that time, together with the belfry, to the left of the chimney stack.

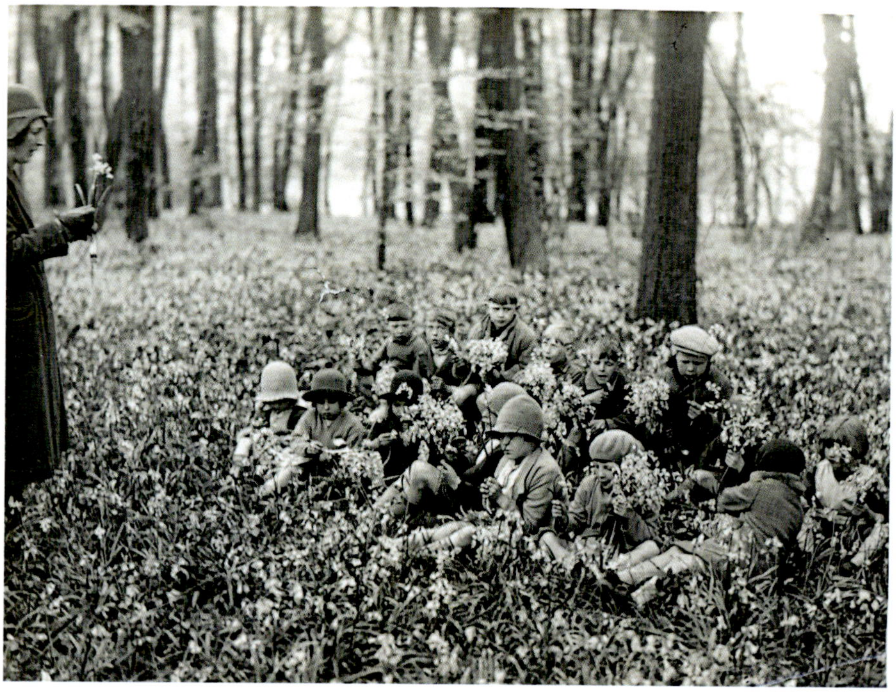

3.22 ***Left:*** Learning also took place away from the classroom. This image, c1927, shows headmistress Edith Tidbury with pupils in the woods at Sulham.

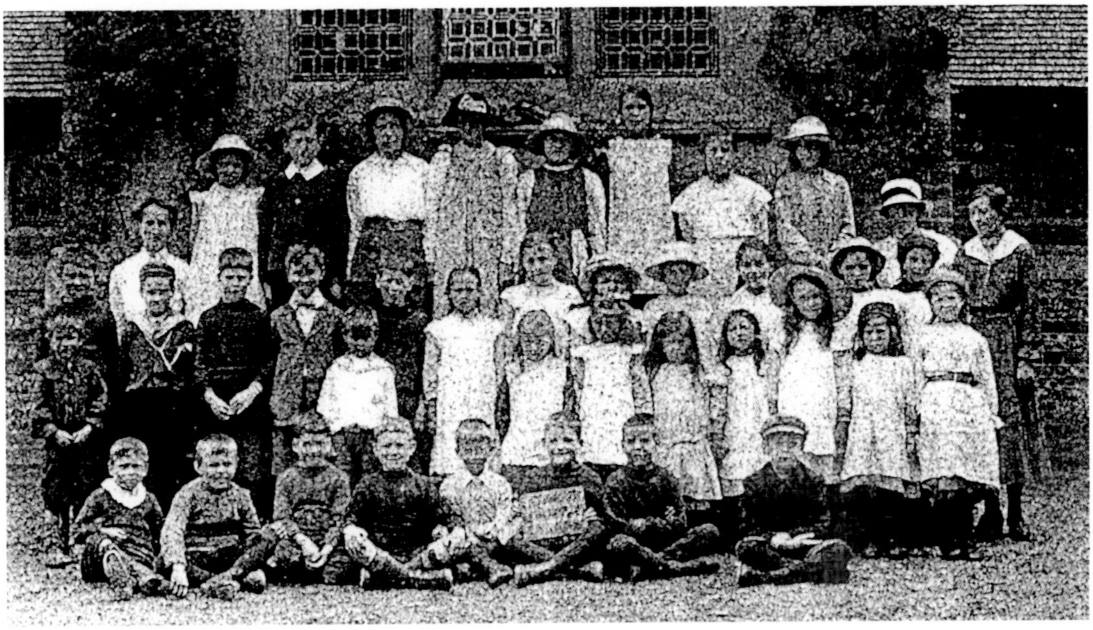

3.23 ***Above:*** Our earliest class photograph from Purley Church of England School dates to the First World War, around the time Miss Dayrell-Reed was the headmistress.

3.24 ***Below:*** By 1921 Miss Mary Edwards had taken over the headship and she is seen here in the centre of the photograph, with assistant teacher Jane (Ginny) Leath to her left.

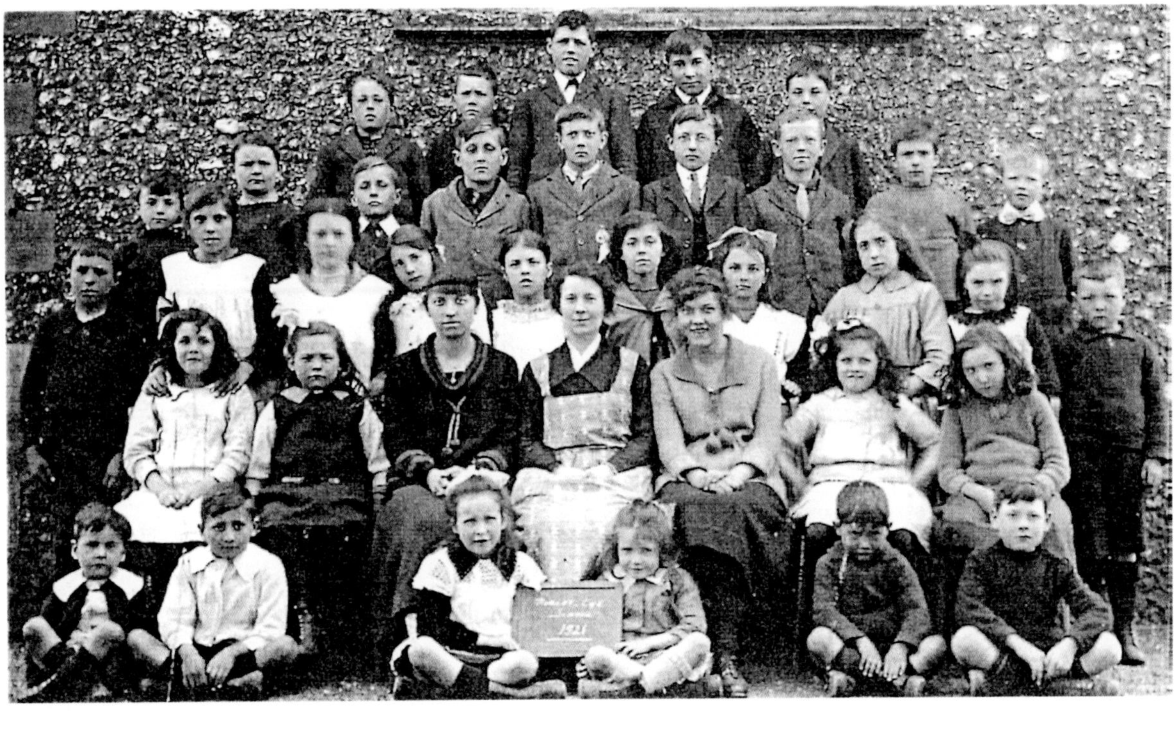

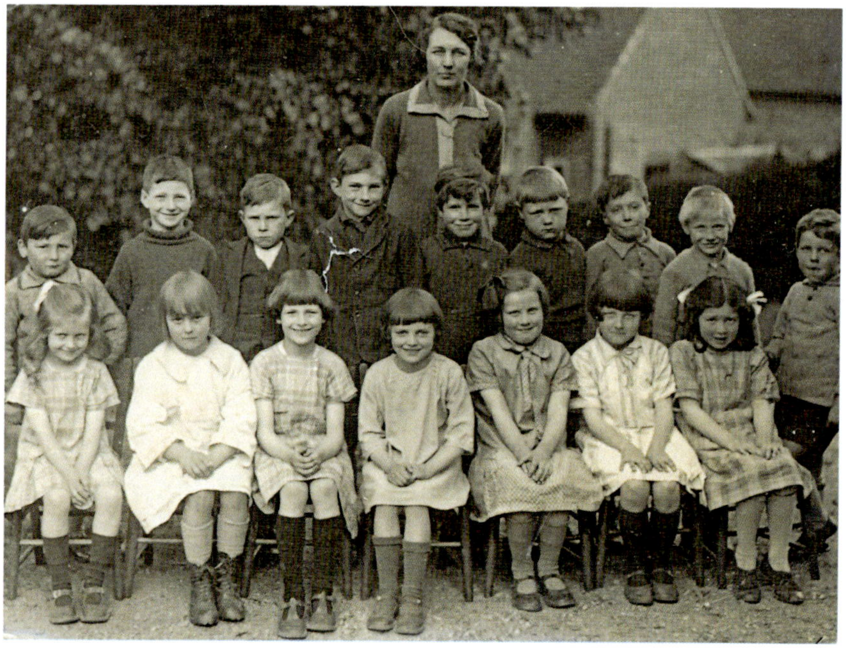

3.25 ***Left:*** Mrs Edith Tidbury was the headmistress between 1925 and 1954 and for a while she and her family lived next door in the school house, now called Hemington. She is pictured here with pupils in 1927.

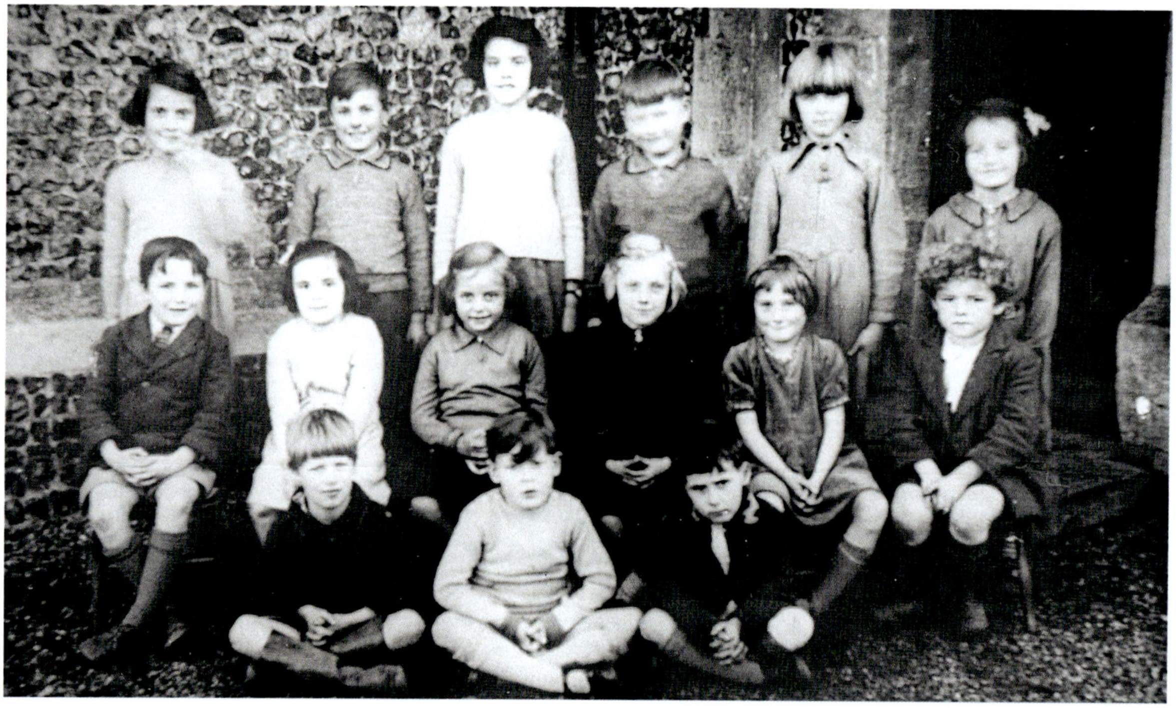

3.26 The class of 1938, from left to right, back row: Jean Miles, Alan Gibbons, Joyce Nicholls, Sam Rodell, Peggy Mott, June Williams, second row: Clarence Bowles, June Nash, Margaret Iles, Mary Miller, Gertie Carter, Derrick Mott, front row: Edgar Carter, Michael Newton,?.

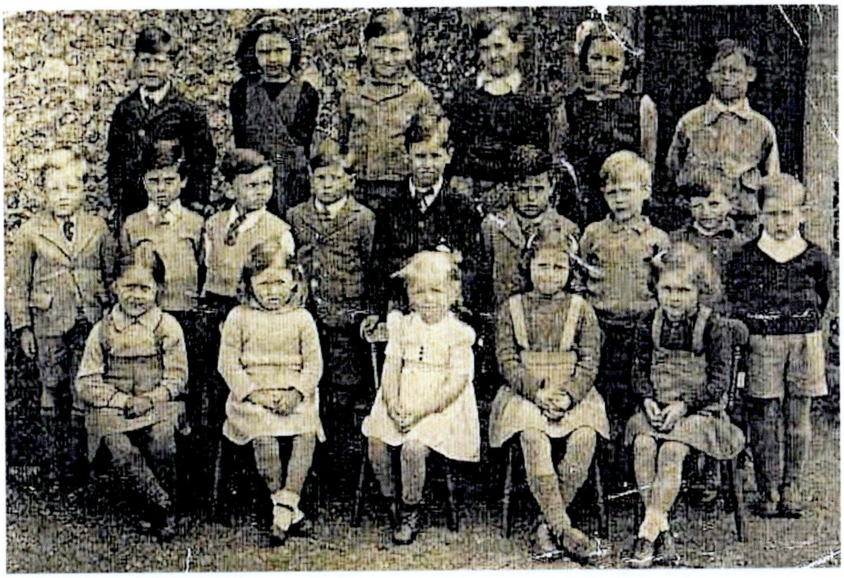

3.27 ***Left:*** The class of 1946. From left to right, back row: Norman Garner, Veronica Pooley, Michael Dunne, Edward Rawlins, Beryl, Albert Clark, middle row: Geoffrey Puttock, David Farr, Terry Casling, Terry Spicer, Brian Woods, Peter May, Kingsley Starling, David Champion,?, front row: Sheila Nation,?, Spicer,?,?.

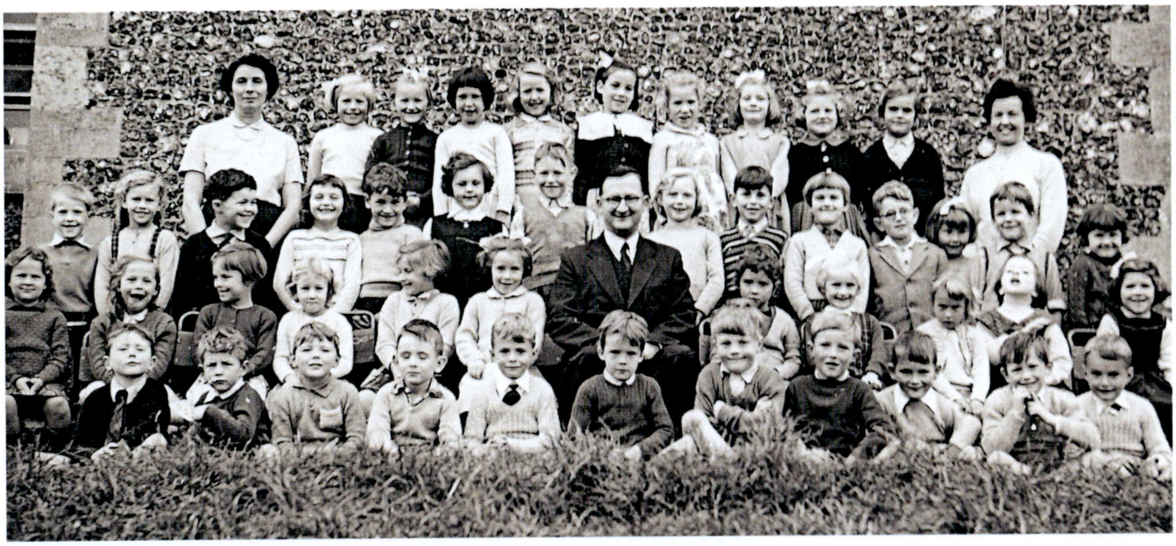

3.28 The class of 1958. From left to right, back row: Mrs McLaughlin, Linda Wright, Theresa Bielanski, Julie Weller, Christina Patterson, Patsy Parr, Janice Allchorne, Nina Gibbons, Denise Twigg, Joy Woodman, Mrs Shaw, 2nd row:?, Janet Duck, Stuart Crook,?, Grenville Annetts, Vivien Walsingham, Peter Clark, Kathleen Horseman, Patrick Reaney,?, John Bird, Sally Apthorpe, Derek Wall, Sharon Windiate, 3rd row: ?,?,?, Pauline Bevan, Marilyn James, Susan Sunderland, Mr Alexander (acting headmaster),?, Fiona Guest, Anne Tomlinson,?, Lynda Skerritt, front row: Colin Schofield, Steven Watts, Martin Corbishley, Keith Goodchild, Michael Gillingham, Graham North, James Day, Stephen Critchell,?, Mervyn Griffiths, Victor Gillingham.

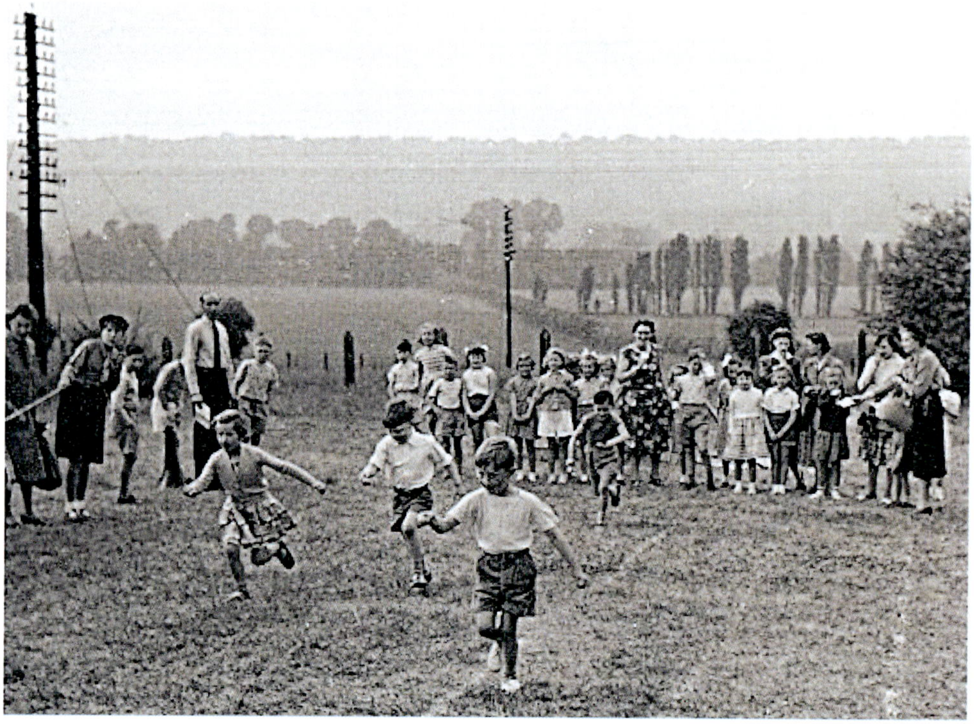

3.29 **Left:** School sports day, 1959.

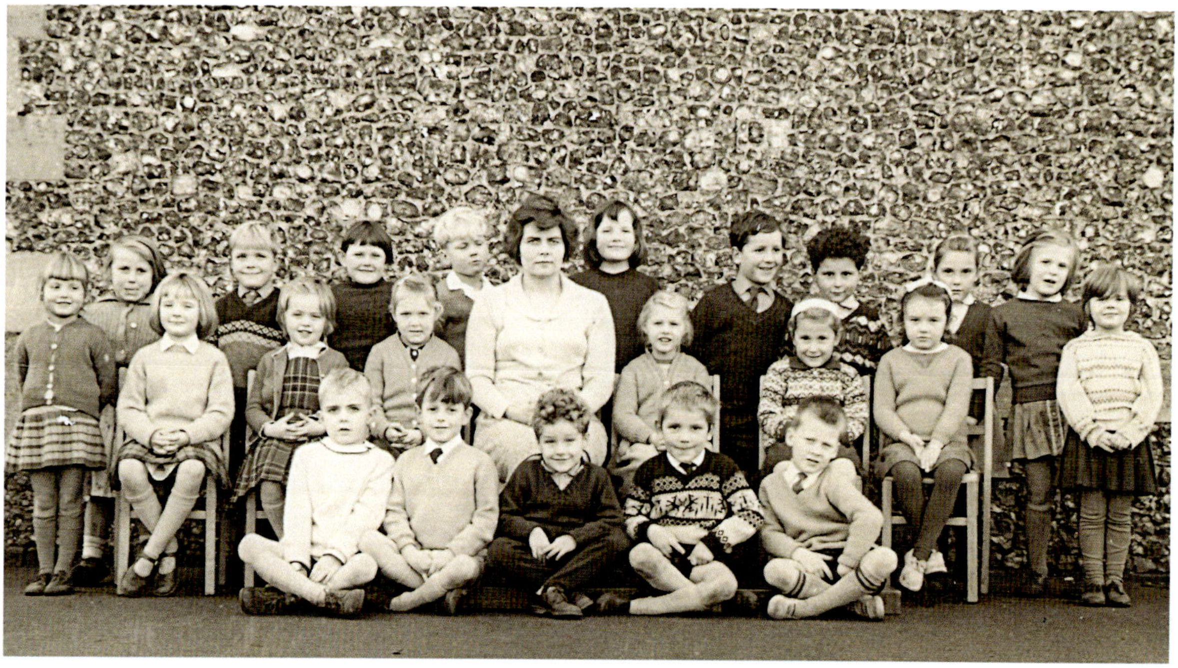

3.30 A class group in 1965 with teacher Pat Deane. Children identified for this picture include on the front row, from left to right: Barry Deane, David Toms, Patrick Hutchings,?,?.

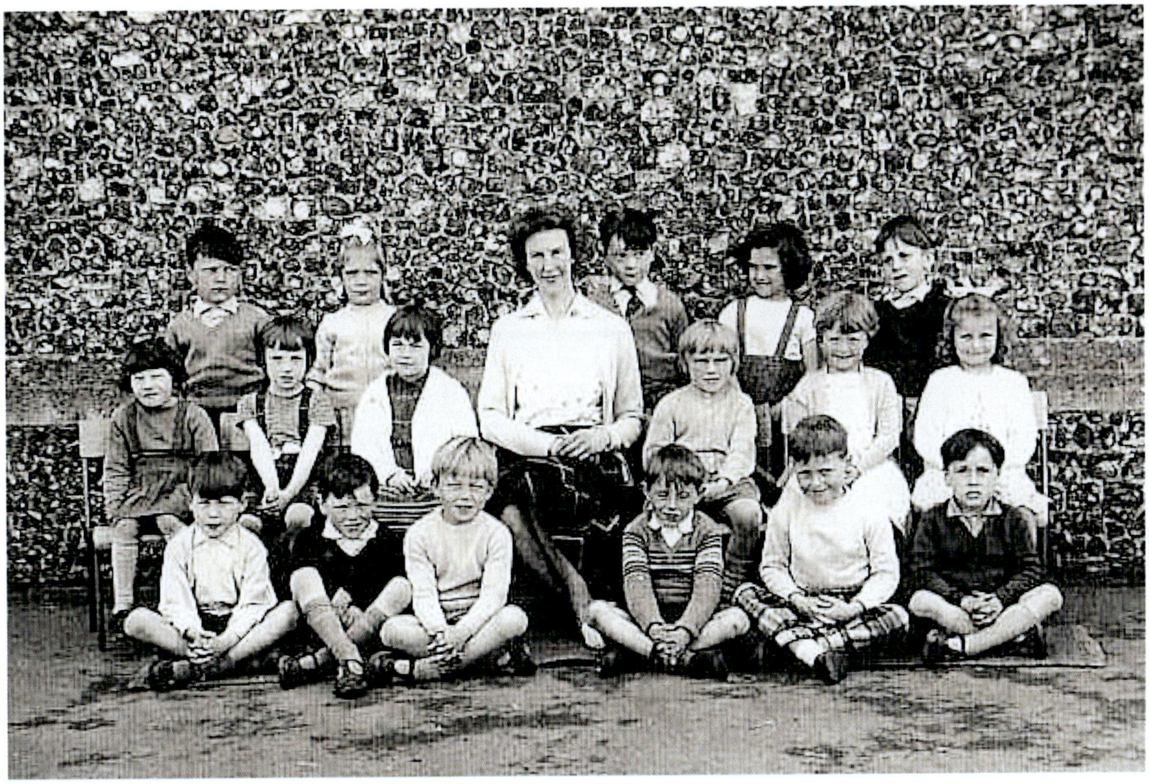

3.31 ***Above:*** The final photograph from Purley Church of England School shows Mrs McLaughlin with her class in 1967.

3.32 ***Below:*** We complete our chapter on the church and school with a photograph of the opening class at Long Lane Primary School in 1966 with head teacher Bill Palmer ***(left)*** and teacher Bert Gonella.

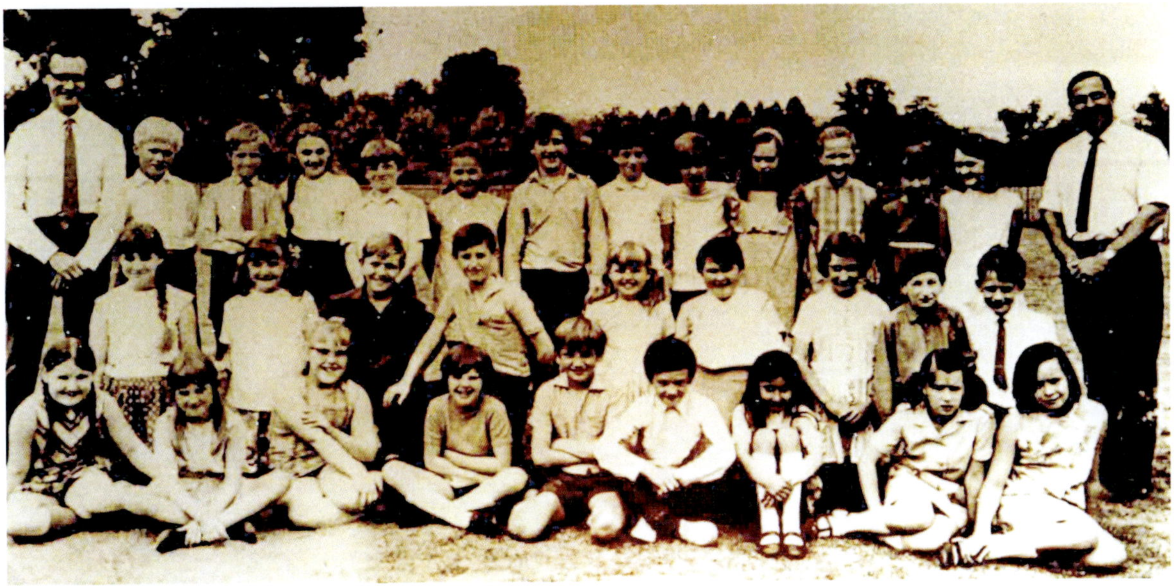

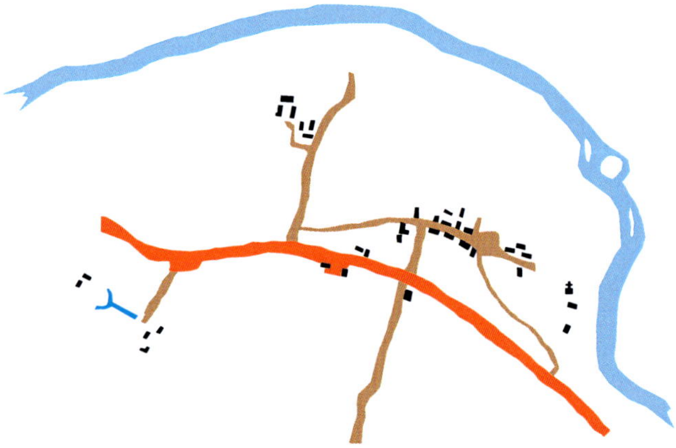

1761

Number of houses: 30
Population: 140

Project Purley estimate

Based on John Rocques map of Berkshire, 1761

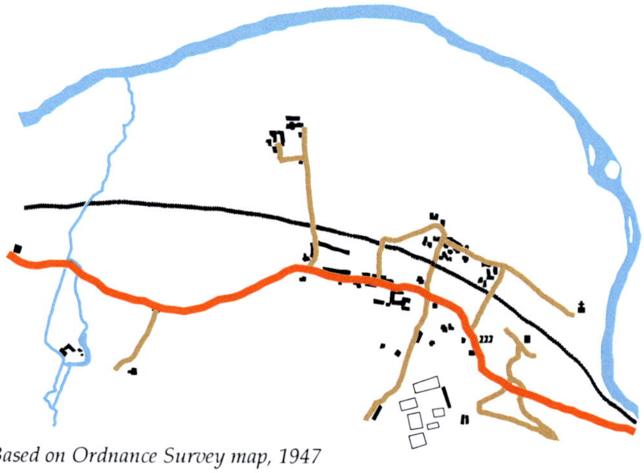

1947

Number of houses: 300
Population: 867

Project Purley estimate

Based on Ordnance Survey map, 1947

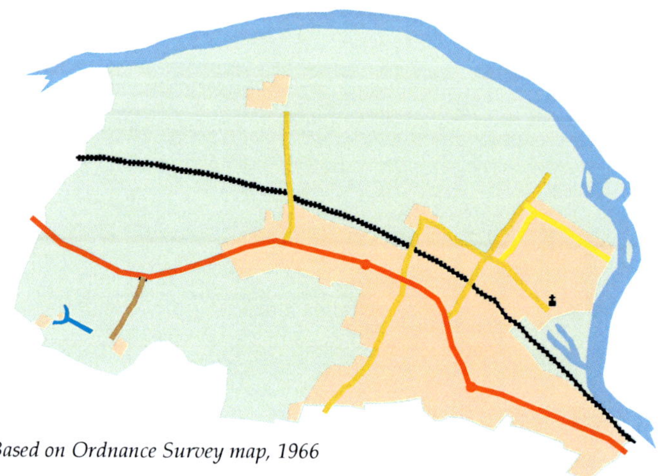

2001

Number of houses: 1,481
Population: 4,232

2001 Census

Based on Ordnance Survey map, 1966

4 *Development of the Village*

One of the characteristics of Purley is that it has no obvious village centre. In medieval times small groups of cottages existed in the three manors, but only one of these manors developed into a more substantive and lasting settlement and this was radically contained when Purley Park was created around 1800. By the early nineteenth century, what remained of old Purley was the village street with Purley Lodge at one end and Home Farm and the village pond at the other, together with a scattering of cottages mainly for the workers of local farms.

In the early twentieth century some limited development took place as land that was previously farmed became available and this accelerated rapidly after the sale and break up, firstly of Purley Park and subsequently of Mortimer Menpes' Fruit Farm. Near to the river, the River Estate grew plot by plot and further up the hill planned developments and infill have substantially increased the village population.

This chapter includes photographs of many of our earliest cottages, several of which date to the early 1600s, together with some of the families who made them their homes. We move on to glimpses of our longer-established roads mid-twentieth century before finishing with the changing of the names of both our village and our main road to those familiar to us today.

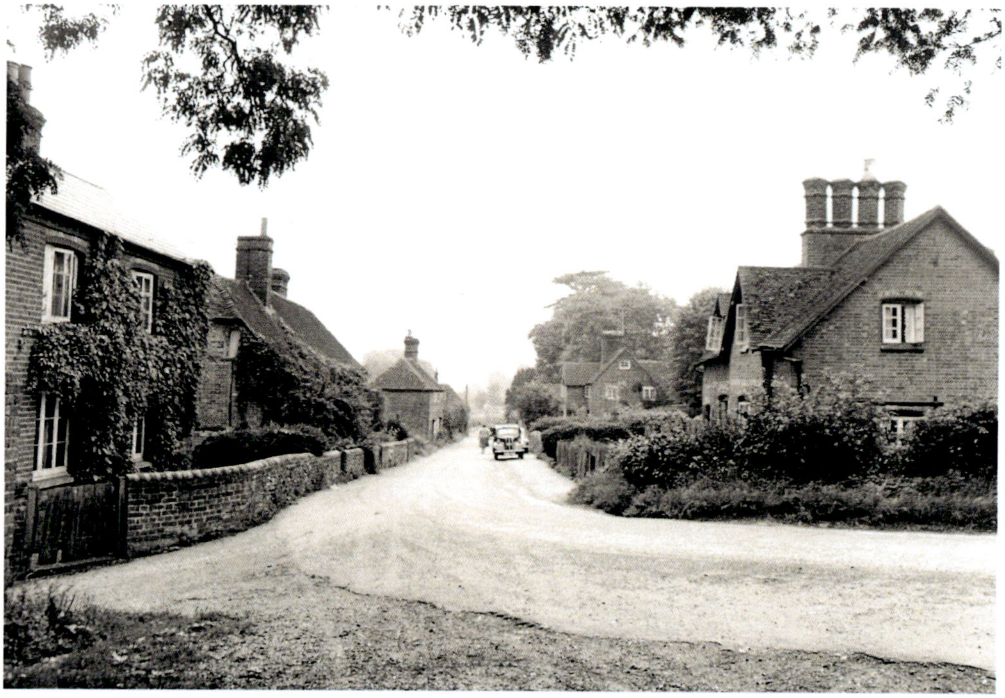

4.1 & 4.2 ***Above and below:*** 'Old Purley' – the scene we would have seen a century ago is still recognisable today. This is where you would find the main concentration of cottages, the rectory, the school, the home farm of Purley Park and the village pond. Of the more obvious changes, in Collier's post Second World War photograph above, we can see the old Corner Cottages, now replaced, on the right, and below, in Tidbury's image taken c1915, the stream which ran along the side of the street, over which the cottagers put small 'bridges'.

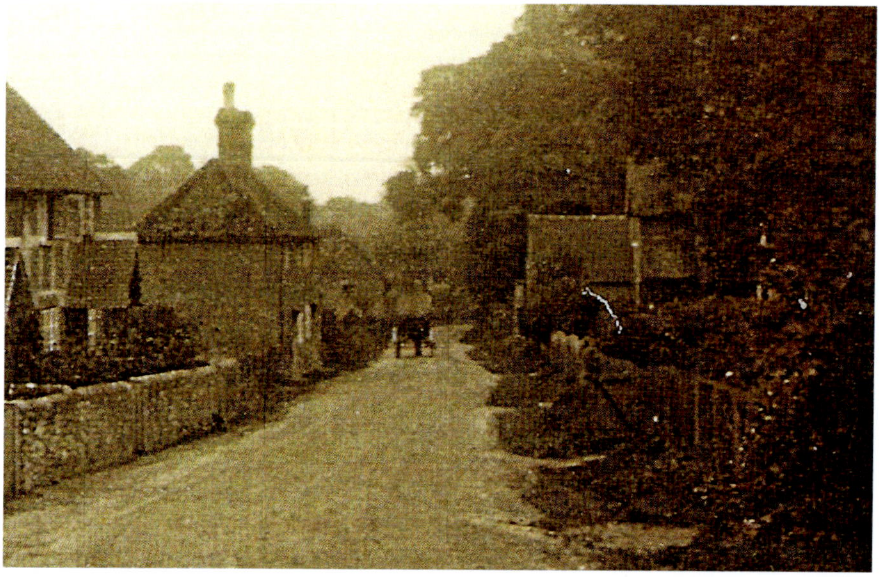

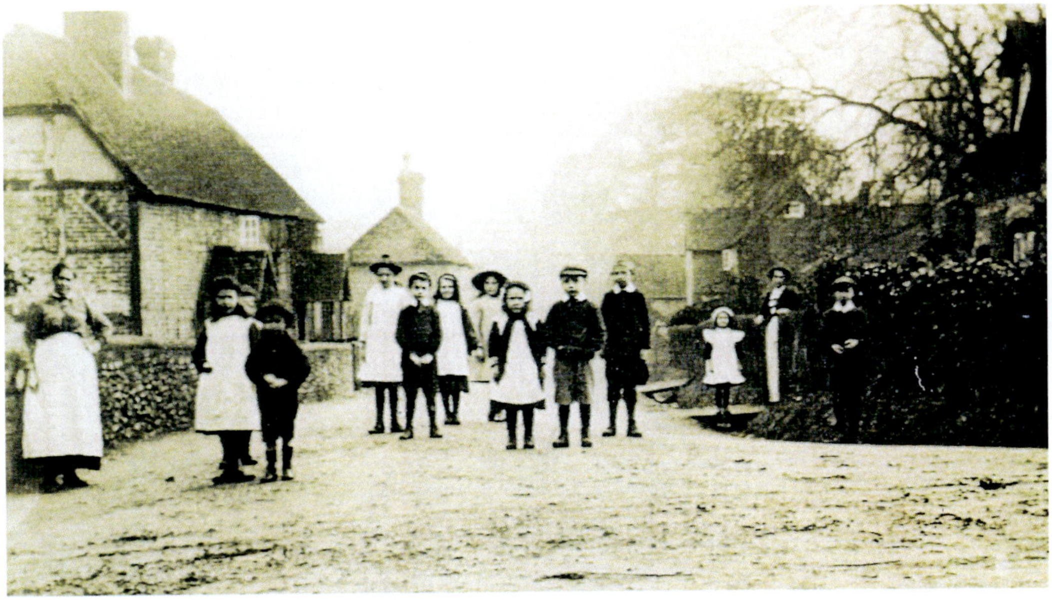

4.3 ***Above:*** A group of village children and mothers pose in 1908 for a photograph taken by Tommy Wright who was the organist at St Mary's Church.
4.4 ***Below:*** On the north-eastern side of The Street lay the village pond, much loved by both the village children and the livestock of Home Farm.

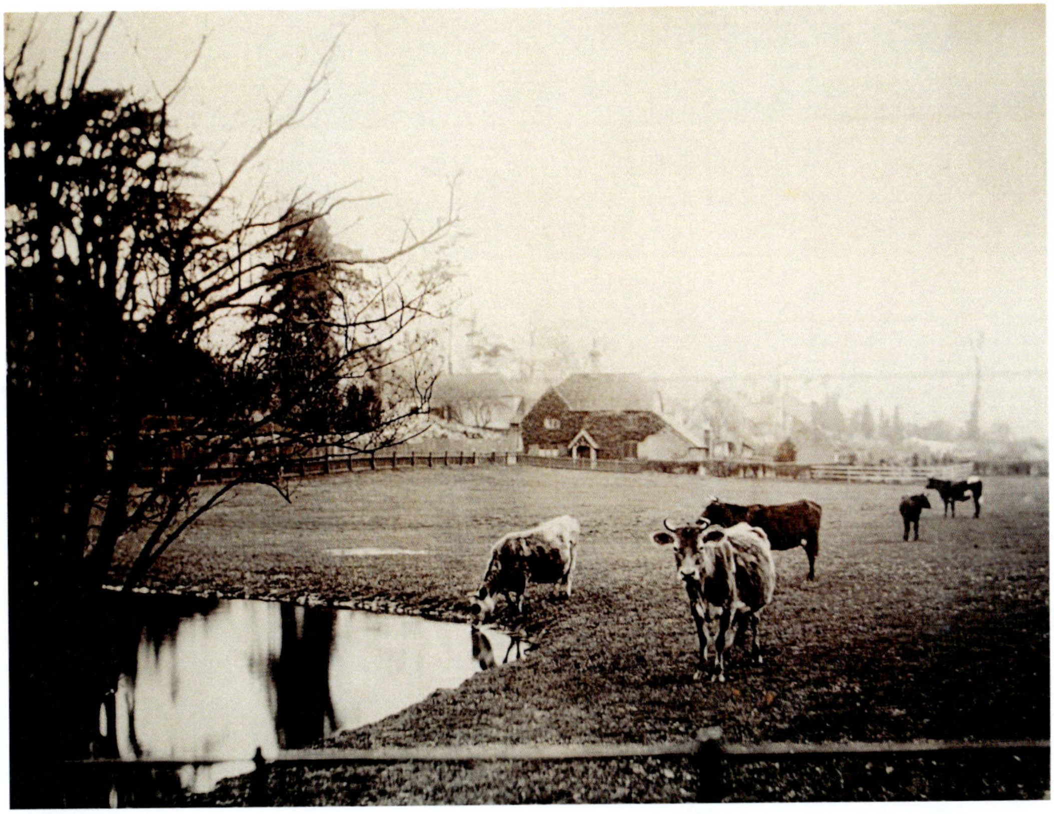

4.5 ***Near Right:*** Henry and Elizabeth Leath pictured in the 1930s in front of Purley Lodge Cottage. Henry was the gardener and coachman at Purley Lodge.

4.6 ***Far Right:*** James Rogers pictured in the 1920s in front of his cottage on The Street. James' wife, Susannah, was a laundress and the garden was often full of drying washing. The cottage was pulled down and Wisteria and Cherry Acre were later built on the site.

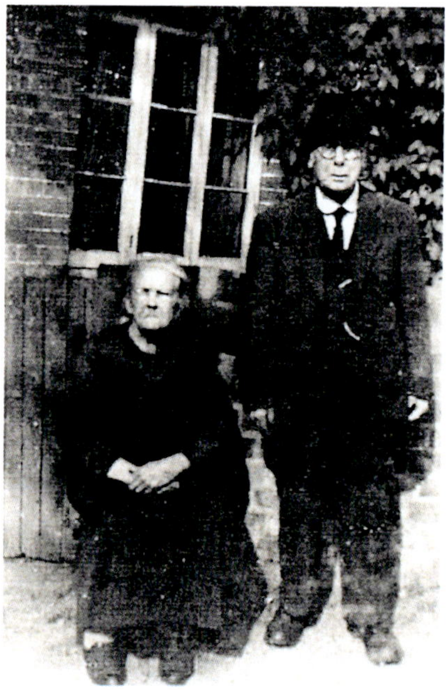

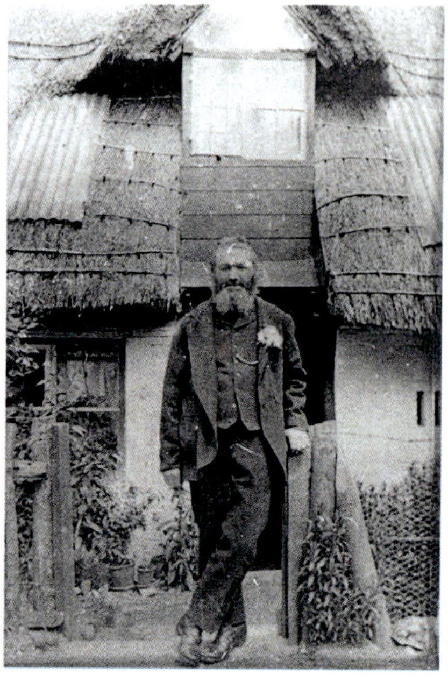

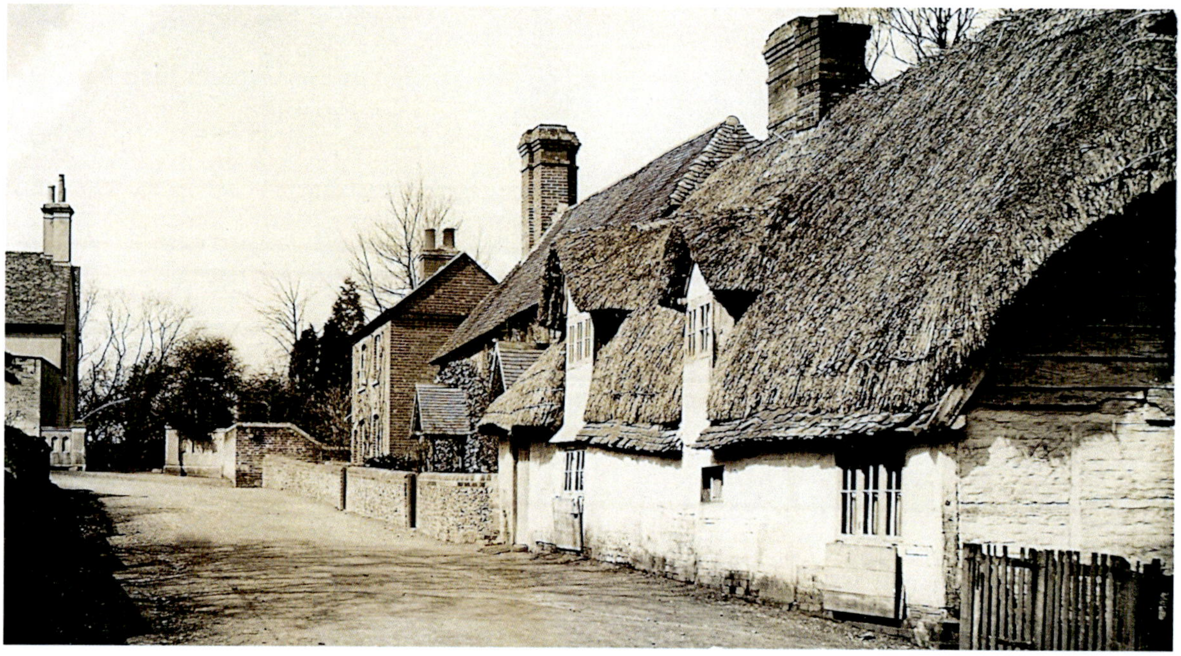

4.7 This cottage was on the site now occupied by The Mimosas and was part of the Westbury Farm Estate. Beyond it you can see Jasmine Cottages and Purley Lodge Cottage.

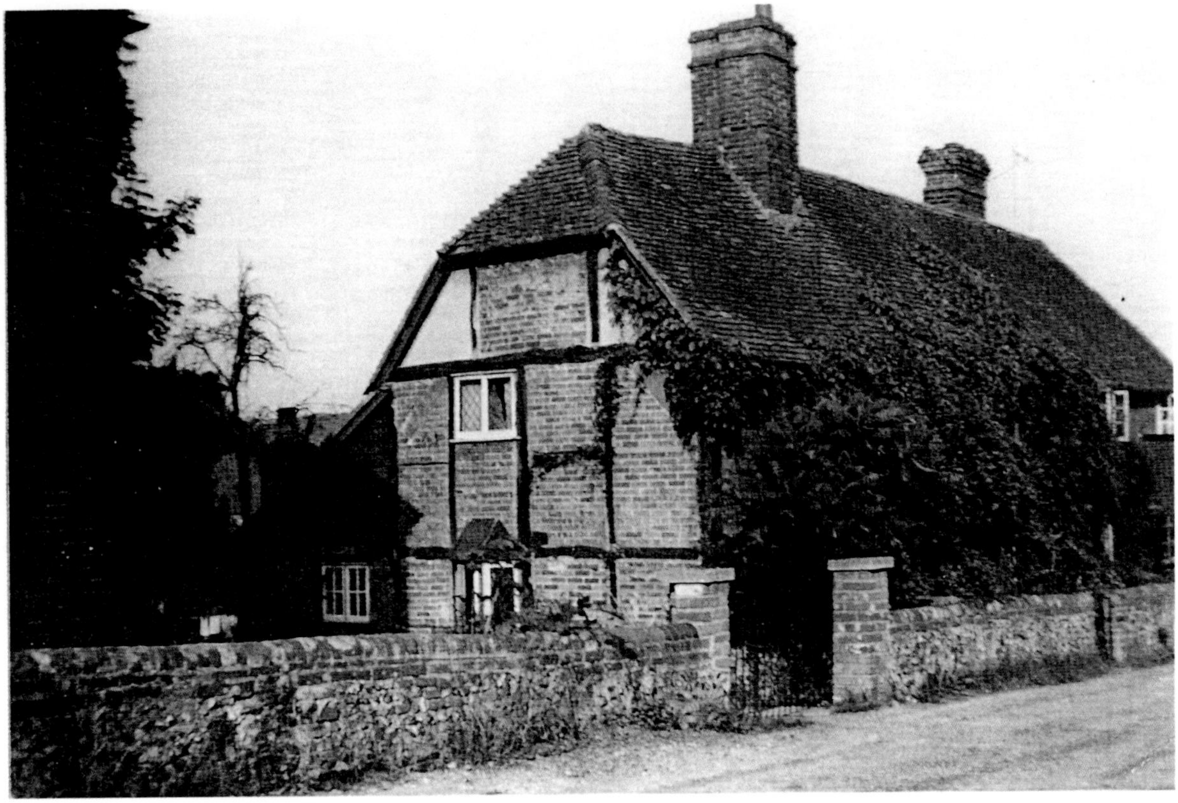

4.8 ***Above:*** Jasmine Cottages, here c1963, were built in the mid 1600s as a single, probably thatched, farmhouse which was later converted into two dwellings for farm labourers.

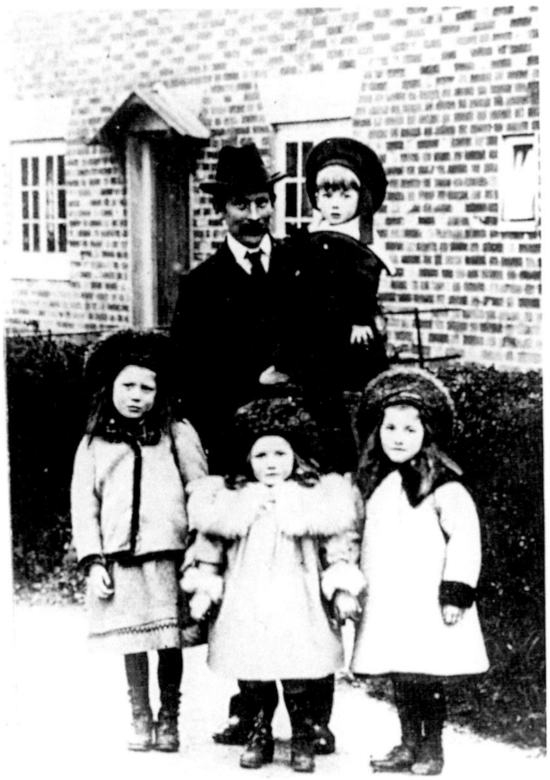

4.9 ***Right:*** Fred Alexander with his son Donald and daughters, from left to right: Augusta, Bessie, and Vera c1904. Fred, a farm labourer, and his wife Lucy moved with their young family from Yattendon to Jasmine Cottages in the early 1900s and the children attended the village school. The family emigrated to America in 1910.

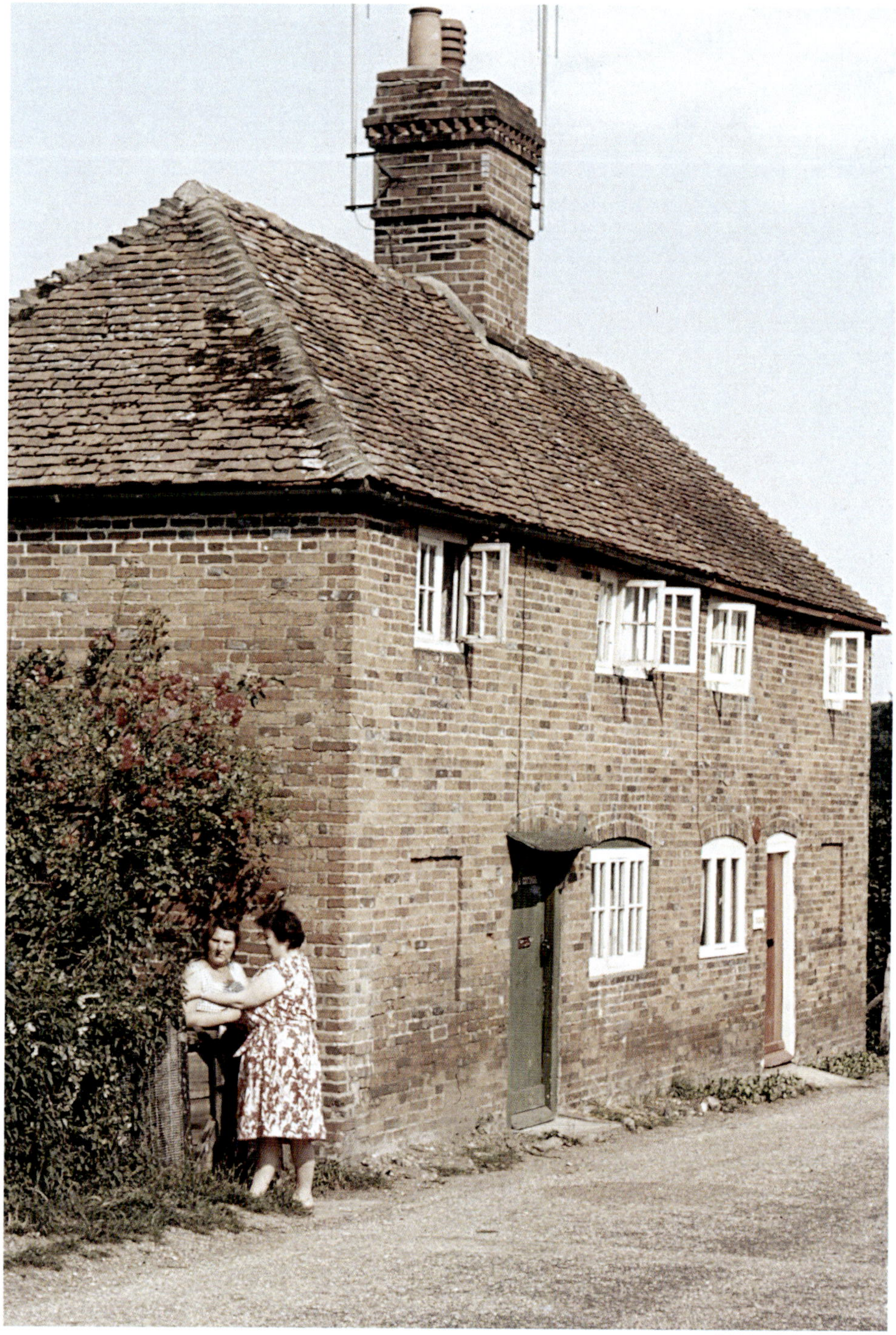

4.10 Jean Mundy and Anne Rawlins of Hemington outside The Cottage in the 1960s, when it was still a pair of tied farm cottages belonging to Westbury Farm.

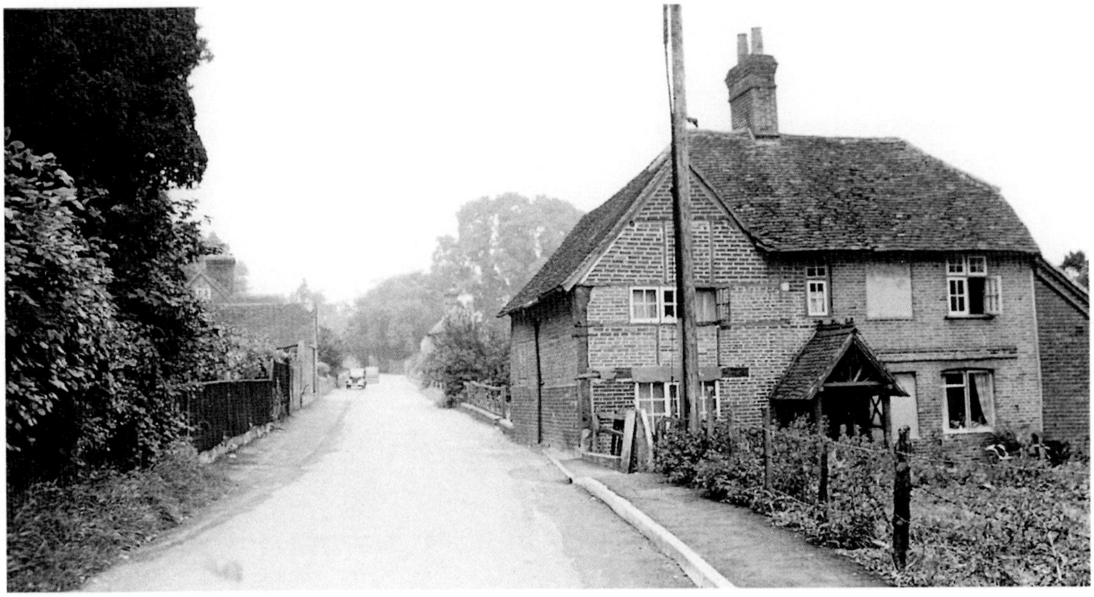

4.11 ***Above:*** Ivy Cottage, built in the 1600s, was originally part of Purley Magna and called 'the old house'. It later became a pair of tied cottages for Home Farm.
4.12 & 4.13 ***Below: (Left)*** Hemington, pictured c1963, dates to around 1730 and has over its history been both a single and a pair of cottages. One cottage was home to the Martin family, shoemakers, before it became the school cottage. ***(Right)*** Corner Cottages, here in the 1950s, were demolished in the 1970s and Stargable and Letgable now occupy this site. Edward Sheppard, a fisherman and a son of William the lock-keeper, lived here with his wife Sarah and their children.

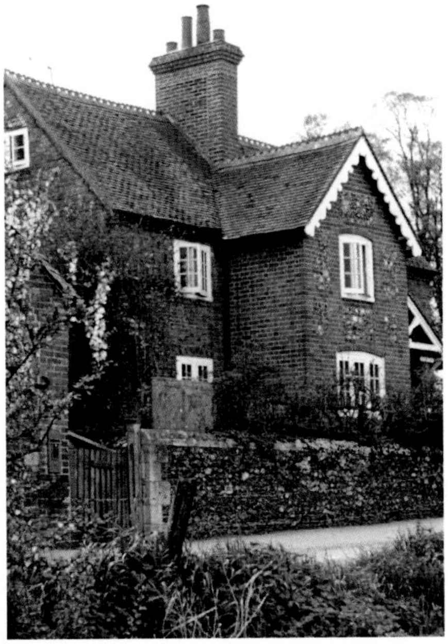

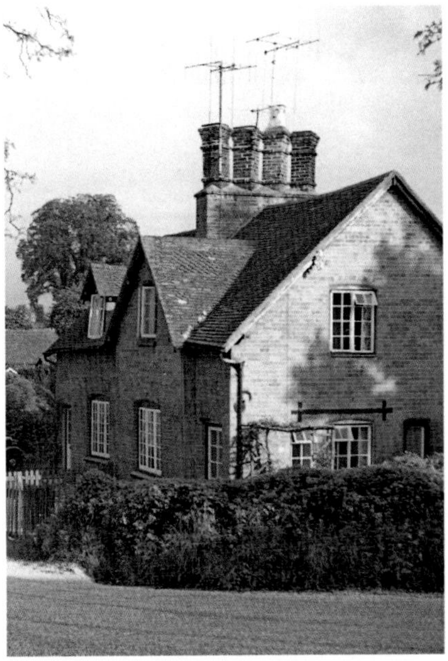

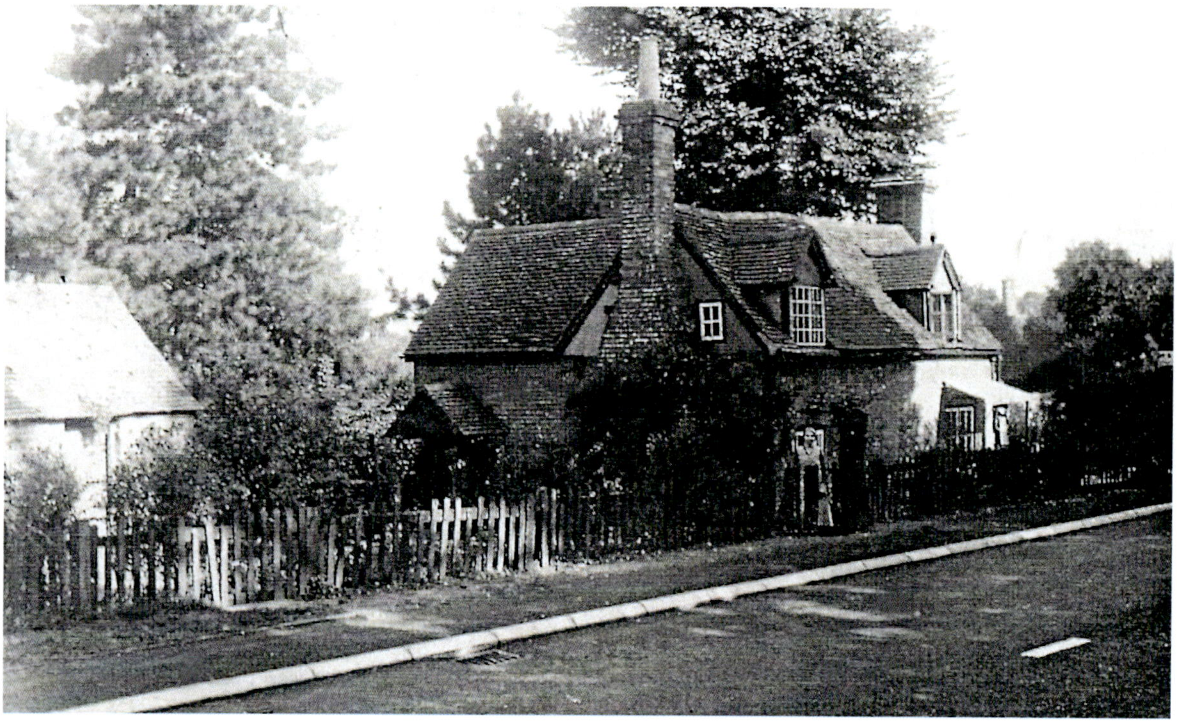

4.14 Well Cottages stood on the main road, approximately where the entrance now is to Nursery Gardens. Fred and Phyllis Rawlins moved into Well Cottages after their marriage in 1935 and lived there until the demolition of the cottages three years later.

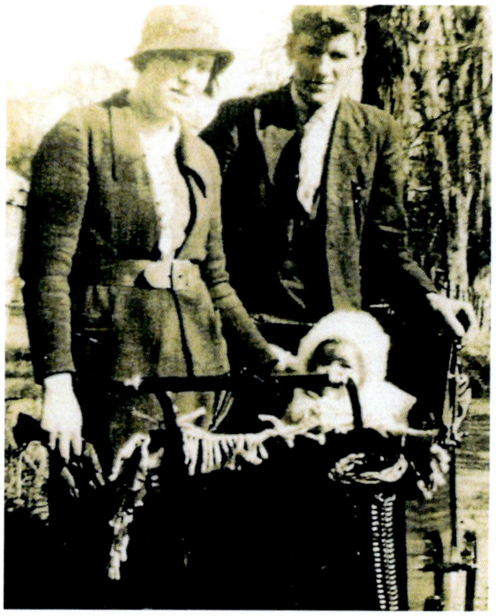

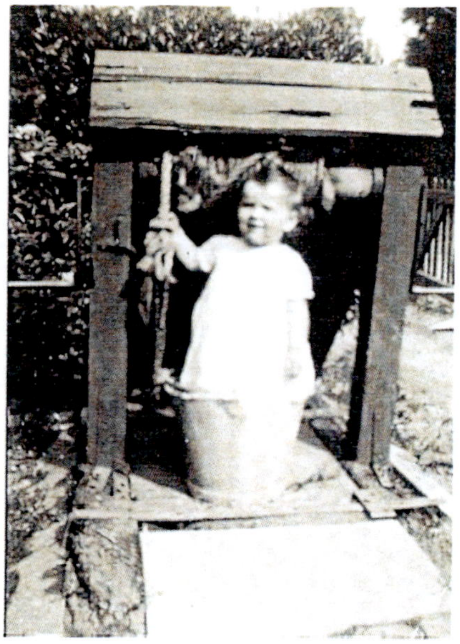

4.15 & 4.16 ***Left:*** Phyllis, Fred and their daughter Anne in Church Walk, c1937, and Anne, at a similar age, standing in the bucket over the well which was the only water supply to both cottages. It was apparently 110 feet to the top of the water.

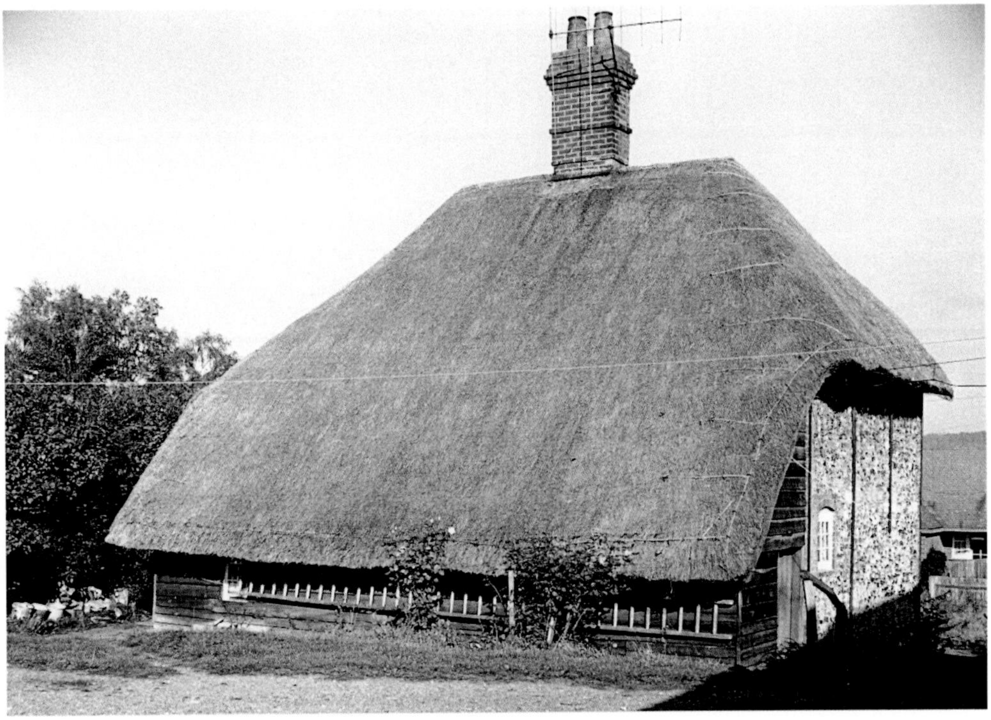

4.17 ***Above:*** Yew Tree Cottage, originally one of a pair probably dating to the 1780s, pictured from the rear in 1978, when it was the home of Joseph and Elsie Kirton.
4.18 ***Below:*** Kennel Cottages were built around 1904 in the grounds of Belleisle for the servants of the South Berkshire Hunt. They were demolished in the 1980s.

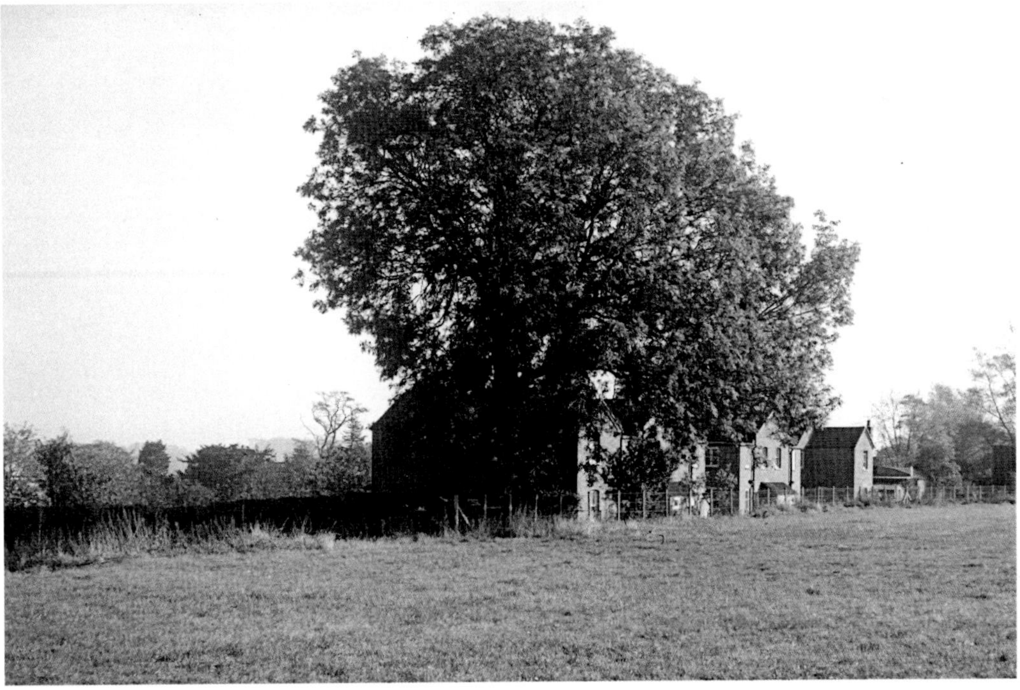

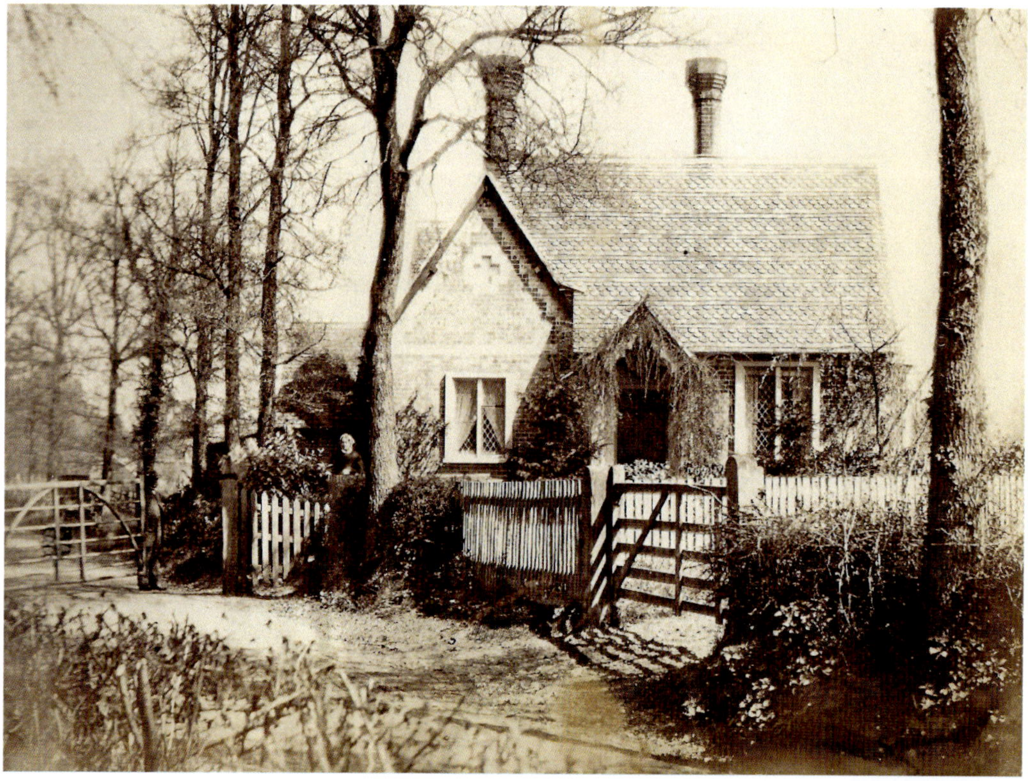

4.19 ***Above:*** Purley Hall Lodge Cottage on Sulham Lane pictured in 1870.

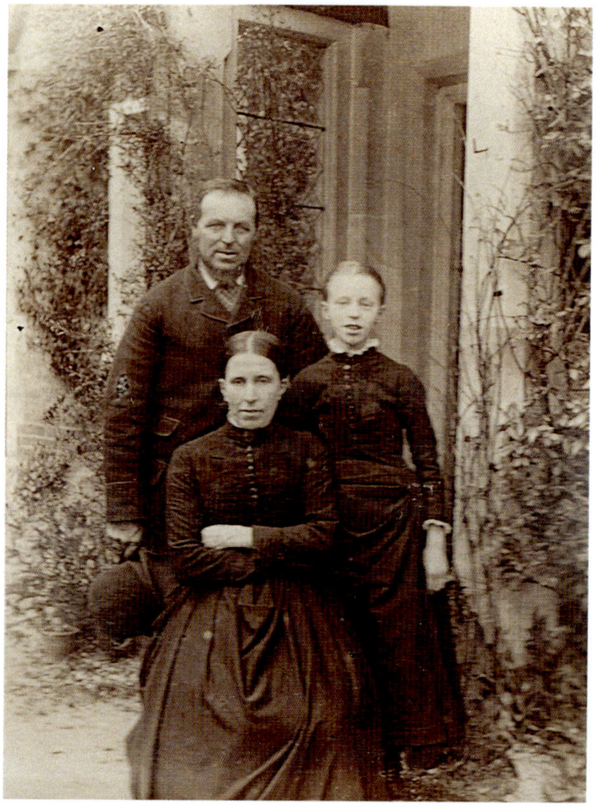

4.20 ***Right:*** The cottage's tenants have included the Simmonds family who are pictured here c1887. Henry Simmonds, standing behind his wife Ann and their daughter Ada, was born in Purley and employed as a gardener at Purley Hall.

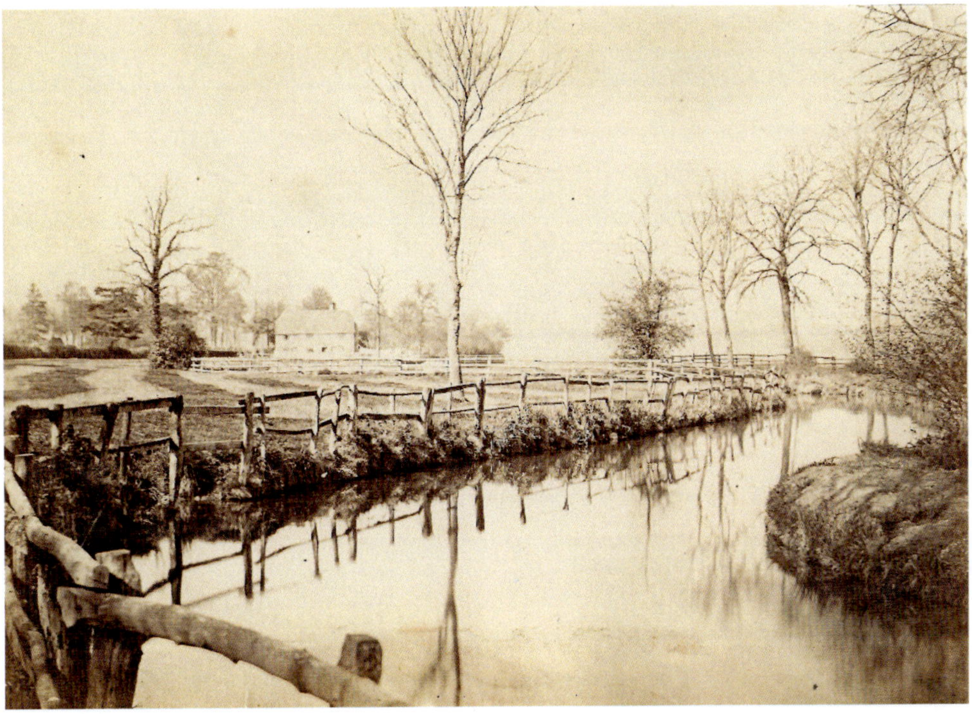

4.21 ***Above:*** Farm Cottage by the Sul Brook and off Sulham Lane in 1870.
4.22 ***Below:*** The Wheeler family pictured outside Farm Cottage c1887 were almost certainly employed as domestic staff at Purley Hall.

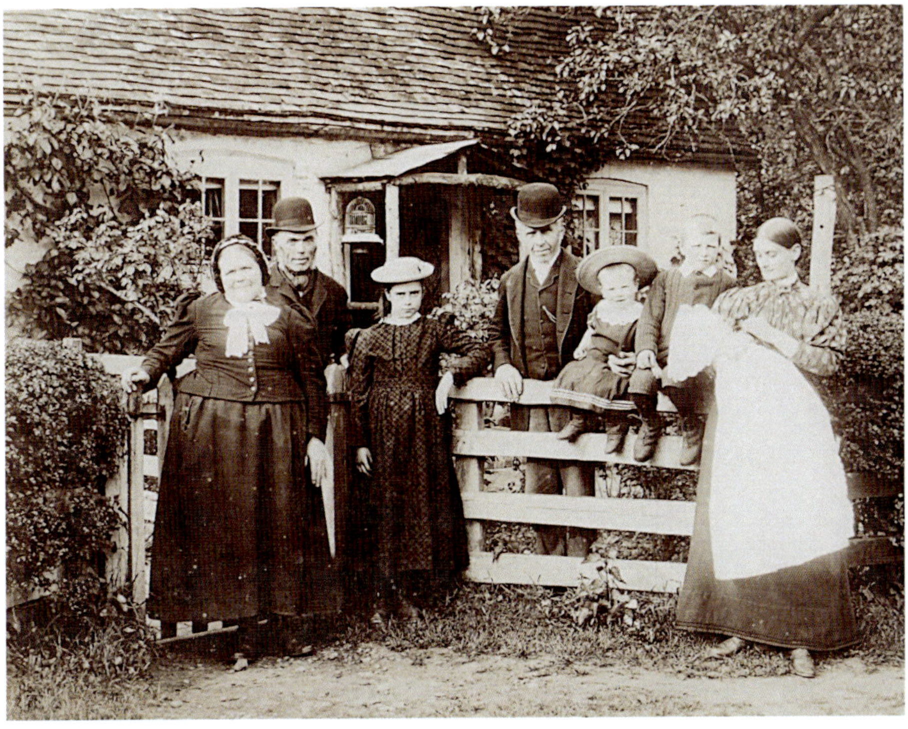

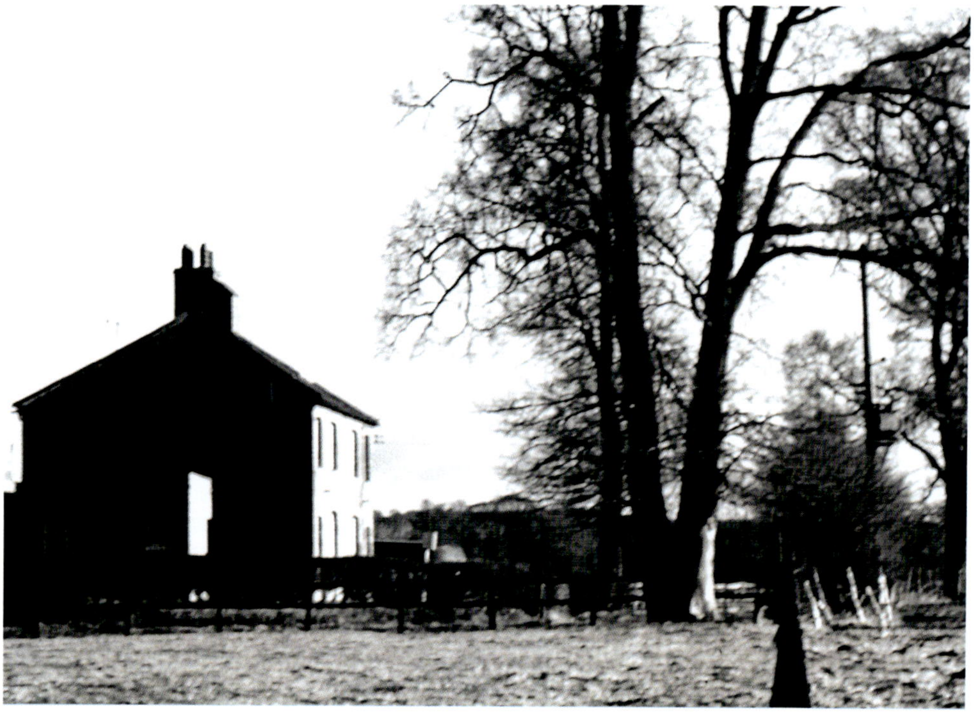

4.23 ***Above:*** Scraces Farm Cottages with the Elm Tree in 1967.

4.24 ***Below:*** Arthur Nash was a carter who arrived at Scraces Farm Cottages with his family in 1915. Here he and his wife Agnes, seated on the right of the photograph, celebrate there the wedding of their daughter Agnes to Albert Strange in 1926.

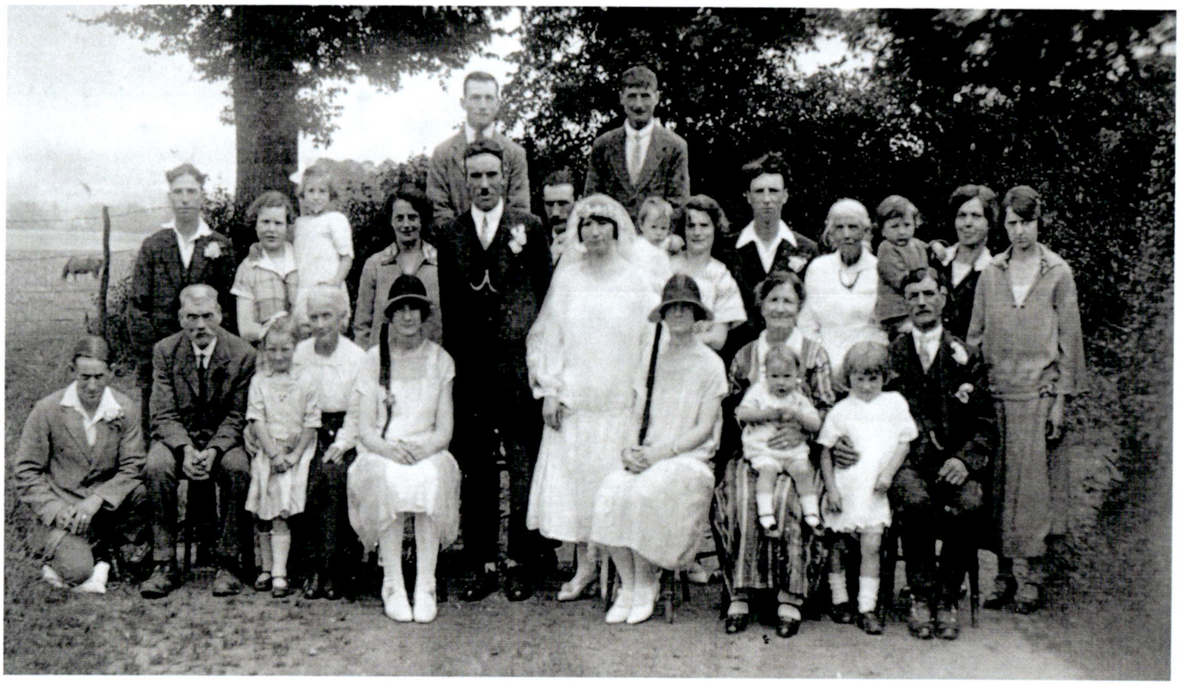

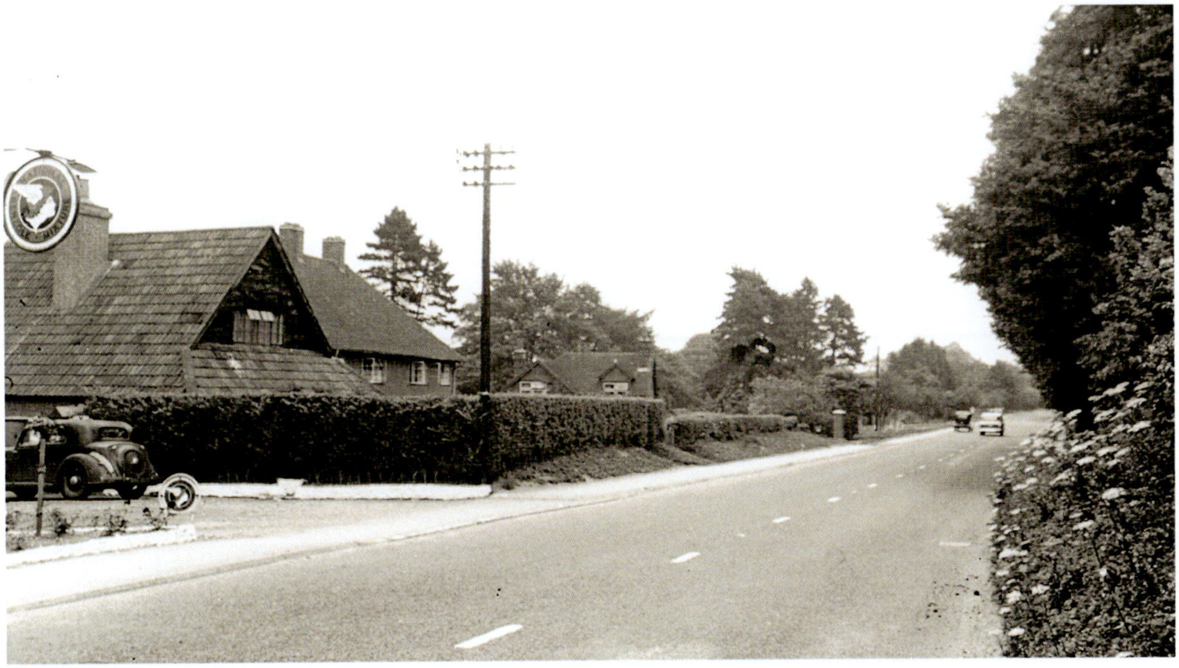

4.25 & 4.26 ***Above and below:*** Differing aspects of Purley Rise, pictured above in the 1950s and below in 1961. In the upper picture the signs for Purley Garage, now Merit Tyres, can be seen to the left of the photograph.

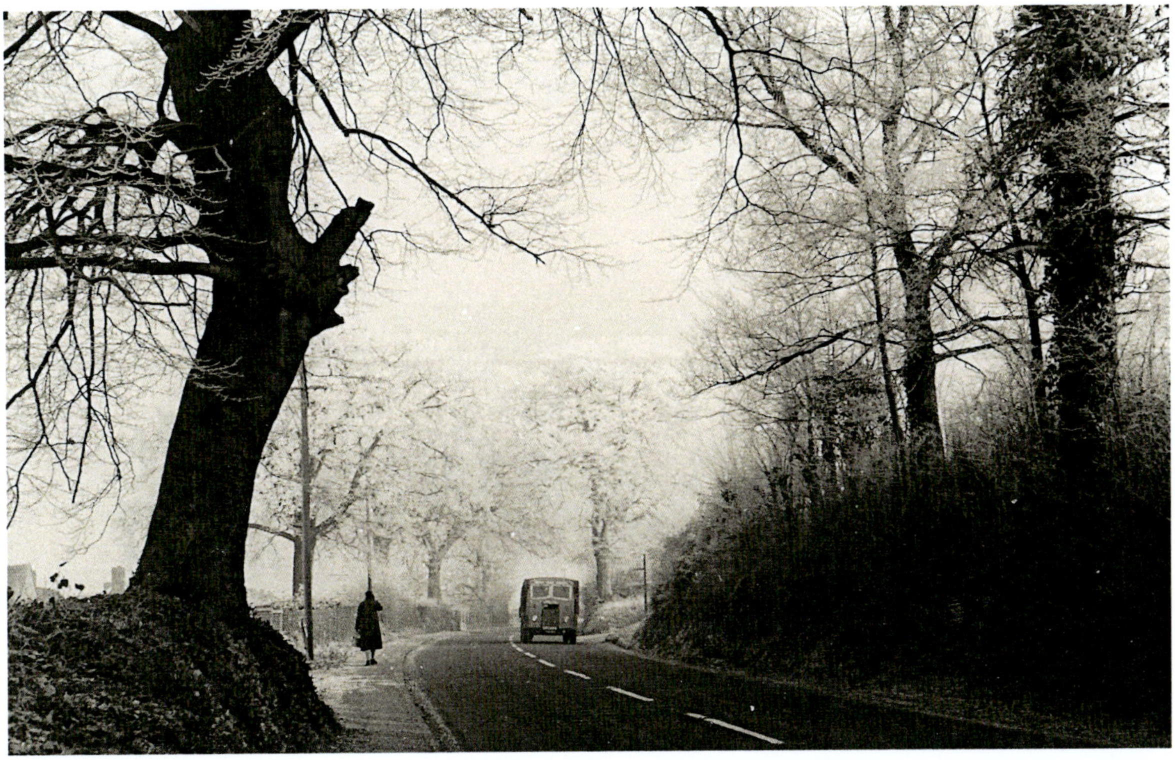

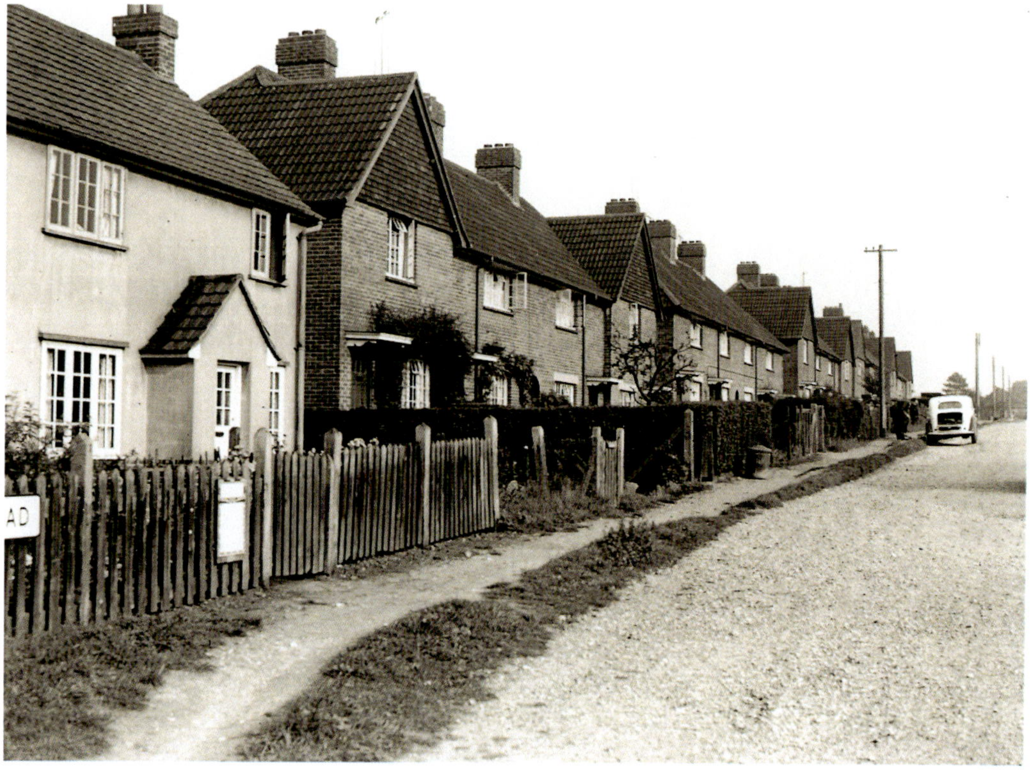

4.27 ***Above:*** Glebe Road, pictured c1950, was named after the land upon which it was built.
4.28 ***Below***: Ian and John Nash enjoy the snow in Glebe Road in the 1940s.

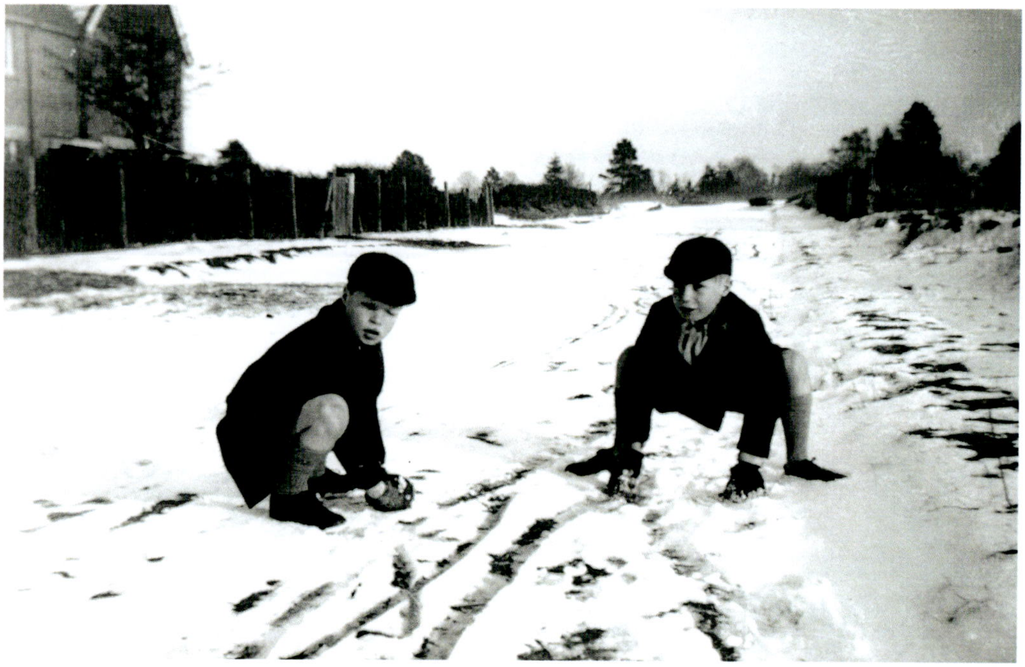

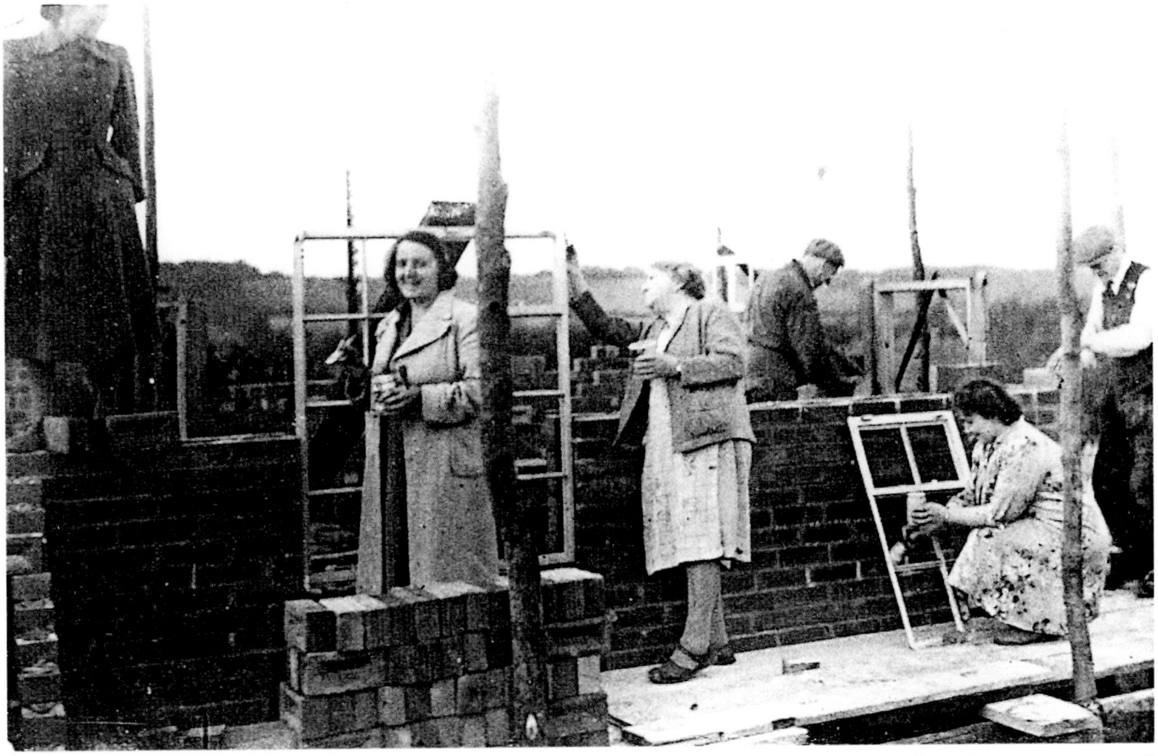

4.29 ***Above:*** The Memorial Hall pictured c1951 under construction by a team of volunteers led by Bert Nicholls. From left to right: ?,?, Florence Goodwin, Ron Winters, Jean Buckmaster, and Bert Nicholls. It was completed in 1953 in time to celebrate the Coronation.

4.30 ***Below:*** Orchard Close on the eastern side of Long Lane, probably in the 1950s.

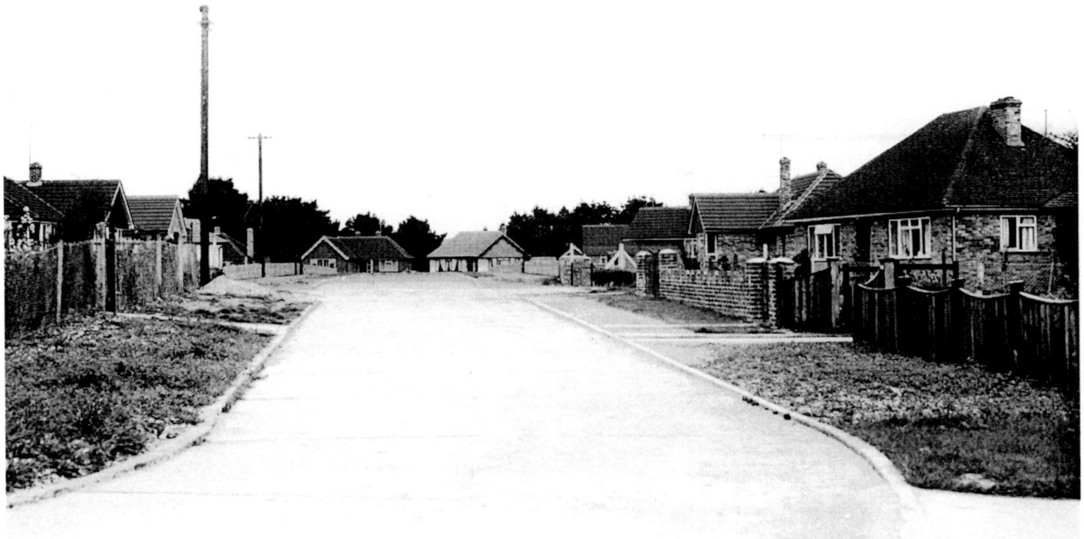

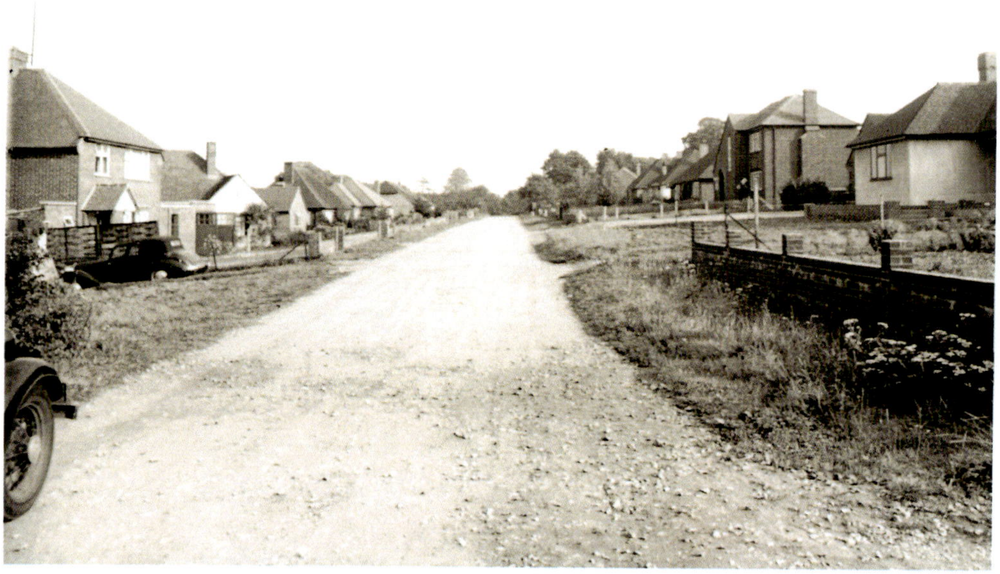

4.31 ***Above:*** Beech Road, possibly in the 1950s.
4.32 ***Below:*** An aerial photograph showing the construction of further houses on Beech Road c1979, after the sale of Yew Tree Farm. To the left of the photograph you can see part of Trenthams with Kennel Cottages behind it.

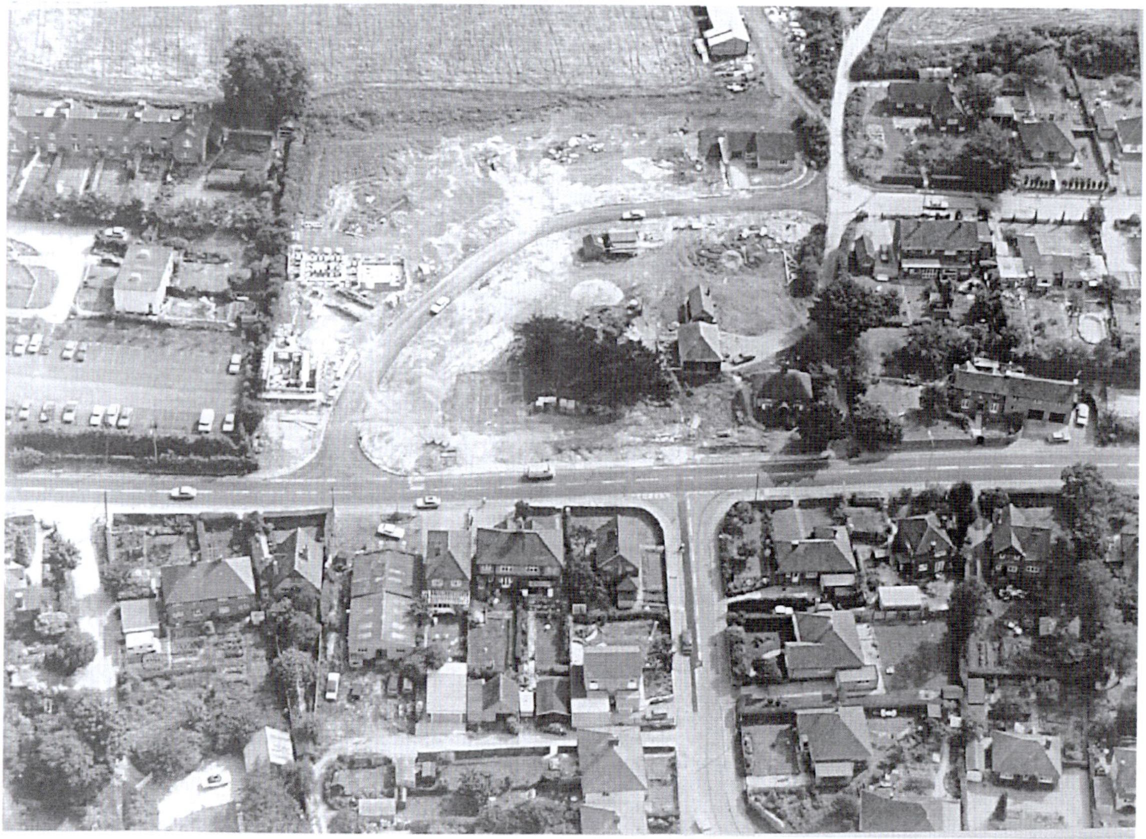

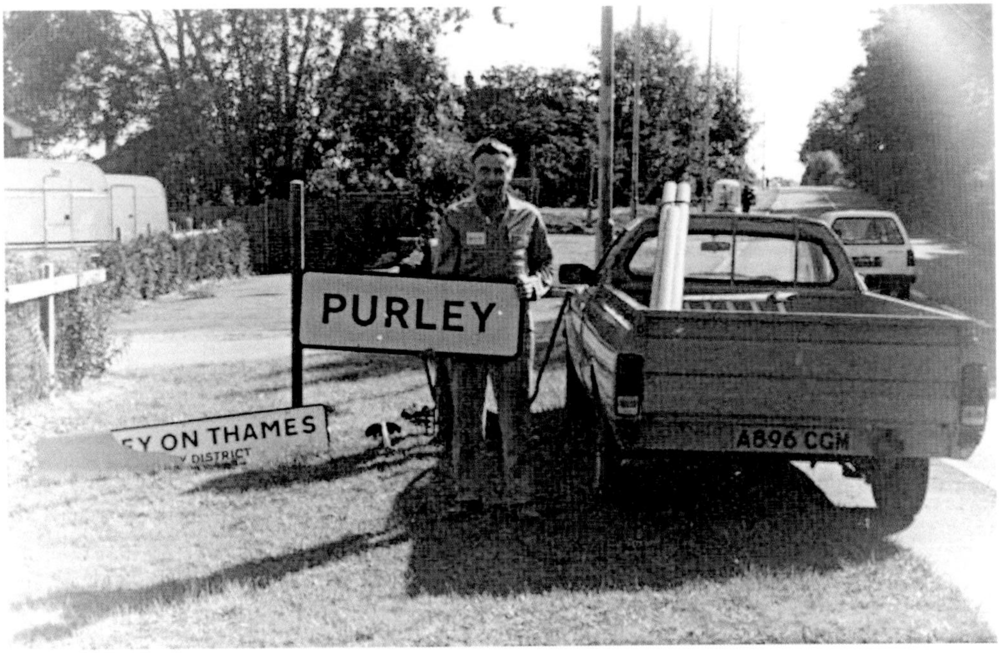

4.33 & 4.34 ***Above and below:*** We conclude our chapter on the development of the village with photographs of two key name changes. The village was renamed in the 1980s, from Purley to Purley on Thames, to avoid confusion with Purley, Surrey and in the image above the signs are being replaced by Council contractors.
Below, Reading Road was renamed Purley Rise in 1983 and here Sybil Pryor, Reg Marshall, Brian Smith and Reg Ayres pose for a photograph with the new sign.

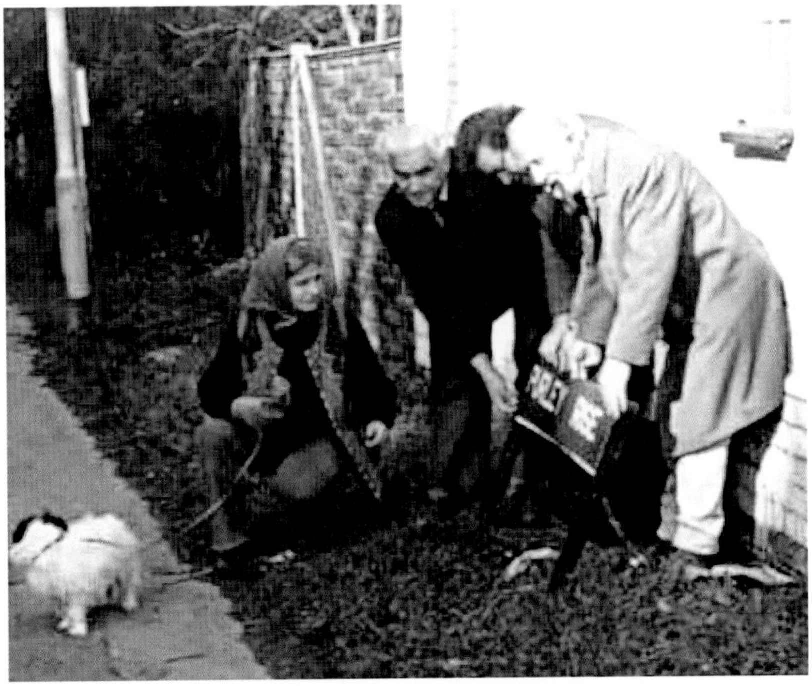

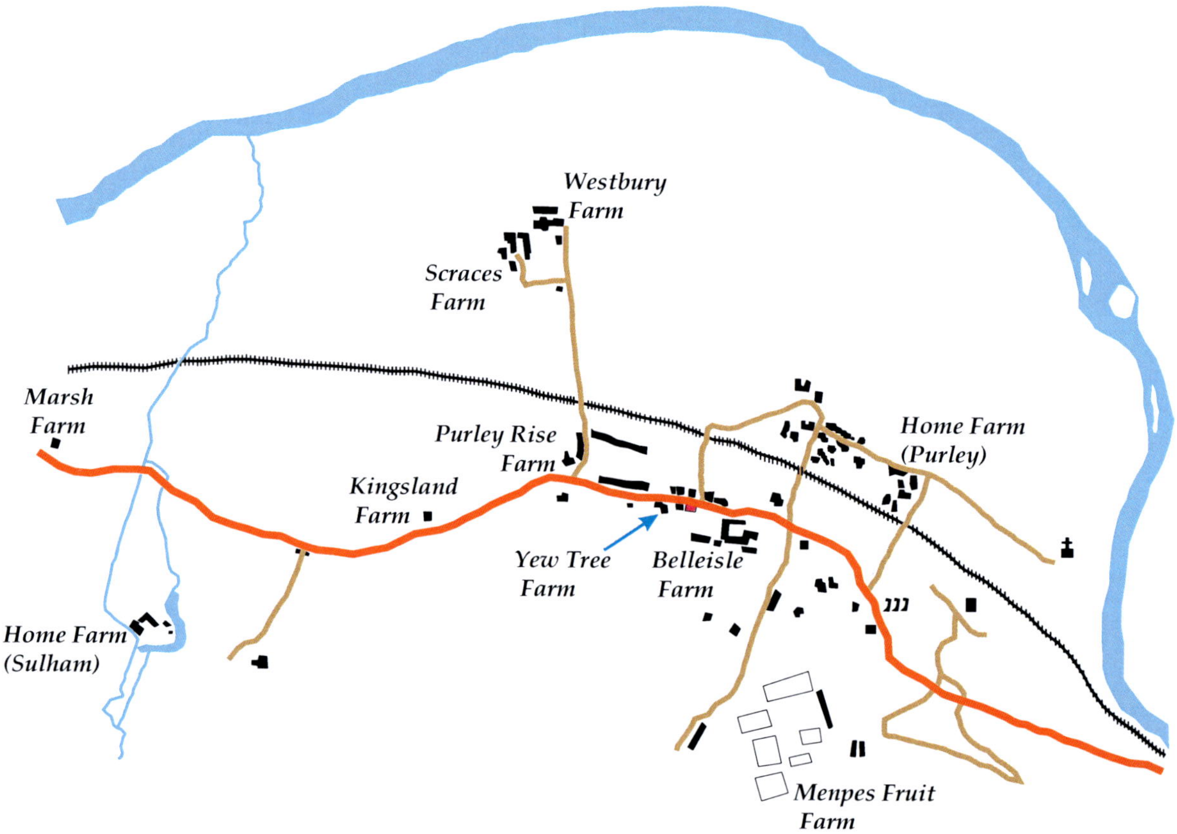
Westbury
Farm
Scraces
Farm
Marsh
Farm
Purley Rise
Farm
Home Farm
(Purley)
Kingsland
Farm
Yew Tree
Farm
Belleisle
Farm
Home Farm
(Sulham)
Menpes Fruit
Farm

5 *Farming and Agriculture*

Purley's rich heritage of farming dates back to the very origins of the village and can still be glimpsed in the topography of the land and in the present-day names given to roads and streets. Our earliest field systems probably date back to Saxon times and some of the early flint boundary markers from this time remain scattered round the fields and village to this day.

Back in medieval times, most of the land in the parish came under manorial control with the villagers holding strips of land to raise crops and also being required to graze their livestock at particular times of the year. There was some common land in the rich meadows close to the river and these would have been deliberately flooded each year to increase their fertility. In the fields crops such as barley, oats, wheat, and beans were sown on a rotation basis.

This landscape and the villagers' way of life remained largely unchanged until relatively recently. The creation of Storer's new estate around 1800 imposed some land restrictions on the villagers, before they were forced to forfeit their common land in 1856 as a result of the enclosure of the open fields and common land. By now the railway had arrived in Purley, the country was embracing industrialisation and Purley began to move away from what had been almost total self-sufficiency. In the 1920s, the sale of Purley Park brought previously undeveloped land on to the market and attracted new entrepreneurs to the village. Many of these new types of business were still linked to the land, such as the chicken and pig farms, a tree nursery, a fruit and flower farm and a trout hatchery. By the late 1960s we even had our own vineyard producing red, white and rosé wine.

In the early twentieth century Purley had several farms: Home Farm in Purley Village, Home Farm off Sulham Lane, Westbury Farm, Scraces Farm (now called Springs Farm), Yew Tree Farm, Kingsland Farm, Purley Rise Farm and Marsh Farm. Nowadays however, we are reduced to the two Home Farms (in Purley and Sulham) doing most of the farming and Yew Tree Farm as a base for farming contractors. We start our photographic journey with a glimpse of some of these farms.

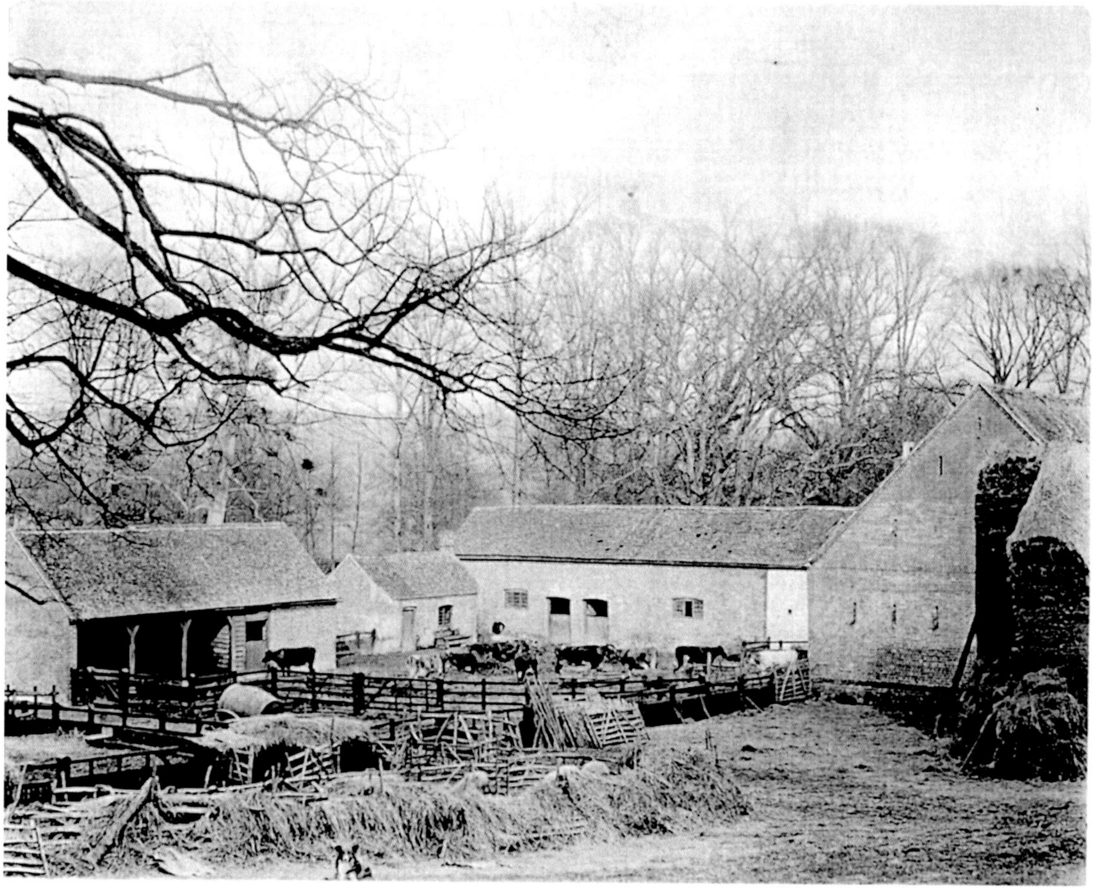

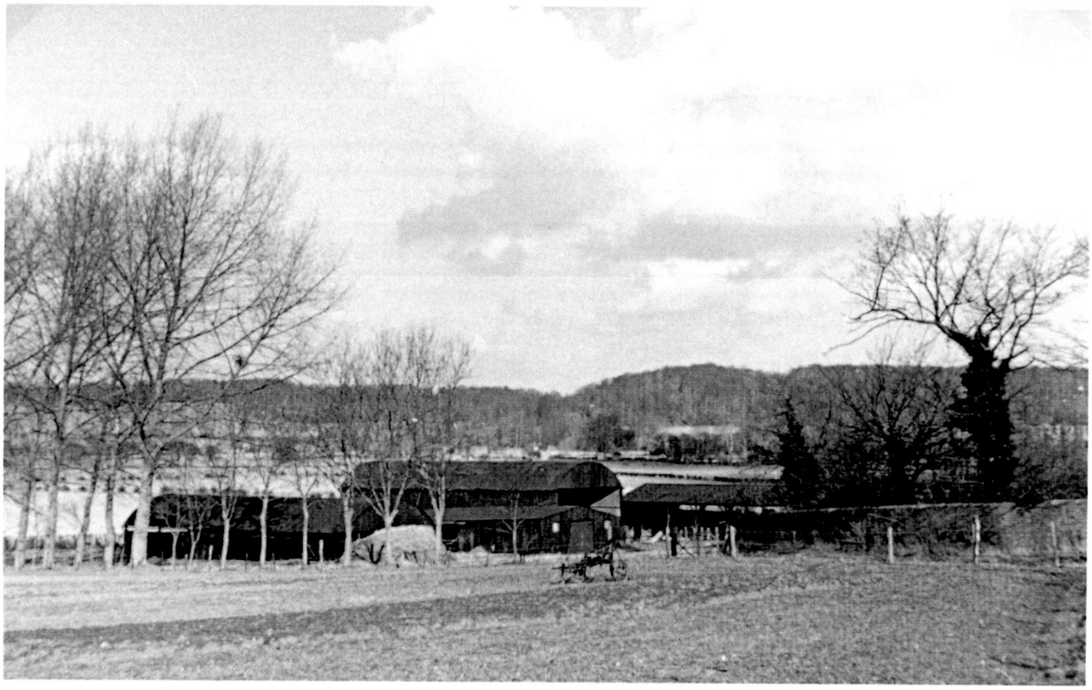

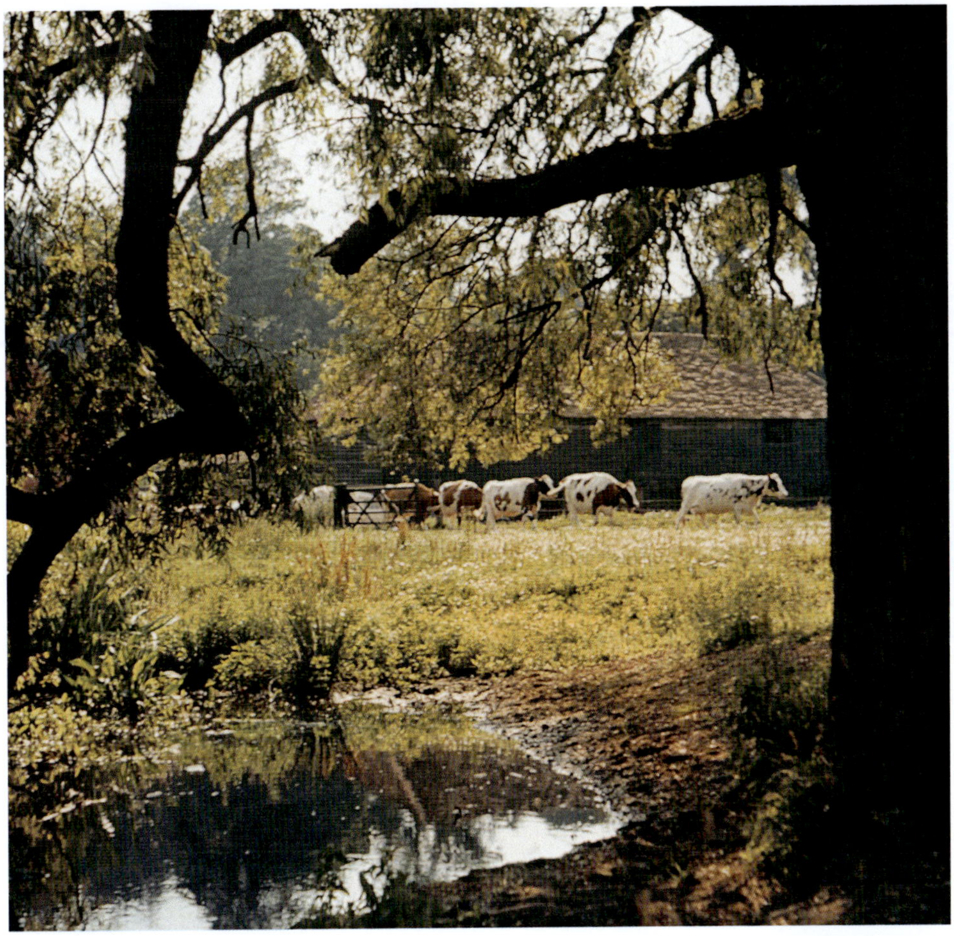

5.1 & 5.3 ***Above and opposite page, top photo:*** The Home Farm of Purley Park was situated on The Street in the village. It is pictured in an early image opposite and from across the village pond, above, in 1963. The slurry from the cows which ran down into the village and the fierce and noisy geese were often a source of frustration for its neighbours. Farm Close now stands on the site.

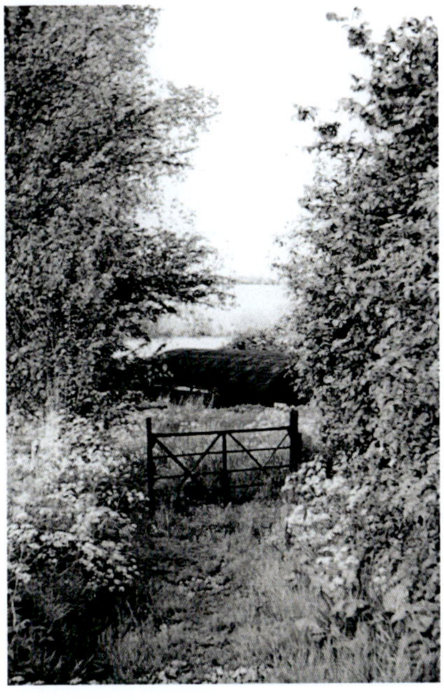

5.2 & 5.4 ***Right and opposite page, lower photo:*** The black barns of Home Farm were situated to the north of The Street and were known affectionately as the 'tin barns'. They are seen here in 1958 (opposite) and the 1960s (right).

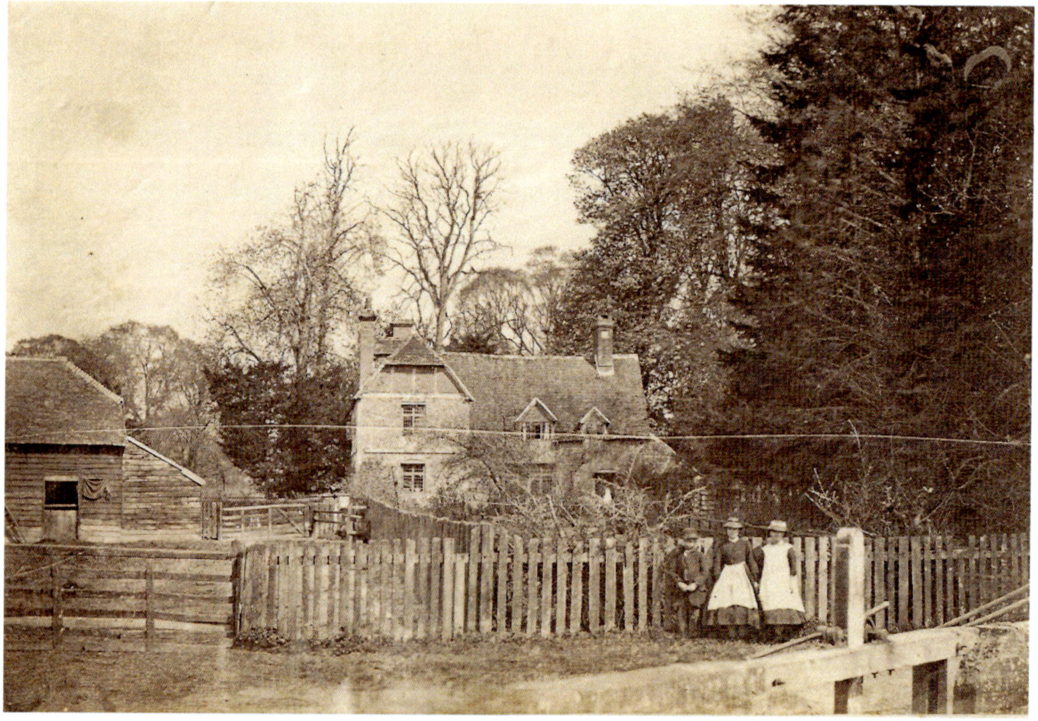

5.5 & 5.6 ***Above and below:*** The current farmhouse of Home Farm, Sulham Lane, above, dates to the sixteenth century. Below we see its watermill which was driven by the Sul Brook. Both images date to 1870.

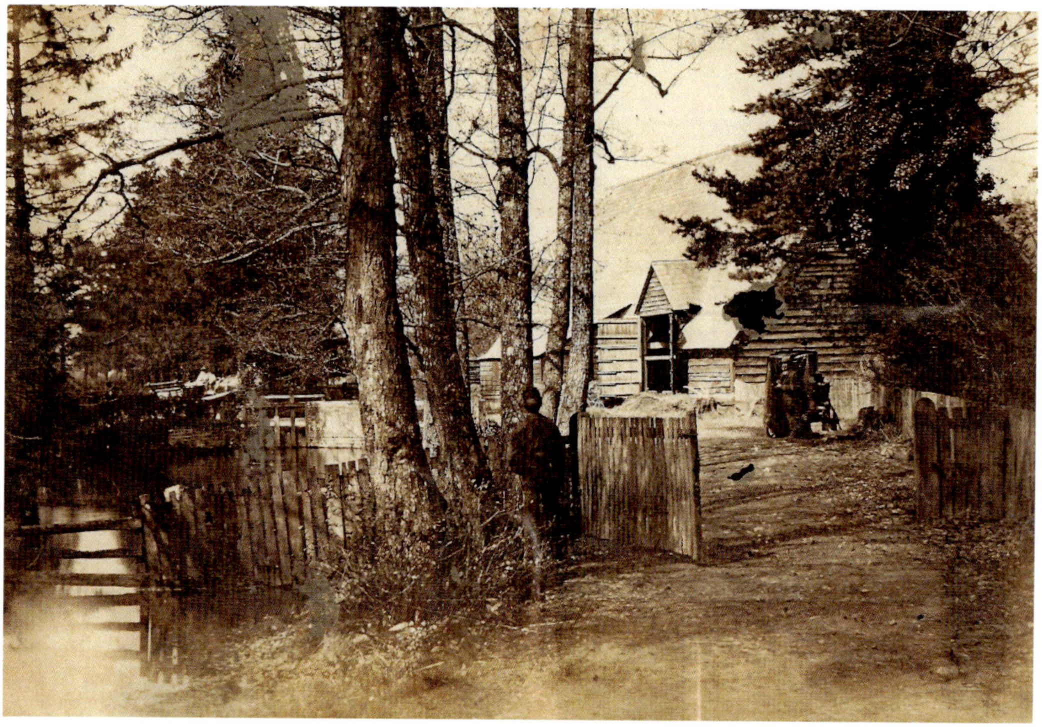

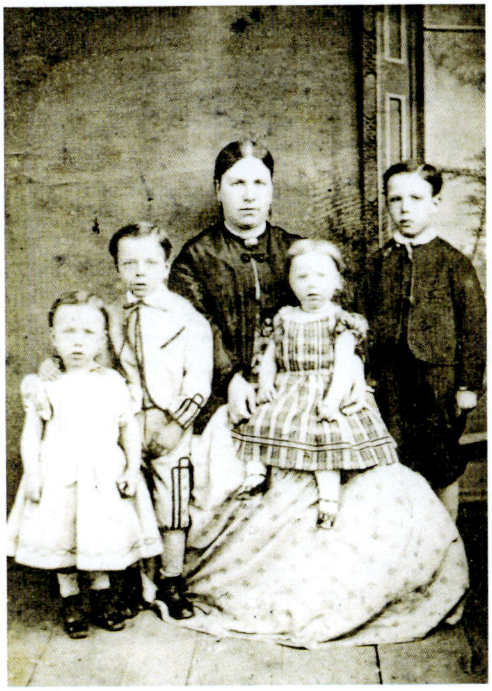

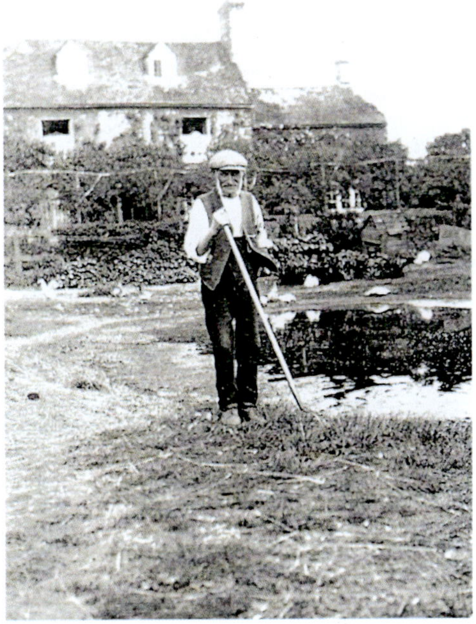

5.7 & 5.8 ***Above: (left)*** Thomas Barnes was the farmer of Scraces Farm in the 1870s. His wife Susannah and children are pictured c1871. ***(Right)*** Frederick Cox, a cowman at Scraces Farm, is pictured in front of the farmhouse c1917.

5.9 ***Below:*** During the Second World War several farms needed extra help after their farm labourers were called up. Land Army girls supported Purley Rise Farm and German prisoners of war worked at Westbury Farm. Here Karl Stephan, on the left, who was imprisoned at Basildon Park whilst he was working at Westbury, poses in the 1940s with two fellow prisoners.

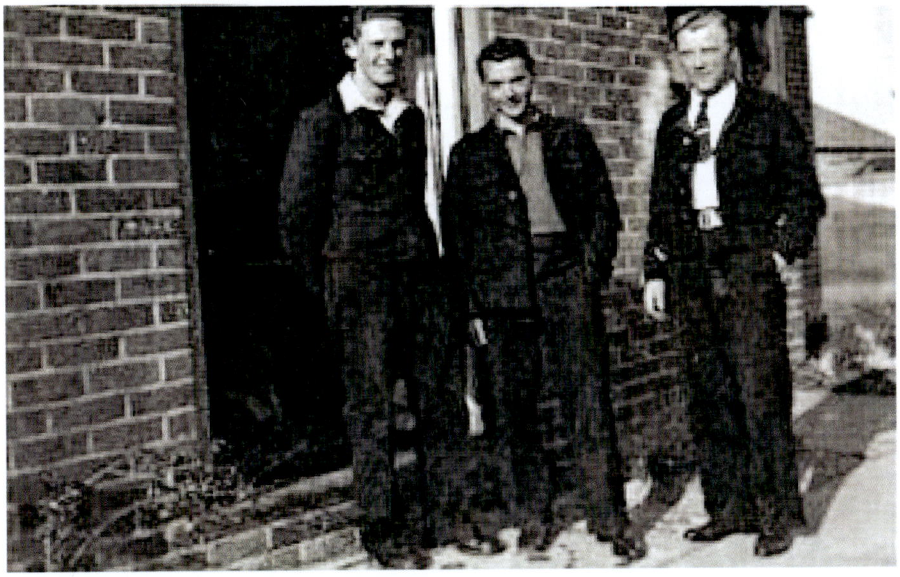

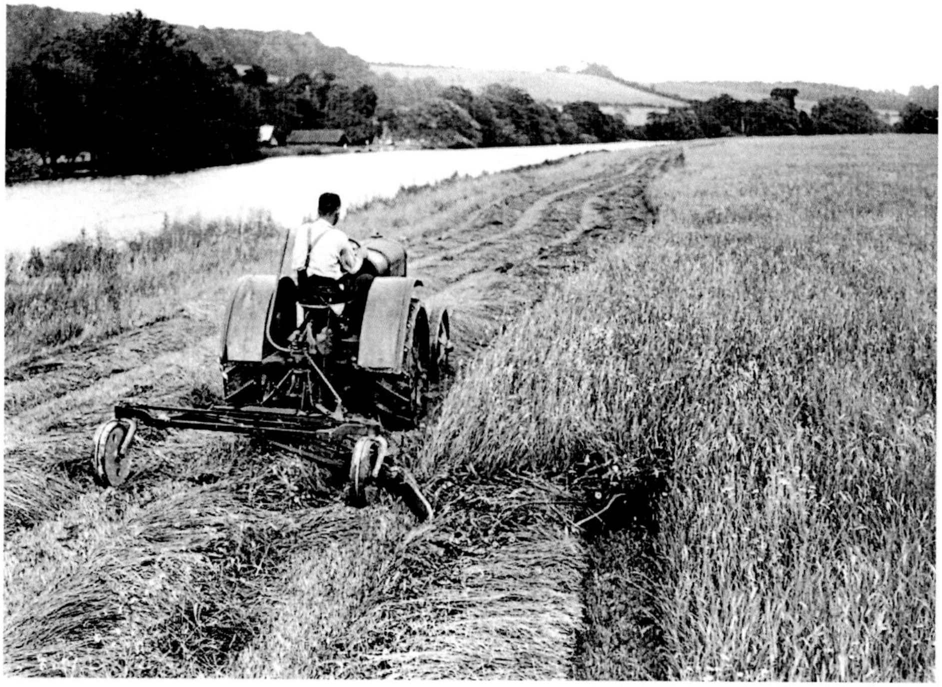

5.10 ***Above:*** In the meadows by the river the crop was hay and here the first yield of the season is cut.

5.11 ***Below:*** Until the 1930s most of the machinery was pulled by horses, as this photograph by Eric Guy of hay being mown near Sulham Woods shows.

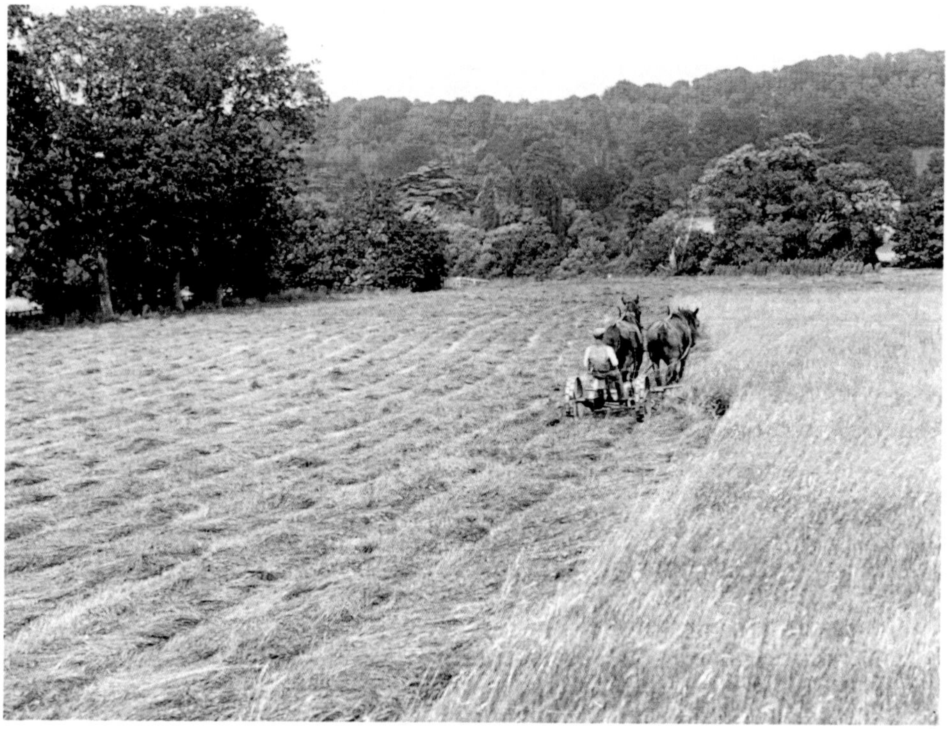

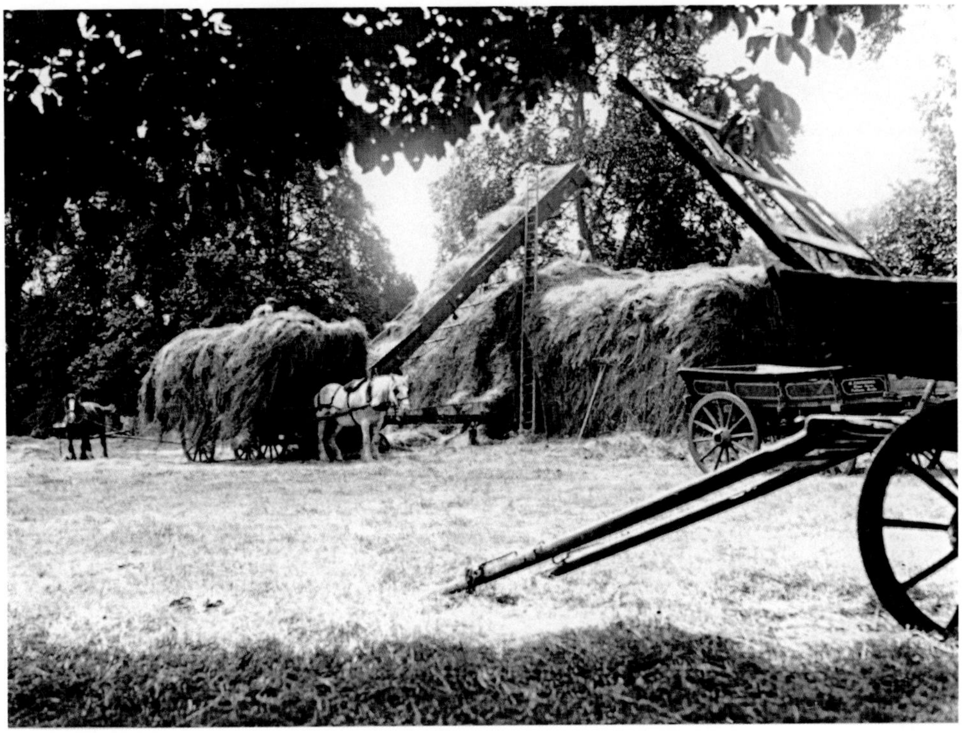

5.12 ***Above:*** Rick building was a skilled craft. Here, at Scraces Farm in the 1920s, a traction engine is used to drive an elevator taking hay to the rick builder.
5.13 ***Below:*** By the 1960s the hay was baled in the fields, as seen in this image taken in 1963 at Yew Tree Farm with Charlie Kirton driving the baler.

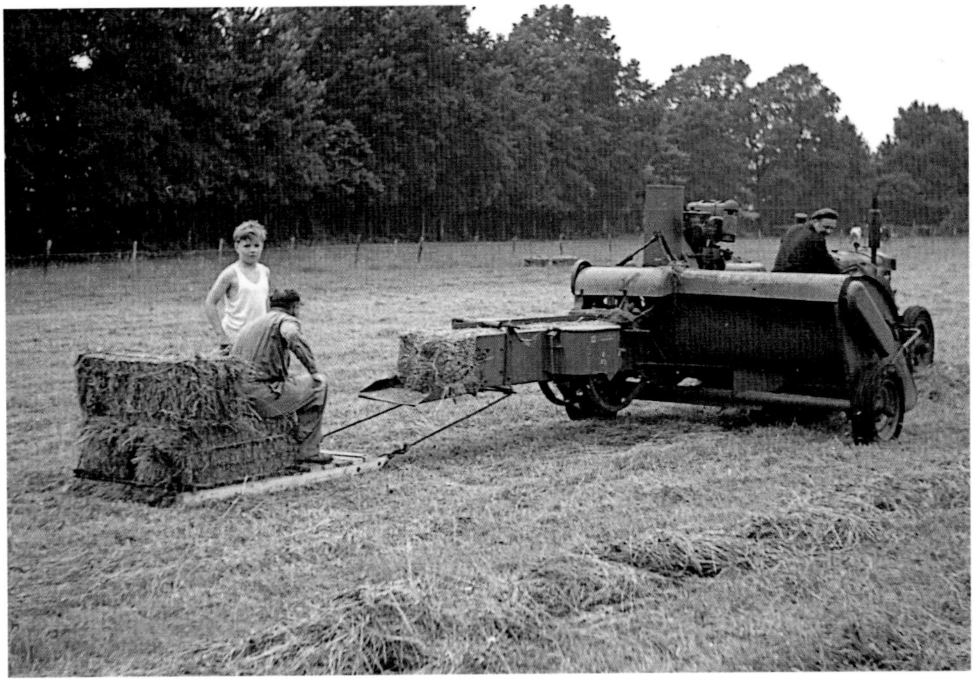

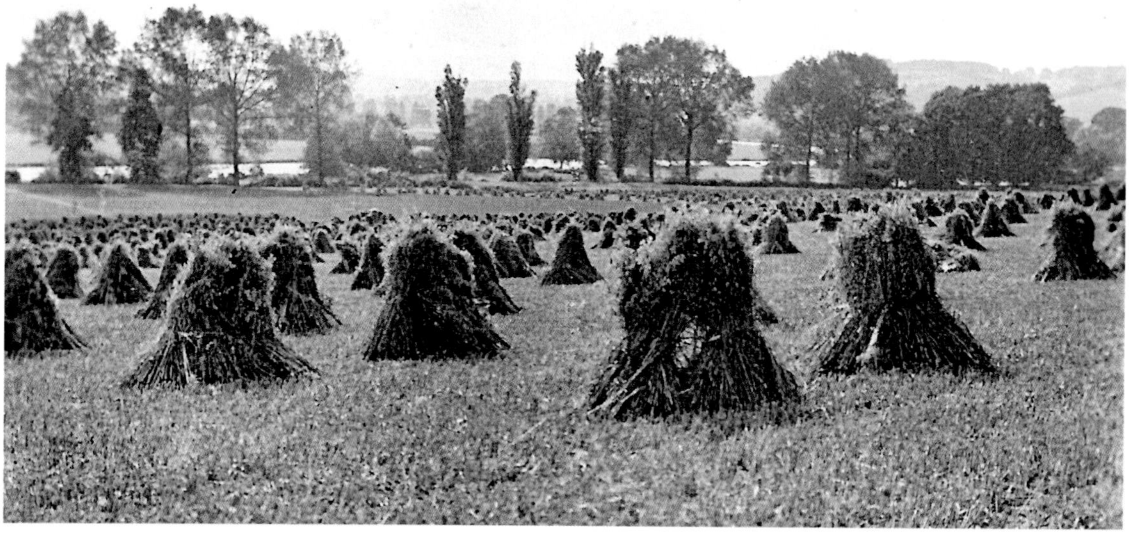

5.14 ***Above:*** Wheat was generally cut by hand with a sickle and bundled into sheaves. Here, in 1908, the wheat is drying out in stooks in fields overlooking the river between Purley and Pangbourne.

5.15 ***Below:*** Winter allowed for other tasks to be completed around the farm. Freddie Miles poses for the camera in December 1968 in a break from hedging in Westbury Lane.

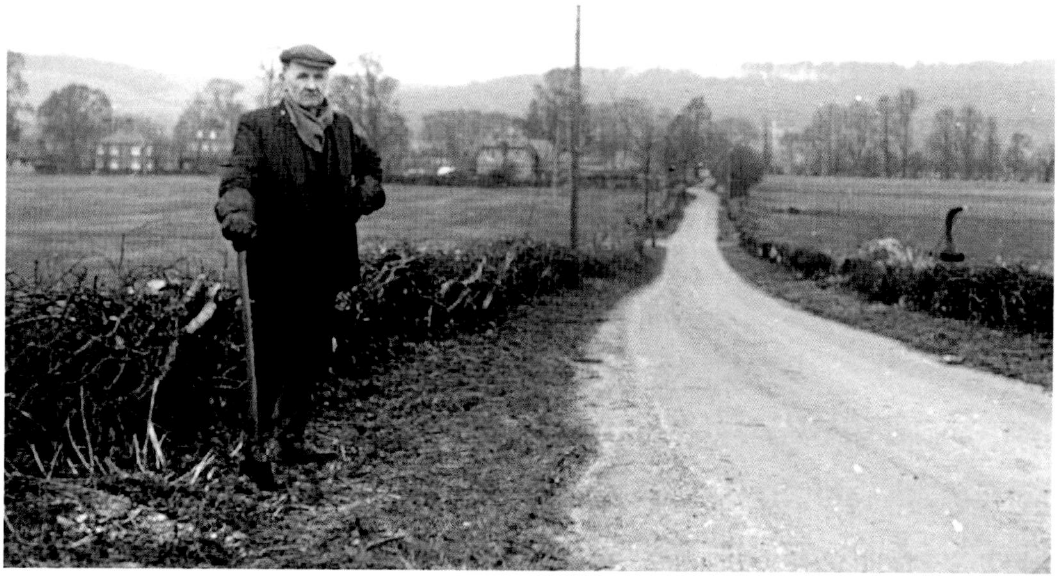

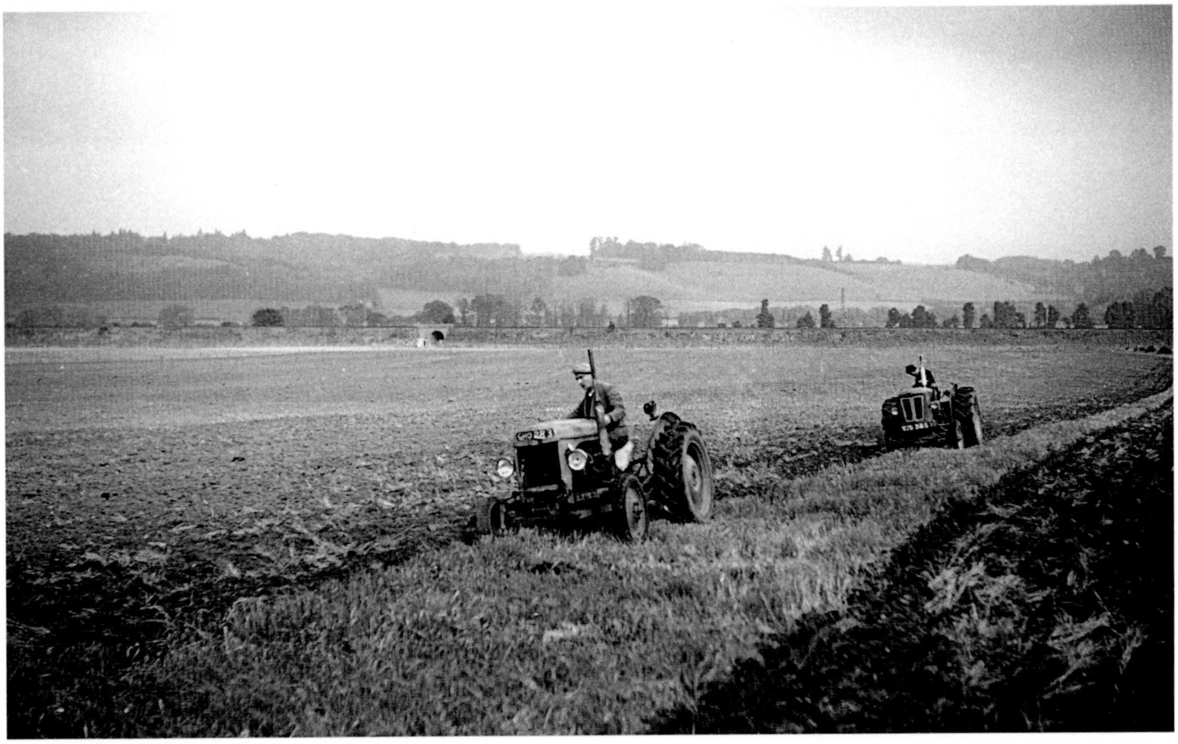

5.16 ***Above:*** Mr Large and his son ploughing on Scraces Farm in 1962.
5.17 ***Below:*** Alec Mundy ploughing on a Fordson Major Tractor by the railway embankment in 1962 with a train vanishing into the distance.

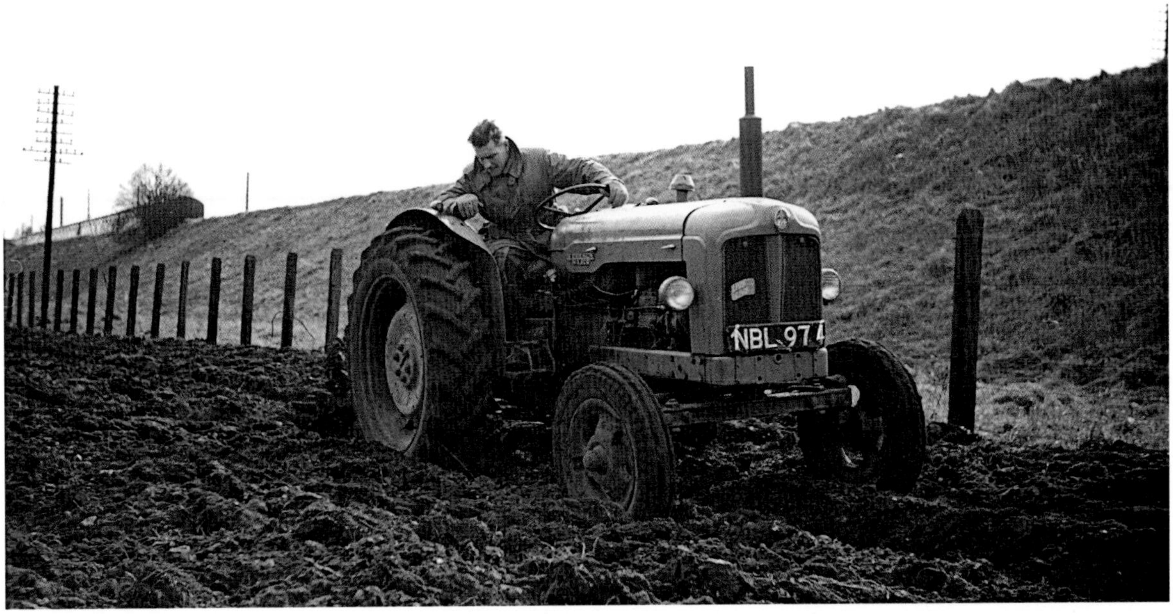

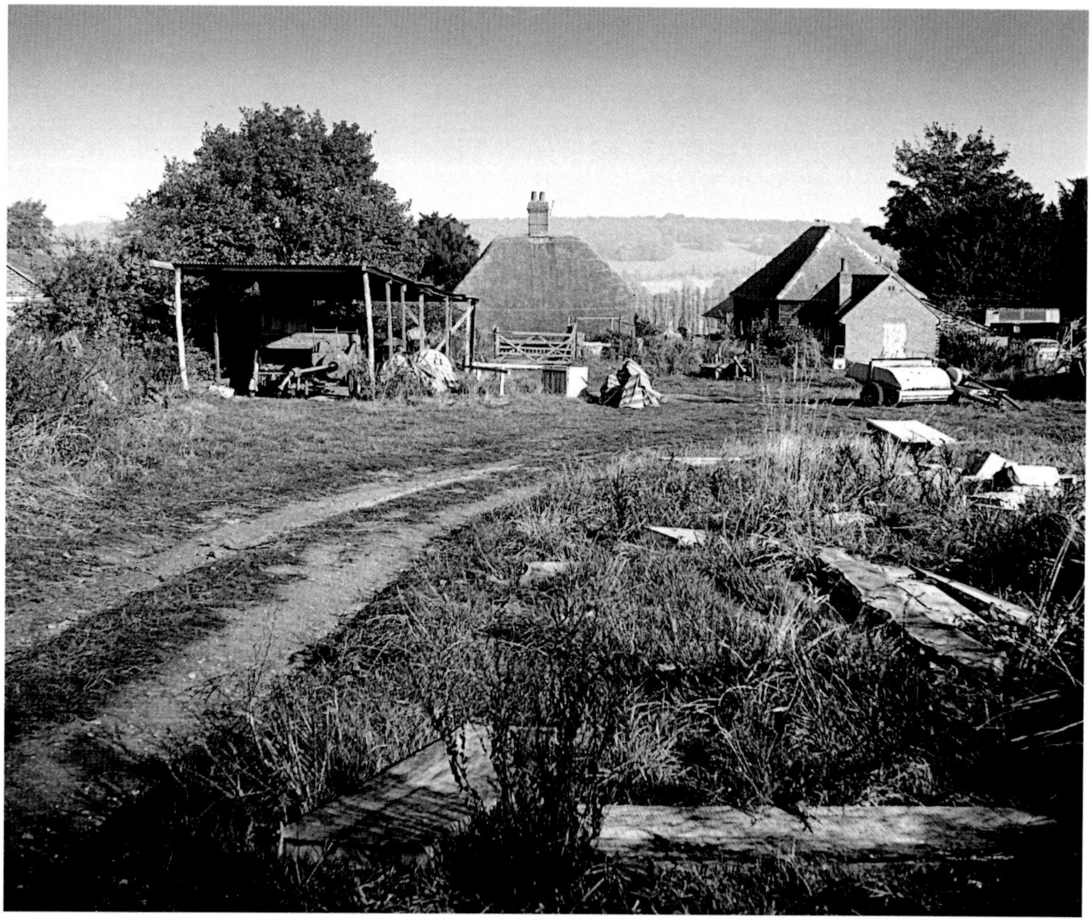

5.18 & 5.19 ***Above and below:*** Yew Tree Farm, also known as Kirton's Farm, in 1978 when it was run by Joseph (Jack) and Elsie Kirton. The upper image shows the back of the farm behind Yew Tree Cottage, the dairy and the barn.
5.20 ***Below, right:*** An old Fordson tractor rusts slowly under the canopy.

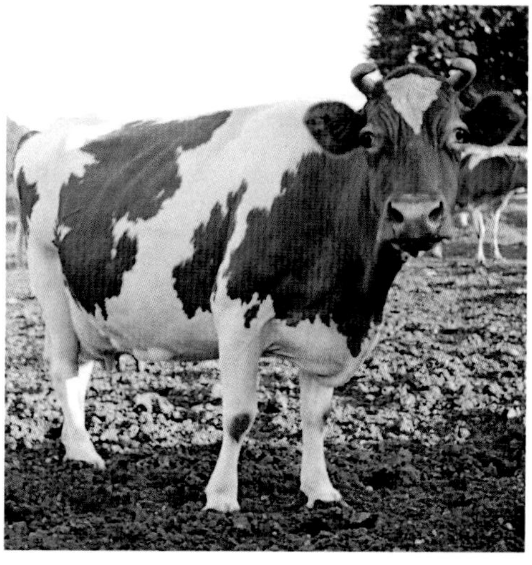

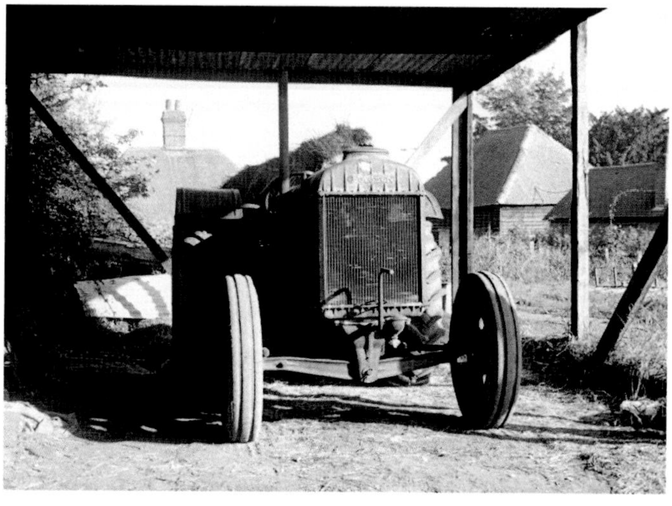

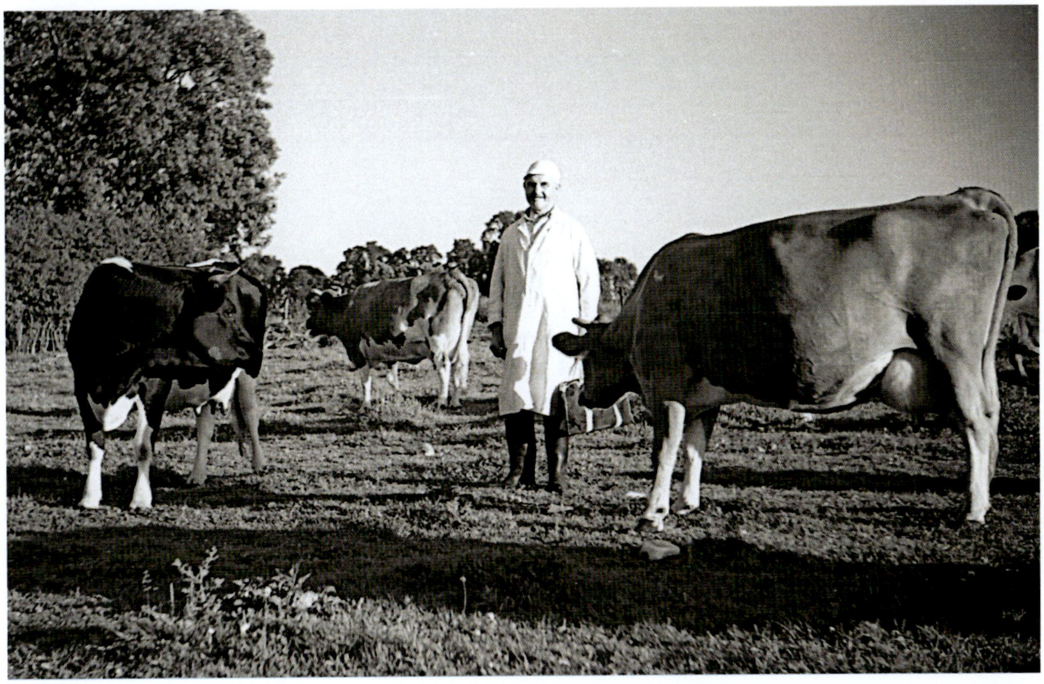

5.21 & 5.22 ***Above and below:*** Jack Kirton in the 1960s with his herd and bottling the milk in the dairy.

5.23 ***Left:*** The end product for customers in 1966.

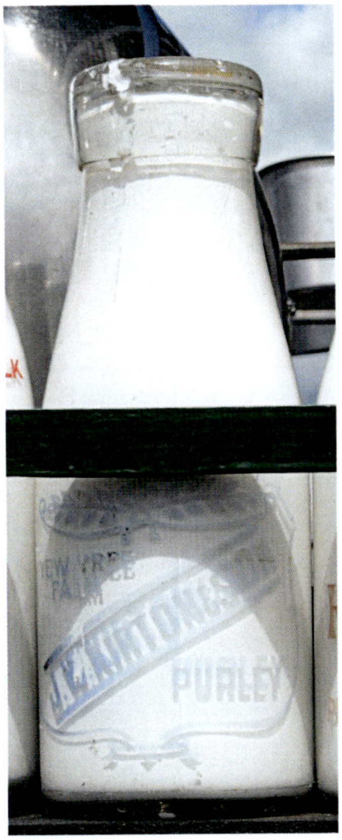

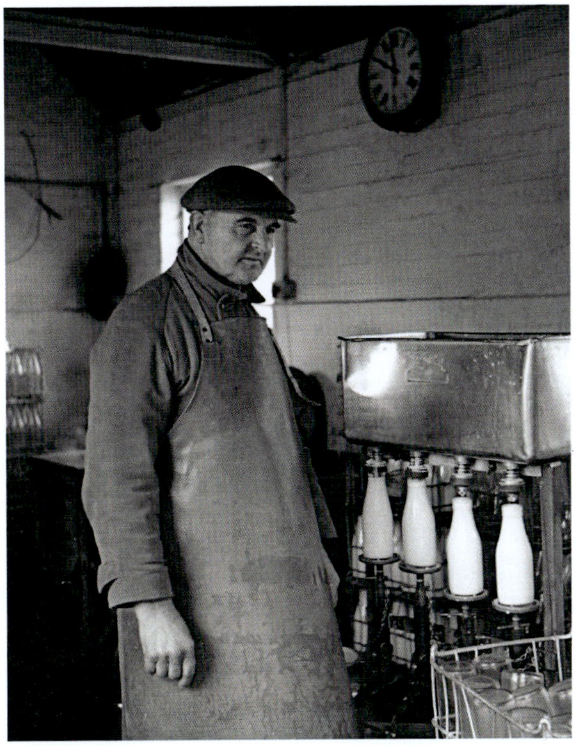

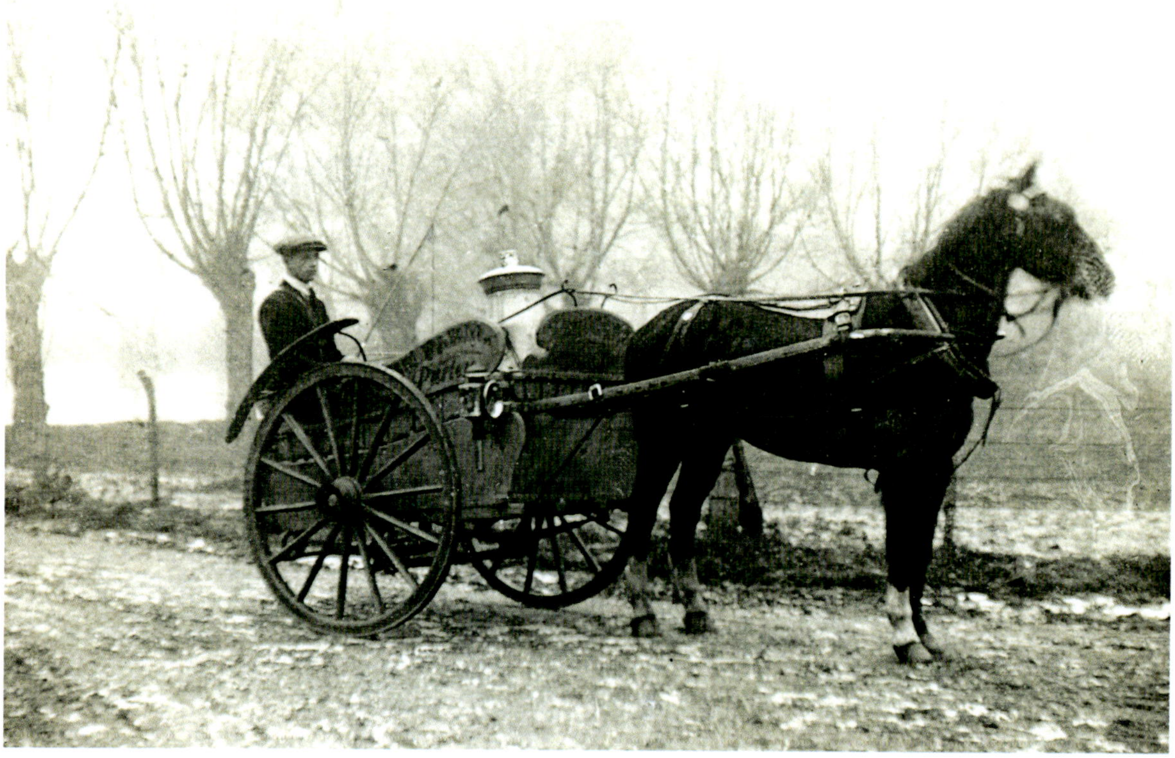

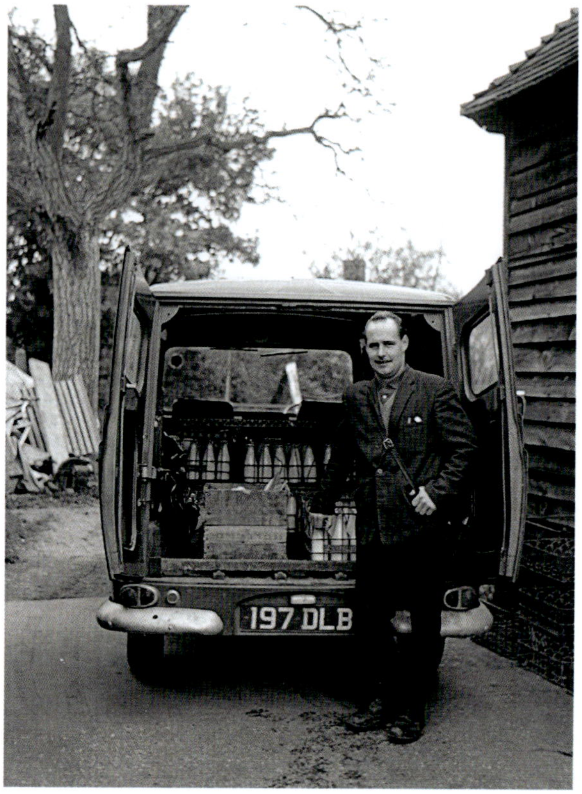

5.24 ***Above:*** A horse and cart from Home Farm, Purley trundles along an unmade road with a churn of milk c1915. Ladles of milk would be poured directly into customers' jugs.

5.25 ***Left:*** Albert Clark, the milkman at Yew Tree Farm, loads up the early morning van in 1966.

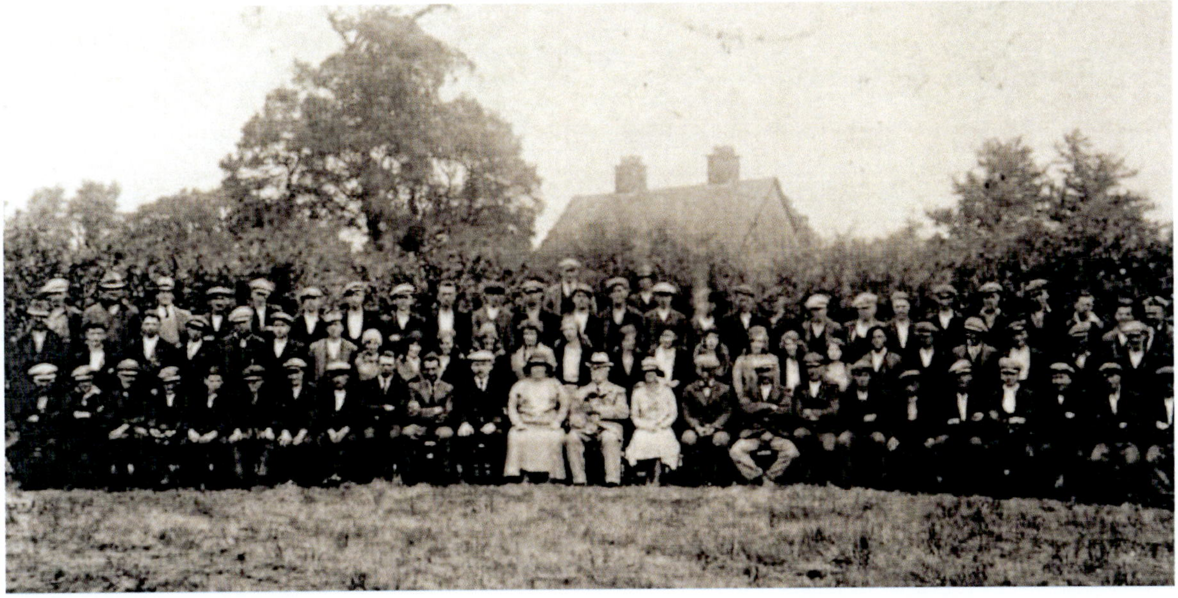

5.26 Mortimer Menpes, artist and co-founder of the Menpes Press in London, his wife and a daughter, pose with their fruit farm workers, c1931. Menpes Fruit Farm Limited, which included the Carnation Nurseries established in 1907, was a large operation based in Long Lane which employed many villagers.

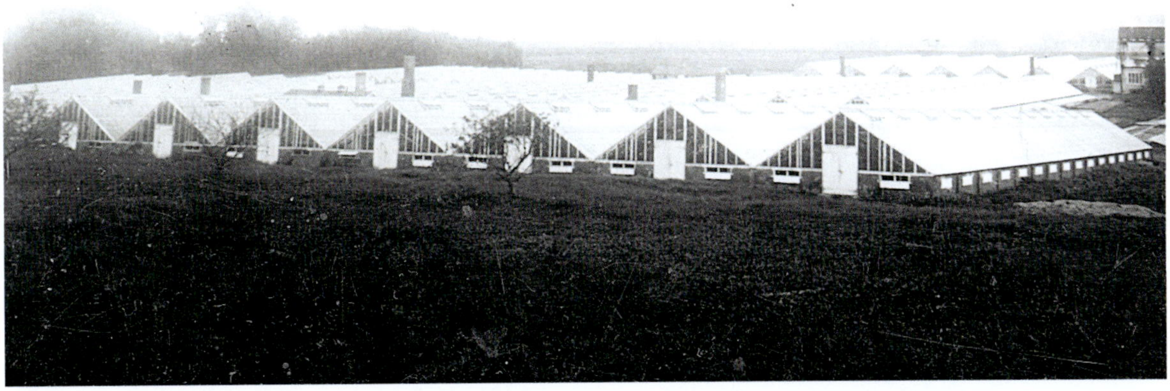

5.27 The greenhouses of the Menpes Fruit Farm, pictured in the 1930s, survived until the 1970s when they were dismantled to build the Wimpey Estate. Menpes used a 9½ inch gauge model railway to transport the fruit across the site.

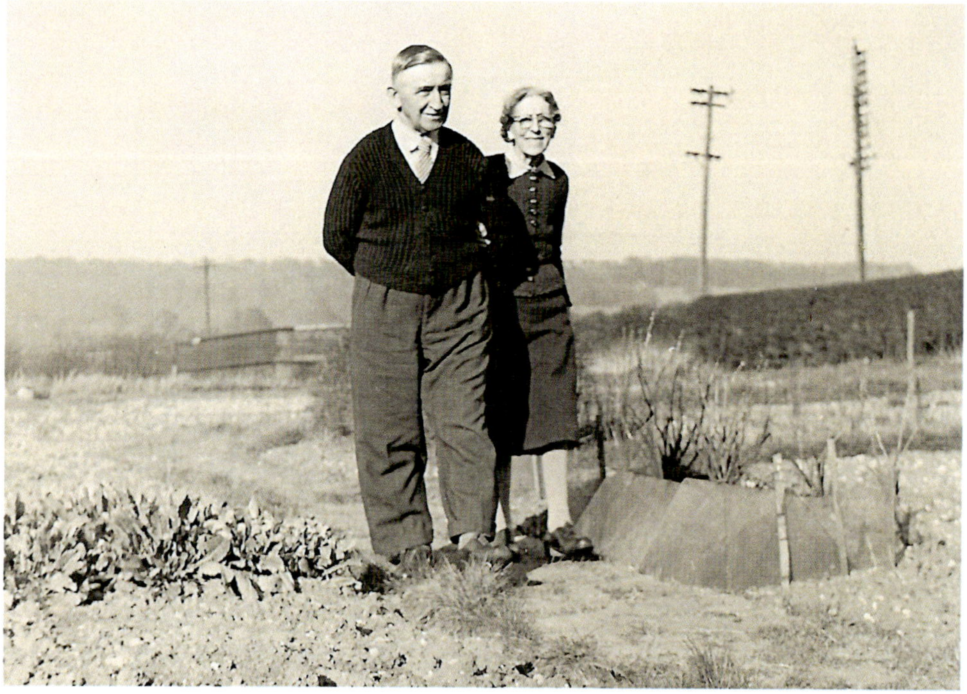

5.28 ***Above***: Joseph and Margaret Venners, here in the 1960s, moved to Purley in 1926 when they purchased 18 acres of arable land on the corner of Purley Rise and Westbury Lane and created Purley Rise Poultry Farm. Later, under the management of their son Kenneth, the farm diversified with glasshouses being added to cultivate tomatoes, flowers and other crops and with pigs and rabbits also being bred.
5.29 ***Below:*** Purley Rise Farm farmhouse, shown here in 1930, was one of a number of houses built on Westbury Lane and Purley Rise by Joseph Venners.

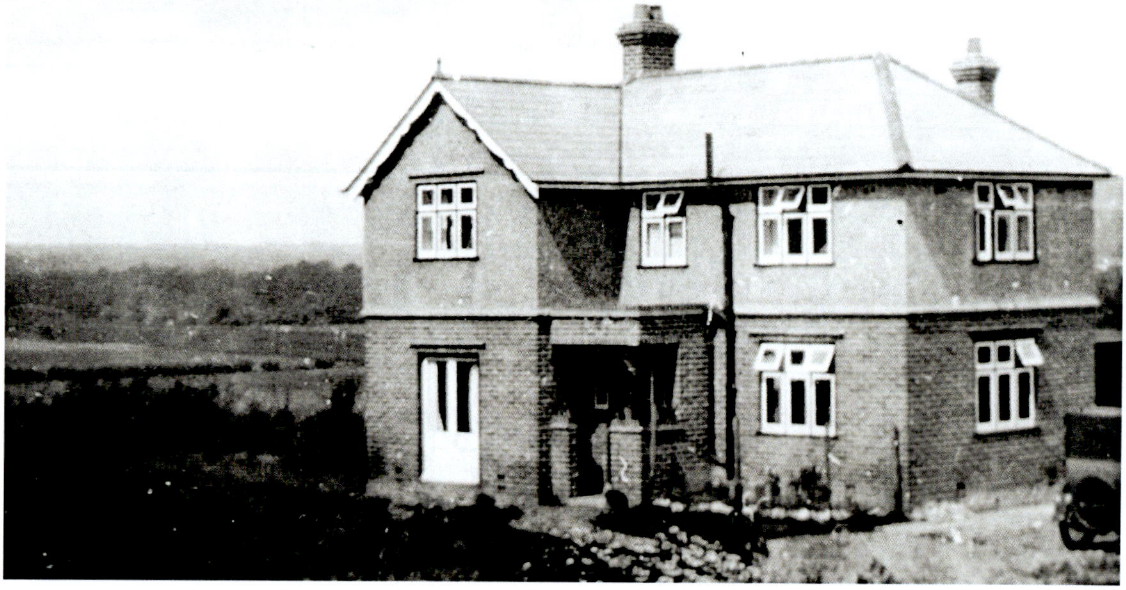

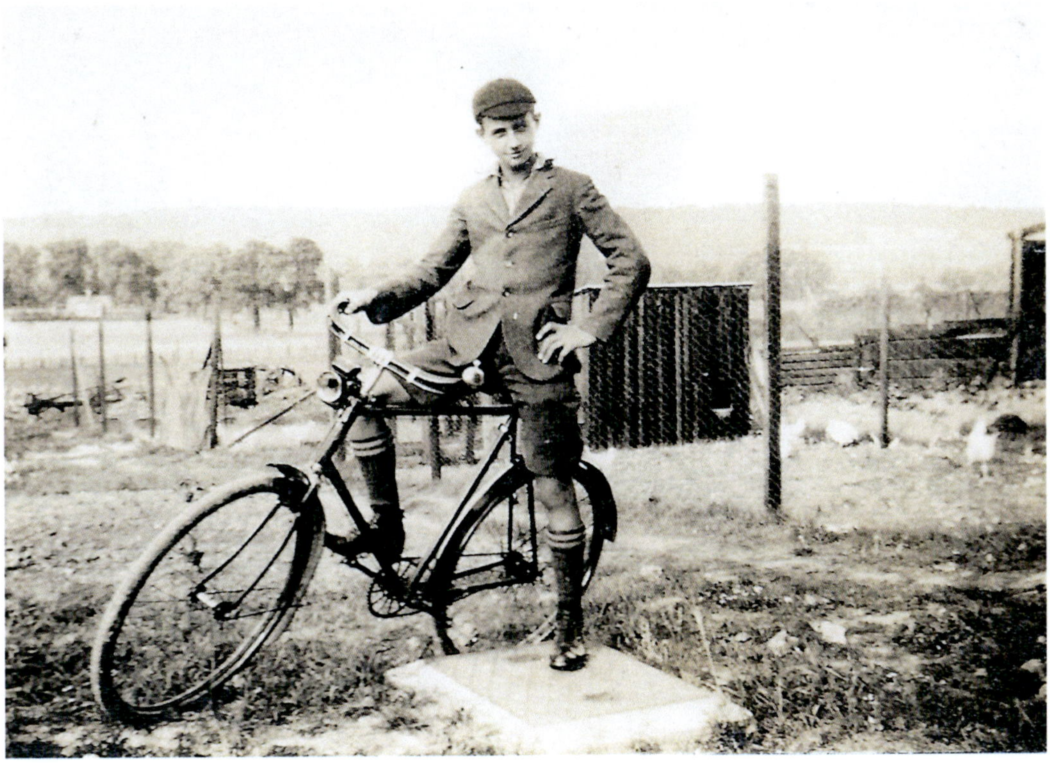

5.30 ***Above:*** Kenneth Venners poses on his bike by the side of one of the chicken coops at Purley Rise Farm, c1927.

5.31 ***Below:*** The main hatchery building of Thomas L Keen, Purley Park Poultry Farm in the 1950s. Thomas L Keen was one of the enterprises which moved onto land formerly belonging to Purley Park, after its sale in the 1920s.

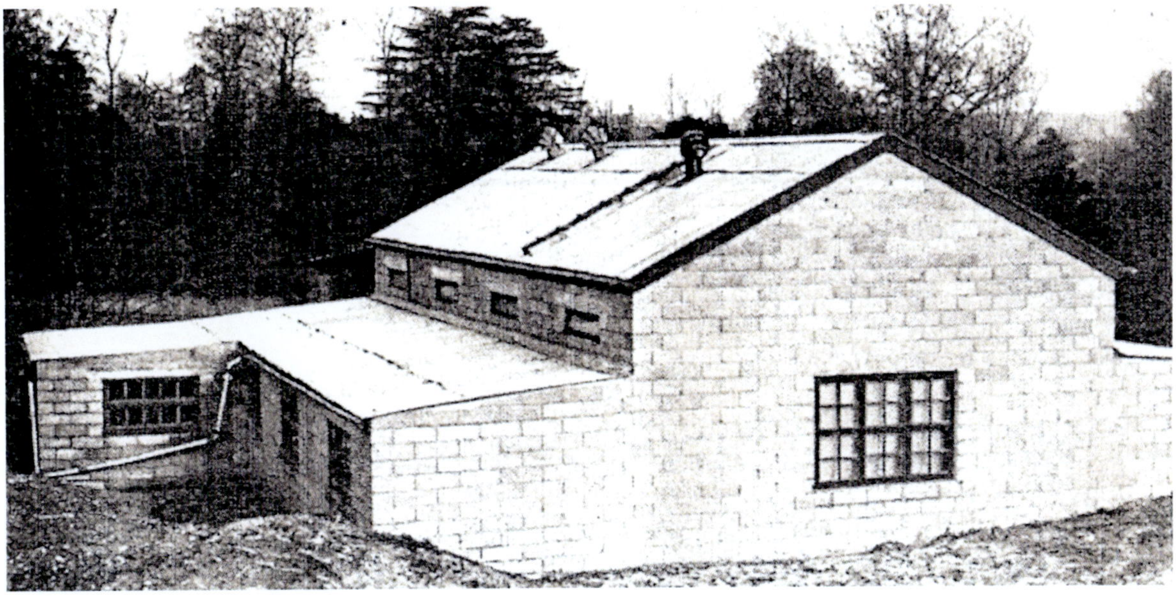

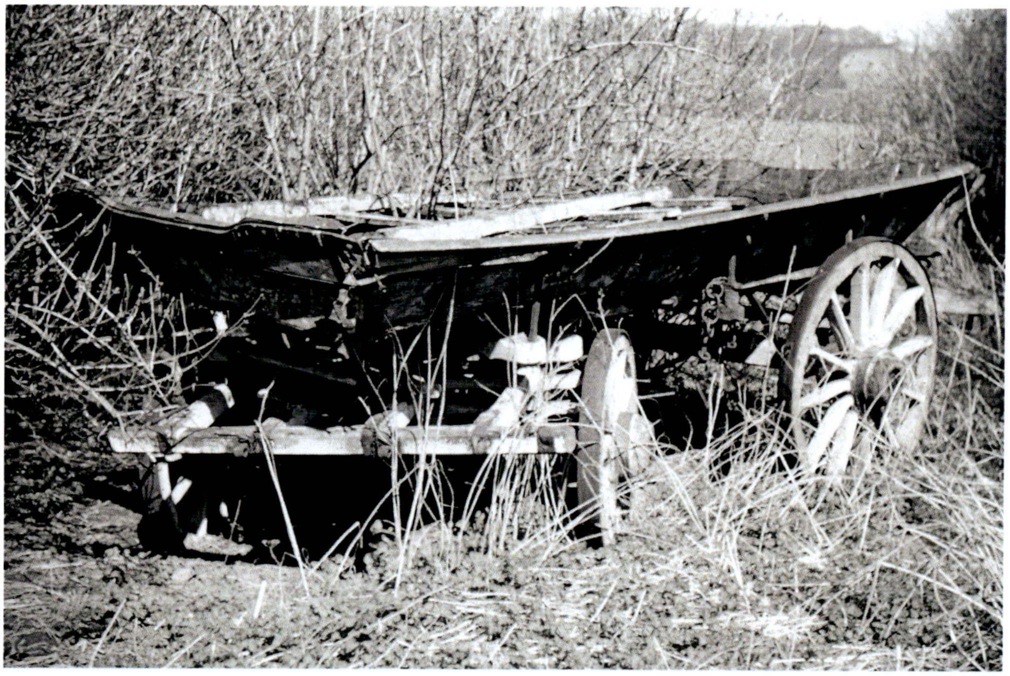

5.32 ***Above:*** As the 'old ways' started to be replaced with new technologies, the casualties included this old horse-drawn boat wagon, pictured in 1961 and said to be the last survivor of its kind in the village.

5.33 ***Below:*** A wine label produced in 1984 from Westbury Vineyard which was established by Bernard Theobald in 1968.

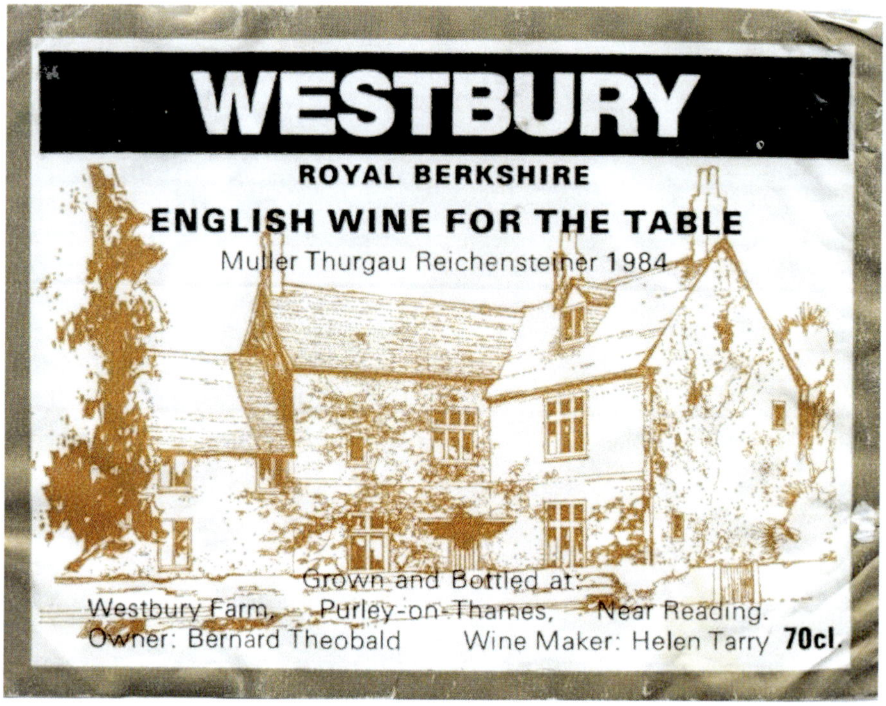

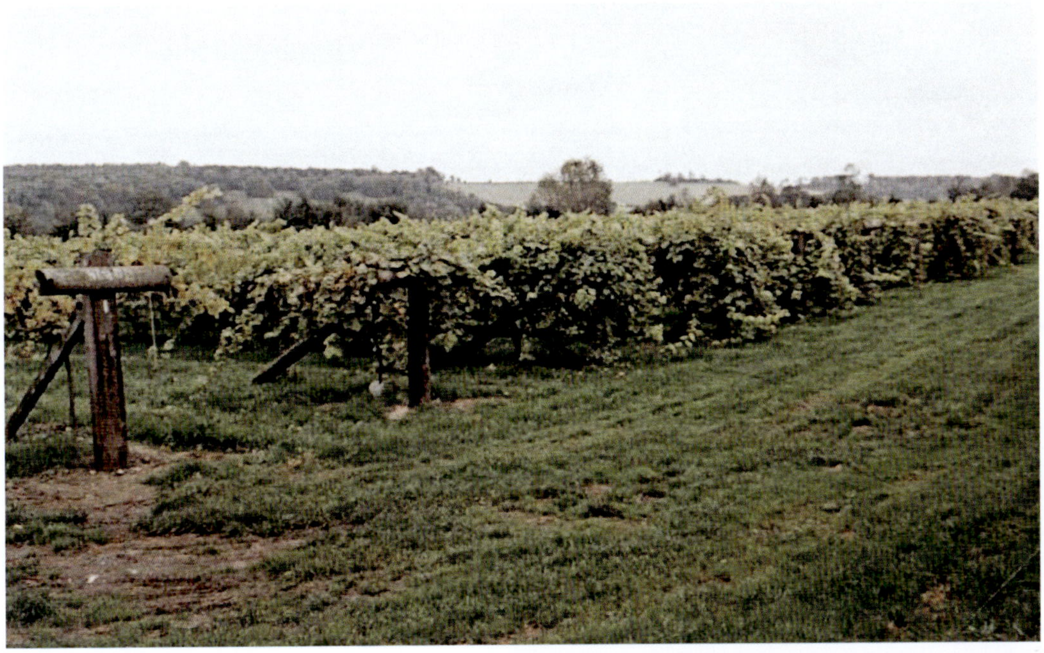

5.34 ***Above:*** We complete our chapter on farming and agriculture at Westbury Vineyard. Sixteen acres of land were devoted to grapes, grown on the Geneva double curtain system, which made it one of the largest vineyards in Britain during the 1970s and 80s.

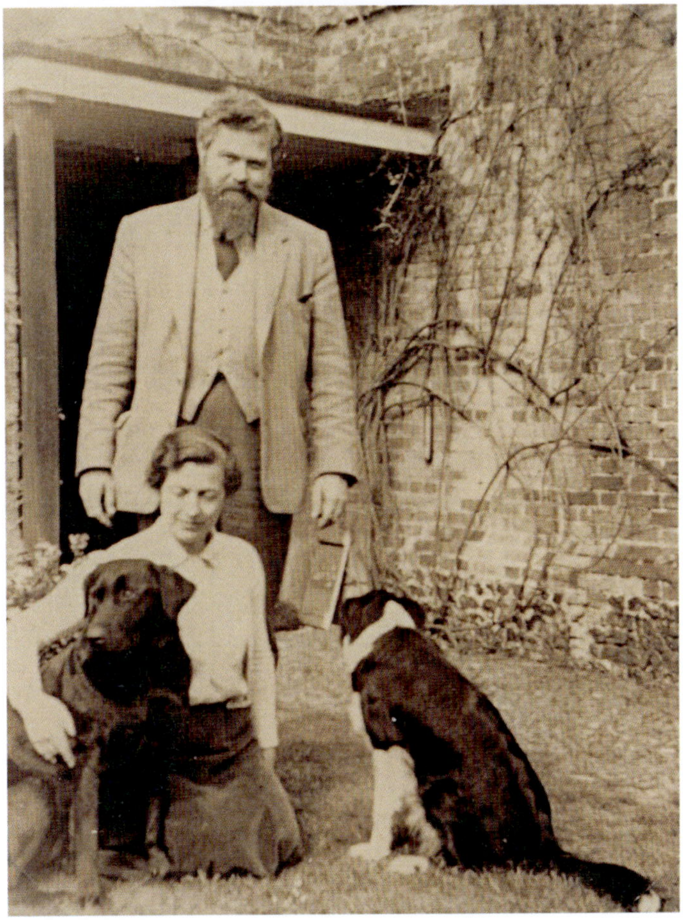

5.35 ***Right:*** Bernard and Gwen Theobald, the creators of the vineyard, in the 1950s in front of Westbury Farm farmhouse.

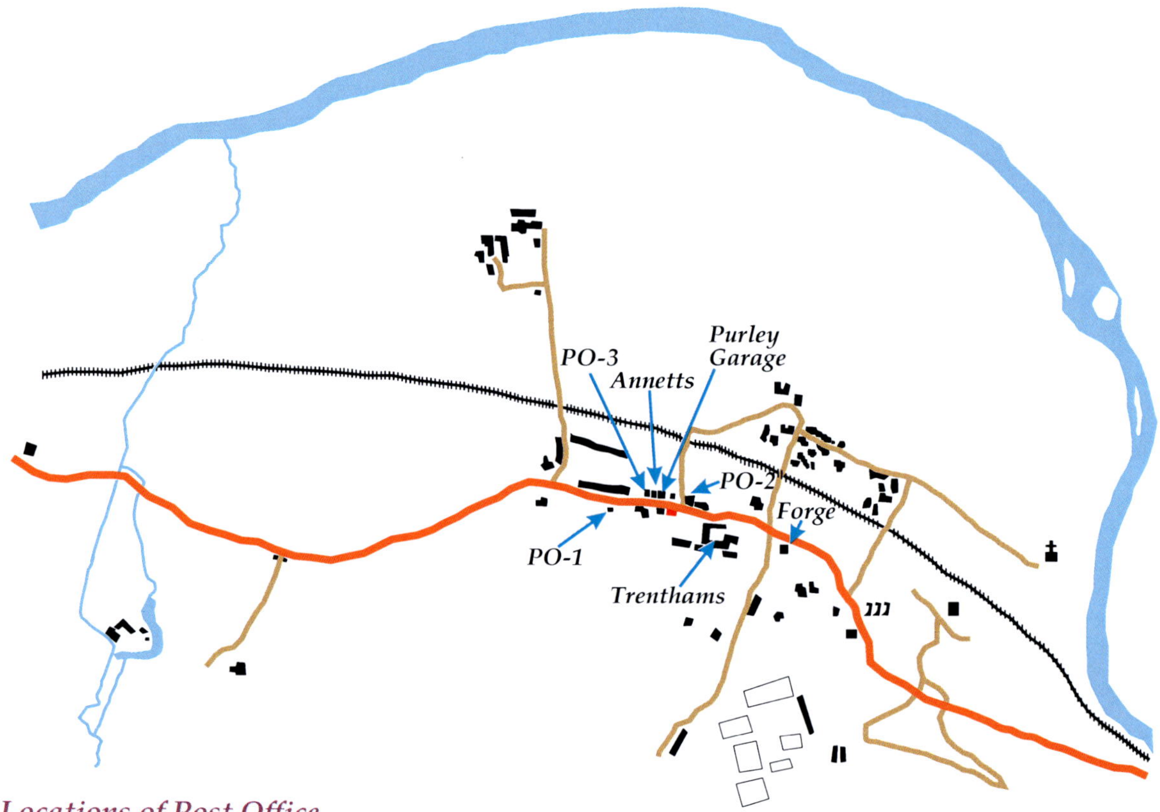

Locations of Post Office
PO-1 : Lichfield Cottage
PO-2 : Gardener's house of Westfield House
PO-3 : Current location

6 *Industry, Commerce & Transport*

There has been limited commercial development in Purley and the little there has been was, in the past, largely focused on satisfying the everyday needs of the villagers. We know, for example, that William Pocock of Lichfield Cottage ran a wheelwright's business, the Martin family of Hemington were shoemakers and a blacksmith's forge was in operation by at least 1600. The last forge was at the corner of Reading Road and Long Lane and served the needs of both the villagers and passing carriers and coaches using the Turnpike Road.

The replacement for the Forge, Purley Garage, established in the 1930s as a small engineering workshop, also sold petrol. During the Second World War it made parts for Spitfires being manufactured at Woodley. The garage was one of several businesses in Purley which supported the war effort and the village also played host to companies escaping the blitz: Sangers occupied Purley Park and the Royal School of Music moved into Westfield House.

The Great Western Railway, which opened through Purley in 1840, provided jobs and improved transport links, but at the cost of splitting the village in half. Until then the villagers had relied on carriers and stage coaches. Our nearest railway station at Tilehurst opened in 1882 and our first bus service started in 1915.

When the GPO was established in 1660 one had to go into Reading to post or collect mail. From around 1790, thanks to the initiative of Godwyn, a carrier, one could use a receiving house in Purley, and this became our first Post Office. From at least 1847 this receiving house was located at Lichfield Cottage on Purley Rise. This chapter includes pictures of the Post Office at Lichfield Cottage and its successors.

Actual industrial activity was limited, although gravel was extracted in several locations and John Purvey and Sons, in the 1920s and 30s, ran a small railway down to a gravel quarry on Home Farm, Purley and then on to the river. Some of this gravel was used in the construction of Caversham Bridge. There was a small industrial estate near where Goodliffe Gardens now stands, on which there were greyhound kennels for the Norcot Greyhound track and several other small enterprises. The nearest Purley came however, to having a commercial development was when G Percy Trenthams brought Belleisle from the South Berks Hunt and used it as their headquarters from 1951 to 1985. We conclude our chapter with photographs of what became Purley's largest employer.

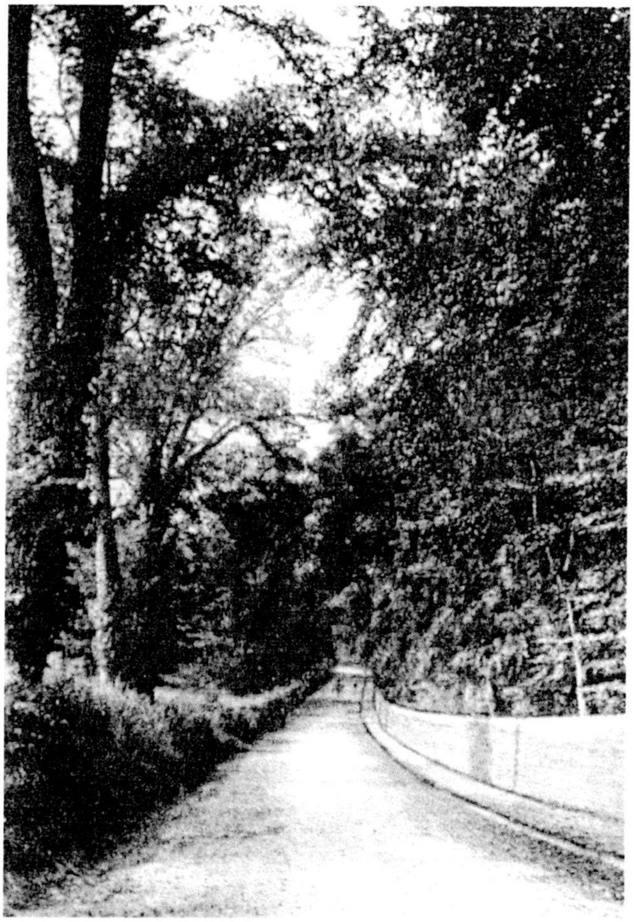

6.1 ***Left:*** Oxford Road, before it was widened in 1917, with the flint wall enclosing Purley Park on the right. This was the 19th century turnpike road along which the carriers and stage coaches passed on their way from Reading to Wallingford and Oxford.

6.2 ***Below:*** The blacksmith's forge is pictured c1908 when it was worked by Thomas Kerr. The older children used to meet here to catch Francis Lee's lorry to school in Pangbourne. On the left you can just see the top of the well and on the right, one of the large elm trees which curved over Long Lane on the way to Tilehurst. The two girls are standing at the spot where the traffic island is now sited in a widened Long Lane junction. The forge was demolished in 1936.

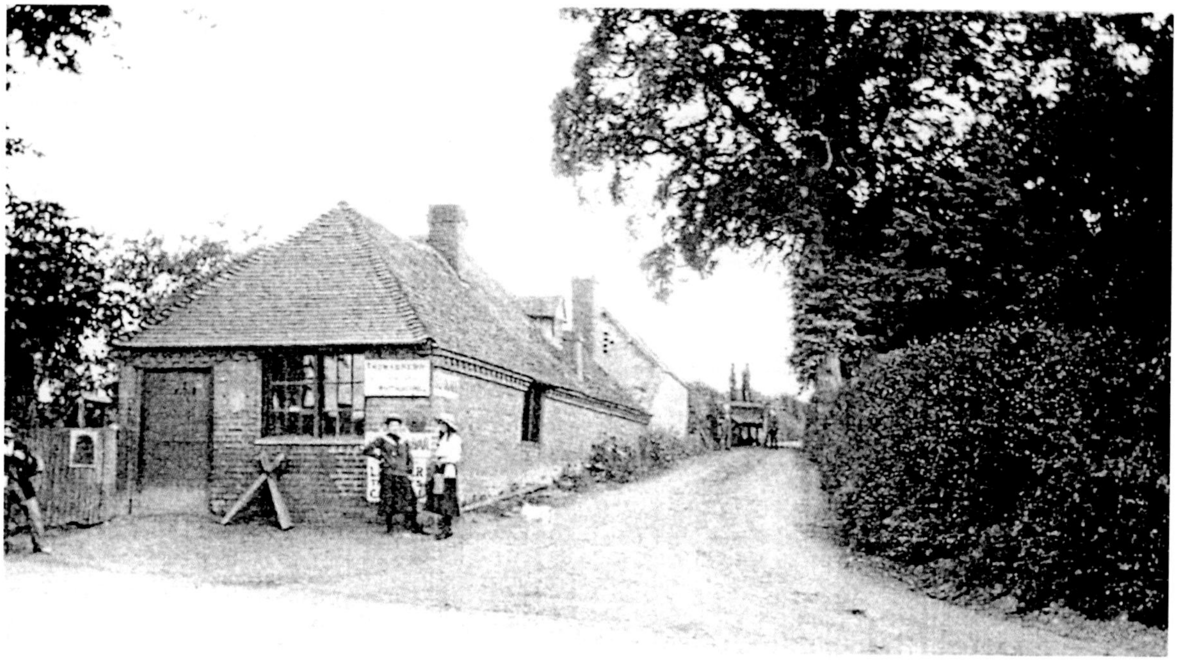

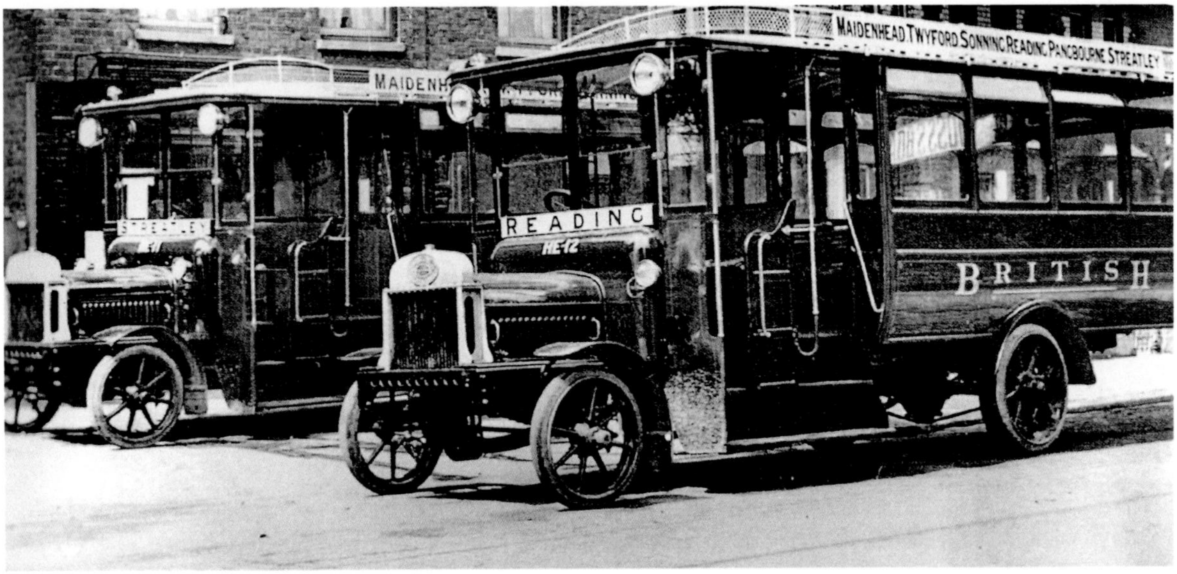

6.3 ***Above:*** In the early twentieth century horse drawn carriages began to be replaced by motorised transport. These buses were part of a collection of six made by the British Omnibus Company for Berkshire's first bus service, which ran from Maidenhead to Streatley, via Purley, in 1915.

6.4 ***Below:*** Waiting to leave Reading Station is this typical Bristol bus which operated the Purley route just after the Second World War.

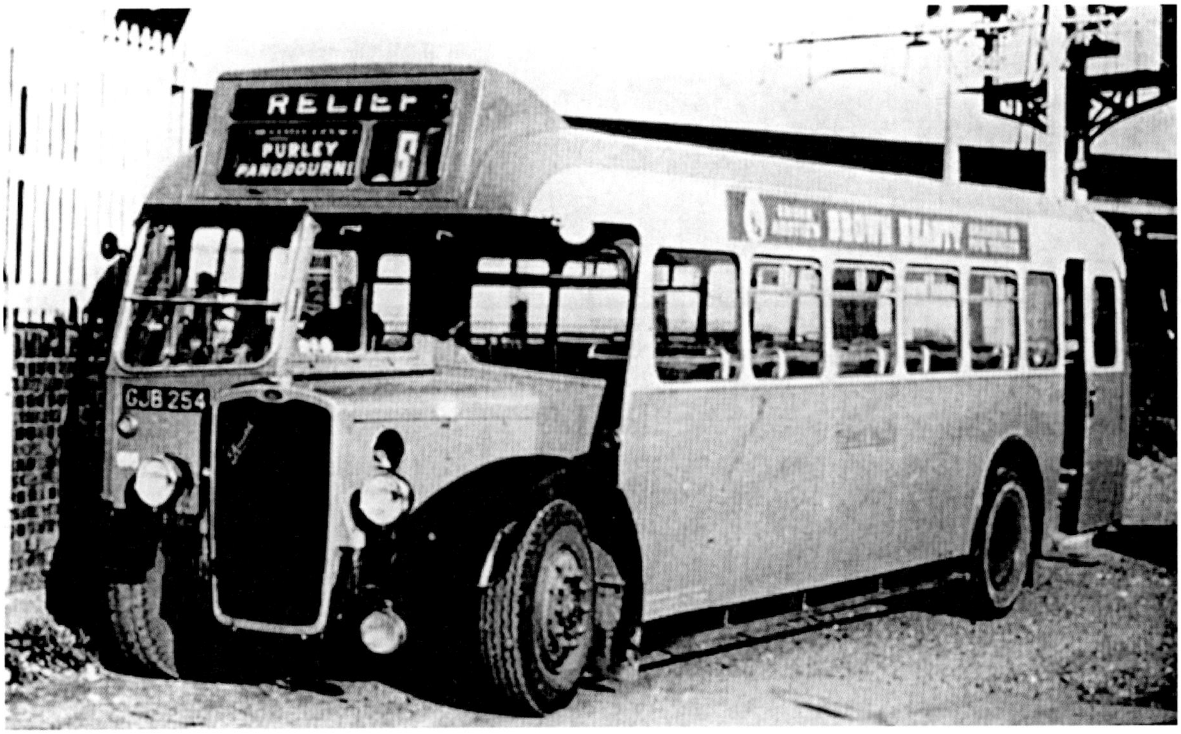

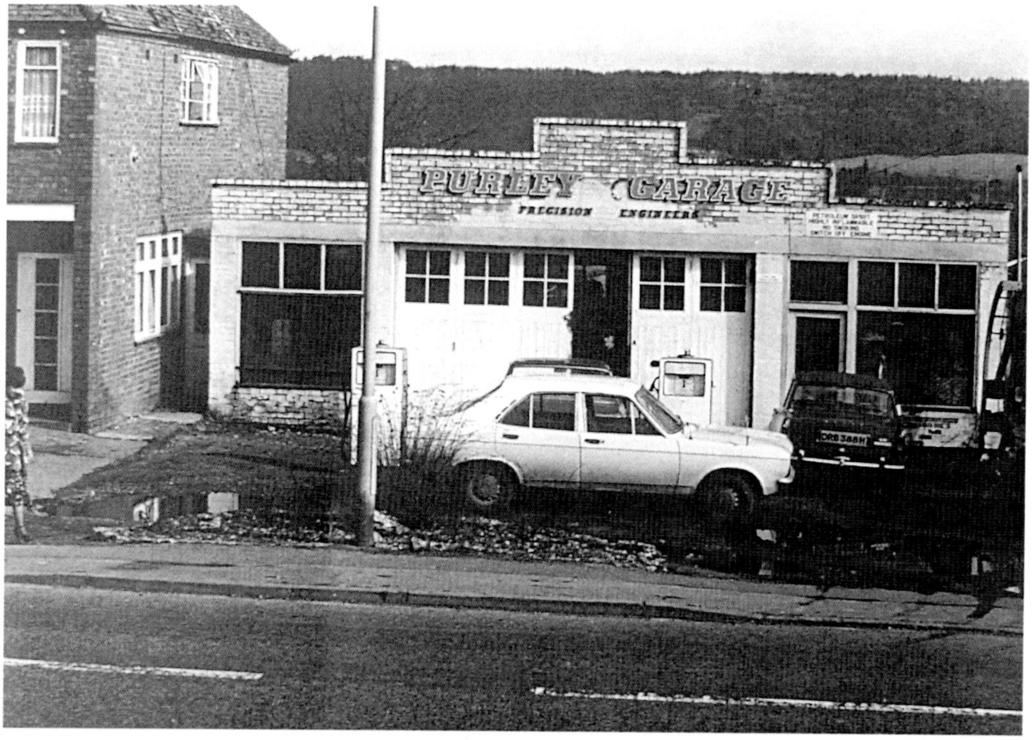

6.5 & 6.6 ***Above and below:*** Purley Garage, pictured above in the 1970s, and more recently below, was established in 1937 to sell petrol as well as repair cars. The bottom photograph shows the business following its development into precision engineering.

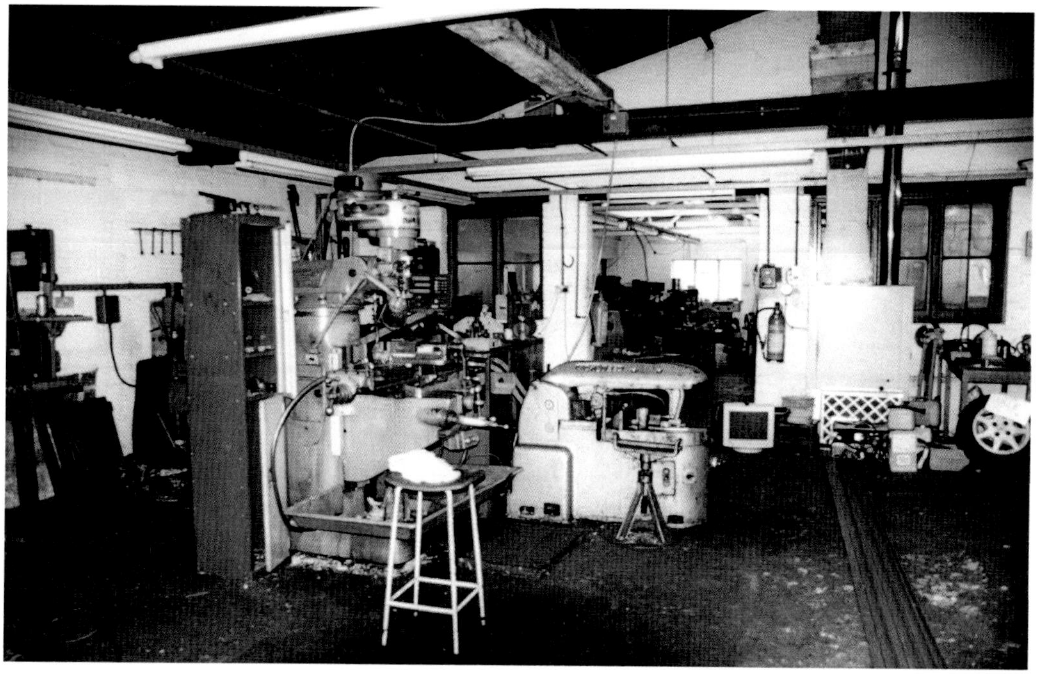

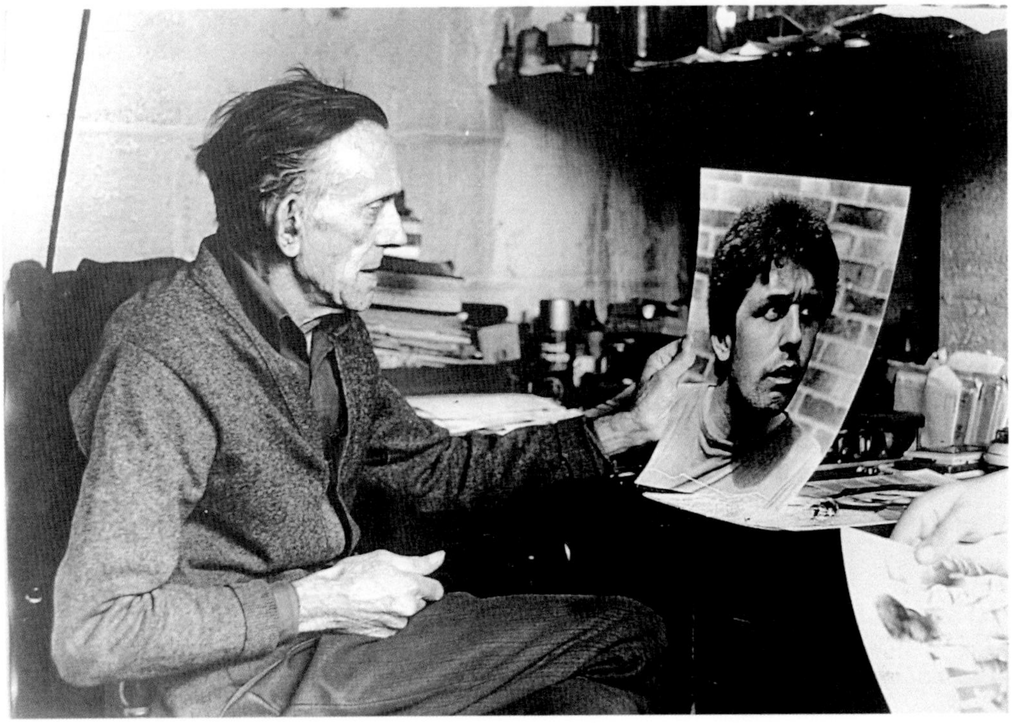

6.7 ***Above:*** Charlie Edwards built the garage and is pictured here in the 1960s. He was also a keen photographer. He held a film show of the village coronation celebrations of 1937 in the garage whilst it was still an empty shell.
6.8 ***Below:*** Charlie's son John, who took over Purley Garage, is pictured in the 1990s working a lathe. The business was sold to Merit Tyres in 2006.

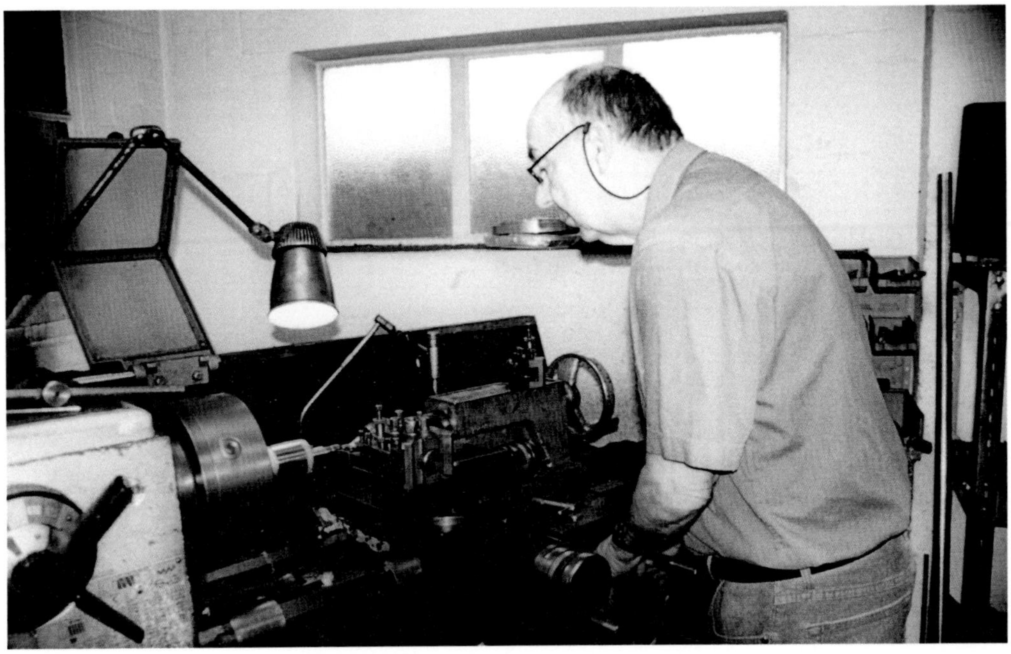

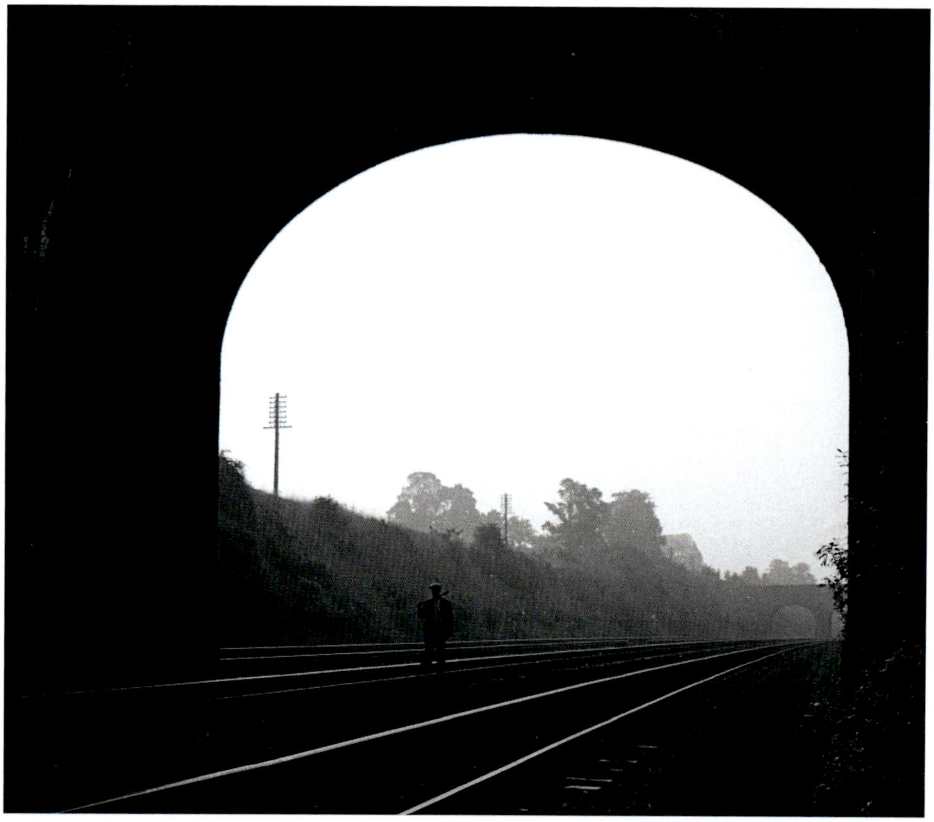

6.9 ***Above:*** Alf Nash, who worked as a ganger on the railway, 'walks the length' of High Bridge in 1961. In the distance you can see the Purley Lane Bridge.
6.10 ***Below:*** Hall class locomotive 4959, named Purley Hall, passes through Purley in 1962.

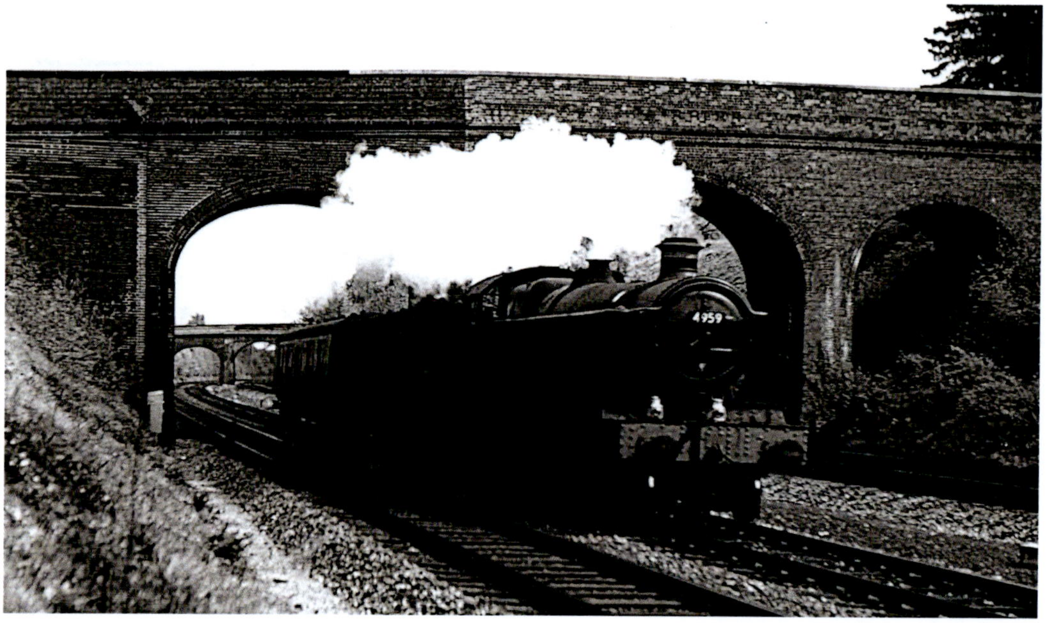

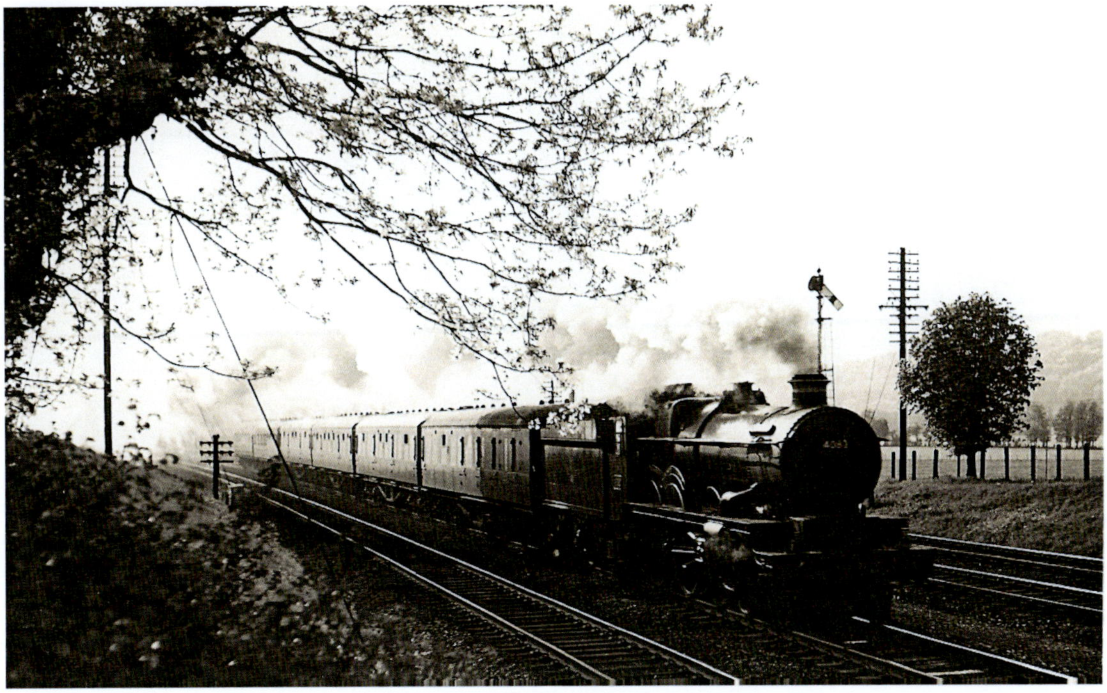

6.11 ***Above:*** The locomotive Windsor Castle, pictured here at Westbury Lane in 1962, had previously pulled the funeral train of King George VI.
6.12 ***Below:*** The 8.10 am Didcot to Paddington train passes the signals at Westbury Lane in May 1962.

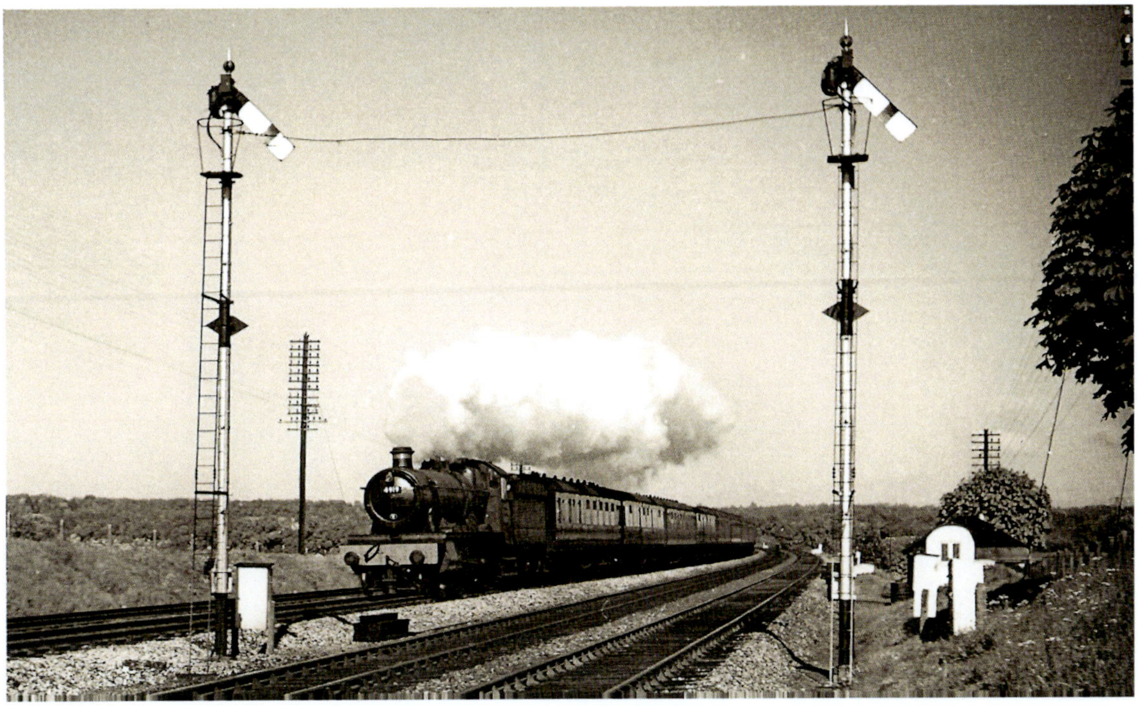

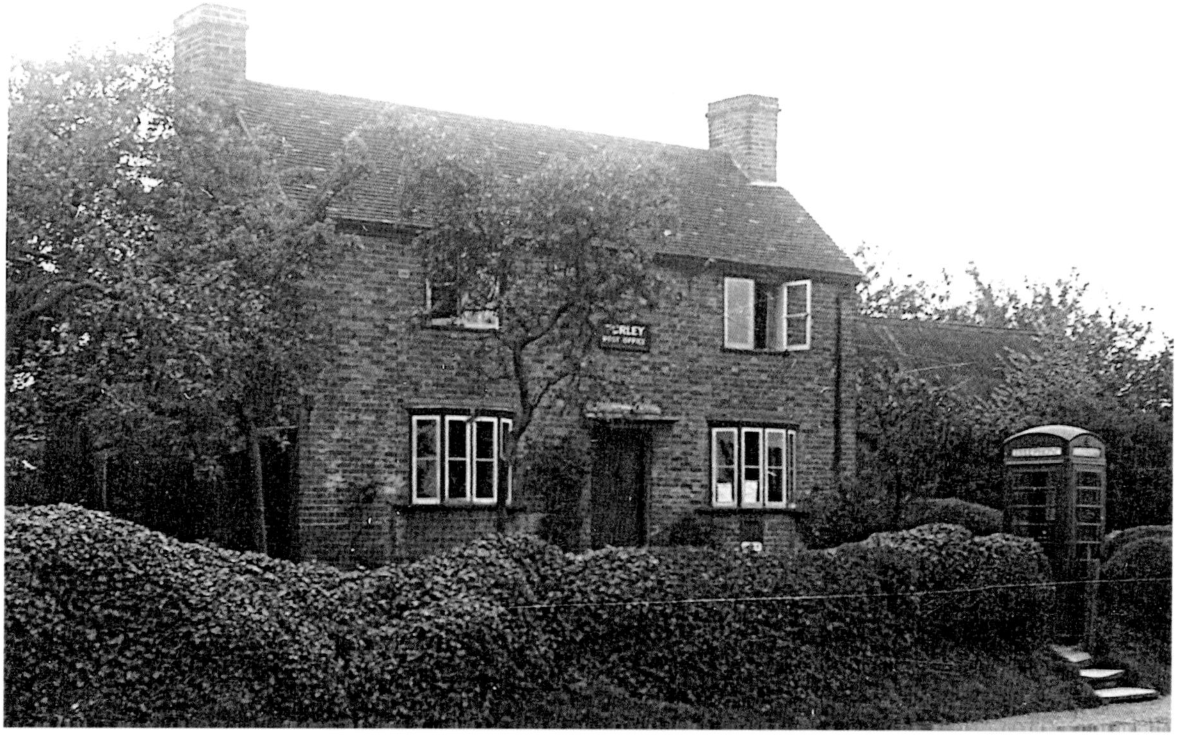

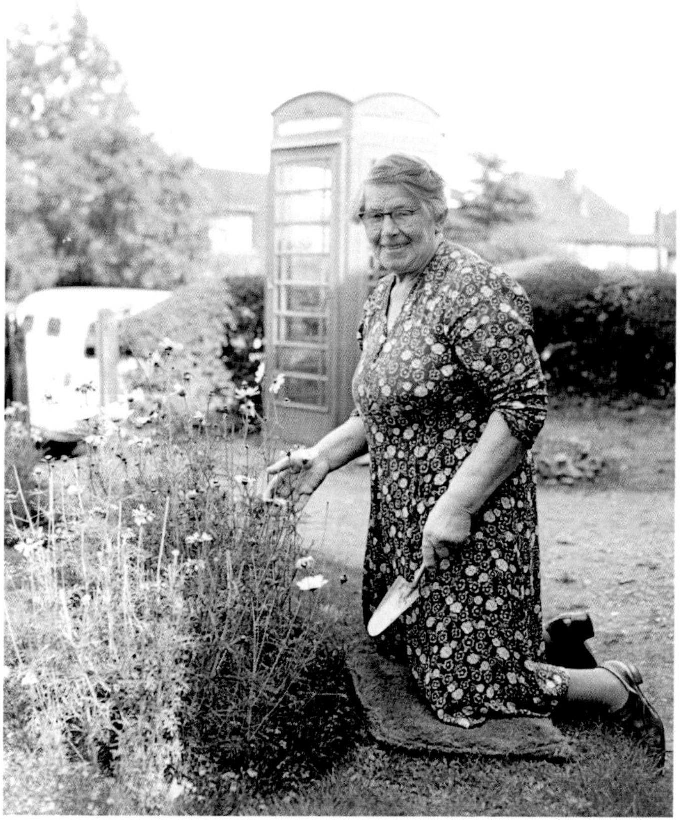

6.13 ***Above:*** Our first known Post Office was Lichfield Cottage on Purley Rise, here in 1955 when it was run by Miss Amy Pocock. In the early 1800s Lichfield Cottage was the village poor house.

6.14 ***Left:*** Miss Amy Pocock pictured at the time of her retirement in October 1955. The GPO then appointed Harold Gutch as sub-postmaster and the Post Office moved to his house across the road.

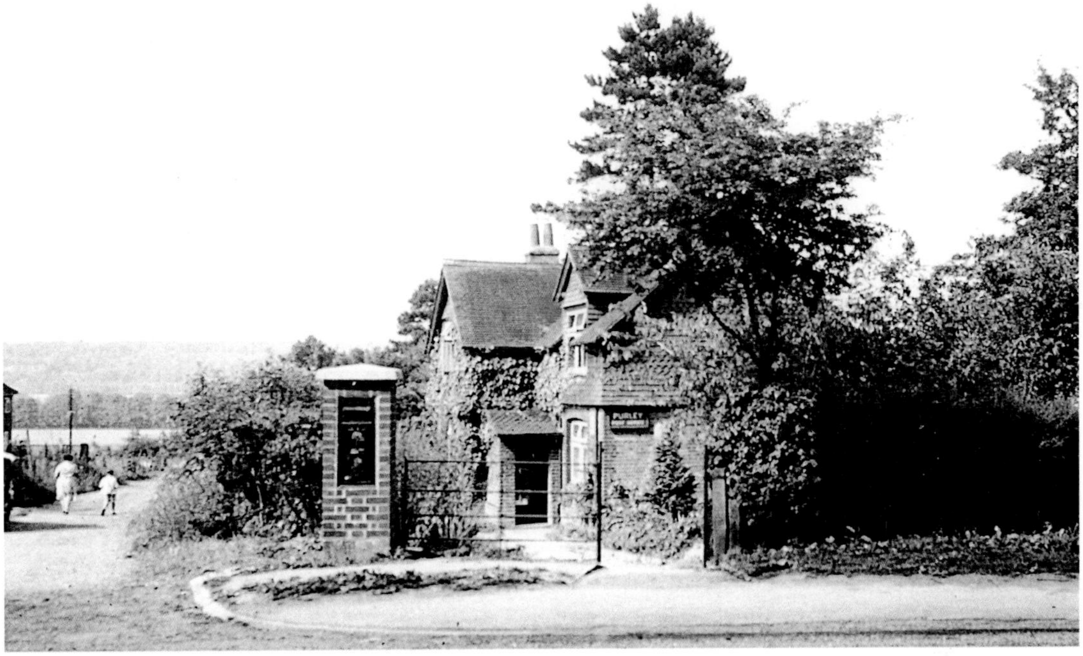

6.15 ***Above:*** Harold and Lucy (Honor) Gutch ran the Post Office between 1955 and 1977 from the former gardener's house of Westfield House, seen here in the late 1950s. Harold Gutch also ran a market garden business which he had set up after the Second World War.

6.16 ***Below:*** After the Gutchs' retirement, the Post Office once again moved premises and this picture shows John Edwards of Purley Garage helping Harold Gutch to remove the Post Office sign.

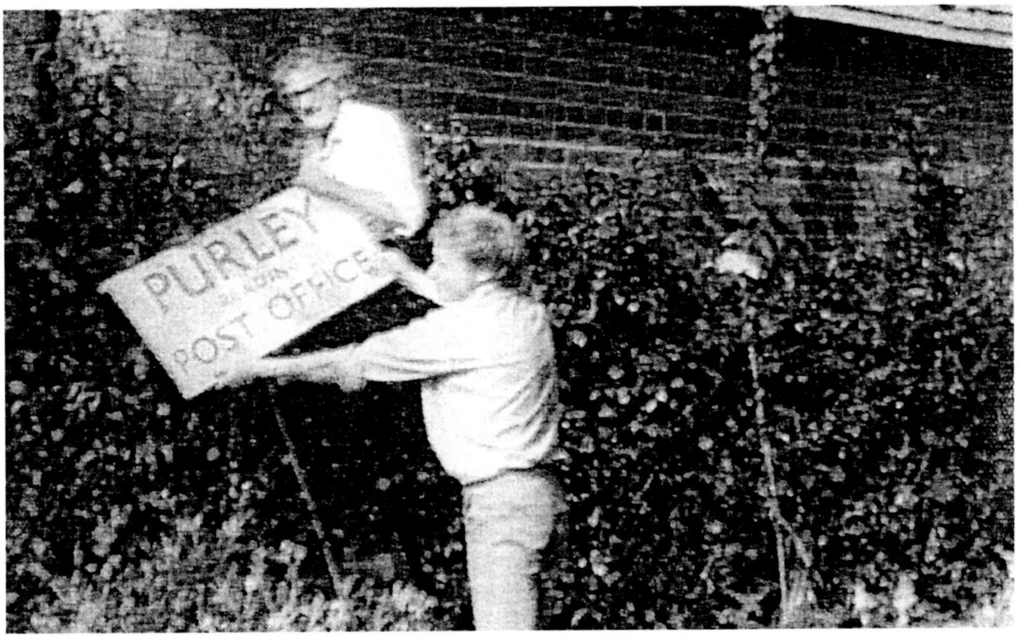

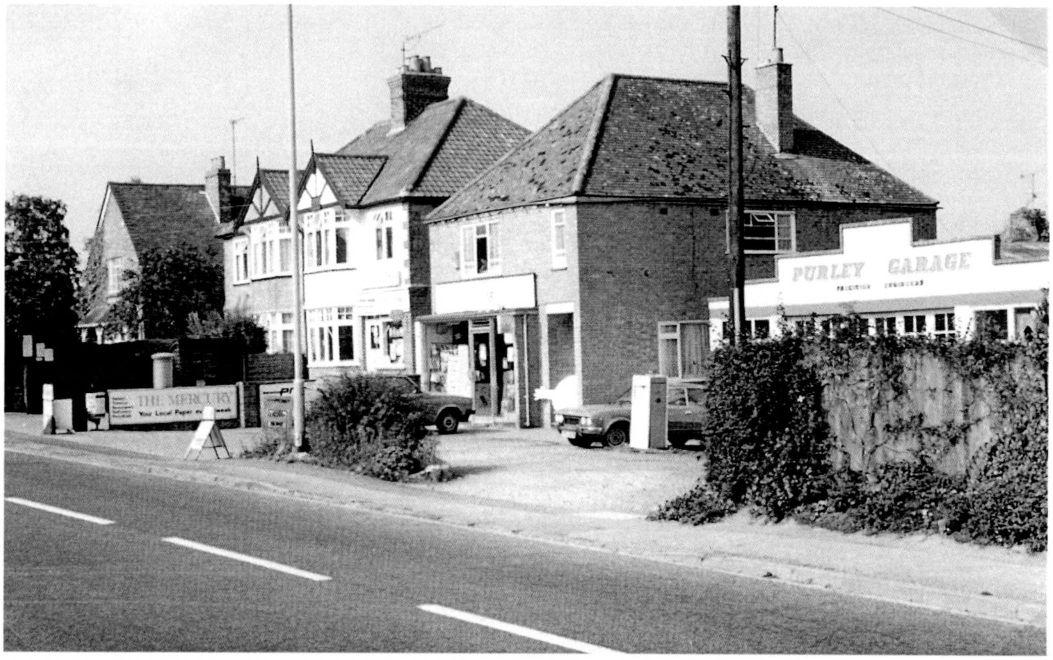

6.17 ***Above:*** The current Post Office was opened further along Purley Rise in 1977. Here it is pictured in the late 1970s alongside the newsagents which was run for many years by Les Annetts.

6.18 ***Below:*** Mobile shops also served the village and here the Baylis mobile grocery van from Reading waits for business in the 1950s in the River Estate.

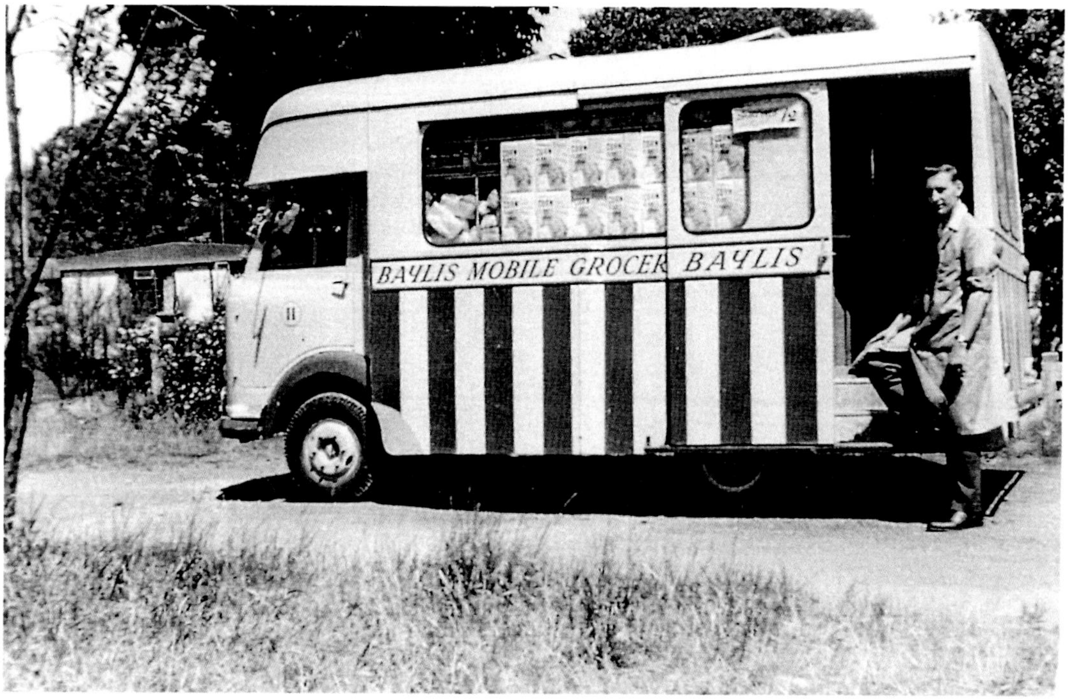

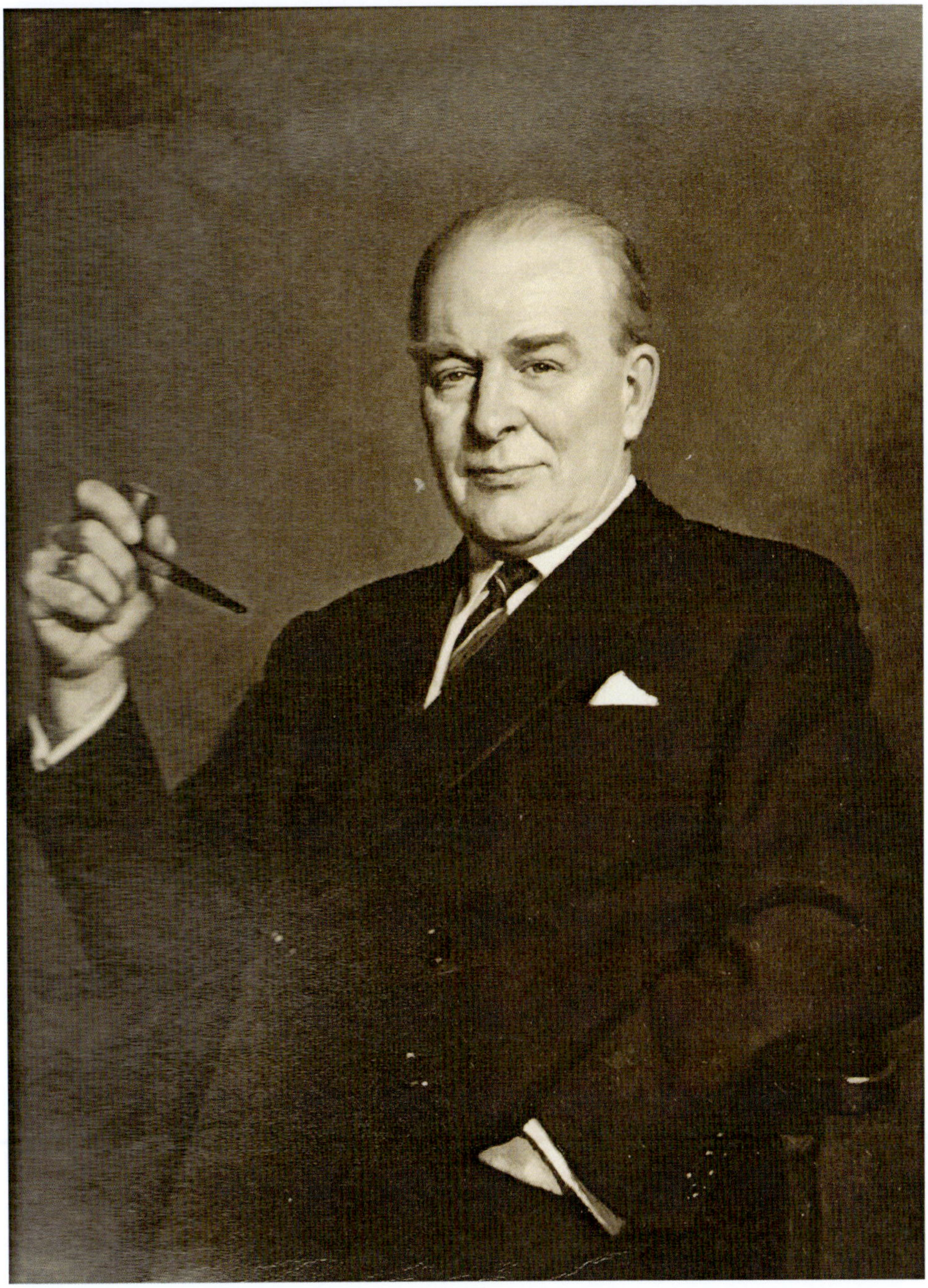

6.19 Our final section of photographs relate to G Percy Trenthams. George (Donald) Trentham, pictured here in 1964 in a painting by Edward Halliday, inherited the chairmanship of Trenthams in 1941 when his father was killed in an air raid, a position which he held until his death in November 1983. During his leadership the Company built the Ford plant at Dagenham.

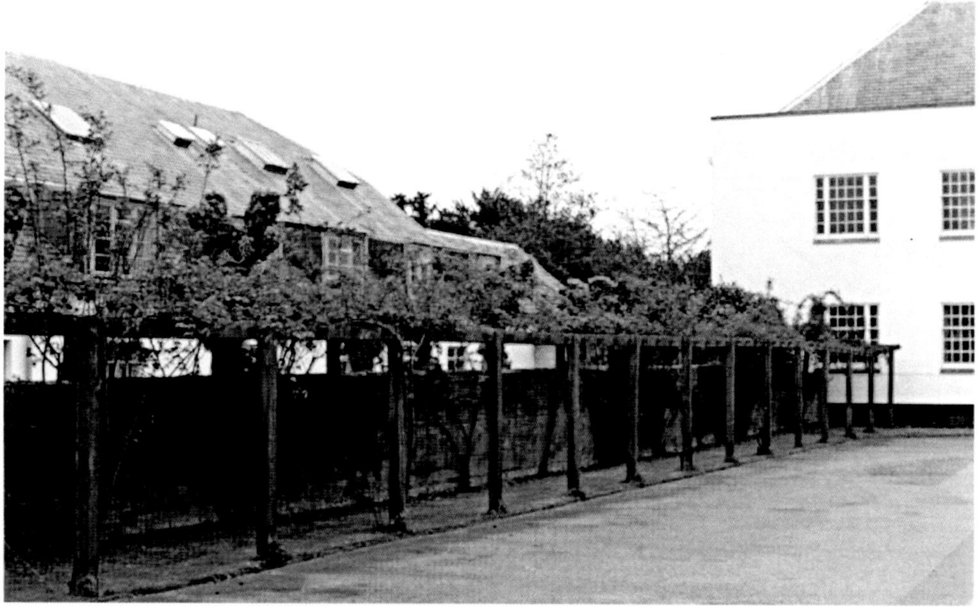

6.20 ***Above:*** Trenthams main buildings were situated around the quadrangle of Belleisle Farm. The rear of the farmhouse is seen behind a row of pollarded oaks, with part of the new office building on the right, shortly before the site was closed and the land and buildings sold in the 1980s.

6.21 ***Below:*** The new office building was designed with great sensitivity to the existing architecture. Trenthams referred to their site as 'The Kennels' after their previous occupiers, the South Berks Hunt.

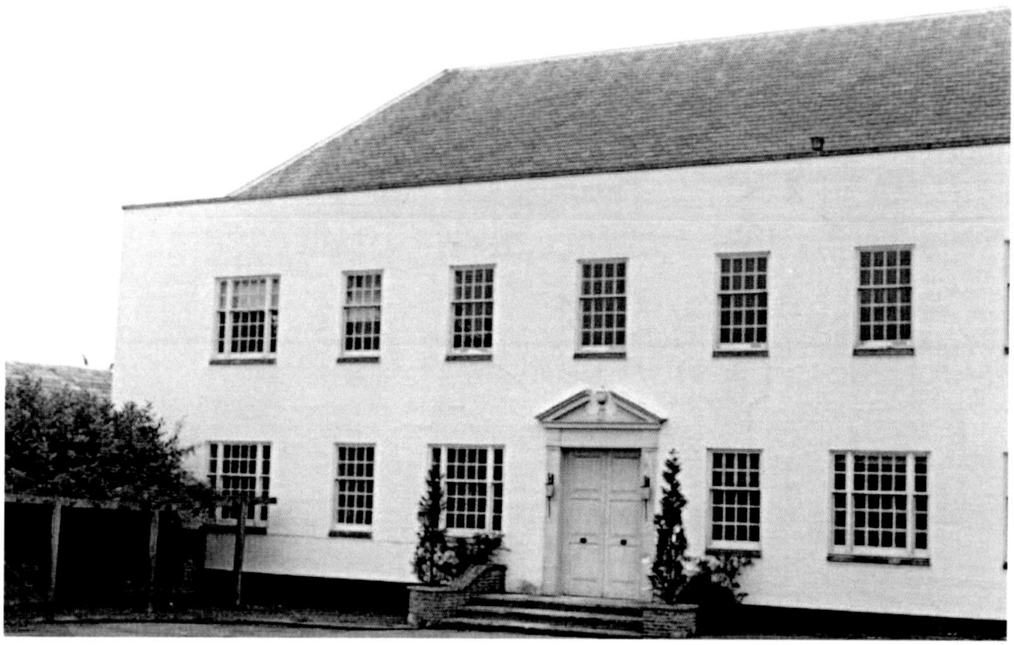

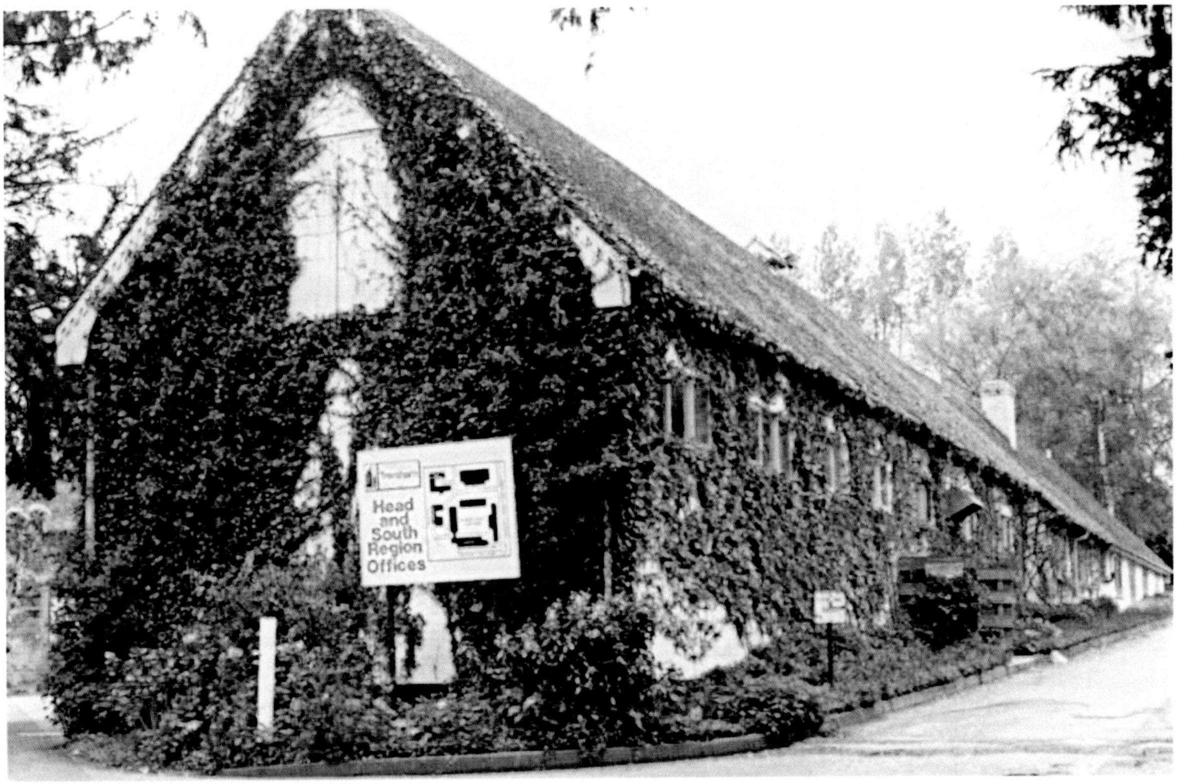

6.22 & 6.23 ***Above and below:*** We conclude our chapter with photographs taken in the 1980s of the two 18th century timber barns which became part of Trenthams Head Office. The medium sized timber barn, above, was the staff canteen and directors' restaurant and the large timbered barn, below, was used as workshops. This larger barn was dismantled and re-erected in the Goosecroft Recreation Ground in 1995.

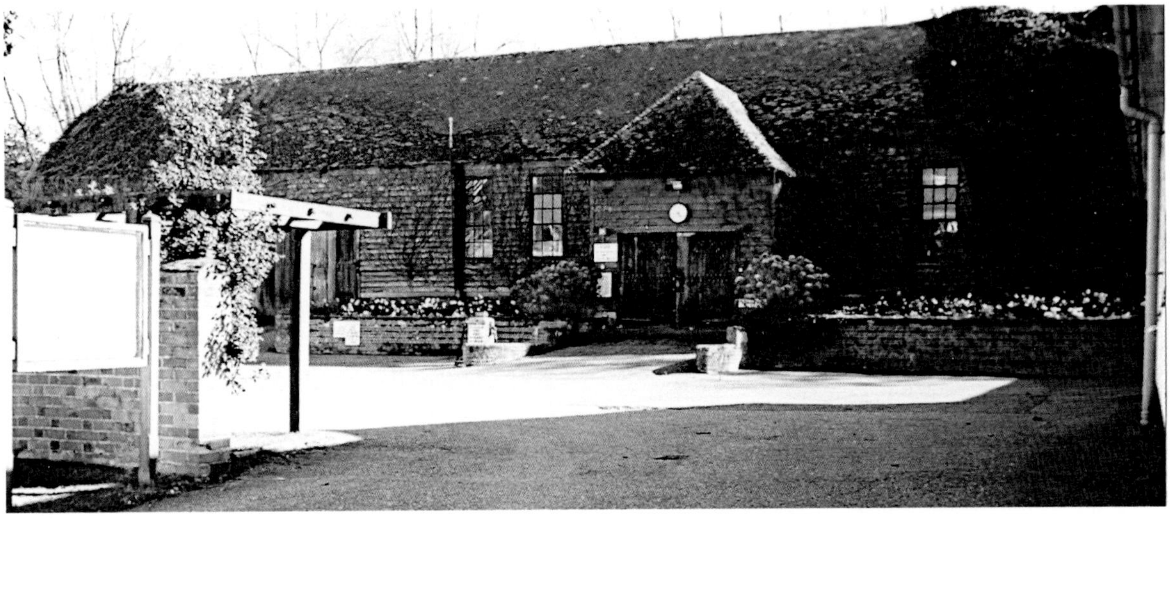

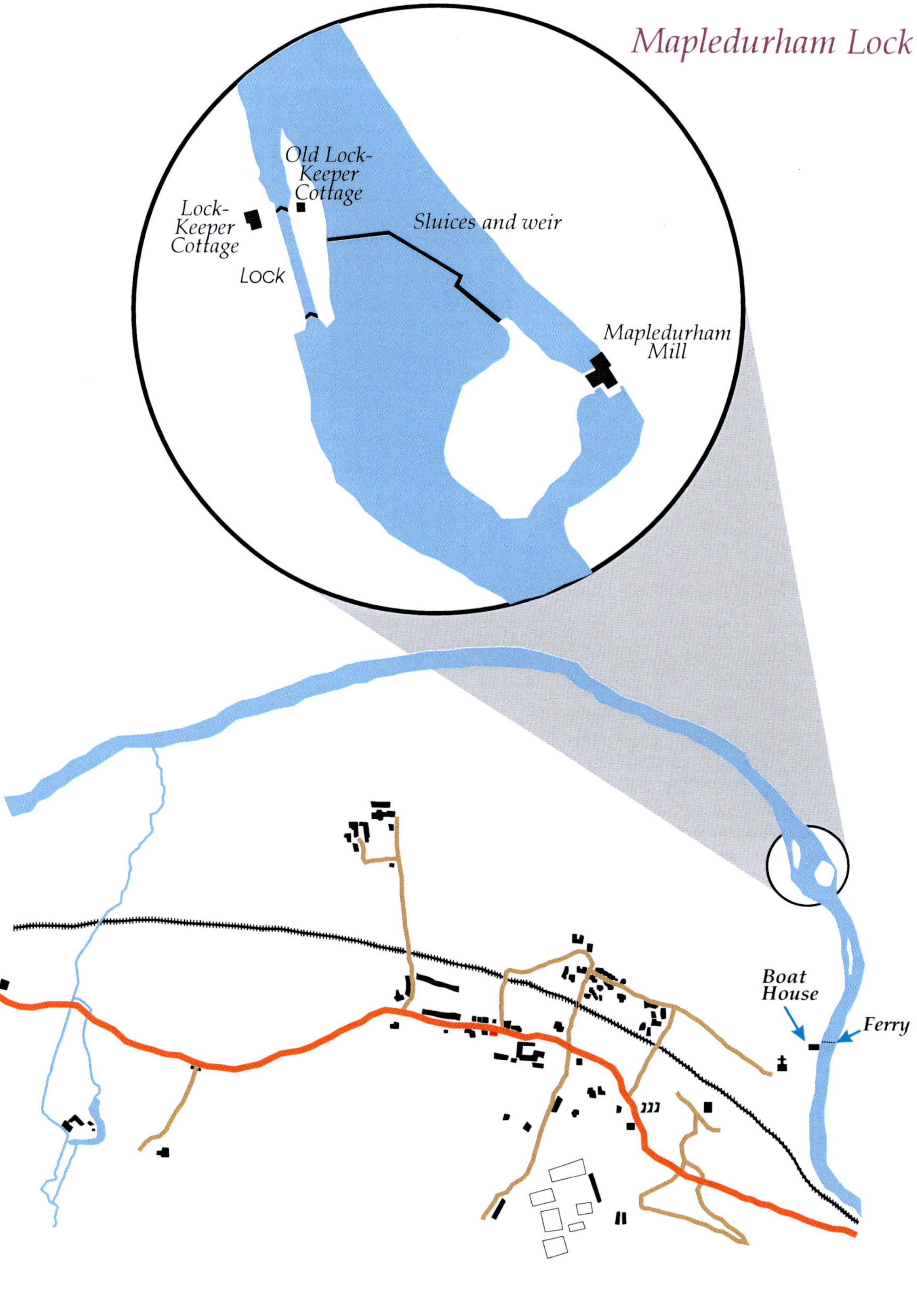
Mapledurham Lock
Old Lock-Keeper Cottage
Lock-Keeper Cottage
Sluices and weir
Lock
Mapledurham Mill
Boat House
Ferry

7 The River

The River Thames has been a quietly significant feature in Purley from the very earliest days of settlement. The lie of the river and its plain influenced where people built their houses and even the types of crops grown in the fields. Only a few villagers in each generation however, would have derived their income wholly from the waters and after the advent of the railways the volume of commercial barge traffic fell away rapidly. In contrast, the number of pleasure boats has increased significantly and boating remains very popular. The river has played host to swimming lessons, fishermen of all ages and even the occasional movie.

From medieval times, a weir over the river was used by the lords of Mapledurham to control the flow of water to their mill and a flash lock enabled boats to pass through it relatively safely. By 1777 river traffic was so great that an alternative was needed and Mapledurham Lock was cut across a headland on the south bank in Purley. The first lock was made from timber with turf sides and barges were charged threepence per ton to pass through it. There was an attempt to rename the new lock as 'Purley Lock' but the old ways prevailed and 'Mapledurham' it has remained. A 'centry' (sic) box for the lock-keeper was first erected in 1798, followed within twenty years by a cottage. This was built on the island and its longest tenant was William Sheppard, who became the lock-keeper in 1822 and served a creditable fifty-four years. The current lock cottage was built in 1931 to replace it, on the Purley side of the lock. The lock has been completely replaced on two occasions and renovated and improved many times.

Alongside the river runs the towpath; today popular with walkers but in the past a continuous path was needed for the horses to pull the barges. In the eighteenth century the then resident of Purley Magna refused permission for the towpath to run through the estate by the church. To ensure barge traffic could continue to use the river the Thames Commissioners were forced to continue this stretch on the opposite bank. A ferry was provided near to the church, where River Gardens ends today, to transport horses and foot passengers to the Oxfordshire bank and a return ferry brought them back to a landing below the Roebuck. We finish our selection of photographs with the towpath and start with the river itself.

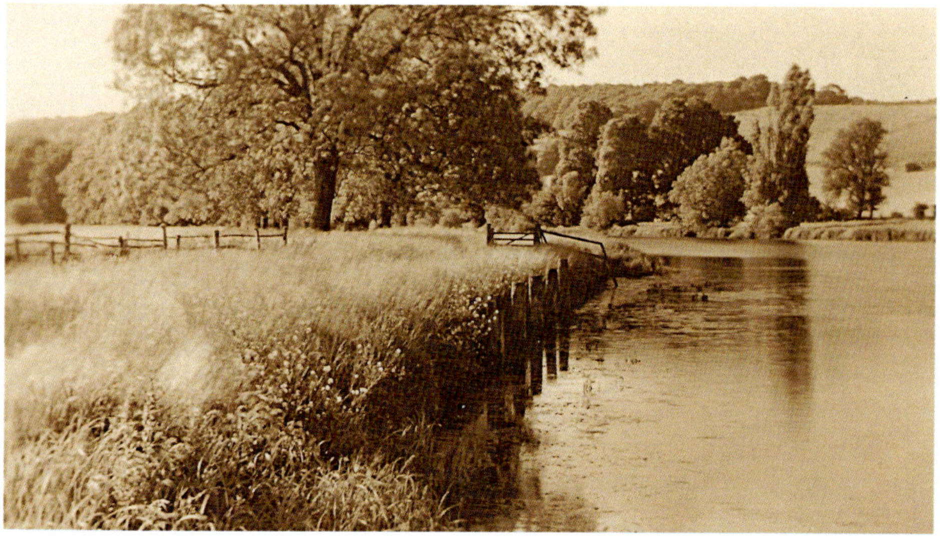

7.1 ***Above:*** The River Thames is arguably Britain's most important waterway as it links London to most of south central England via its tributaries and linking canals. The stretch between Purley and Pangbourne has been described as its most picturesque.

7.2 ***Below:*** Mapledurham Lock c1870 before its last rebuild, showing Lock Island with the old lock-keeper's house and part of the weir. William Sheppard, the lock-keeper in 1870, also rented the fishing rights on the river and was reported to have sent up to half a ton of fish at a time to Leadenhall Market in London.

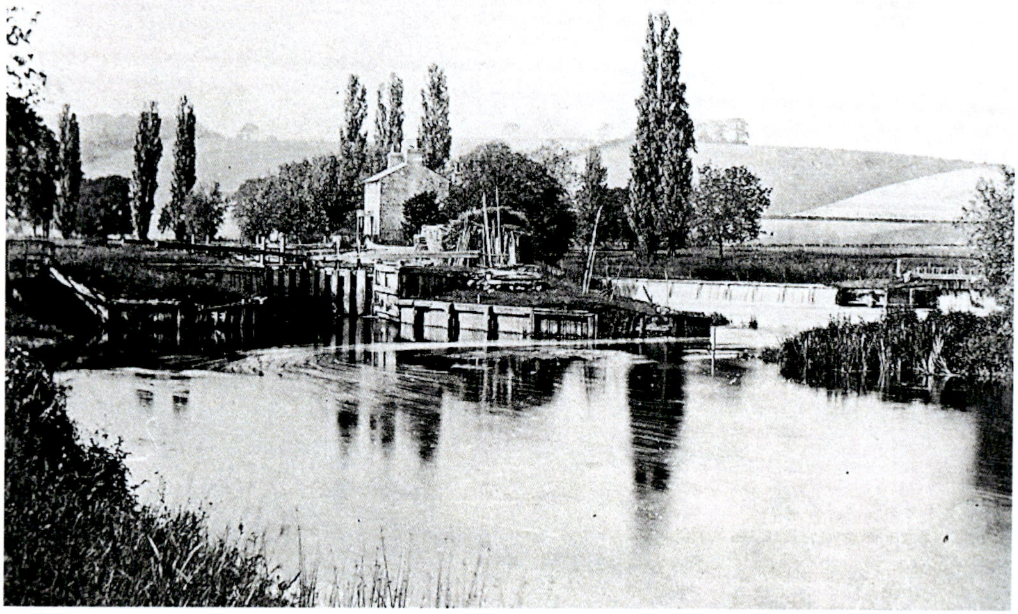

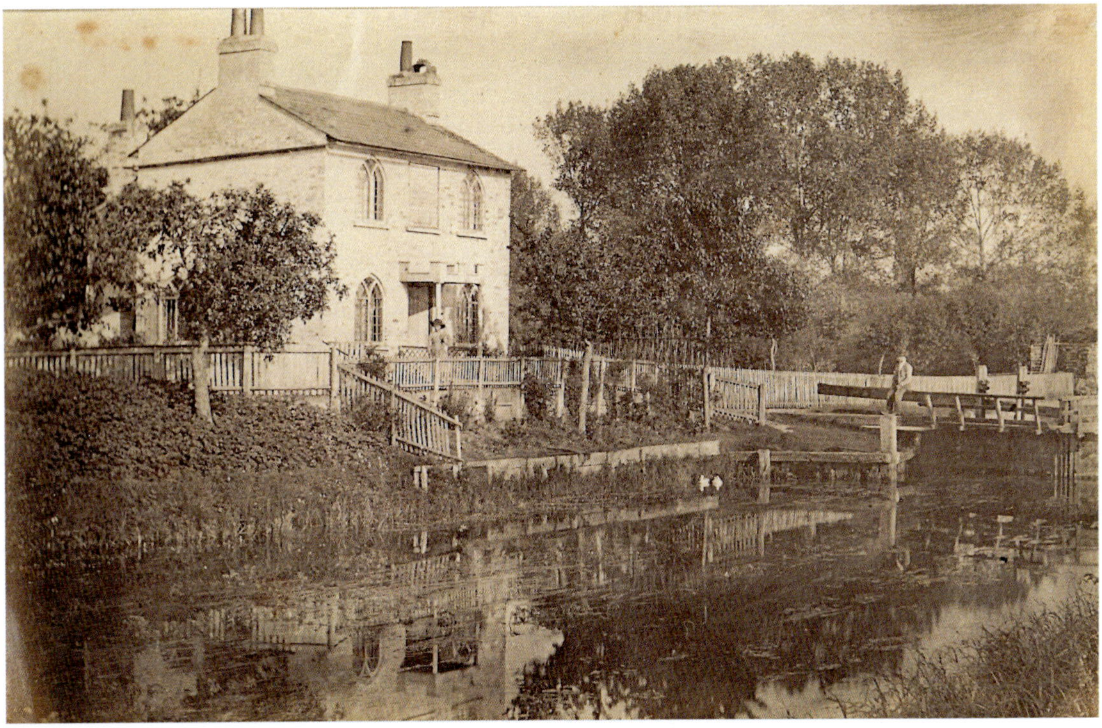

7.3 ***Above:*** The old keeper's cottage, c1890.
7.4 ***Below:*** Mapledurham Lock in the 1950s, with the replacement keeper's cottage, was still manually operated at this stage. The lock regularly won awards for the beautiful gardens which the keepers cultivated.

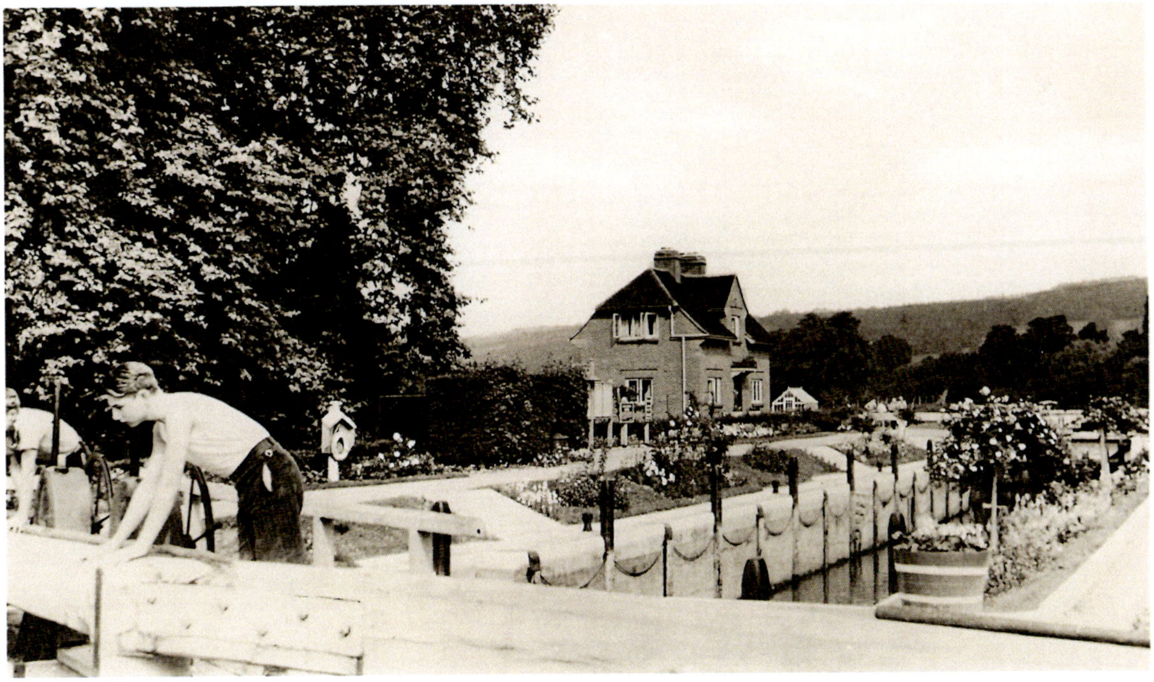

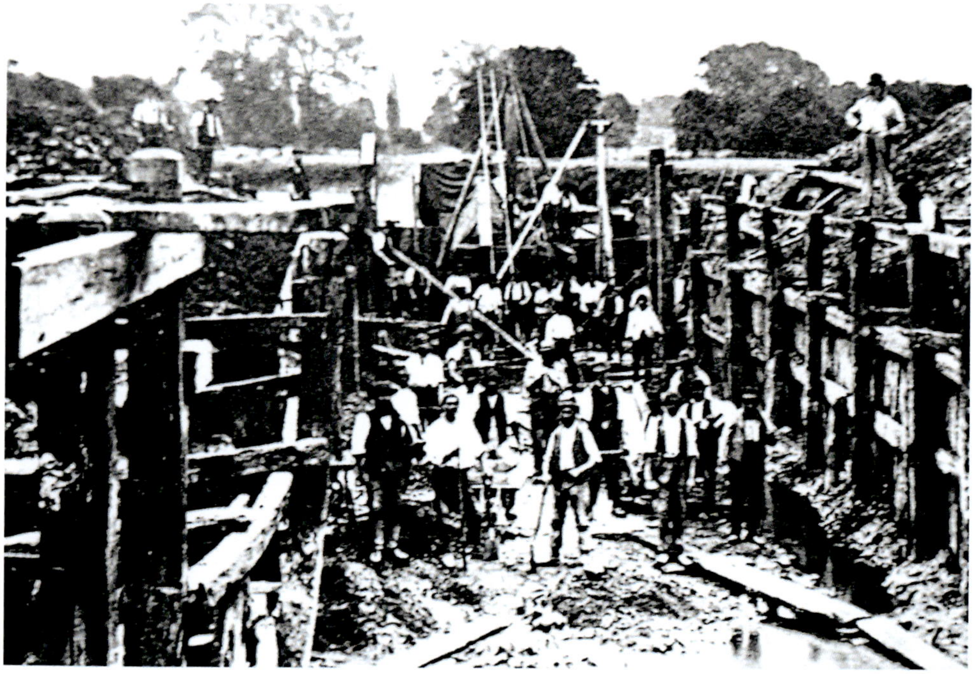

7.5 & 7.6 ***Above and below:*** The first rebuild of Mapledurham Lock in 1865, above, depended on considerable manual labour. The 1908 rebuild, below, utilised the available technology of the day and provided an extensively enlarged lock with brick sides which required far less water.

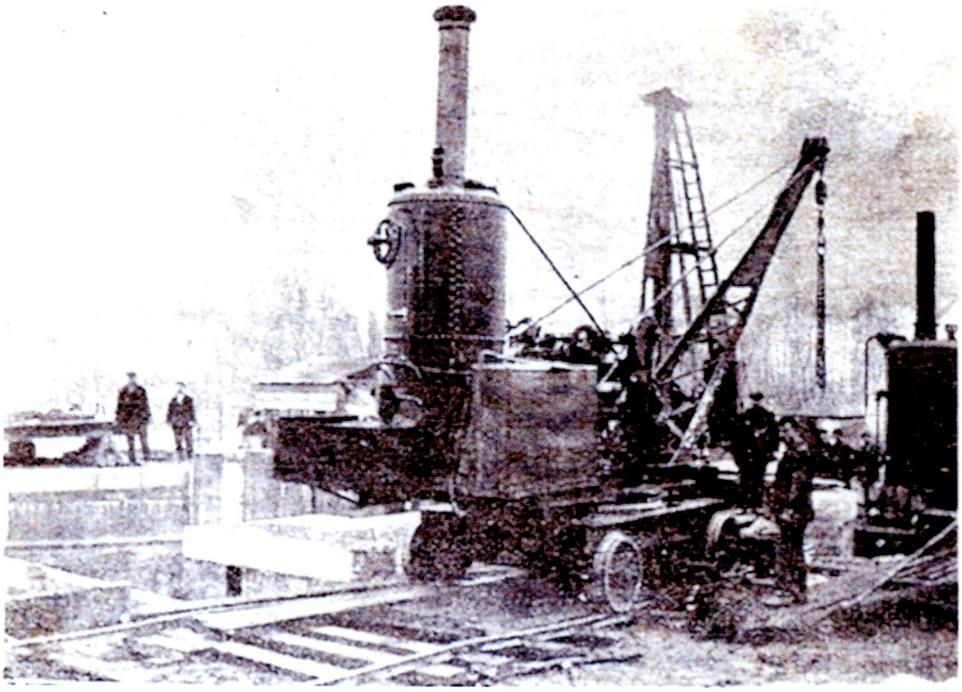

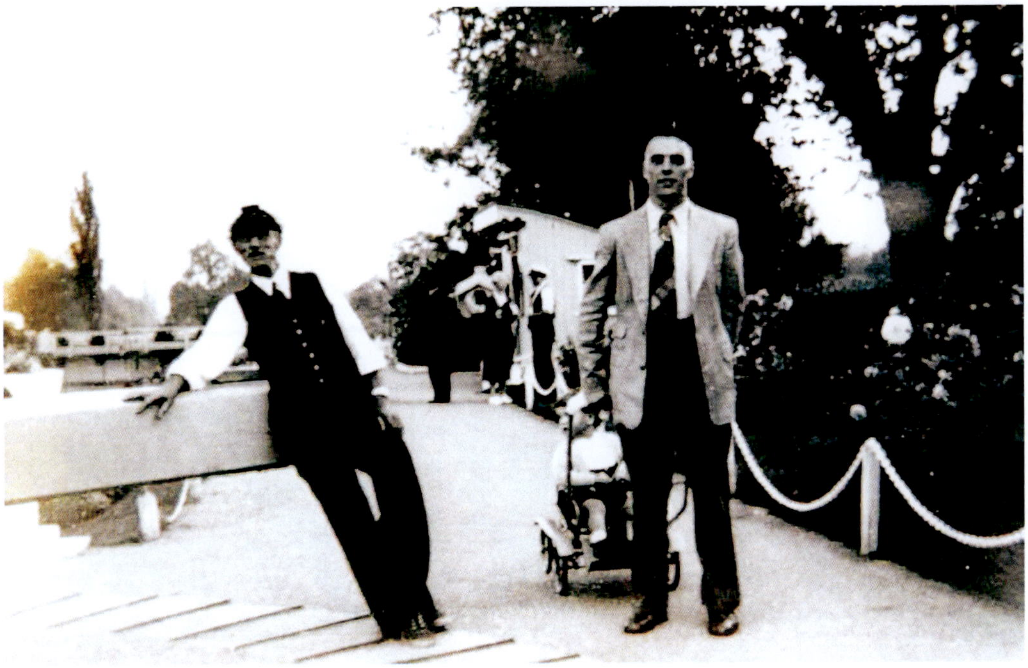

7.7 ***Above and below:*** The lock-keepers have always been at the centre of the community. Leslie Ledgerwood, above, opens the lock gates in 1956 as Jack Iles passes, Fred May, (***below left,*** *7.8*), poses with the Sir Reginald Hanson Challenge Cup for the best kept lock in 1952 and George Fielder, (***below right,*** *7.9*), who later became Purley's first Villager of the Year, demonstrates the use of the rymers and paddles in the 1970s.

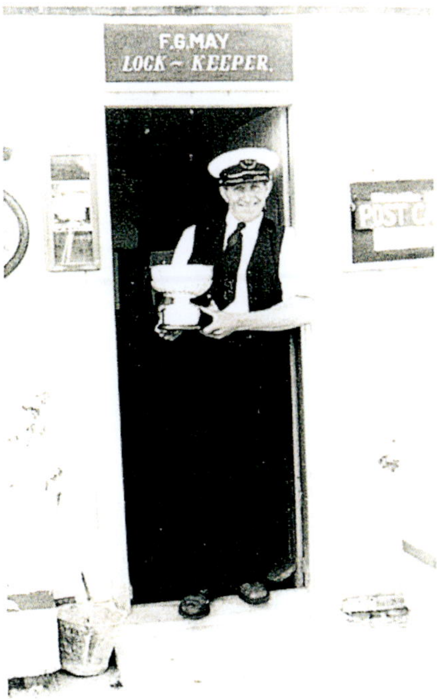

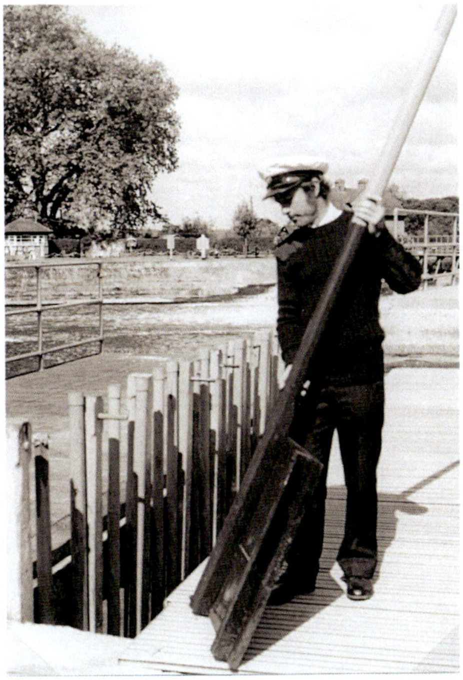

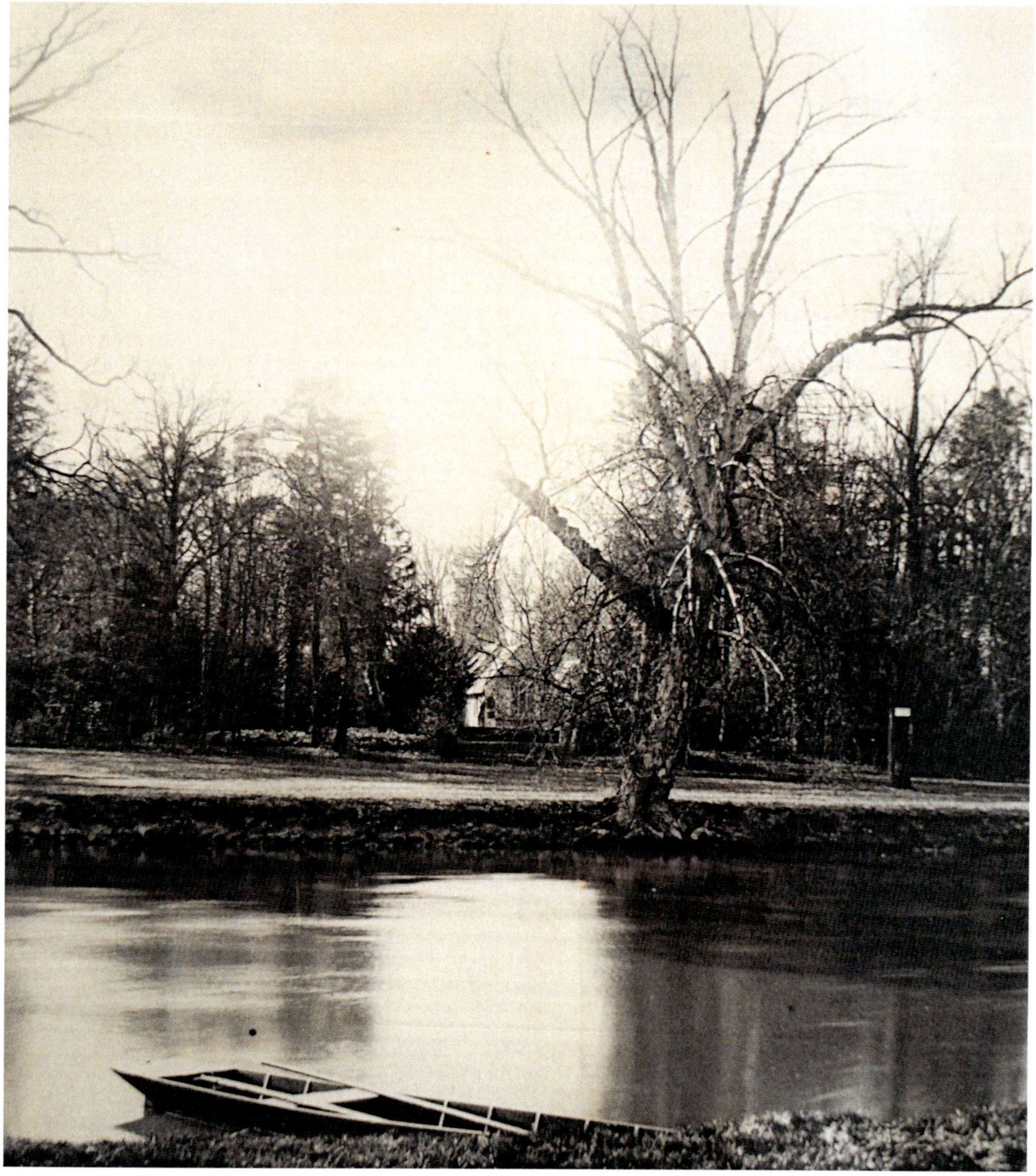

7.10 At the eastern end of Purley's stretch of the river the church was, until recent times, visible to passing boats and barges. This image dates from c1905.

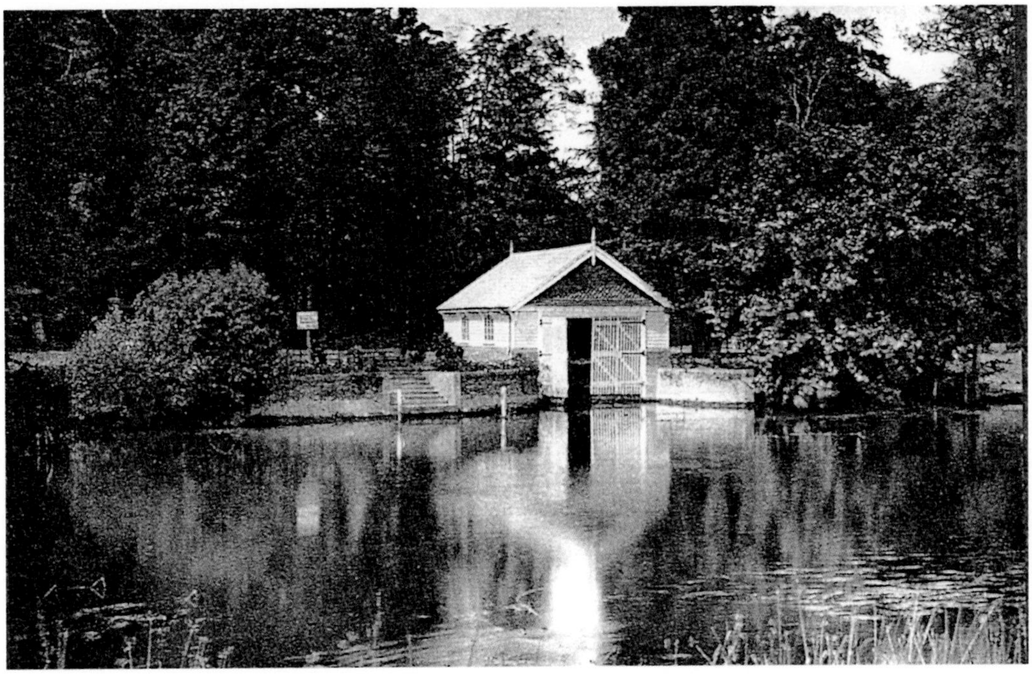

7.11 ***Above:*** The boathouse belonging to Purley Magna in the 1920s. This was located near the church.
7.12 ***Below:*** The horse ferry, which operated near Purley church, in an engraving from 1811 with the new Purley Park mansion visible on the hill above. The lords of the manor of Purley Magna controlled the ferry for many years.

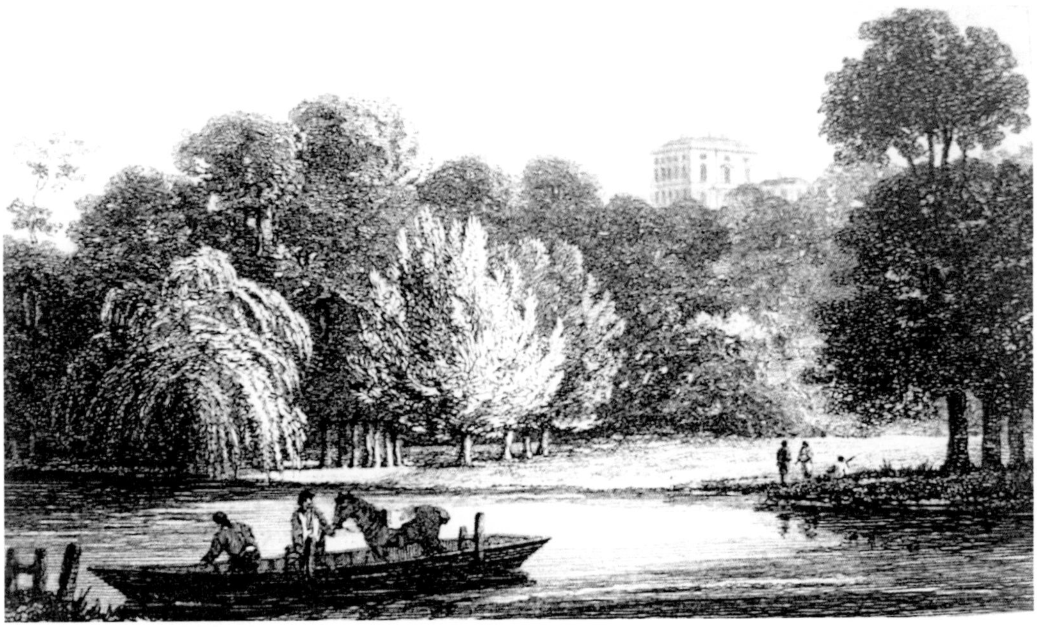

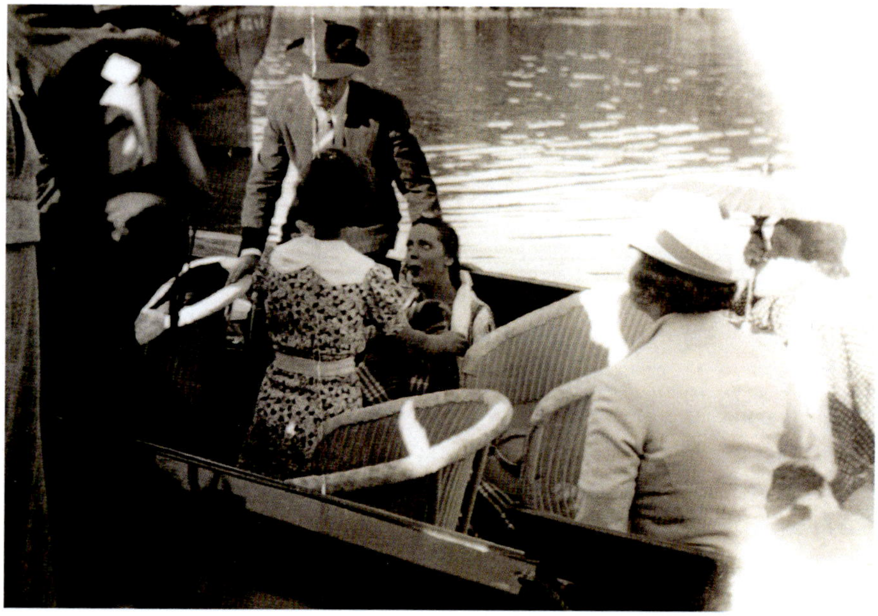

7.13 ***Above:*** 'Sailing Along' starring Jessie Matthews, Roland Young, Barry Mackey and Jack Whiting was filmed on the Thames in Purley in 1937. The Thames is popular with film makers and several other notable films have been shot here.
7.14 ***Below:*** The annual Swan Upping, pictured here in July 2008, is always an enjoyable pageant for spectators.

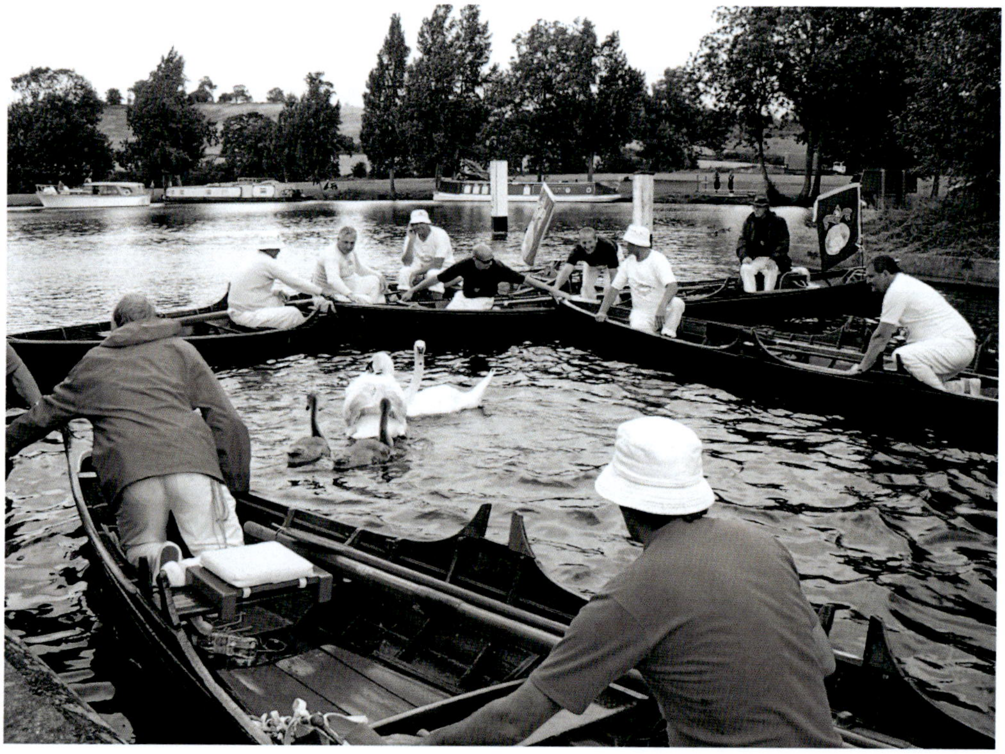

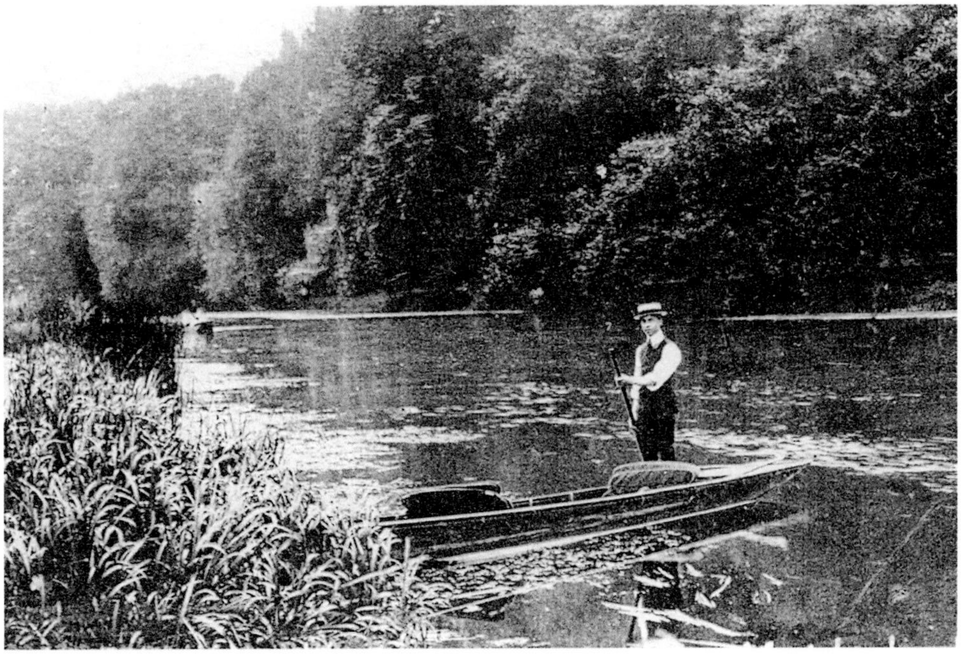

7.15 ***Above:*** A young man punting on the river near Mapledurham Reach c1890.
7.16 ***Below:*** A punt on the river with Mapledurham House in the distance, c1905. Punts and rowboats were the most popular river craft in the latter half of the nineteenth century.

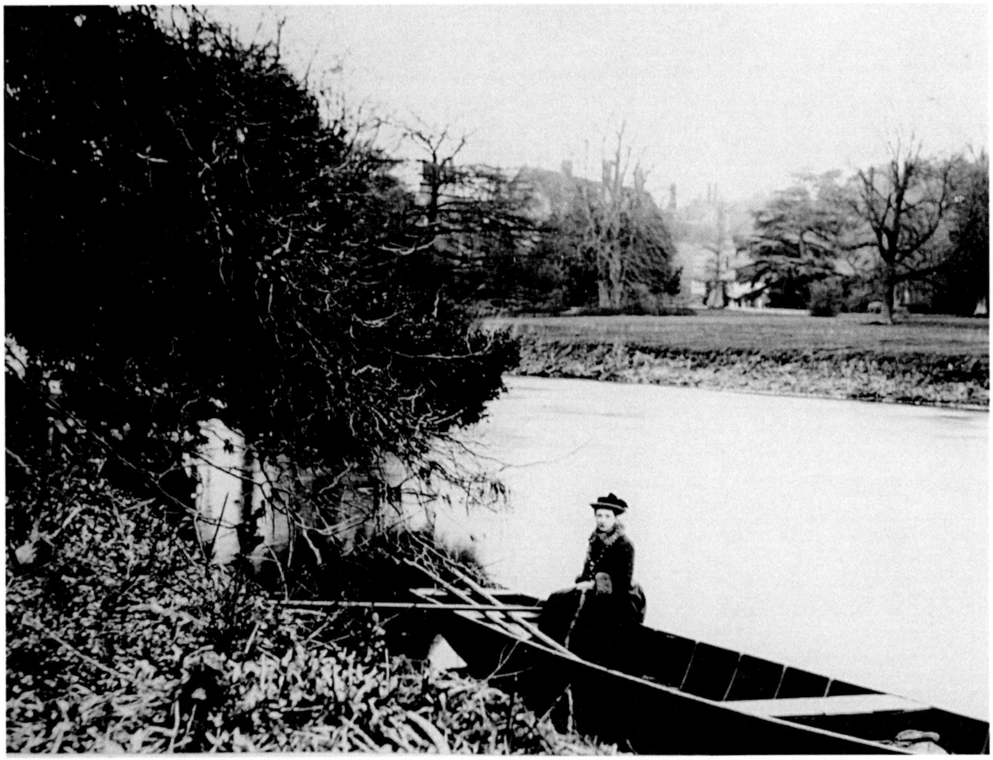

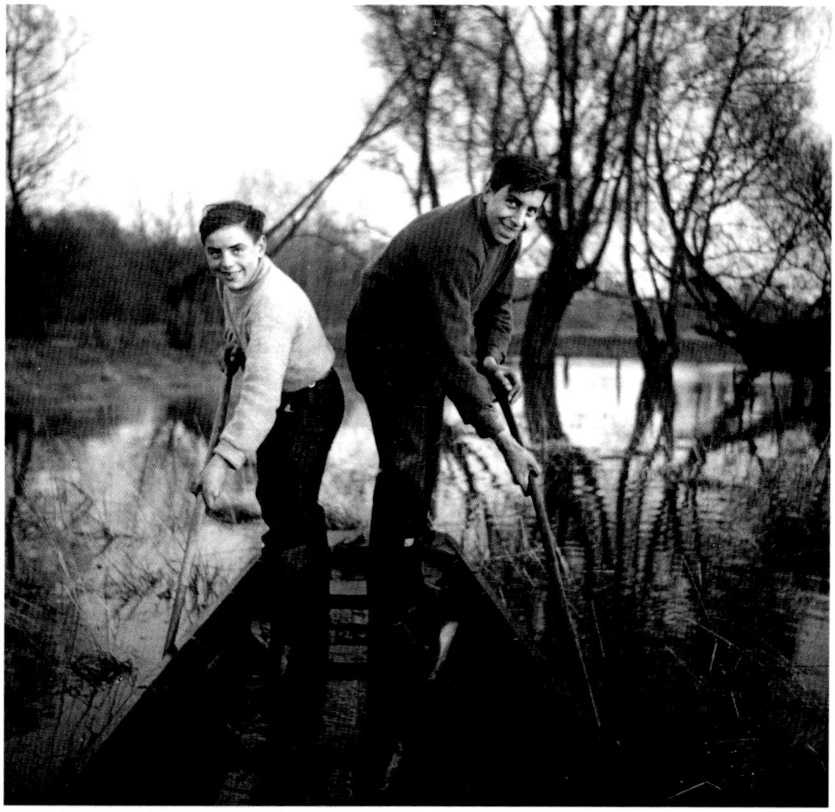

7.17 ***Left:*** Peter and Tony May of Lock Cottage enjoy messing about on the river in 1954.

7.18 ***Below:*** Pleasure boats wait to enter Mapledurham Lock c1963.

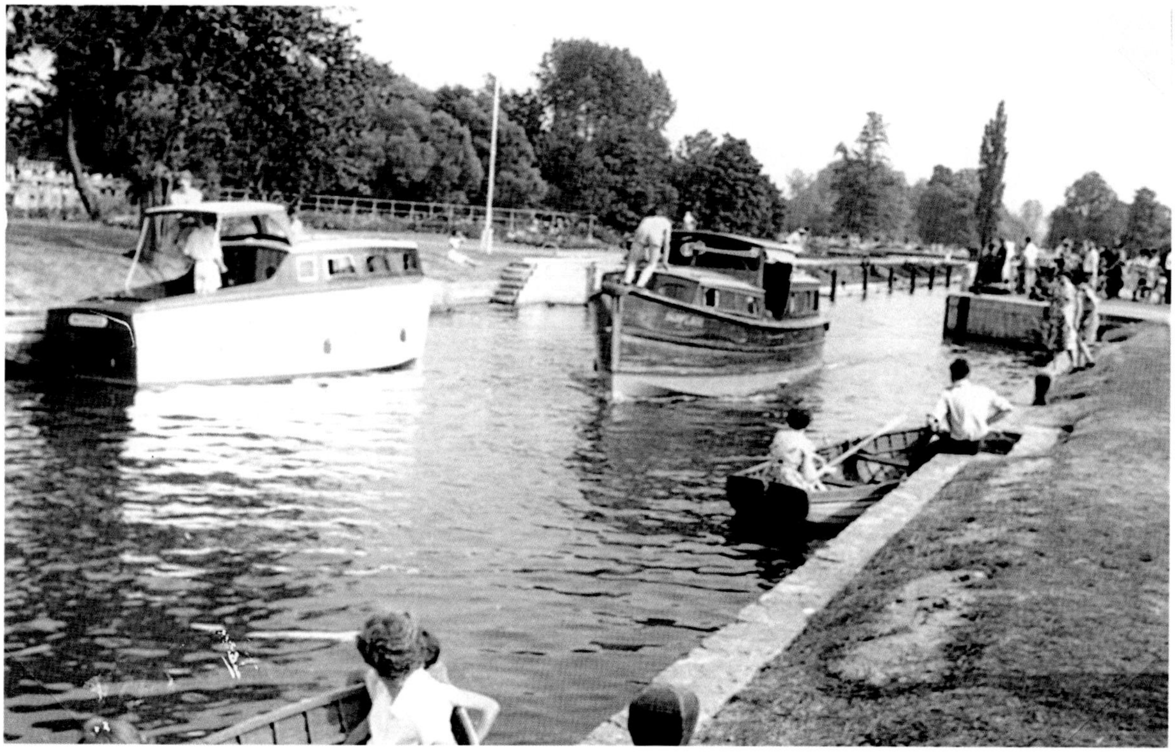

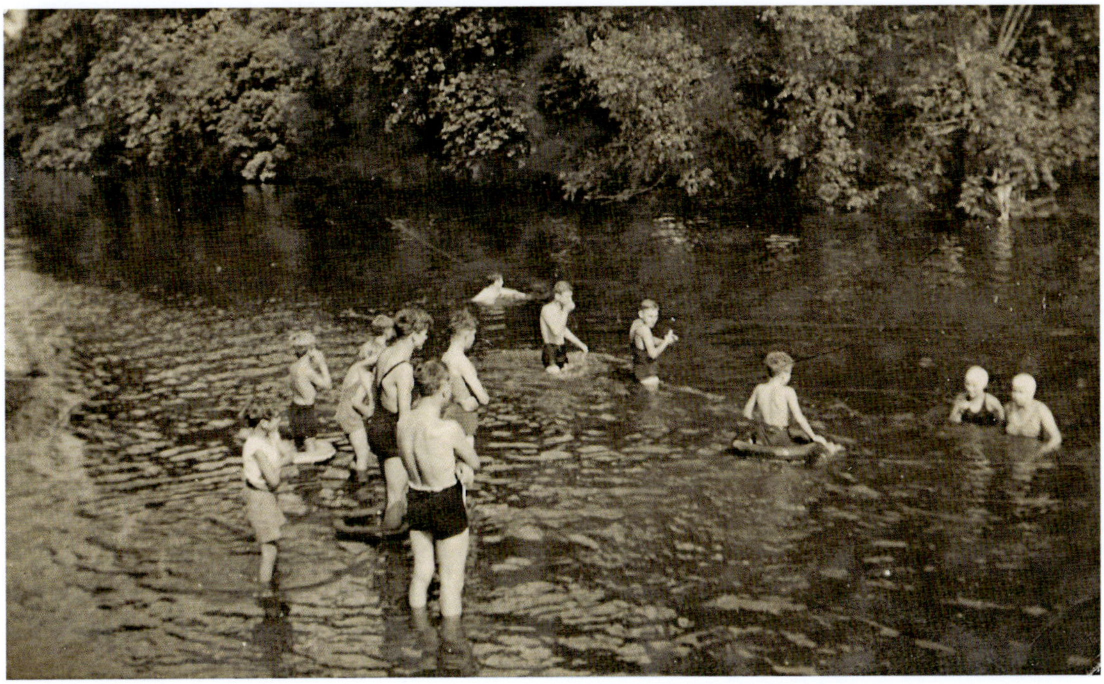

7.19 ***Above:*** Swimming in the river in the late 1930s. The shallow part of the river near the island, was where many of the village children learnt to swim. Walter Hasemore is the gentleman standing nearest to the camera watching his son Sidney, fourth from right, swim.

7.20 ***Below:*** We finish our chapter on the river bank with a photograph of a family strolling by the river on a sunny day in the 1950s, perhaps the most popular of all ways in which people now enjoy the river.

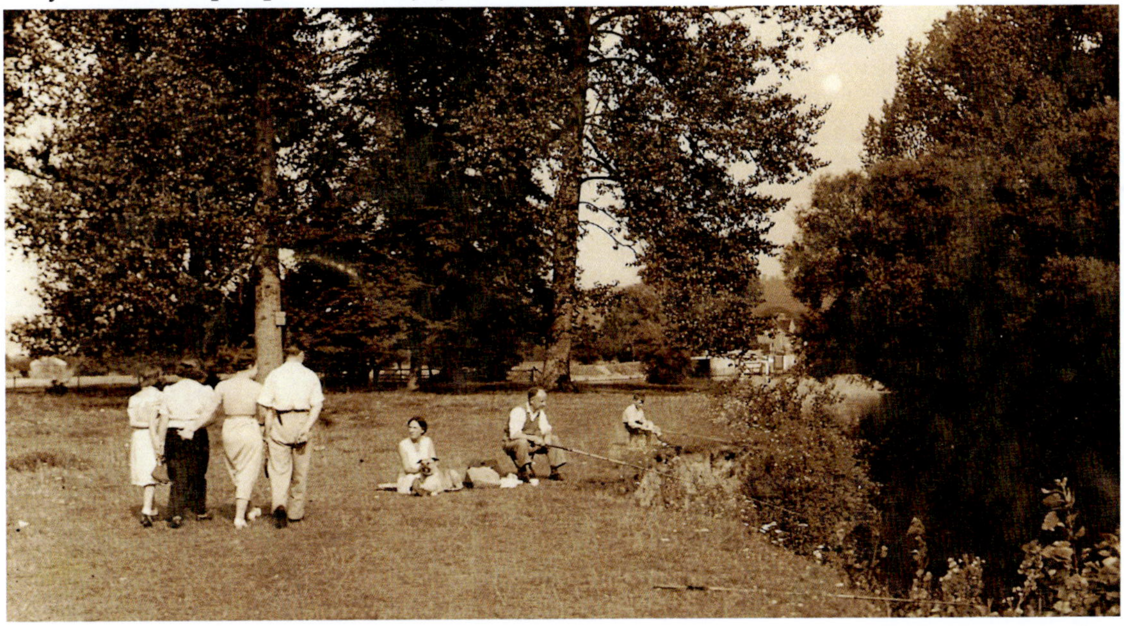

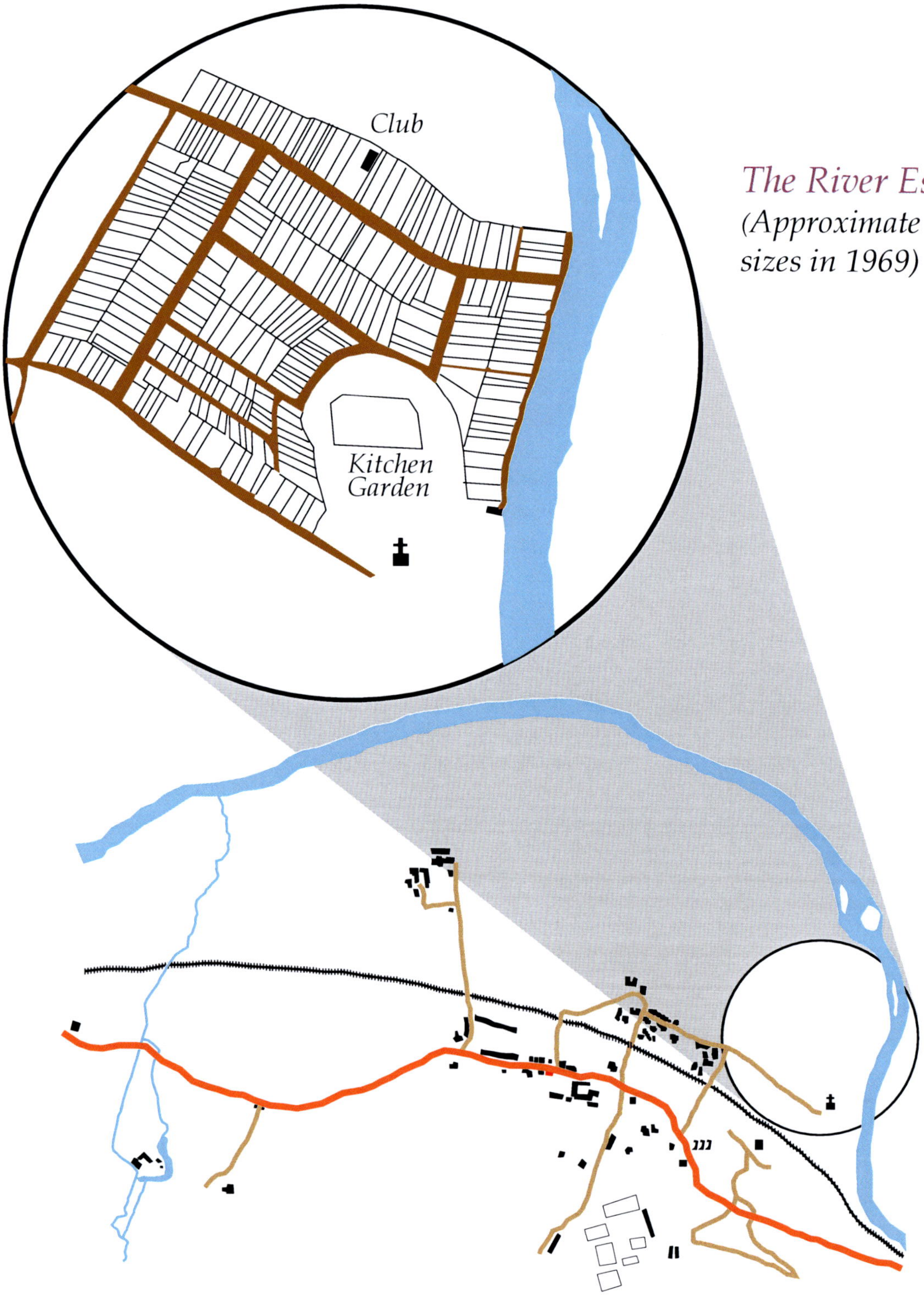

The River Estate
(Approximate plot sizes in 1969)

8 The River Estate

Following the death of Major Storer in 1902 Purley Park was broken up and sold in 1920 by his granddaughter. The parkland adjoining the river was bought by the Mountain family, but they soon realised that the land was prone to flooding which would prevent them receiving permission to build. To recoup their investment they devised a scheme offering plots of land for sale as camping or caravan pitches. A standard plot measuring 60 by 11 feet cost £5.00 and these were soon sold typically to professional families from London who would come down to Purley for weekends and holidays.

When war broke out, many of these families took up permanent residence in Purley to escape the blitz and began to construct more permanent homes. Some of these were made from decommissioned carriages from the Great Western Railway, others from old buses and many were simply wooden huts.

After the war Berkshire County Council attempted to enforce planning regulations and demanded that all structures should be capable of being moved. This started a memorable period when many of the huts gained wooden wheels, which were propped against them in an attempt to persuade planning officers they were really caravans. Gradually the plots began to be merged and the old caravans, carriages and buses were replaced by brick structures until, by the early 1970s, almost all had gone.

The supply of services and the condition of the roads were continual issues for the residents and it was not until the 1970s that the houses were connected to mains sewerage and four of the roads made up and adopted by the County Council. Nowadays a small number of older properties remain amongst what is a uniquely developed area with some very fine houses.

The River Estate has always been characterised by a close community spirit, especially in the early days, and we see this in many of the pictures in this chapter. We begin our chapter with the sale of the parkland.

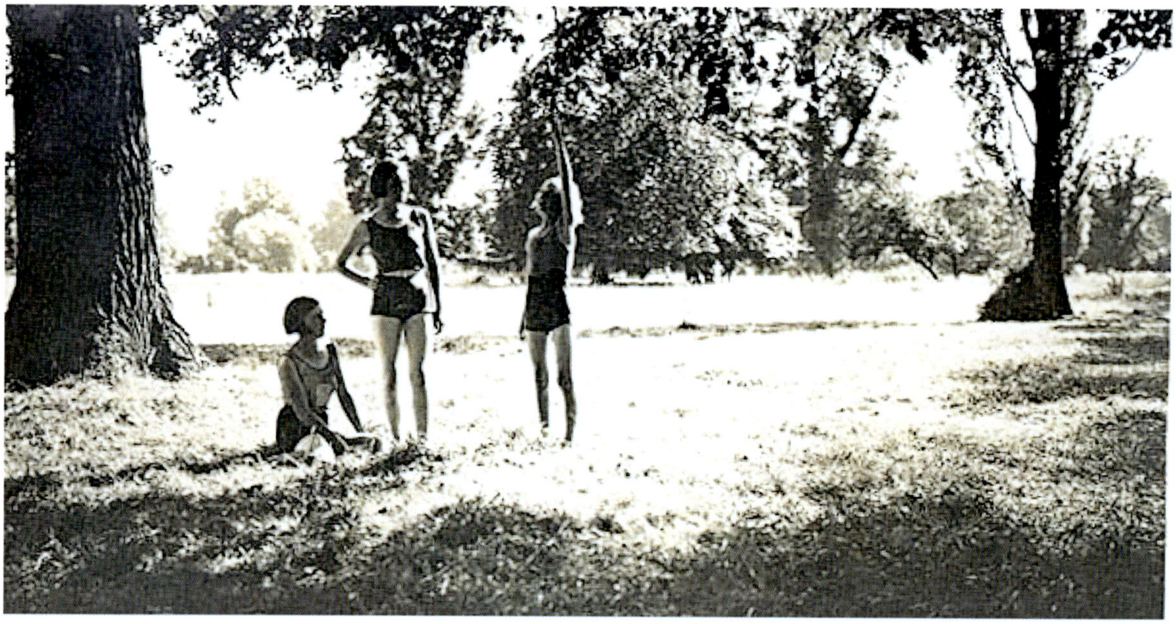

8.1 ***Above:*** Children play in the Purley Park parkland c1929, before the sale of camping plots commenced.

8.2 ***Below:*** An image taken from the booklet advertising the sale of the camping and caravan plots. The brochure was aimed at professionals who could afford to buy a permanent holiday plot.

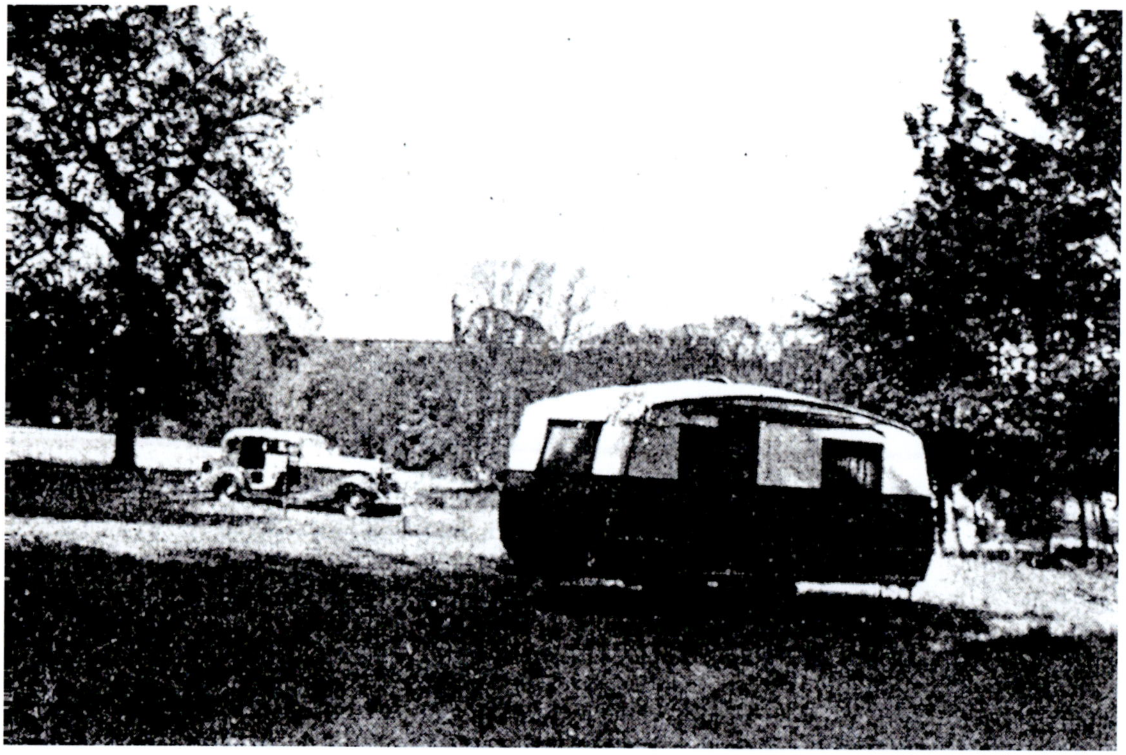

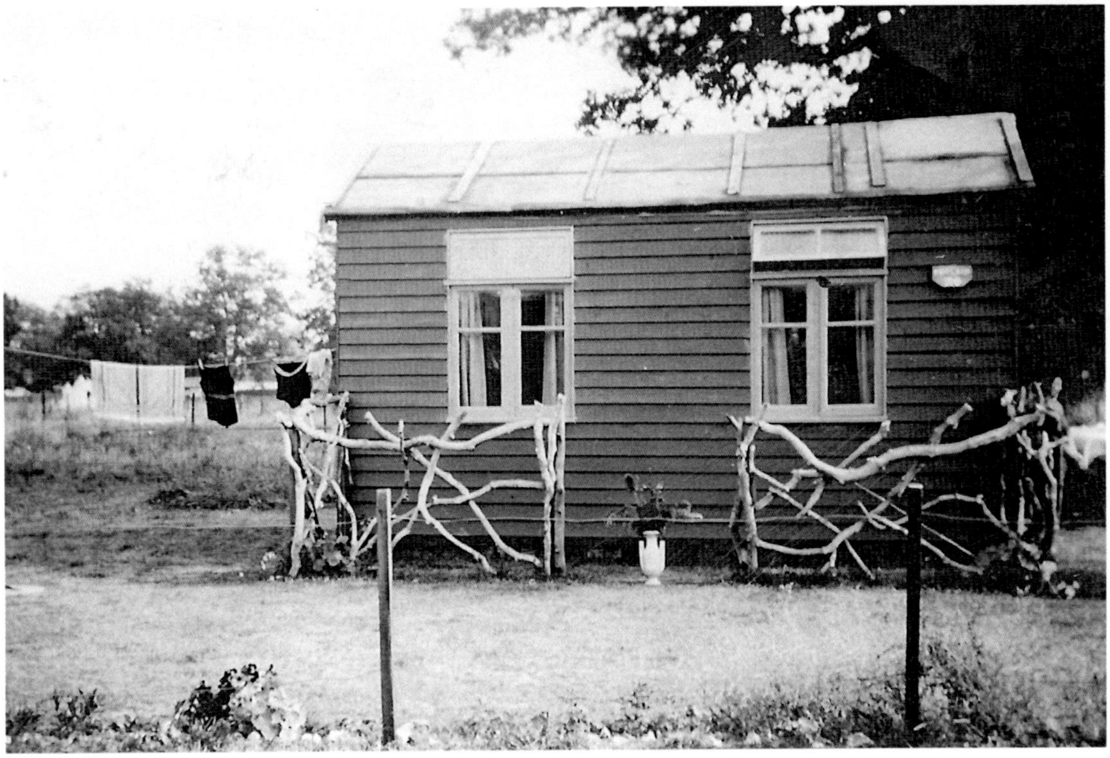

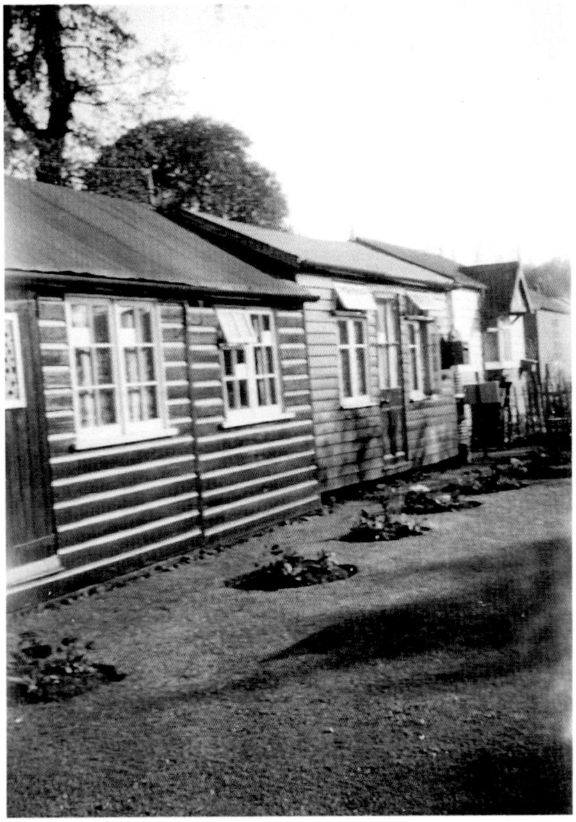

8.3 & 8.4 ***Above and right:*** Walter and Eva Hasemore from Edmonton bought a plot for their family in the 1930s on what is now Colyton Way. They started with a tent which they brought down for holidays and then by 1940 had progressed to a small wooden hut, above. This became extended over time until it was replaced with a brick building. The period rustic fence and immaculately kept garden are typical of the care the residents took of their homes.

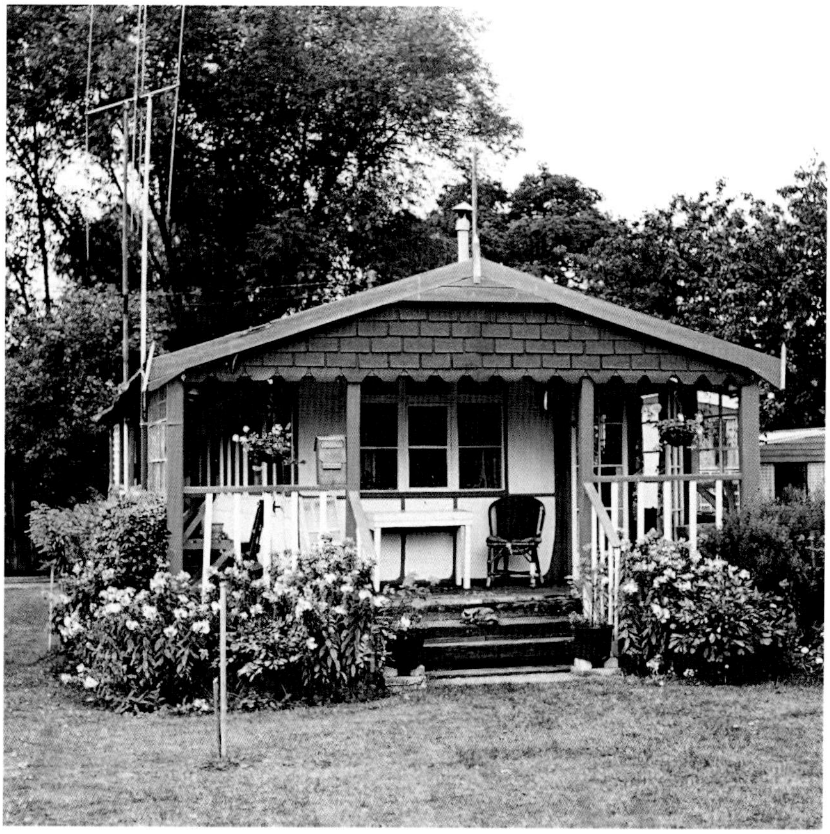

8.5 & 8.6 ***Above and below:*** A number of the homes were made from converted railway carriages and buses, some less obvious than others as these photographs of 10 River Gardens in 1969 show. The body of the 3rd class saloon number 2511, built in 1894 by the Great Western Railway did not become apparent until you stepped on to the veranda.

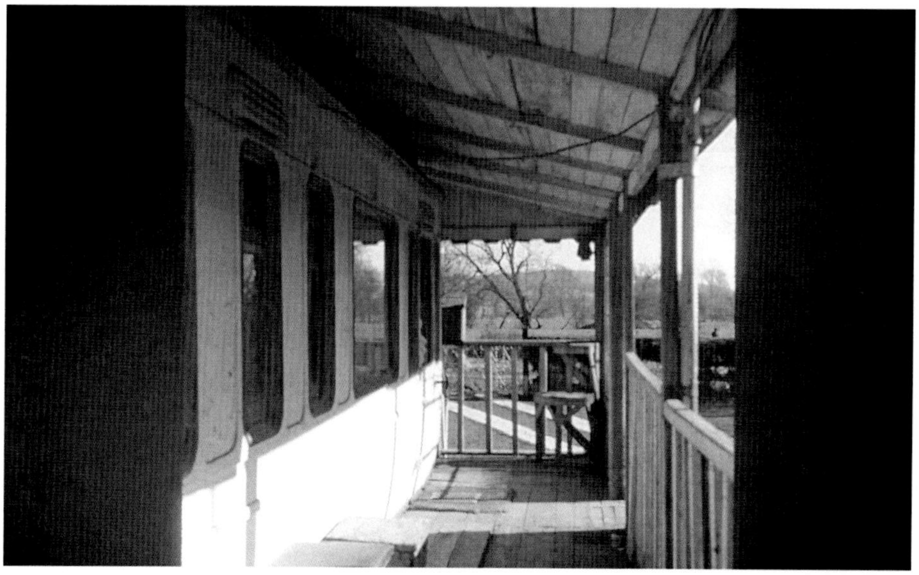

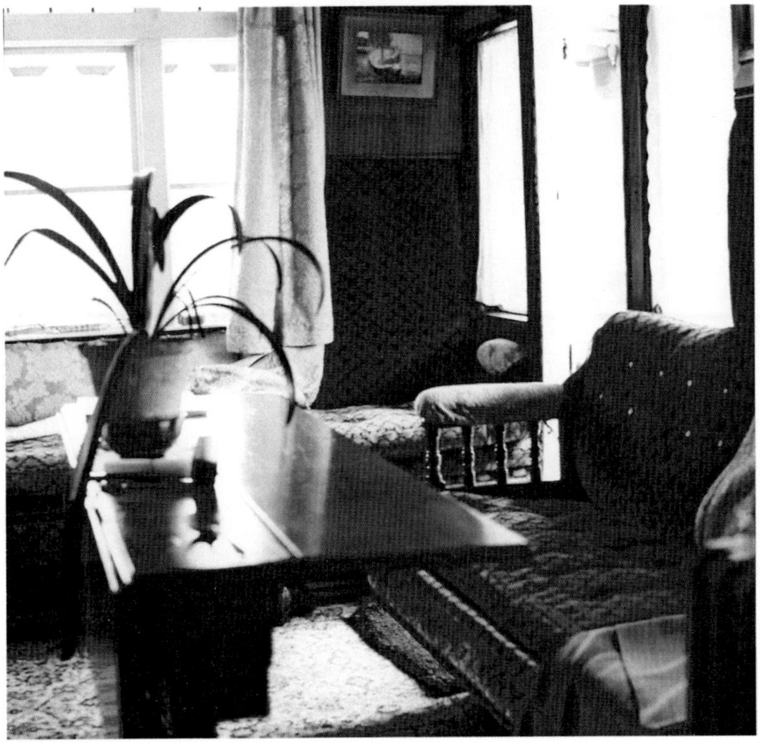

8.7 ***Above:*** Inside, the carriage at 10 River Gardens retained many of its original features.

8.8 ***Below:*** This maroon coloured carriage at 58 Wintringham Way also pictured in 1969 belonged to Archie White. Previously it had been GWR saloon number 2547.

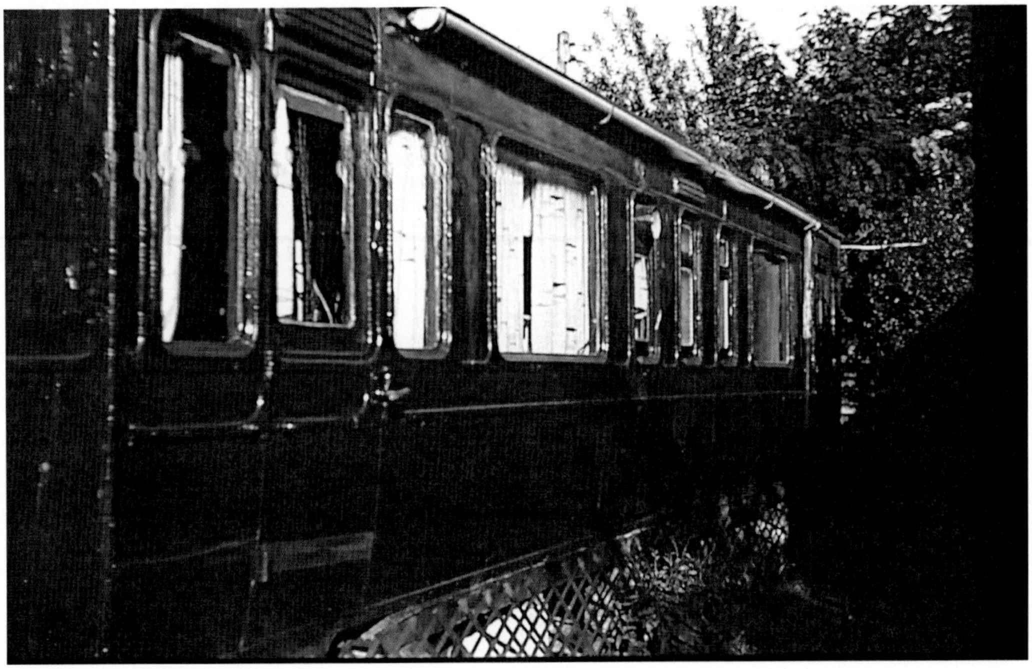

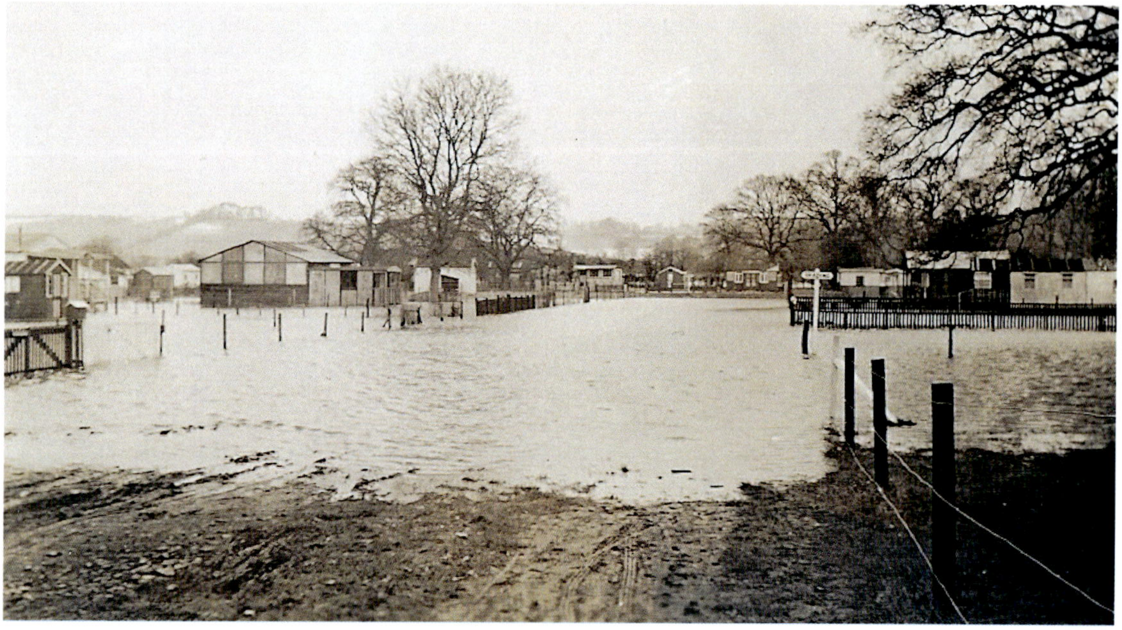

8.9 & 8.10 ***Above and below:*** The floods in 1939/40. The plains upon which the River Estate developed are prone to flooding and steps have been taken to alleviate all but the most extreme conditions. The posts which marked out each individual plot can be seen clearly in these pictures. The picture above is of Colyton Way, with the sign indicating the entrance to Brading Way on the right and Wintringham Way in the distance. Below the view is across Wintringham Way.

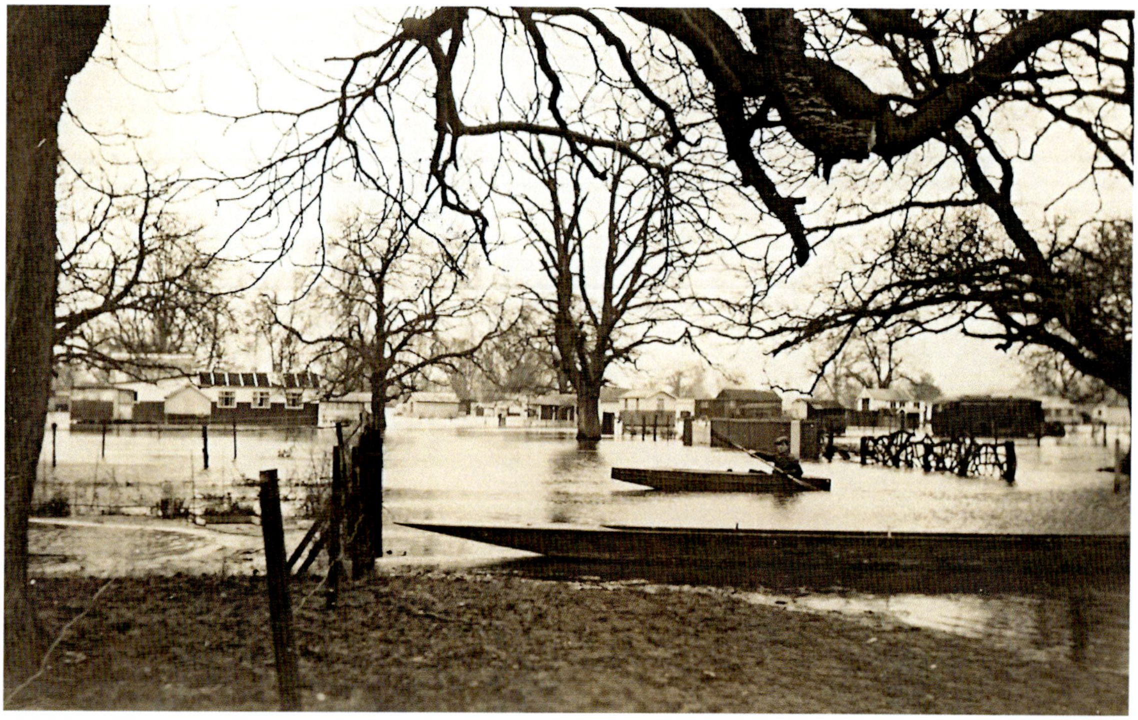

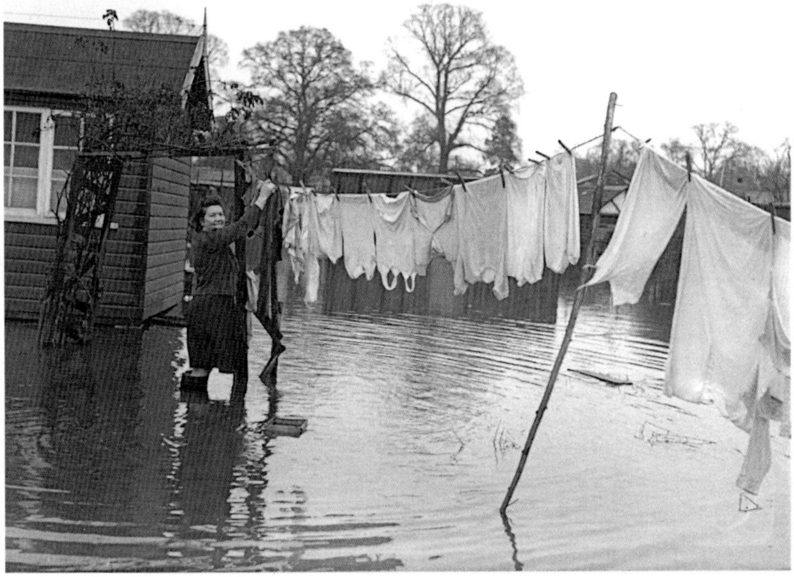

8.11 ***Above:*** The 1947 floods were more severe and caused extensive flooding to the lower part of Purley, but the villagers maintained normal life as far as possible.
8.12 ***Below:*** An aerial view of the 1947 floods. At the bottom of the image the railway line is visible with New Hill crossing over it. The island of higher ground, on which the church and Purley Park's kitchen garden stand surrounded by trees, is in the lower right of the image with the River Estate in the centre. Home Farm, Purley is in the bottom left of the picture.

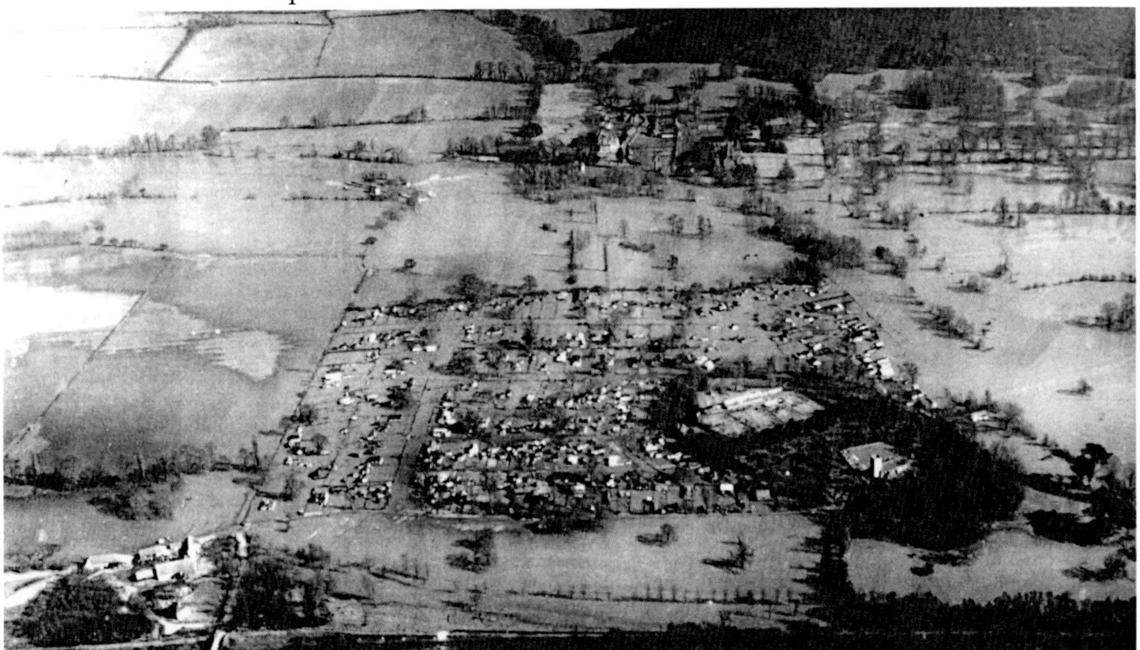

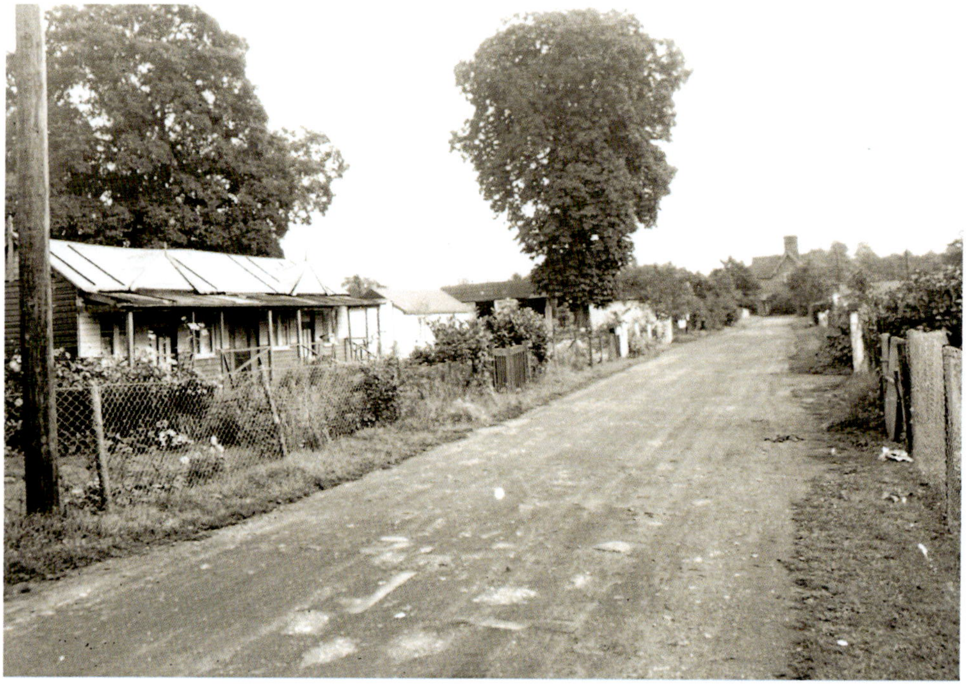

8.13 & 8.14 ***Above and below:*** During the 1940s and 50s the development of more permanent buildings continued. They were erected around a network of unmade roads, seen here in these two photographs of each side of The Short. The gardener's cottage of Purley Park is visible at the far end of the road.

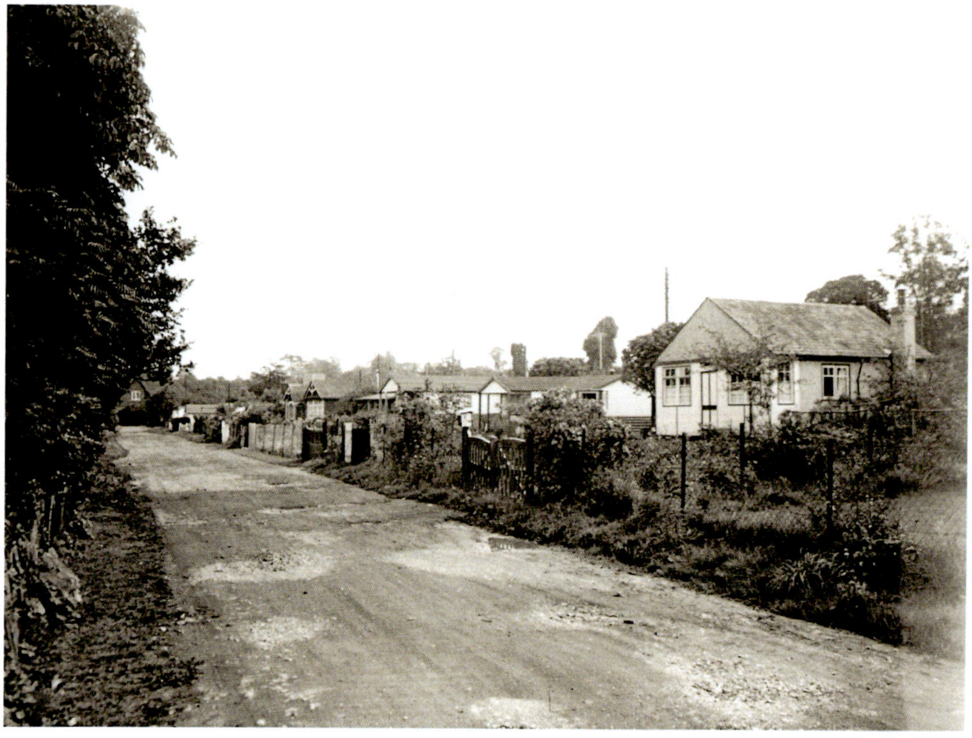

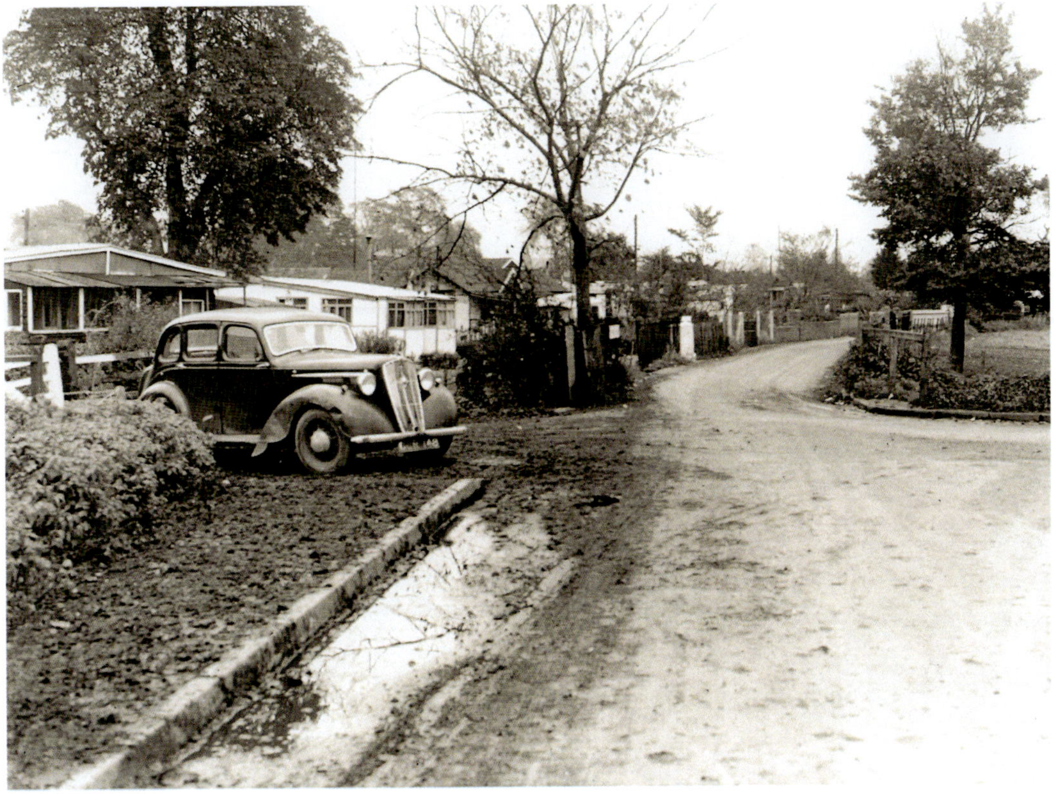

8.15 ***Above:*** The crossroads of St Mary's Avenue, looking towards the church with New Hill on the right and Mapledurham Drive on the left, c1950.
8.16 ***Below:*** Wintringham Way c1950.

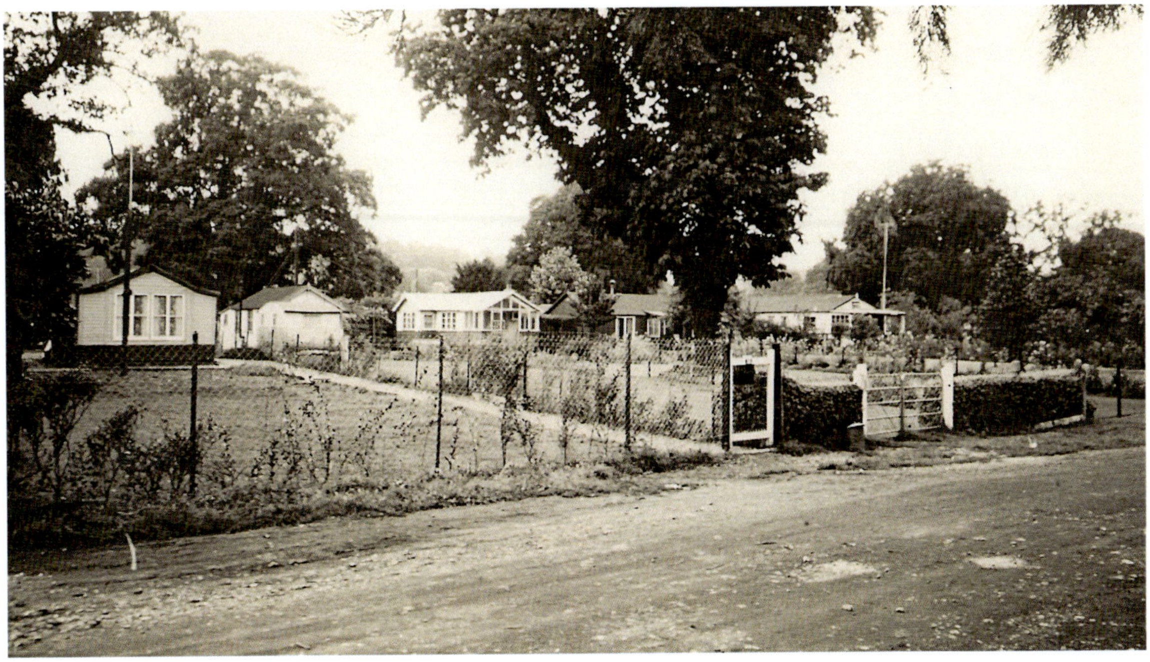

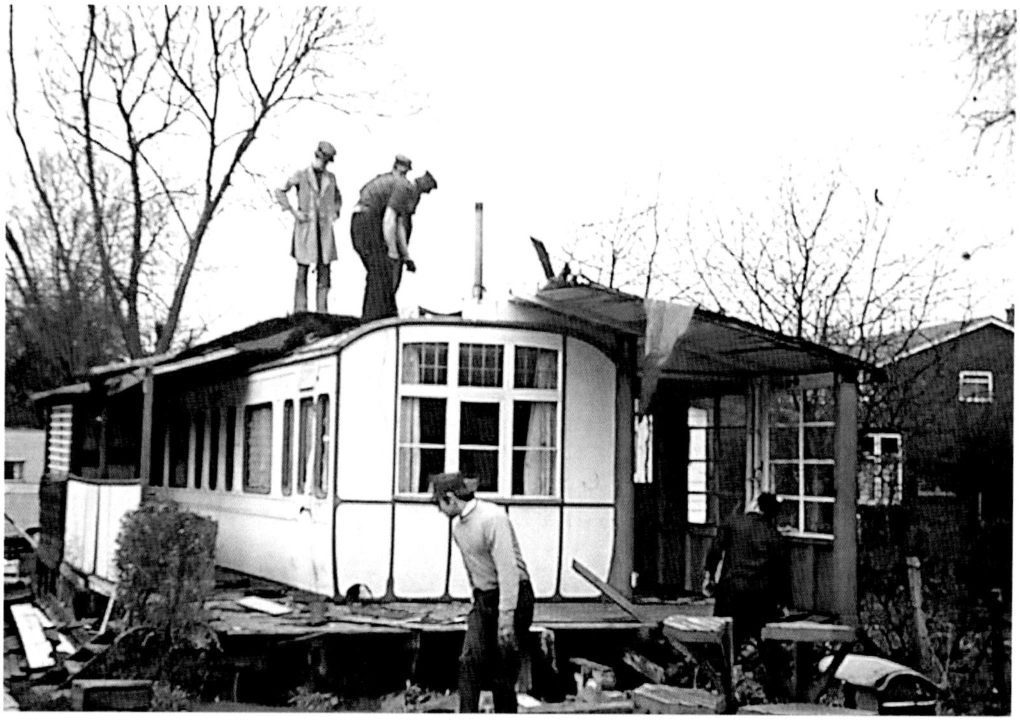

8.17 & 8.18 ***Above and below:*** 10 River Gardens being dismantled in 1972. The railway carriage was saved from being scrapped by Kevin McCormack, then secretary of the Great Western Society, and taken on the back of a flat loader lorry to the Didcot Railway Centre where restoration is ongoing.

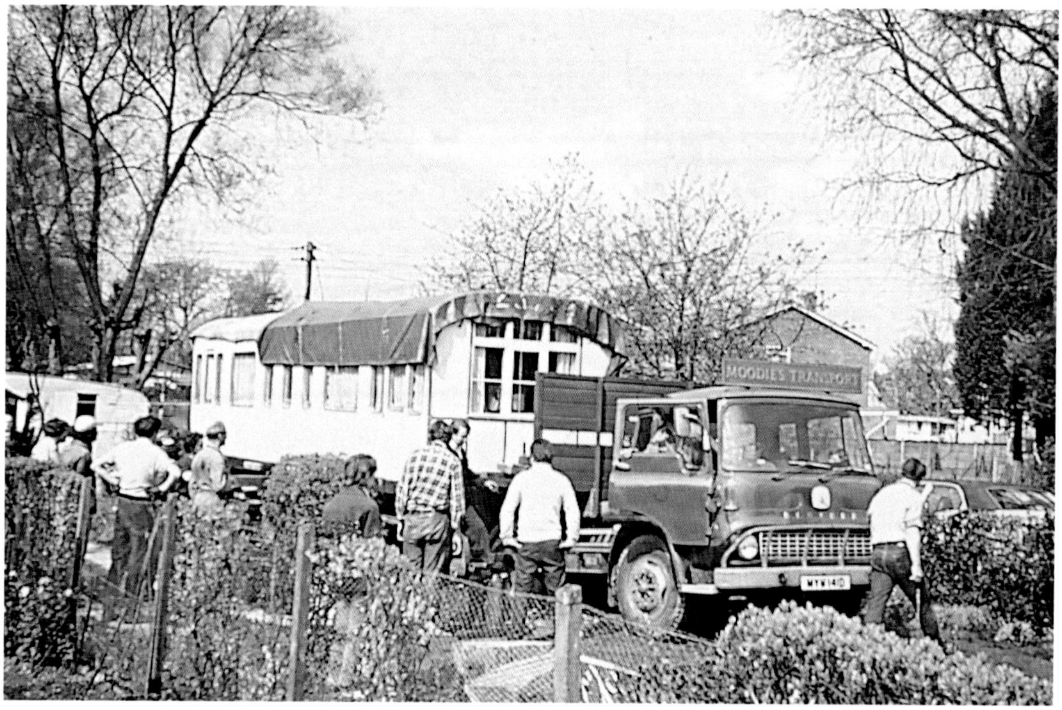

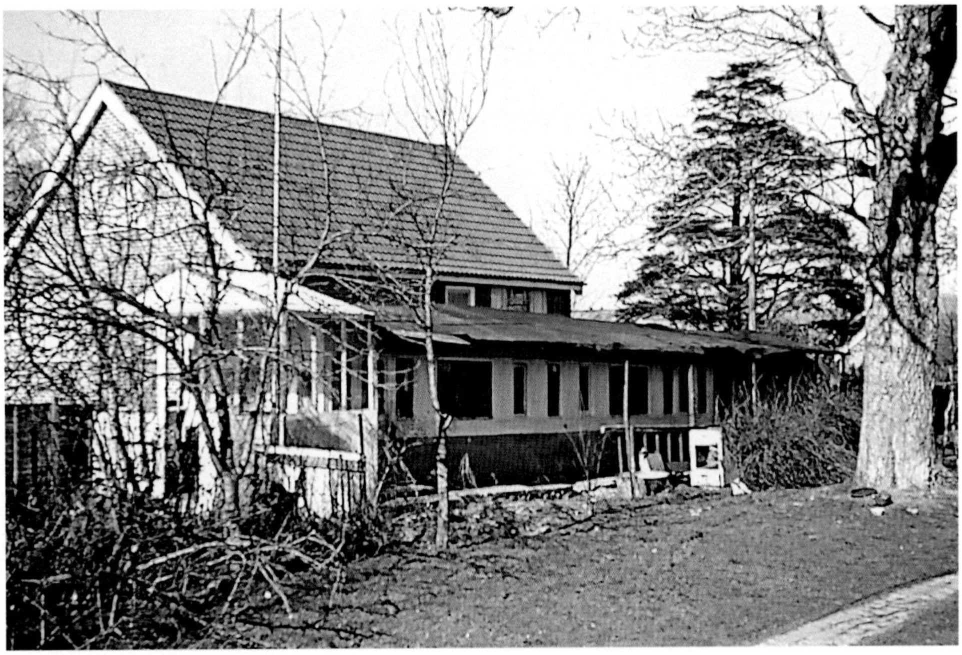

8.19 ***Above:*** The railway carriage at 24 Brading Way in 1972. This was the former home of Thomas (Lewis) and Lynette Barnes and was being dismantled.
8.20 ***Below:*** The remains of a London General Omnibus Company bus, believed to be an S-type single decker dating from the early 1920s, was discovered when the new owners demolished the chalet at 35 Wintringham Way in 1985.

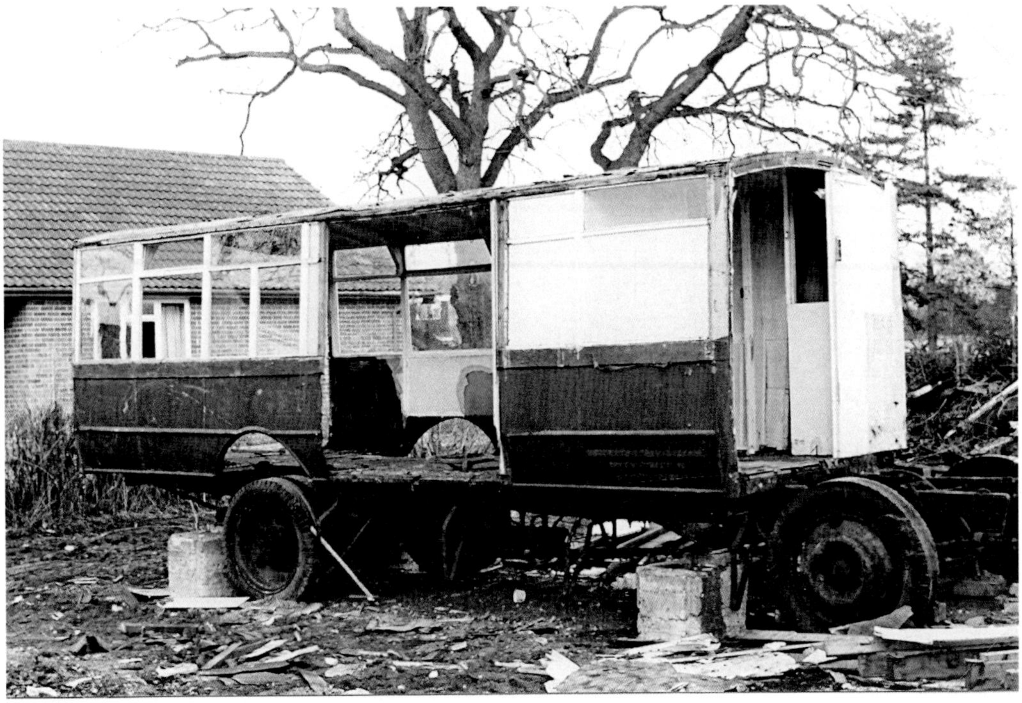

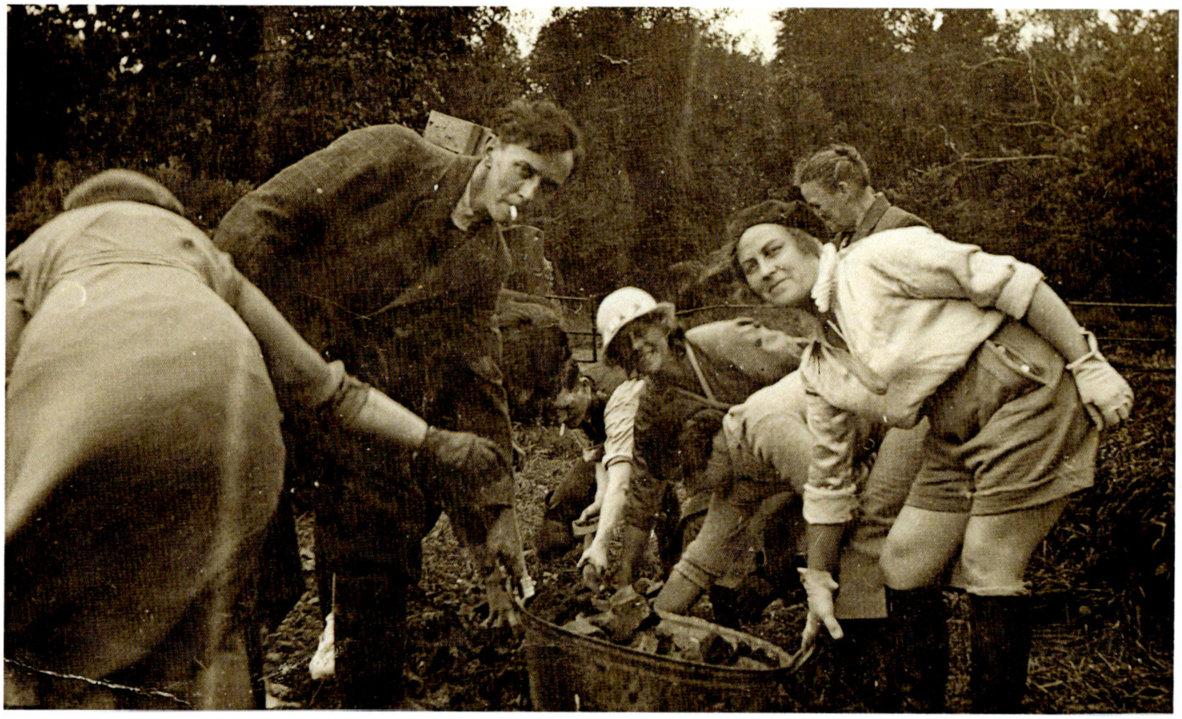

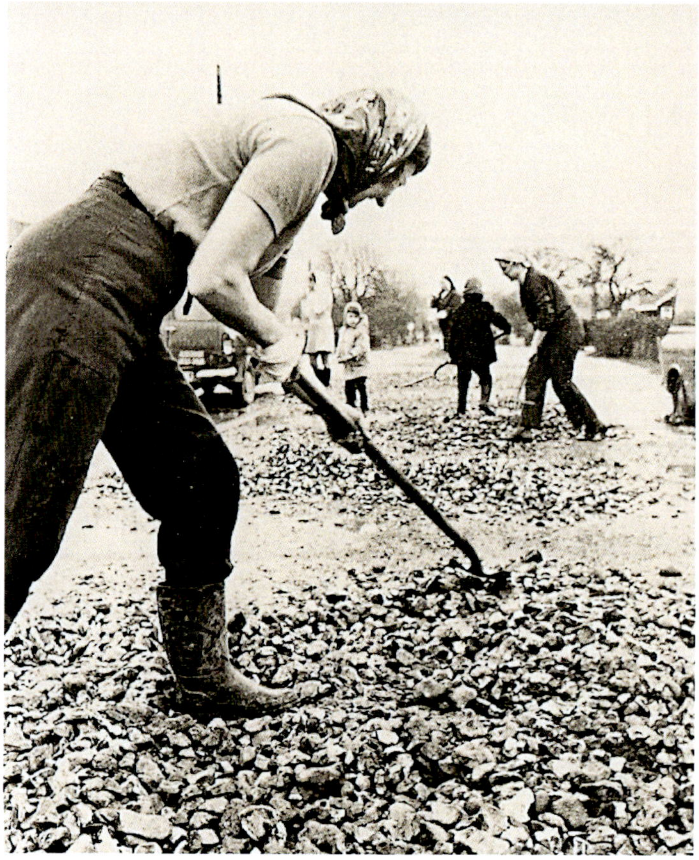

8.21 ***Above:*** The roads around the river estate were in constant need of attention and the community regularly organised repair days. Eva Hasemore, in a beret and shorts, and Rebecca Skerritt, in a white hat, lend a hand during the 1940s.

8.22 ***Left:*** Lynette Barnes, closest to the camera, is part of a working party in Colyton Way in the 1960s.

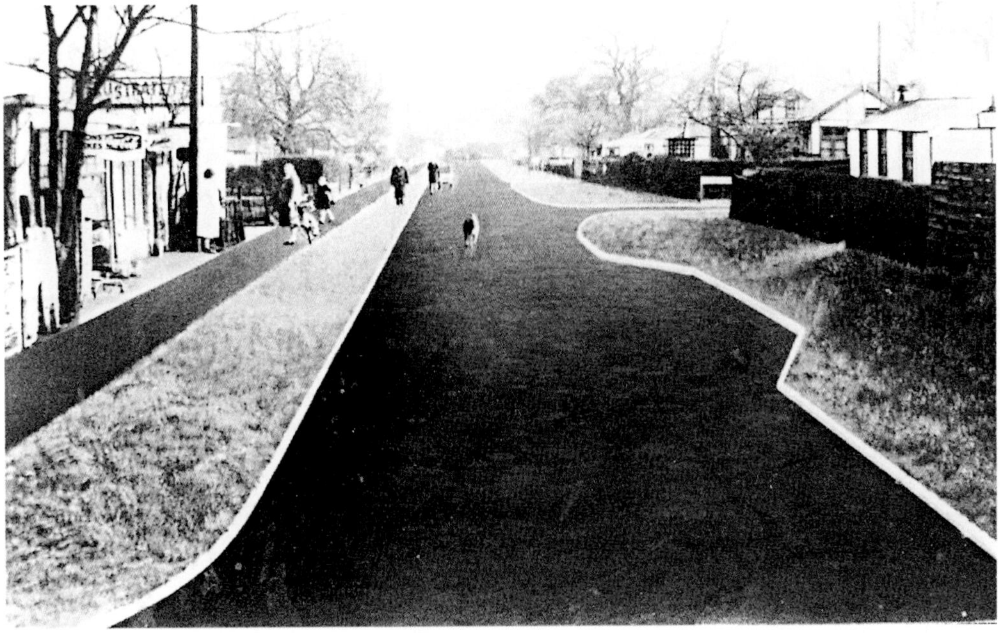

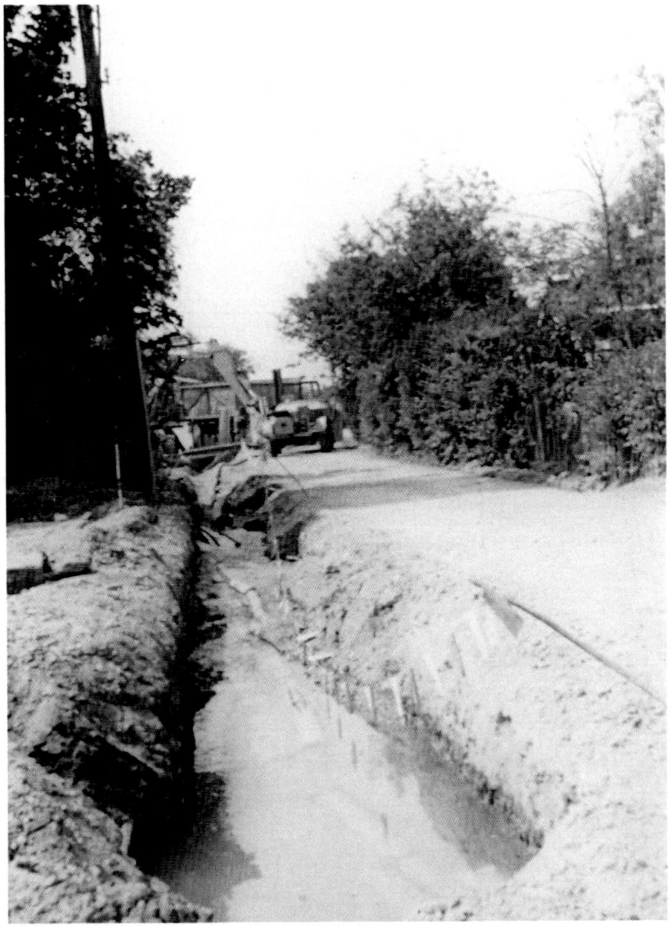

8.23 ***Above:*** Bob Skerritt put together this doctored photograph in the 1950s to show how the roads might appear if they were surfaced.

8.24 ***Left:*** Sewers were finally installed on the estate in 1977 after which four of the roads were brought up to the full highway standard required for adoption by Berkshire County Council. The high water table, evident in this image of Brading Way, prevented the residents building septic tanks. Until this time houses had relied upon the services of a domestic lavatory engineer, Dan Smith of Westbury Lane, who is remembered affectionately by older residents as 'Dan, Dan the lavatory man'.

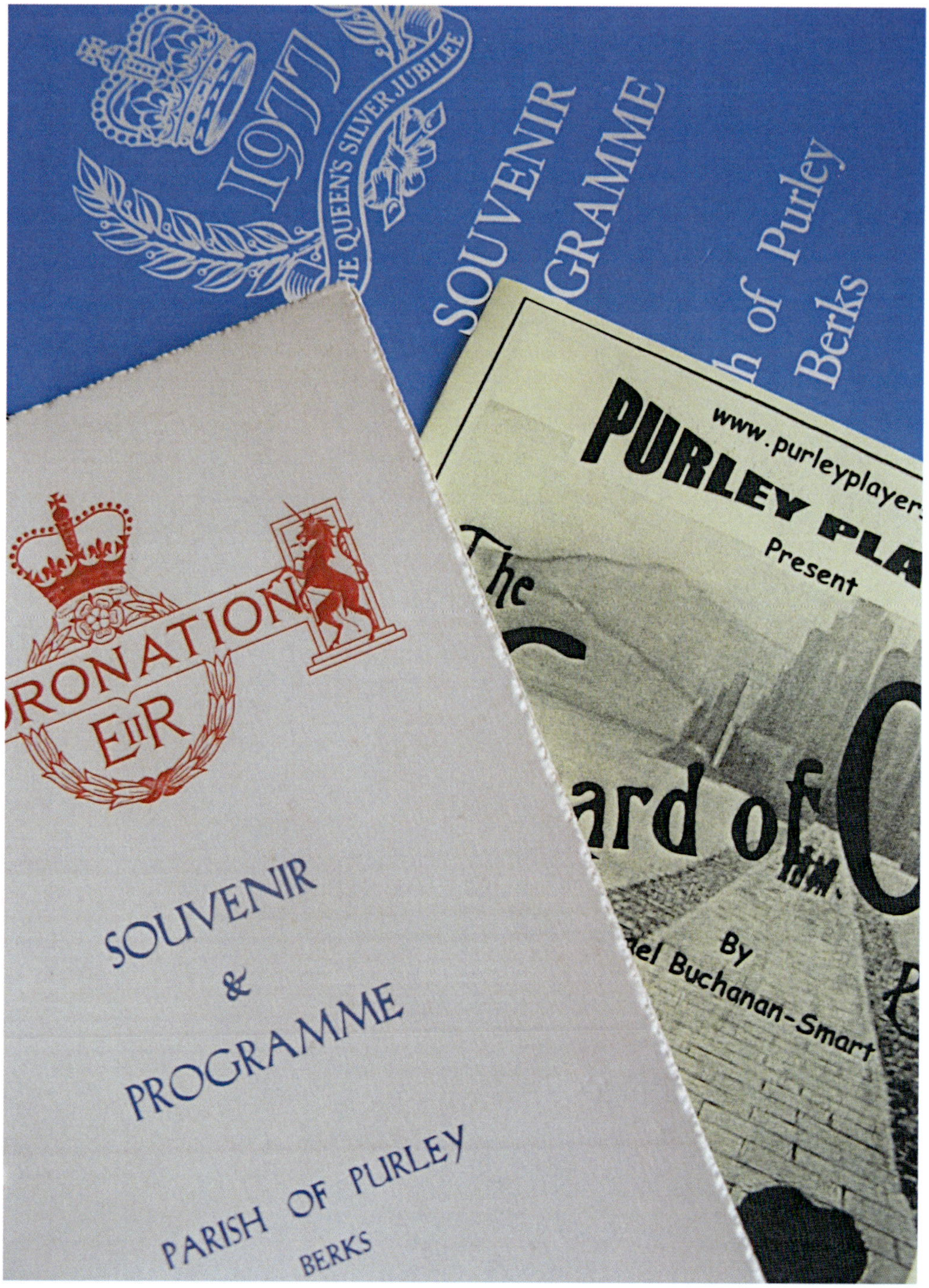
1977
THE QUEEN'S SILVER JUBILEE
SOUVENIR
GRAMME
h of Purley
Berks
PURLEY PLA
www.purleyplayers
Present
The
ard of
By
el Buchanan-Smart
RONATION
EIIR
SOUVENIR
&
PROGRAMME
PARISH OF PURLEY
BERKS

9 *Pastimes and Events*

Our final chapter contains images of some of the multitude of clubs, societies and charities that are or were active in Purley, together with photographs marking a range of events that have taken place in the village over the last century. Some of these marked occasions of national or historical importance, such as the two World Wars, the coronation of our monarchs and their anniversaries plus the journey of Sir Winston Churchill's funeral train in 1965; others were simply local events such as dances and carnivals. What shines through in all of these photographs is the strong sense of community that typifies the village and the willingness of people to commit time and energy for a common cause.

The Sunday School is perhaps the oldest of our organisations, predating even our earliest school in the village and so playing an important role in providing education to the children. Records exist for the Purley Tennis Club back into the 1800s and of cricket matches in the 1700s. By the end of the twentieth century both the cricket club and the football club were fielding teams in county competitions.

The Guides and Brownies also have a considerable history in the village. Purley has a personal association with the Guide Movement through Olave St Clair Soames, who lived briefly with her family at Purley Hall before her marriage to Lord Robert Baden-Powell. She went on to become the World Chief Guide and was responsible for the development of the Guide Movement after 1918.

The Women's Institute was founded in the village in 1936 and we include photographs from their fortieth and seventieth birthday years.

We hope you enjoy this glimpse back in time.

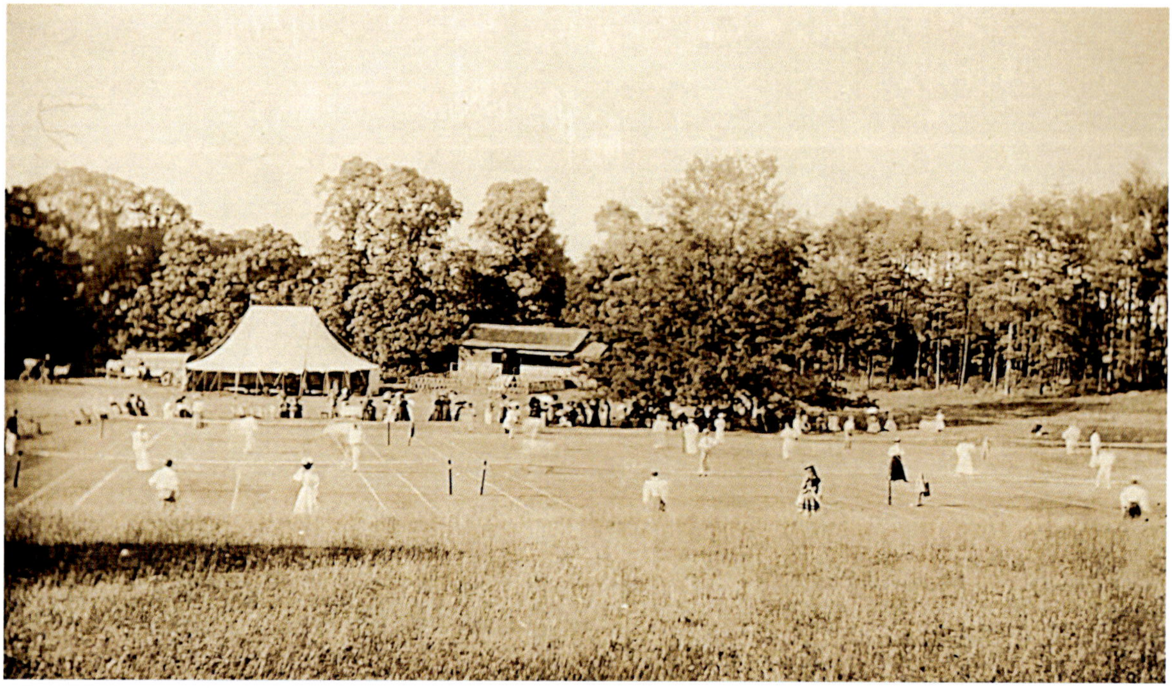

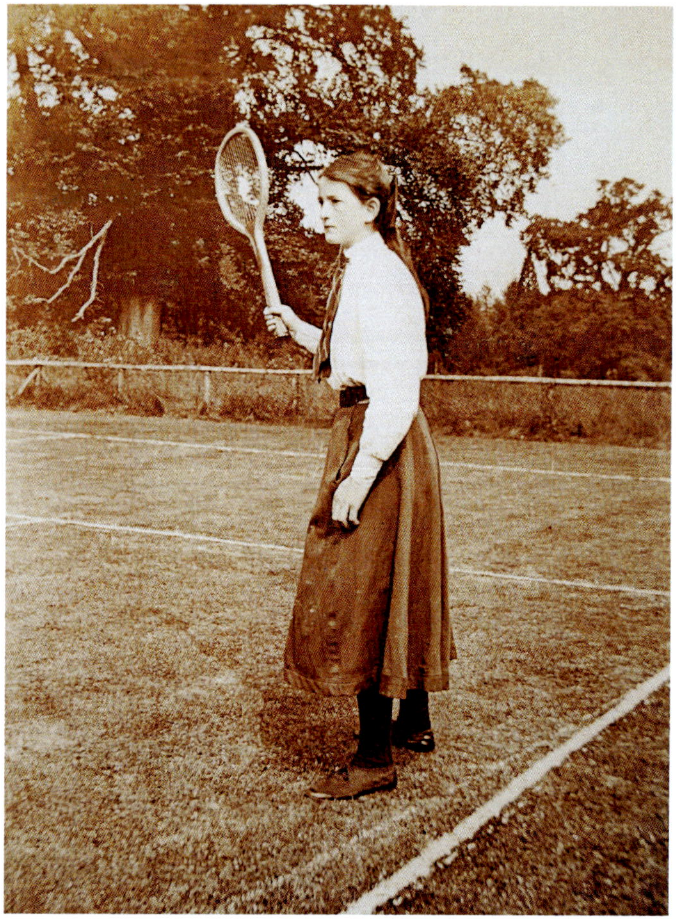

9.1 ***Above:*** Purley Tennis Club tournament, 1895, in the grounds of Purley Hall.

9.2 ***Left:*** Myra Fullerton, granddaughter of Major Storer, playing tennis in 1912 at Purley Park.

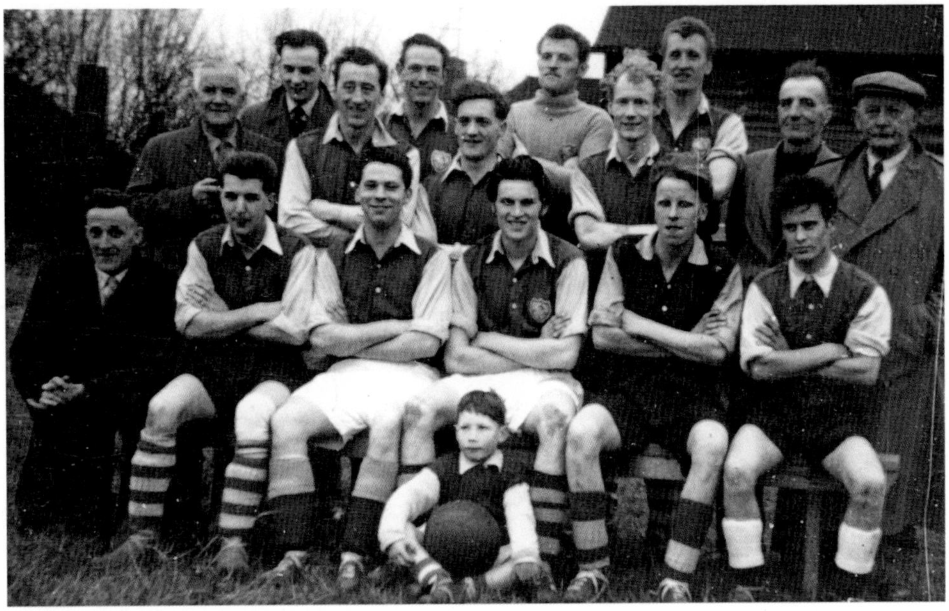

9.3 ***Above:*** Purley Football Club in the 1950s. From left to right, back row: ?,?,?,?,?,Derrick Mott, ?, ?, Alf Nash, Mr Russell, seated: ?,?, Eric Gibbons, David Mott, Pierce Bennellick, ?. Team mascot is Alan Nash.
9.4 ***Below:*** Purley Football Club, 1983-84 season. From left to right, back row: John Sunderland, Max Eales, Ian Sawyer, David Moulds, Paul Sawyer, Ron Gurney, Tim Francis, Chris Wickens, Mark Guest, Geoff Druce, Trevor Jones, Cecil Fright (Manager), front row: Colin Murgatroyd, Maurice Williams, Colin Leighton, Robert Ives, Lyndsay Maskell.

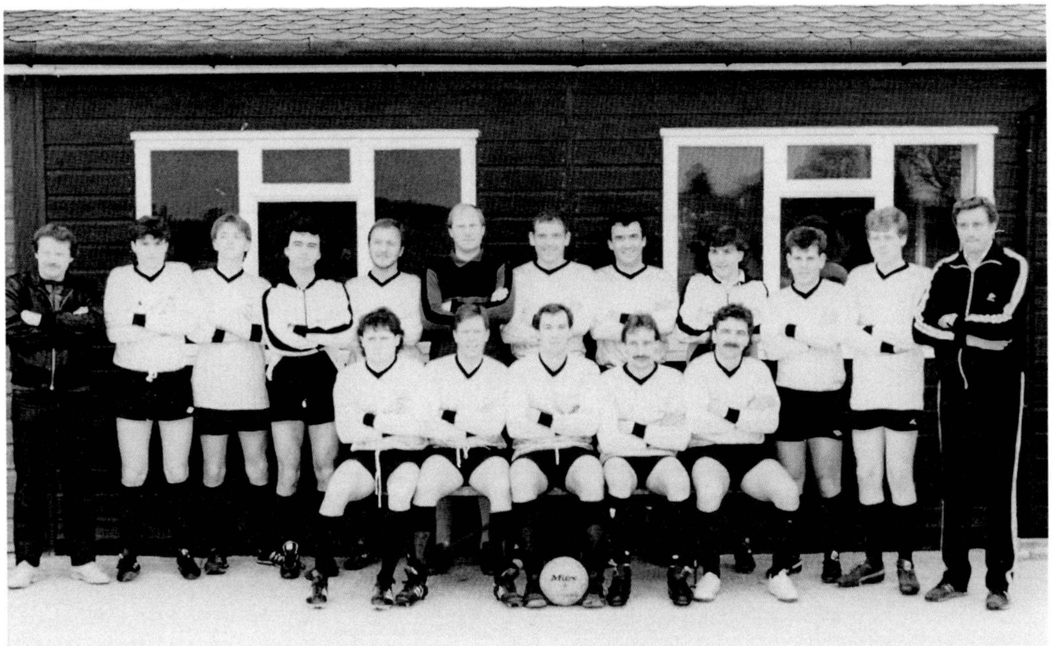

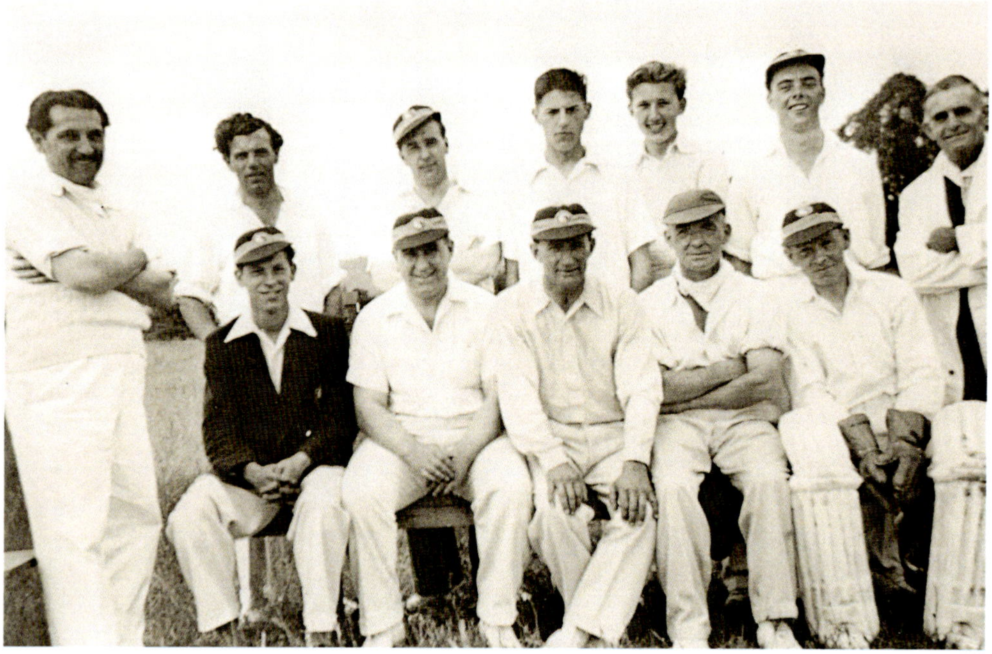

9.5 ***Above:*** Purley cricketers in the 1950s. From left to right, standing: Les Annetts, Hind,?, Lillington,?, Jack Iles, Fred King, seated: Eric Gibbons, Peter Fitchew, Maurice Gardiner, Benny Williams, Fred Saunders.

9.6 ***Below:*** Purley Cricket Club in the late 1970s/early 80s. From left to right, standing: Brian Kingston, Charlie Cook, Mick Clark, Peter Hemmings, Chris Morris, Kevin Hardwicke, seated: Martin Bishop, Richard Francis, John Duffin, Neville Jackson, Andrew Lewendon.

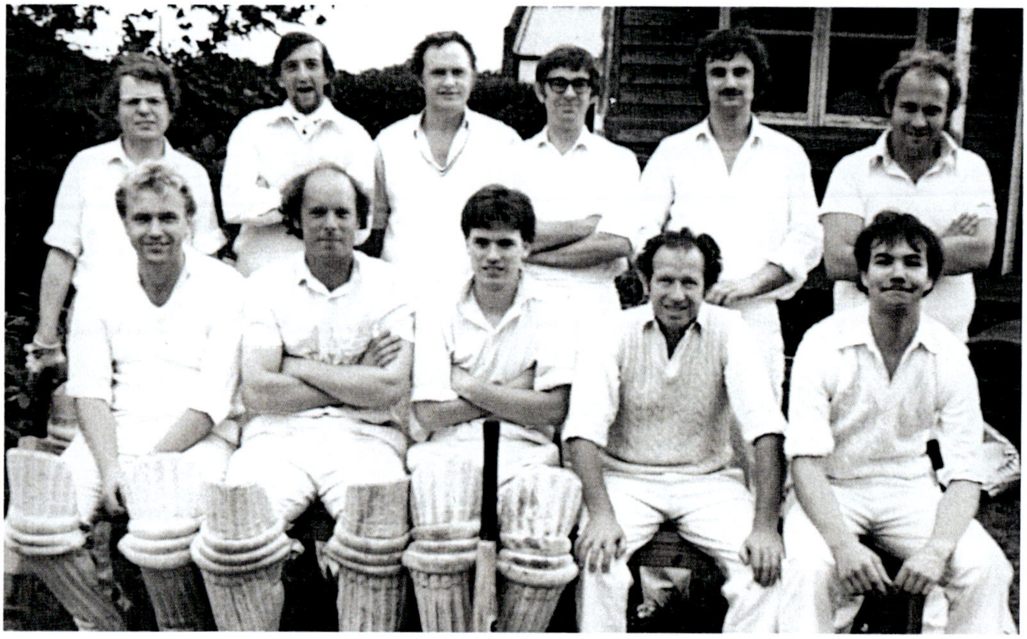

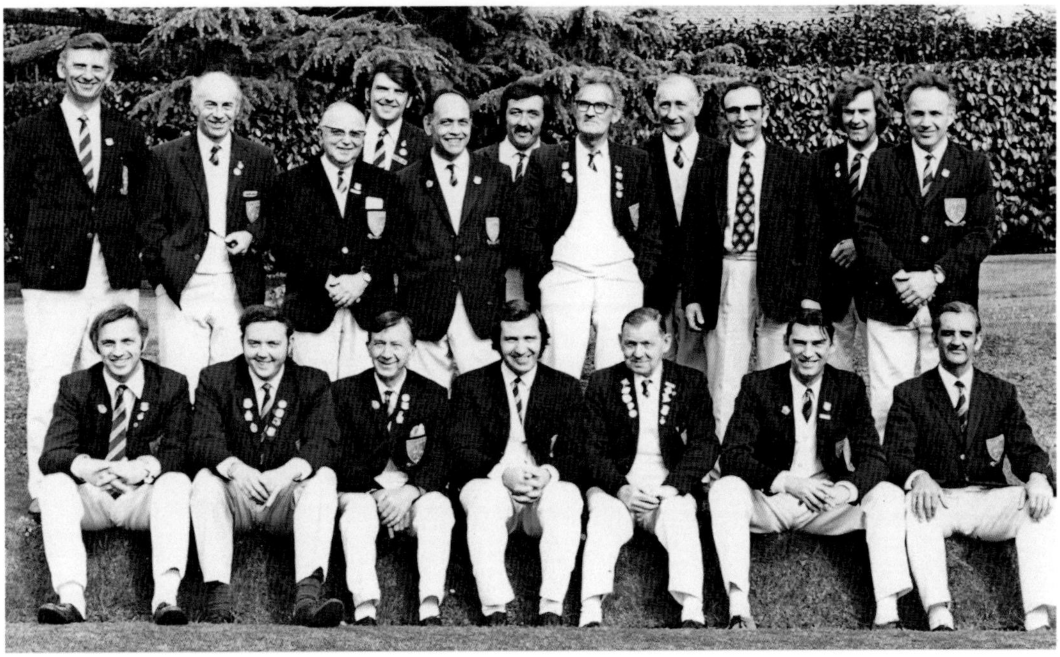

9.7 Trentham Bowling Club in the 1950s with Fred Tassel (second from left, bottom row) and Fred Saunders (fifth from left, bottom row).

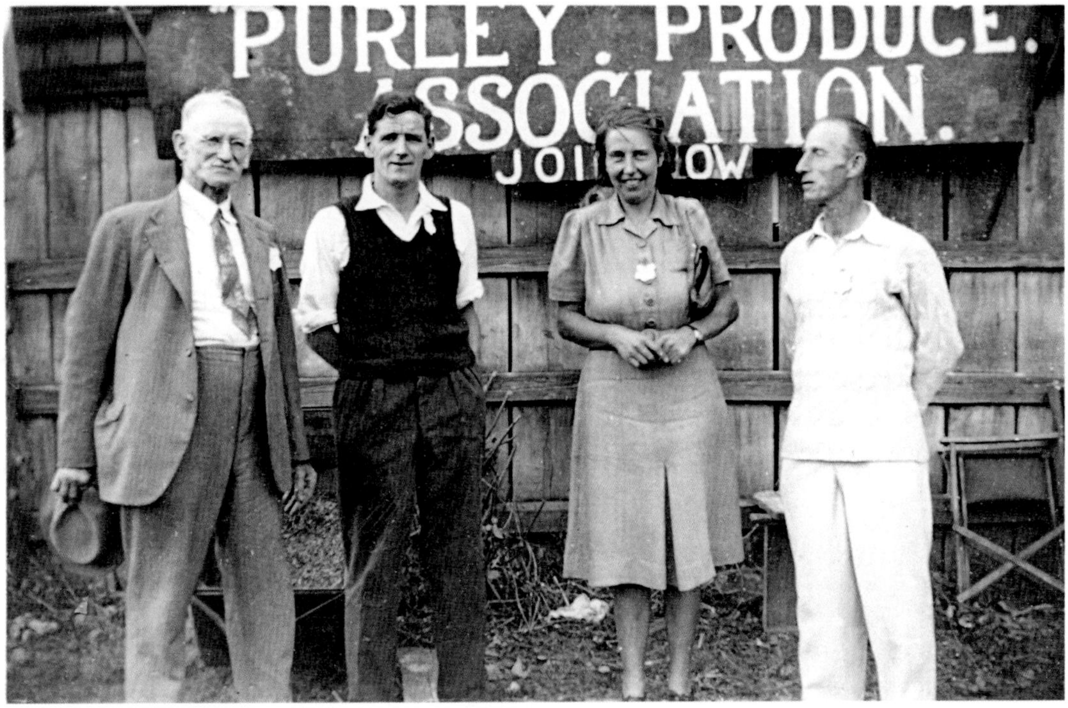

9.8 Purley Produce Association show in the late 1940s with James Rawlins, Fred Rawlins, Miss Moore and Teddy Pailes wearing their winners' rosettes.

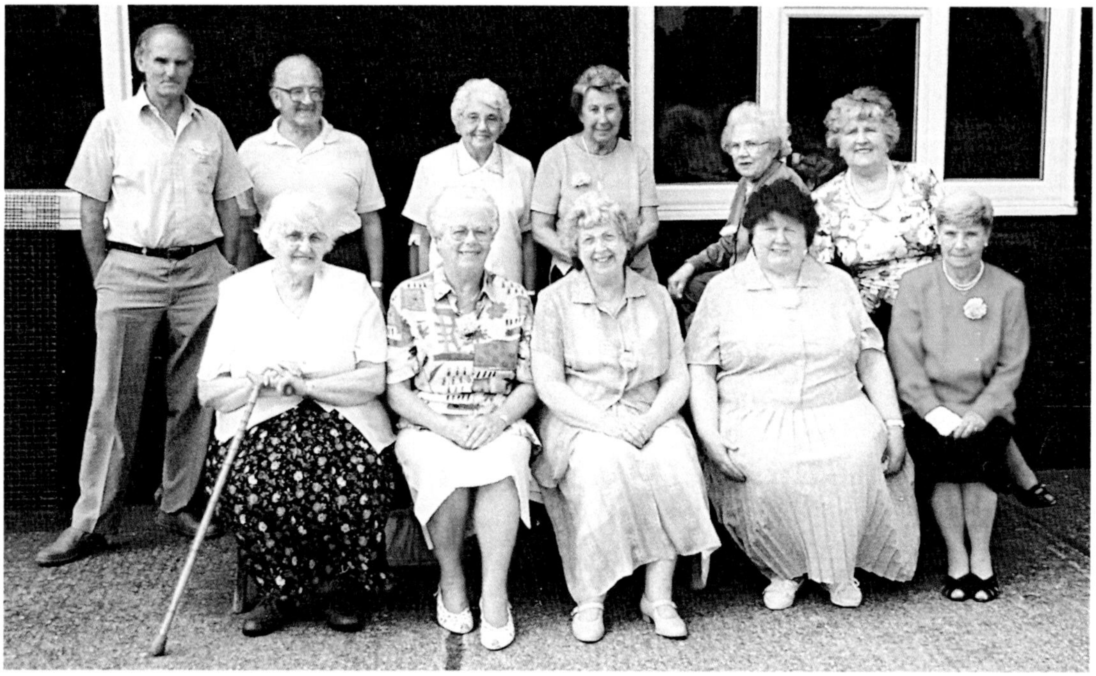

9.9 ***Above:*** The Wednesday Club enjoy a summer buffet in 1999 at Purley Sports and Social Club. Left to right, back row: Harry Capel, Les Jamieson, Joyce Selby, Gladys Jamieson, Barbara Mercer, Margaret Schofield, front row: Edith Gilliland, Wyn Capel, Rita Denman, Pat Morgan, Vicky Fidler.

9.10 ***Below:*** Elsie Kirton, a founder member of Purley WI, at a celebration in September 1976 to mark their fortieth anniversary.

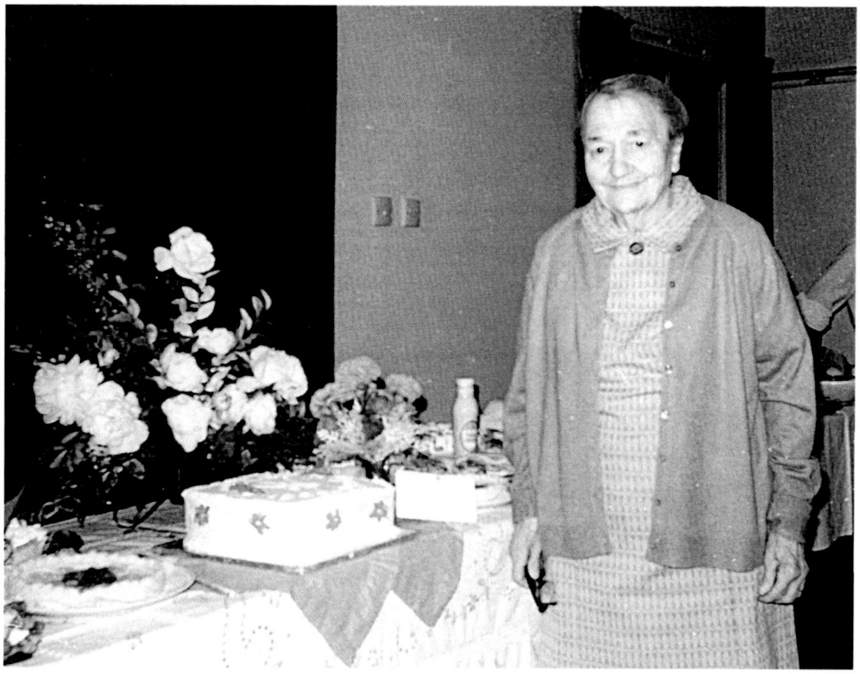

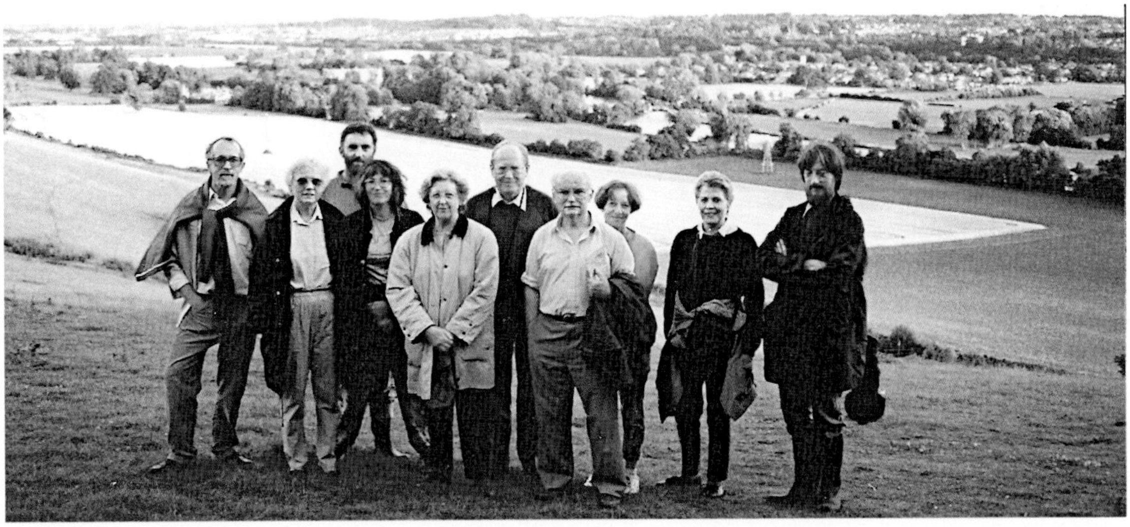

9.11 ***Above:*** Members of Project Purley and guests at Hardwick overlooking Purley, July 1993. From left to right: Ben Viljoen, Patricia Heslop, Patrick Holton, Liz Holton, Rita Denman, John Chapman, James Heslop, Dorothy Viljoen, Edna Bint and Trevor Cotton.

9.12 ***Below:*** Purley Sunday School members attend their teacher Jerry Fisher's wedding to Lynne in 1967. From left to right, back row: Paul Pocock, Terry Pocock, Lynette Barnes, Alan Winters, Paul Marshall, Sandra Rhodes, middle row: Janet Carlton, Fay Jordan, Julie Cameron, Terry Snelling, Mark? Snelling, Tara Starling, Caroline Holder, Jackie Cameron, front row: Michael Holder, June Griffiths, Karen Heddington, Angela Rearman, Karen Maxwell, Ian Maxwell, Christa Pearman, Lisa Inkpen, Katrina Sellafield, Wendy Sellafield, Mark Reave?.

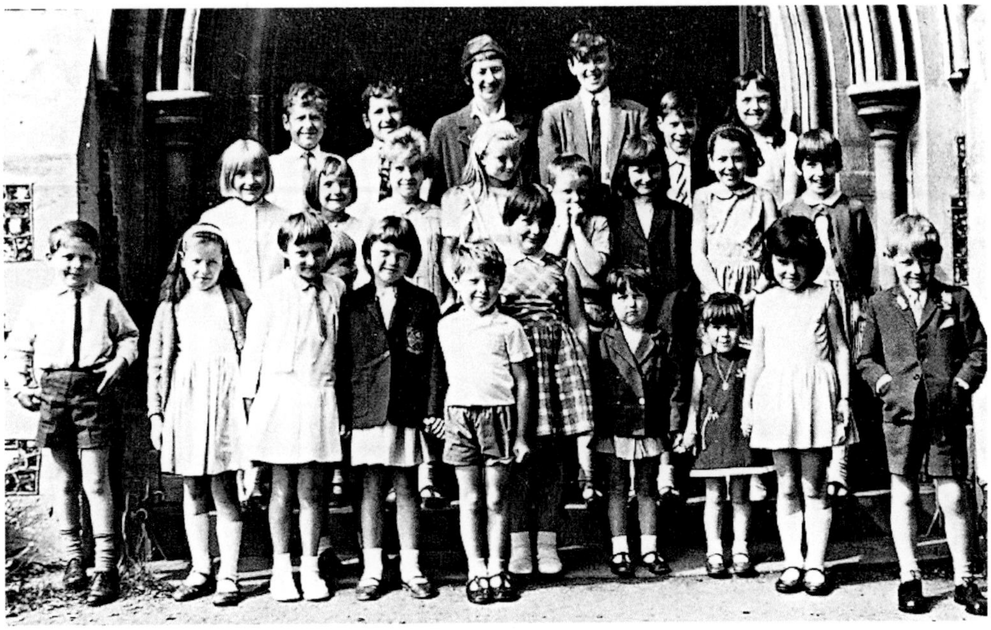

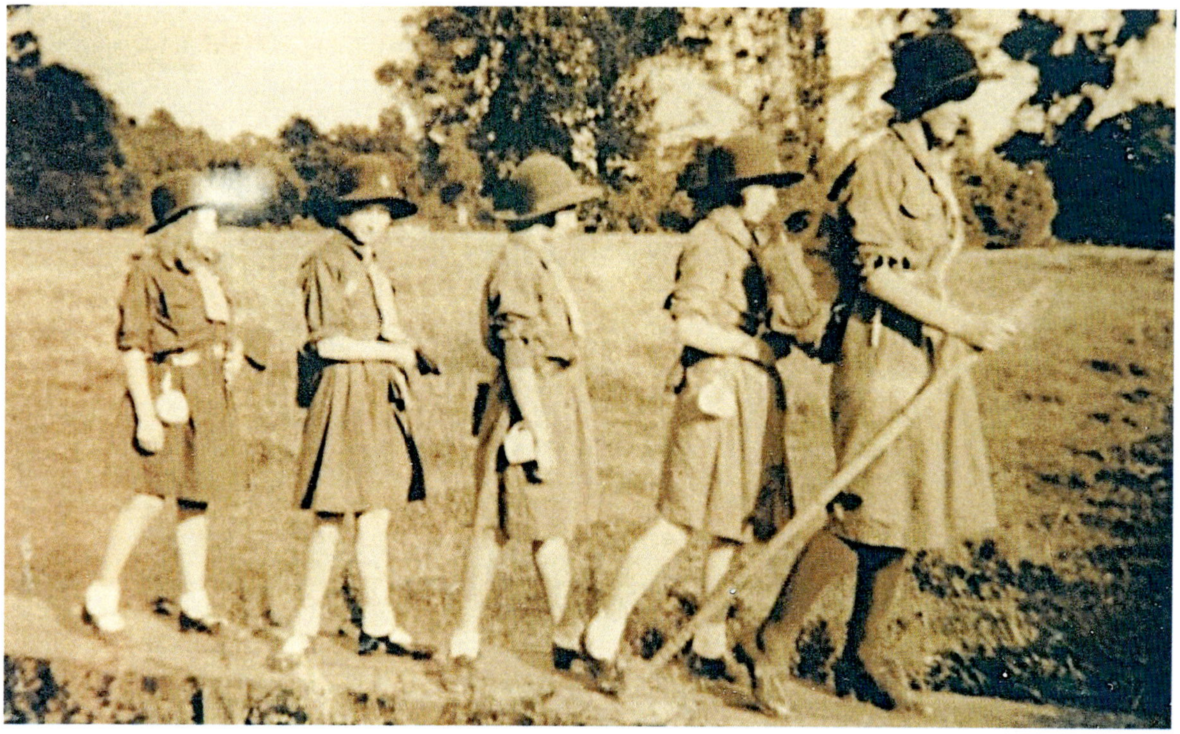

9.13 Purley Guides on a hike in the 1930s.

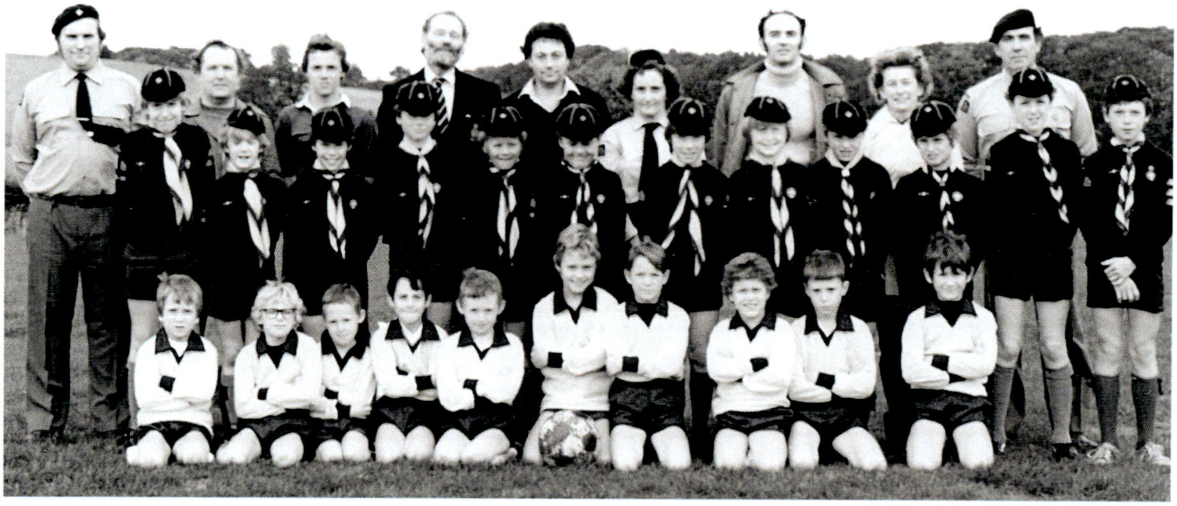

9.14 Purley Cubs and leaders, c1981. From left to right, back row: Colin Richmond, ?, ?,Ken Mercer, ?,Des Smithurst, ?, Marion Dabbs, Robert Clark, middle row: Alex Mason, Nathan Clark, Scott Richmond,?, Justin Smart, Andrew Humphreys, ?, Roger Hawkins, Ian Noakes, Ian Dabbs, Darren Noakes, ?, Front row: David Rees,?, Robin Purcell, ?, James Purcell, ?, ?, Chris Smithurst, ?, ?.

9.15 ***Right:*** Phyllis Leath of Purley Lodge Cottage in her Brownie uniform in the early 1920s. The Brownies were only formed in 1914 making this an early photograph.

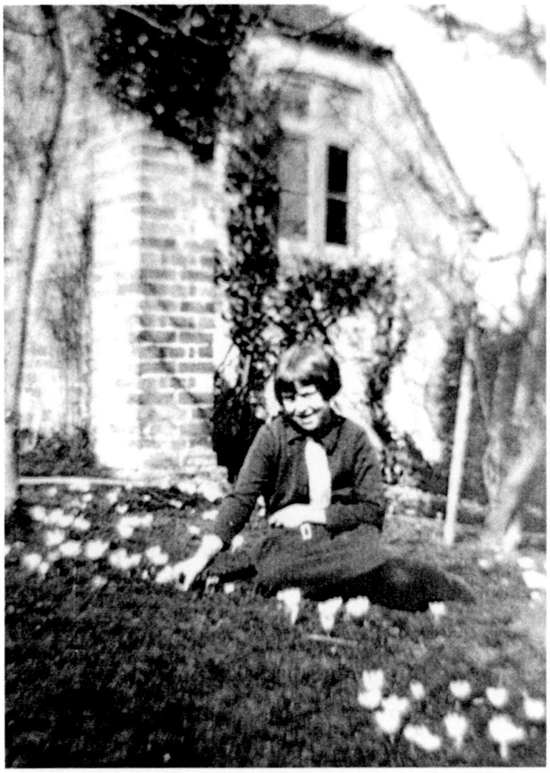

9.16 ***Below:*** 1st Purley Brownies with their brightly coloured toadstool in 1963.

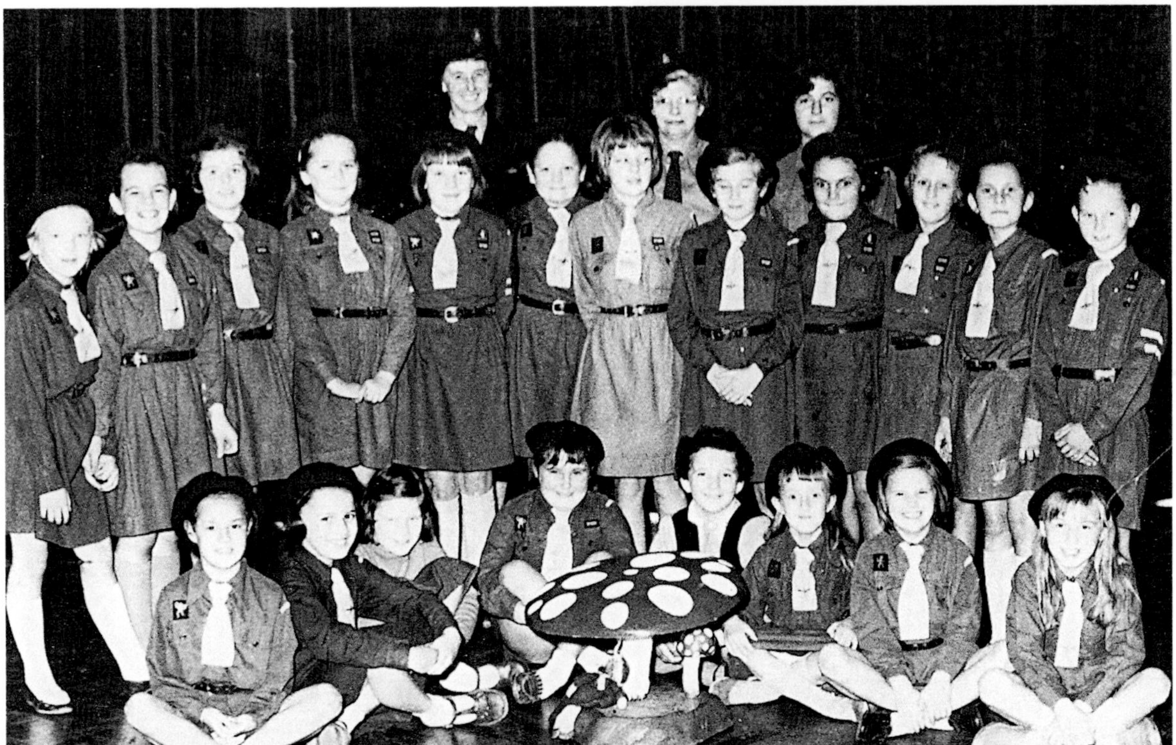

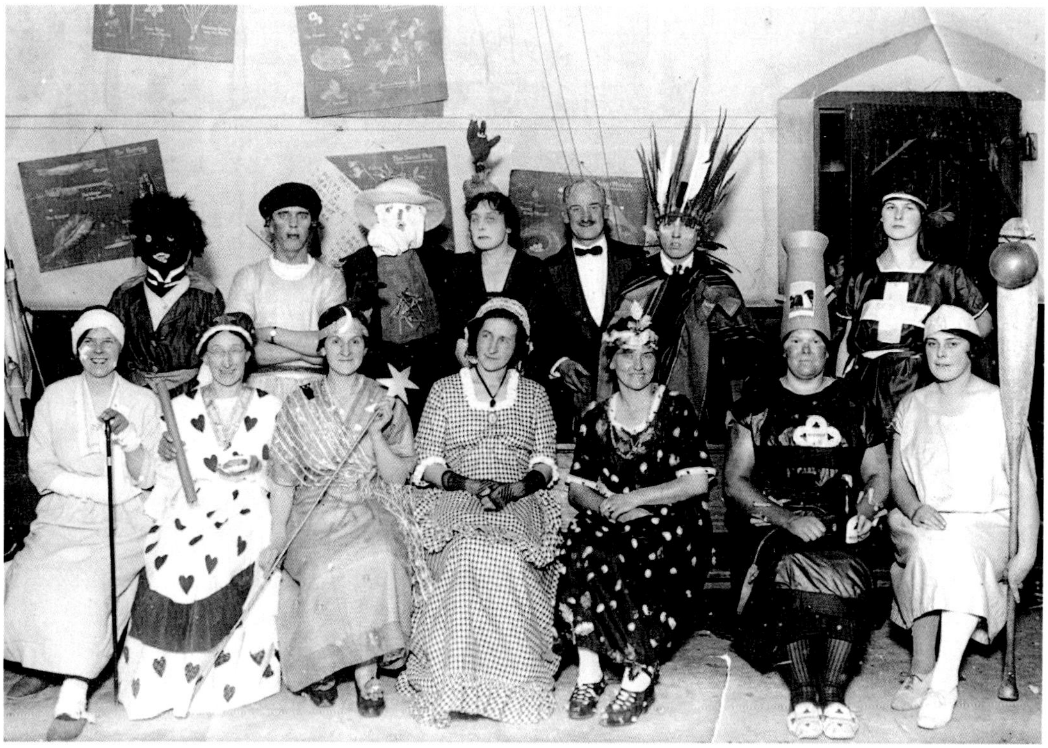

9.17 & 9.18 ***Above and below:*** A fancy dress party held at the school room in 1924 showing an imaginative range of costumes together with a glimpse of the pictures displayed on the walls. Attendees include, in the upper image, left to right, back row: ?, Edward Young,?, Rita Aldin, Cecil Aldin, Arthur Mott,?, front row: ?, the three 'Sheppard sisters'; Mary, Jess and Nell, Mrs Sheffield, Floss Leath,?.

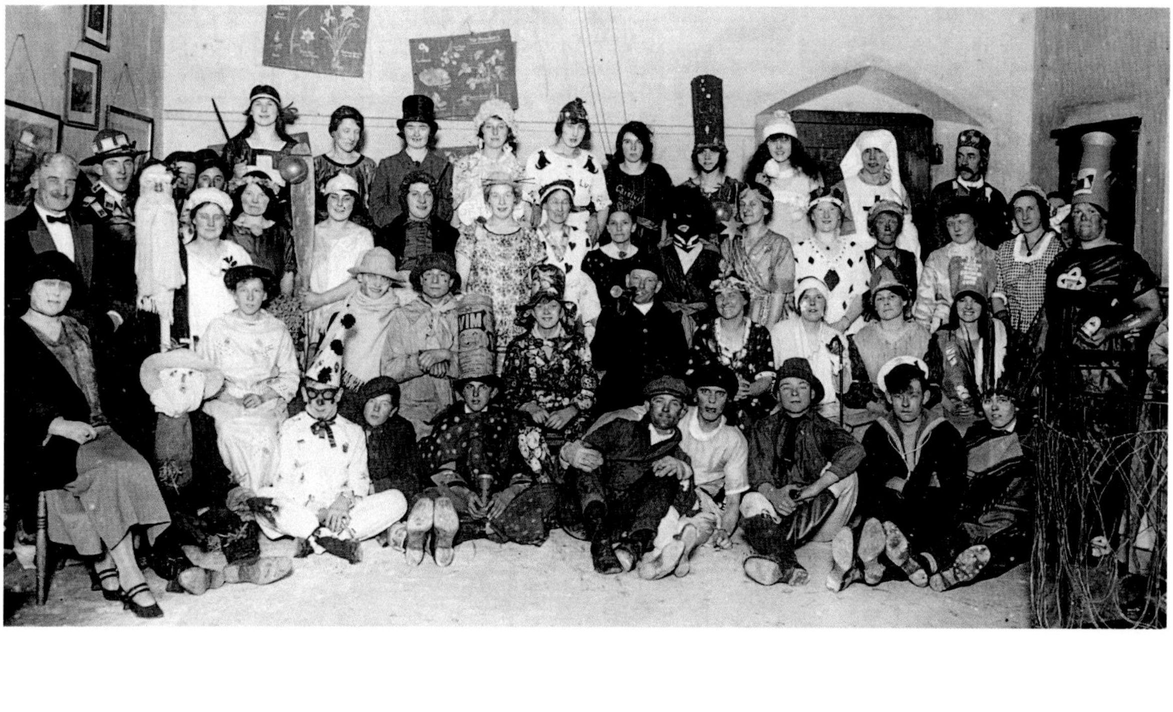

9.19 ***Right:*** Sarah Sheppard of Corner Cottages collects her King George V Silver Jubilee Commemoration Medal in 1935. The table was set up in front of the school.

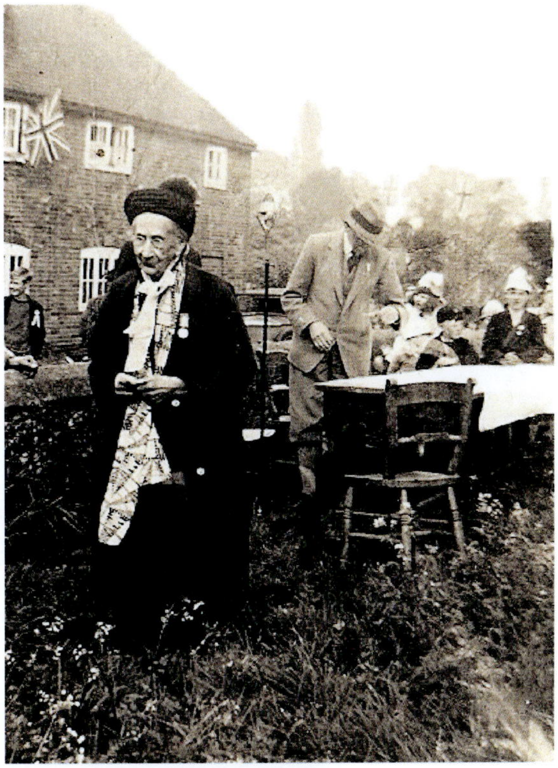

9.20 ***Below:*** Revd Ernest Skuse presents a prize for the best decorated bicycle competition at the village celebrations to mark King George V1's Coronation in 1937. The first prize went to Ronald Rawlins who was encased in a thatched cottage with the upper windows open so he could see to steer. Jean Skuse, the rector's daughter, is on the right of the picture with her bicycle on its stand.

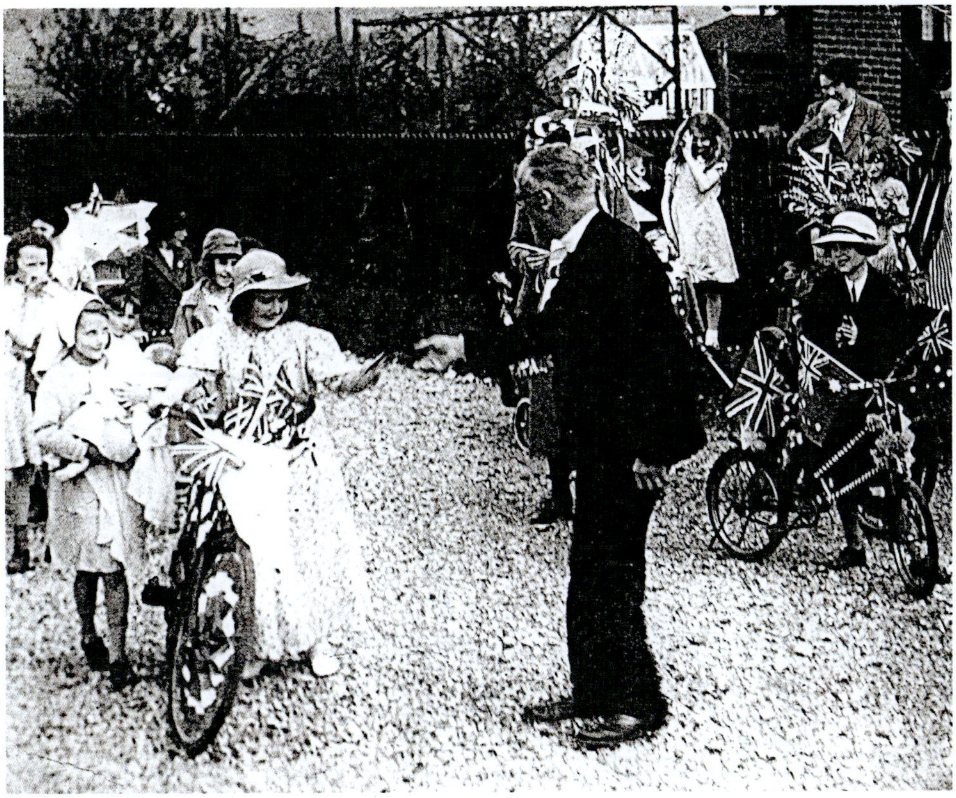

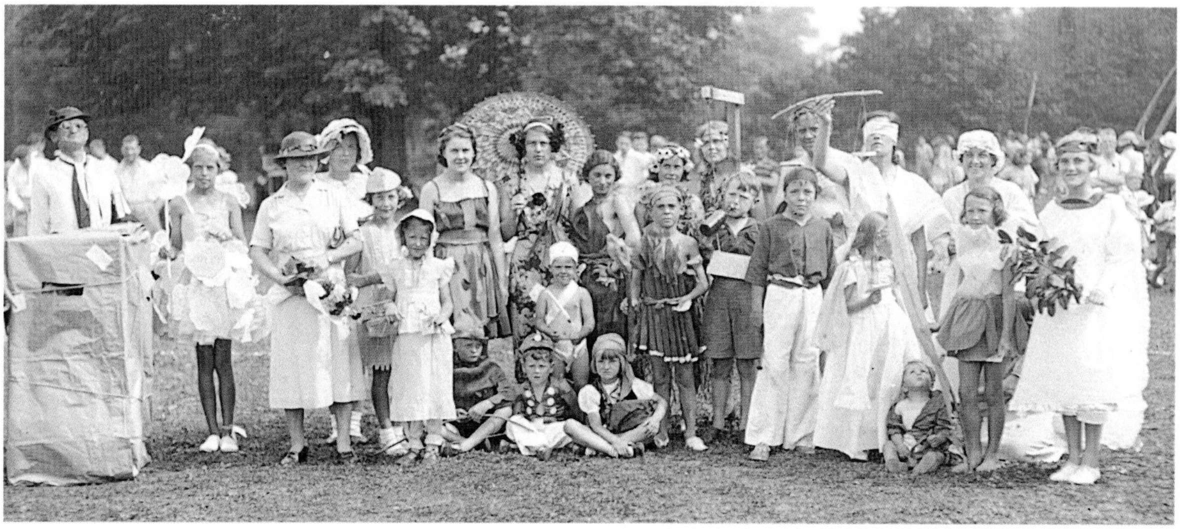

9.21 The River Estate Sports Day in 1938 included a Fancy Dress competition. Phyllis Hasemore is 'peace' on the far right of the group with Hilda Whatley next to her.

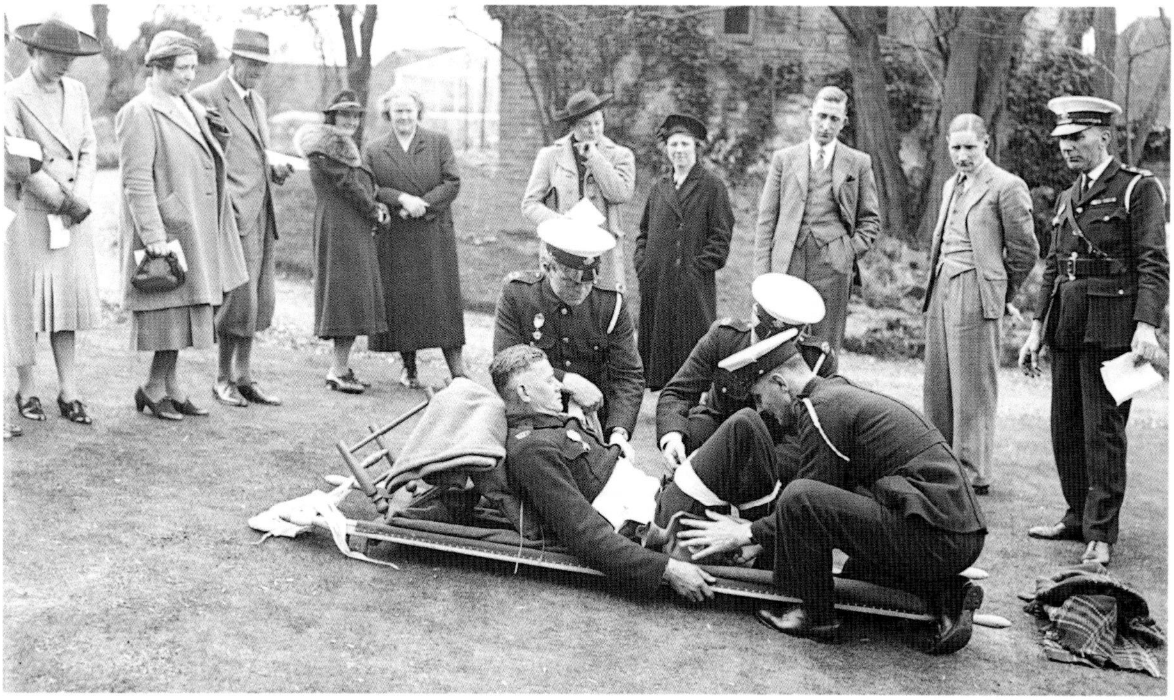

9.22 A first-aid demonstration led by Mr Marshall of the Red Cross, held at Purley Lodge in 1940. Charles Hodgkin, owner of Purley Lodge on the left with his wife, organised regular first-aid training for the village including the ARP wardens. Floss Leath is thought to be 5th from left.

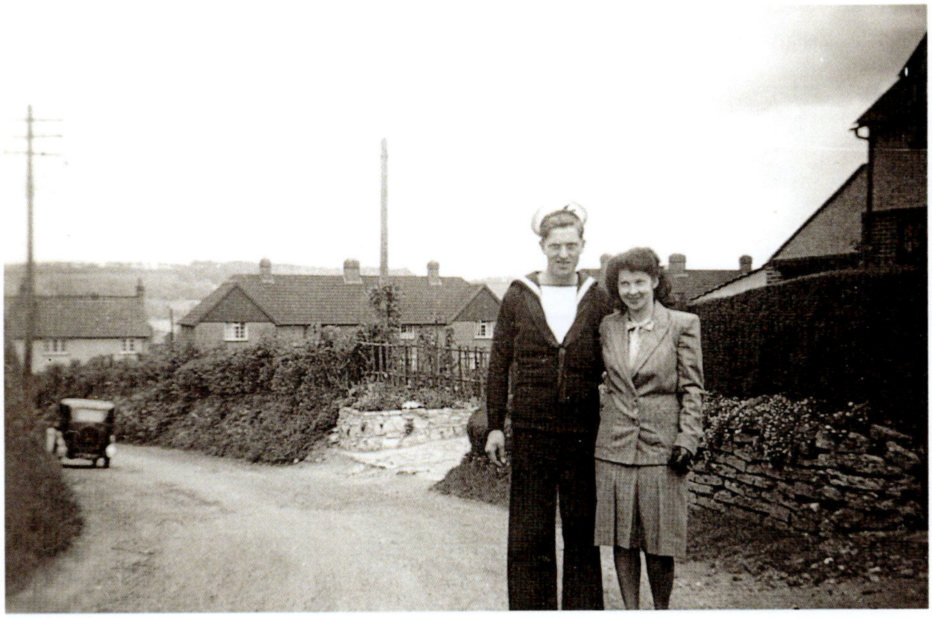

9.23 ***Above and below:*** Many of our villagers served in the forces in the Second World War; here are just a few of them. Above, Bill Leat is pictured with Christine Reed in Westbury Lane in 1946.

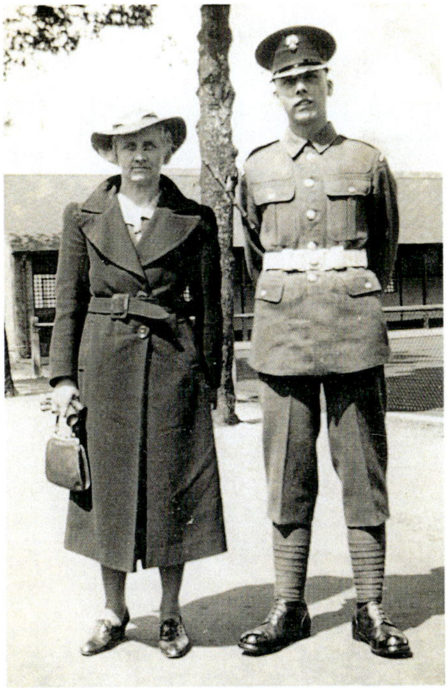

9.24 Guardsman Peter Warwick of Glebe Road with his mother in the 1930s.

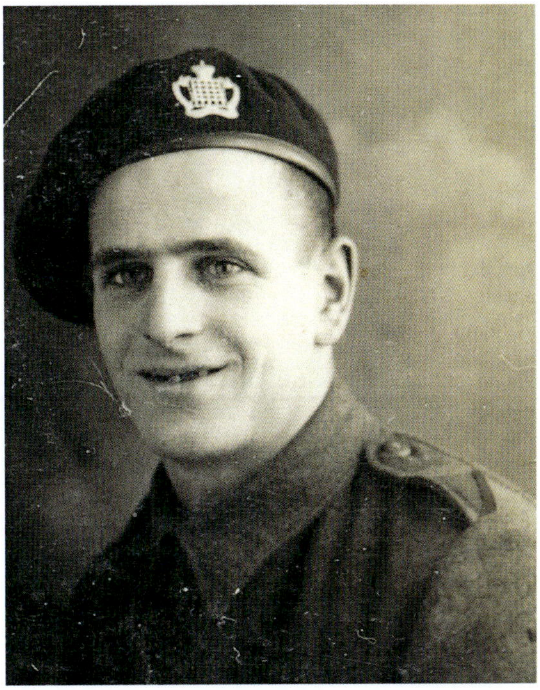

9.25 Ronald Rawlins of Long Lane was killed in action in 1945 with the Royal Tank Regiment.

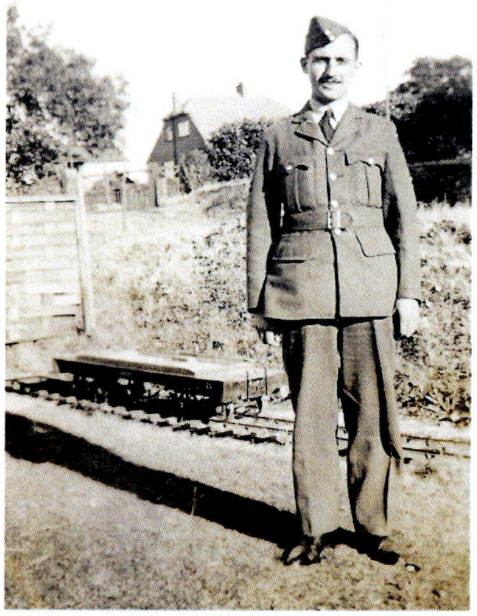

9.26 ***Left:*** Kenneth Venners of Purley Rise Farm, c1942. The miniature train behind him was used to transport eggs and had previously been in use at Menpes' Farm.

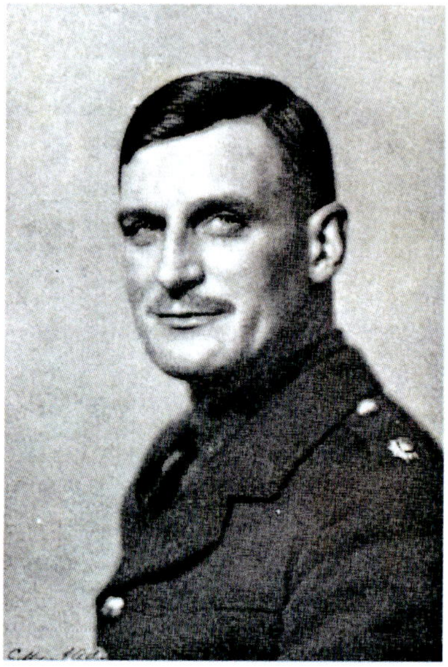

9.27 ***Right*** Hugh Lister of the Old Rectory was a nephew of Lord Lister of antiseptic fame and ordained a priest in 1922. He was killed in action in 1944.

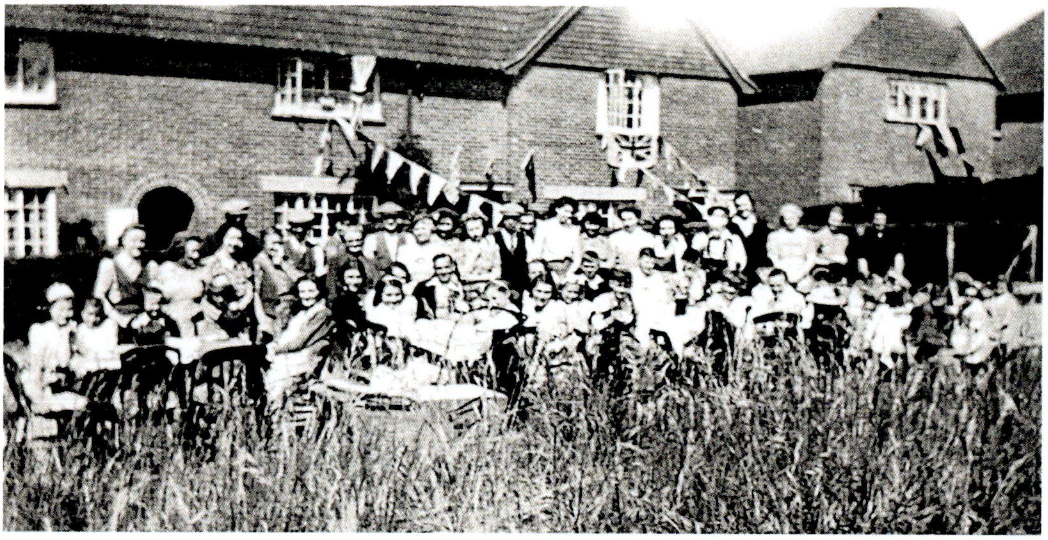

9.28 VE Day celebrations in Glebe Road, May 1945. Standing left to right, back row: Sybil Gibbons, Gwen Bowles, Gwen Fisher,?, Lynne Fisher,?,?, Mrs Bowles, Bert Nicholls, Joan M Hope,?, Evelyn Fisher, William Hope, Donald Hope, Joyce Nicholls, Phyllis Clark, Myra Hope, Joan Hope,?, Mrs Iles, ?,?,?. front row: ?,?,?,?, Violet Mott?, Peggy Mott, June Williams,?, Mr Champion?, Margaret Iles, Pearl Newton, Jean Miles, Gibbons, Newton, ?,?, David Mott,?,?,?,?,?,?.

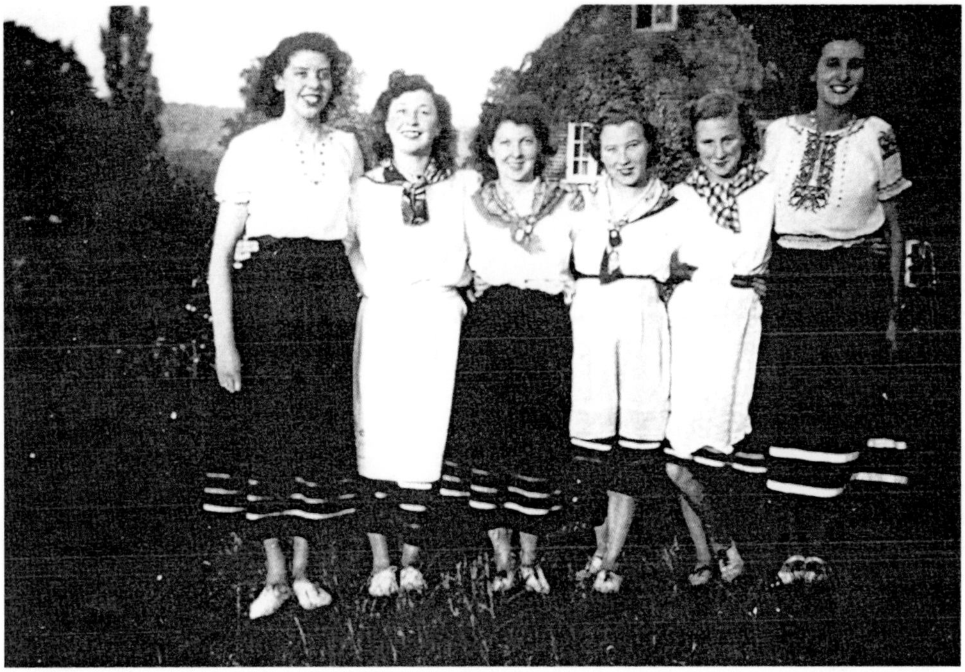

9.29 ***Above:*** Members of Purley Girls' Club who danced at the Berkshire Association of Girls' Clubs Dance Festival in 1947, taken in front of the school. From left to right: Joyce Nicholls, Doris Kirton, Christine Reed, Gwen Bowles, Margaret Bowles and Betty Wren. The girls' skirts were probably made from blackout material of which there was a surplus after the war and decorated with bands of braid.

9.30 ***Below:*** Judging underway in Glebe Road for the best dressed house competition, part of Purley's extensive Coronation celebrations in 1953.

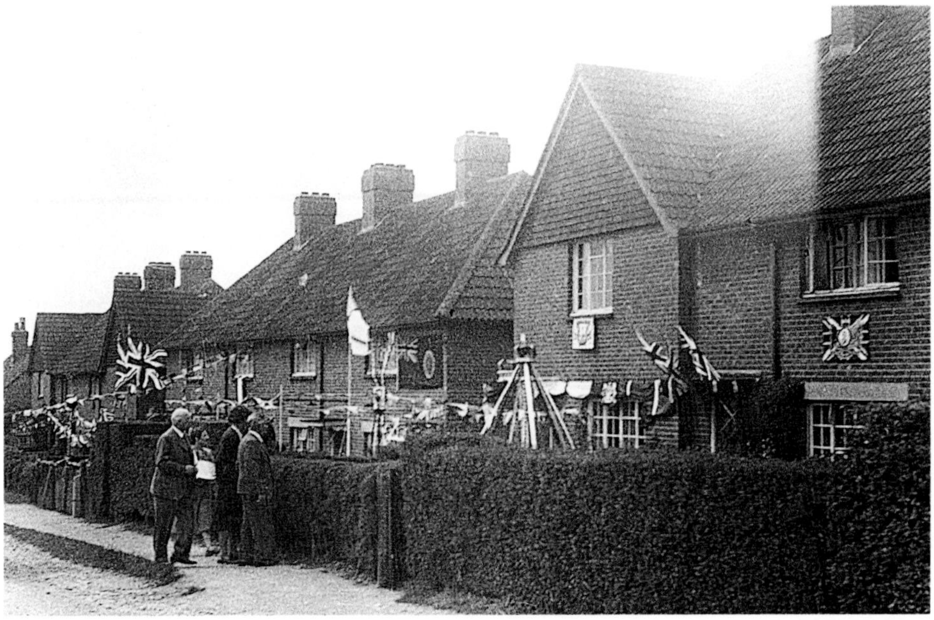

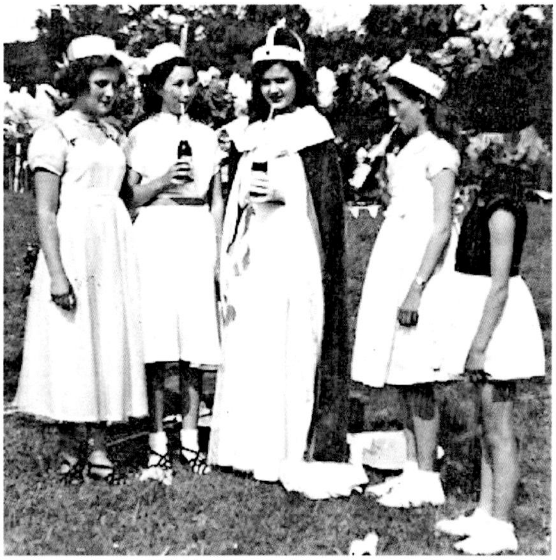

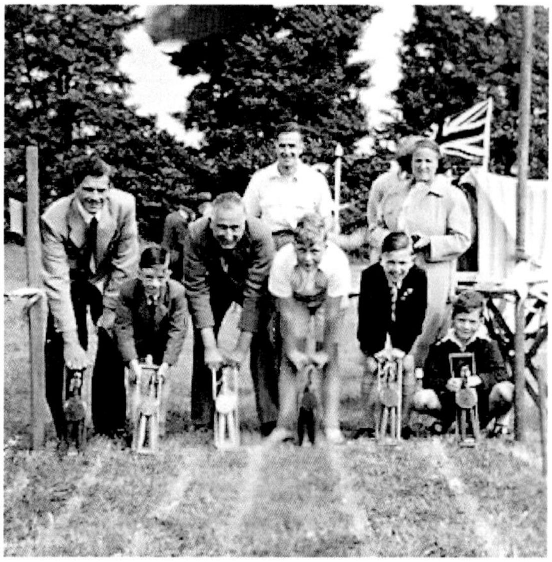

9.31 & 9.32 Other events organised in 1953 to celebrate Queen Elizabeth II's Coronation included a carnival, complete with Veronica Pooley as 'Queen' and from left to right Patricia Twigg, Melanie Sutton, ?, and Sandra Twigg as her attendants. There was also a sports day, here with a 'horse' race, on the newly completed Memorial Hall field.

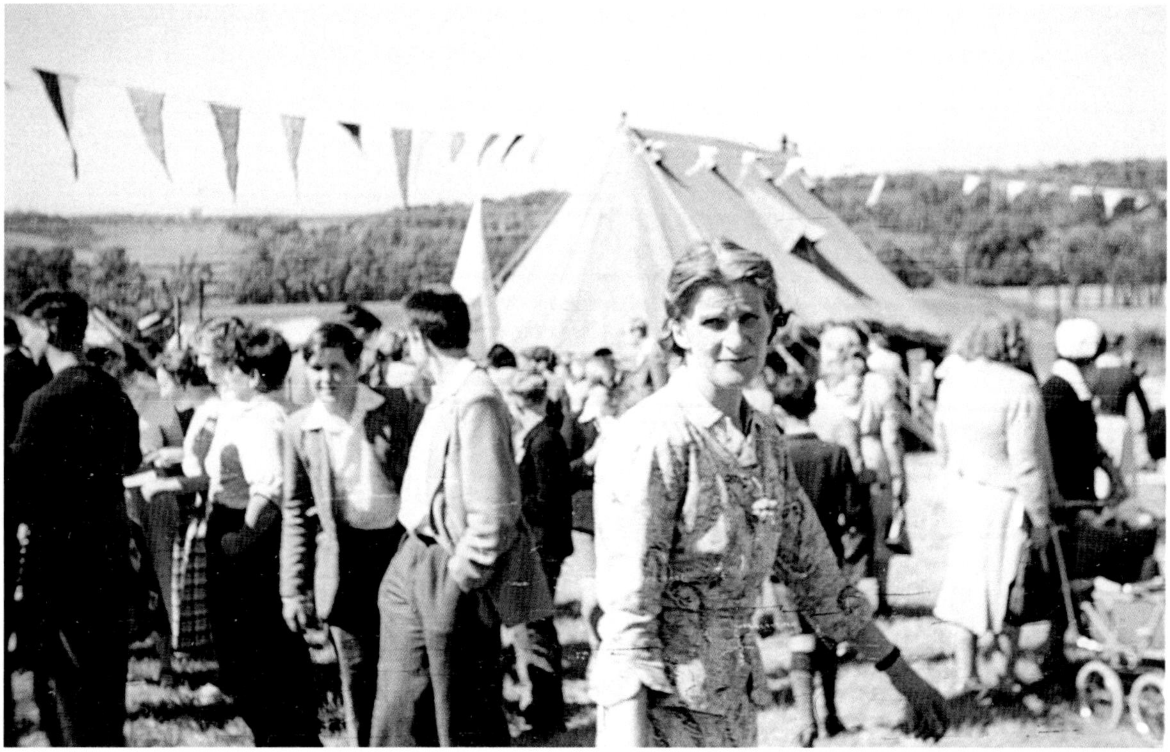

9.33 Carnivals and fairs were regular events in the 1950s. Elizabeth Pryor enjoys the festivities in this event.

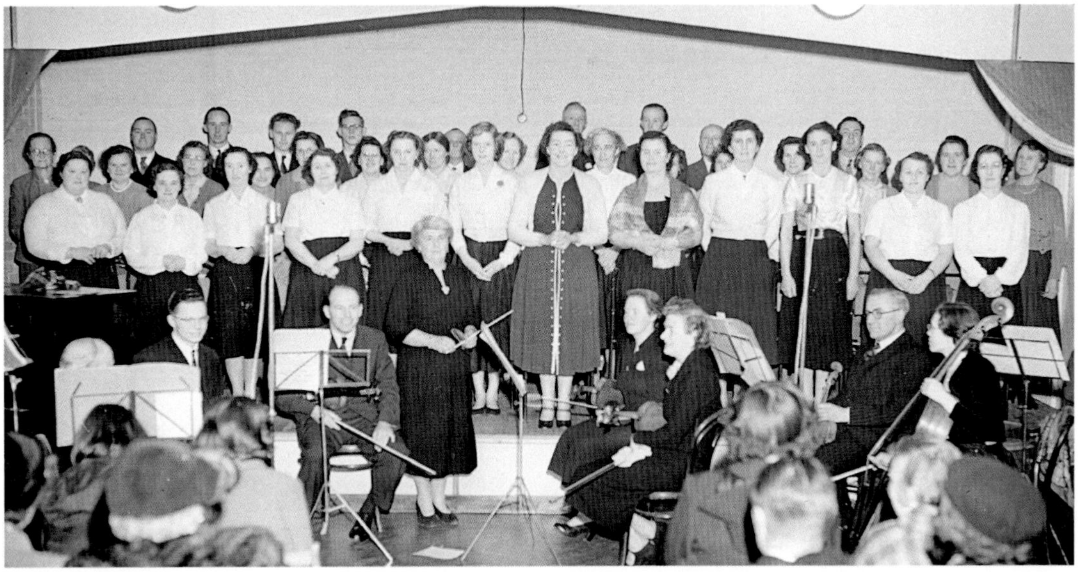

9.34 ***Above:*** A combined choir from Purley, Sulham and Tidmarsh WIs, augmented by male voices, perform Handel's 'Messiah' in the Memorial Hall, 1954. The conductor was Mary Richards; the WI choir later became Thames Vale Singers.

9.35 ***Below***: The retirement of Edith Tidbury as headmistress of Purley Church of England School, c1954. From left to right, back row: Mrs Iles, Phyllis Rawlins, Pat Patterson, Mrs King, Mrs Butler, Elizabeth Pryor, Edith Tidbury, James Rawlins, Revd Ernest Skuse, Arthur (John) Bucknell, Nelson Cooper, Ernest Spong, front row: Frederick Dutton, I Allchorne, Barbara Wright, Judith Higgins.

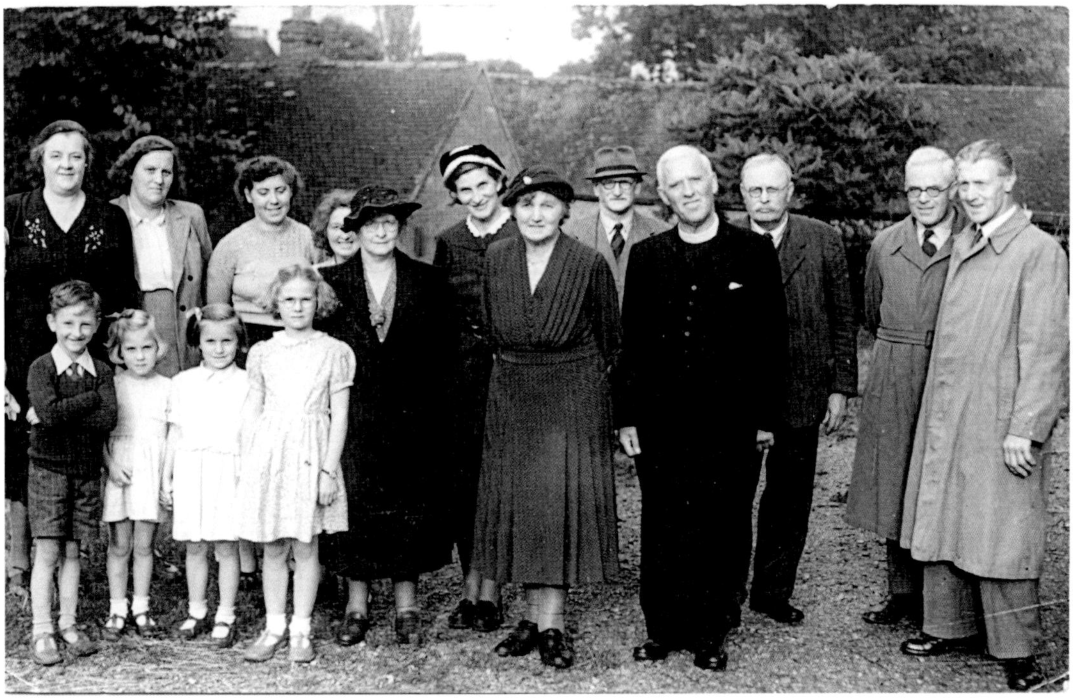

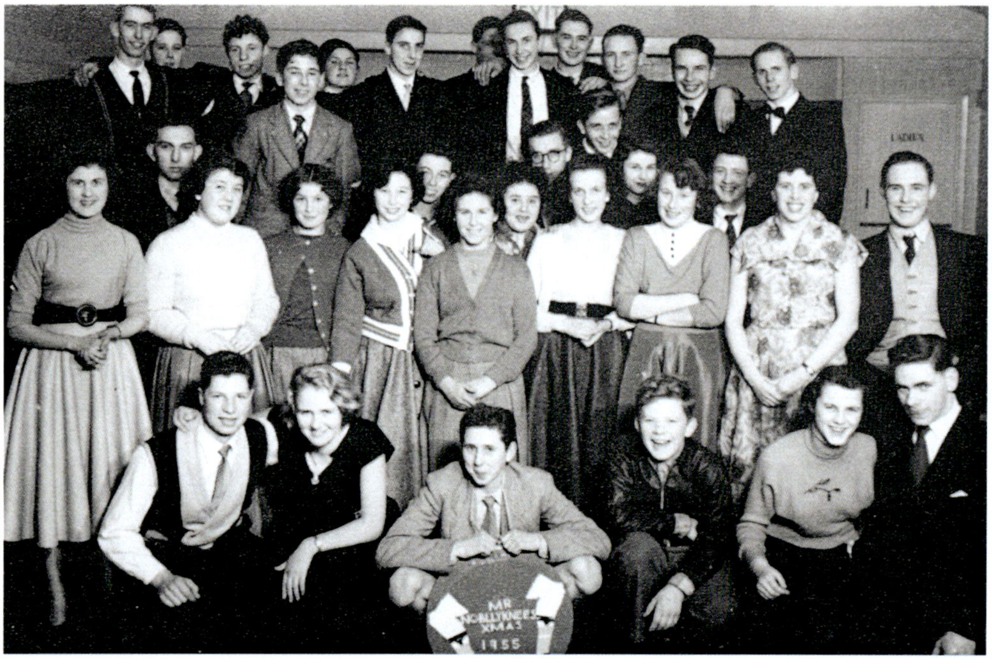

9.36 ***Above:*** A Village dance, Christmas 1955, which included a 'Mr Knobbly Knees' contest. From L-R, back row:?, Edward Rawlins,?, John Jones, John Fisher, Tony May, John Nash, David James, Michael Toomey, Roderick Venners, Dennis Beale, Raymond Giles, 2nd Row: Fred Cook, Victor Leforte, Donald Beale, Brian Beale, Betty Collins, Norman Garner, 3rd row: Jean, Joy Mumford, Susan Sloper, Melanie Sutton, Maureen Emerson, Jean May, Peggy Garner?,?, Teacher, Albert Clark, front row: Ian Nash, Jeanette Griffiths, John Clark,?, Susan Emerson, Michael Mace.

9.37 ***Below:*** Purley villagers pay their respects to Sir Winston Churchill as his funeral train passes in January 1965.

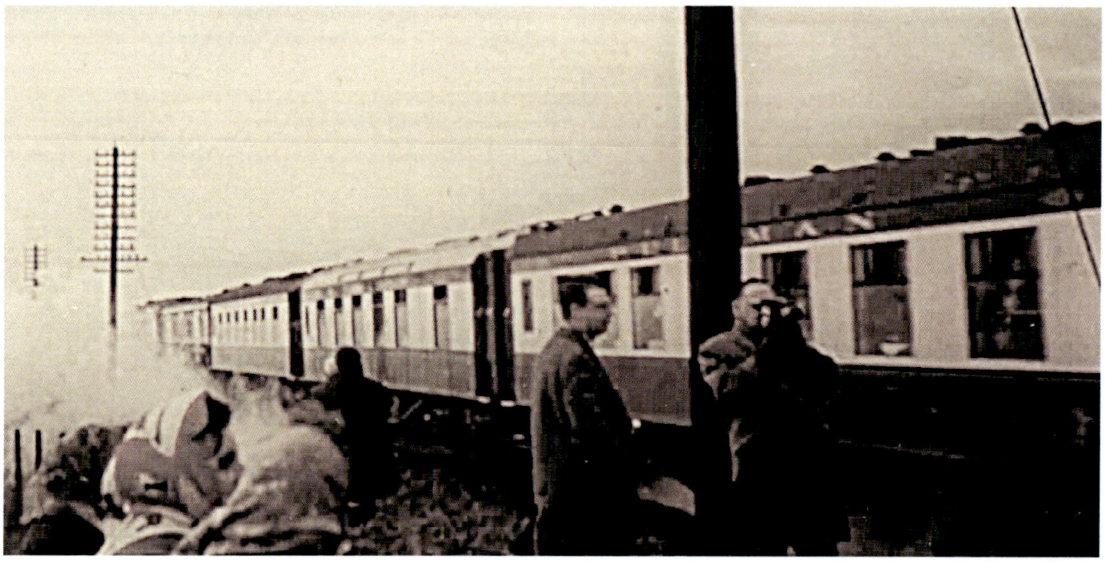

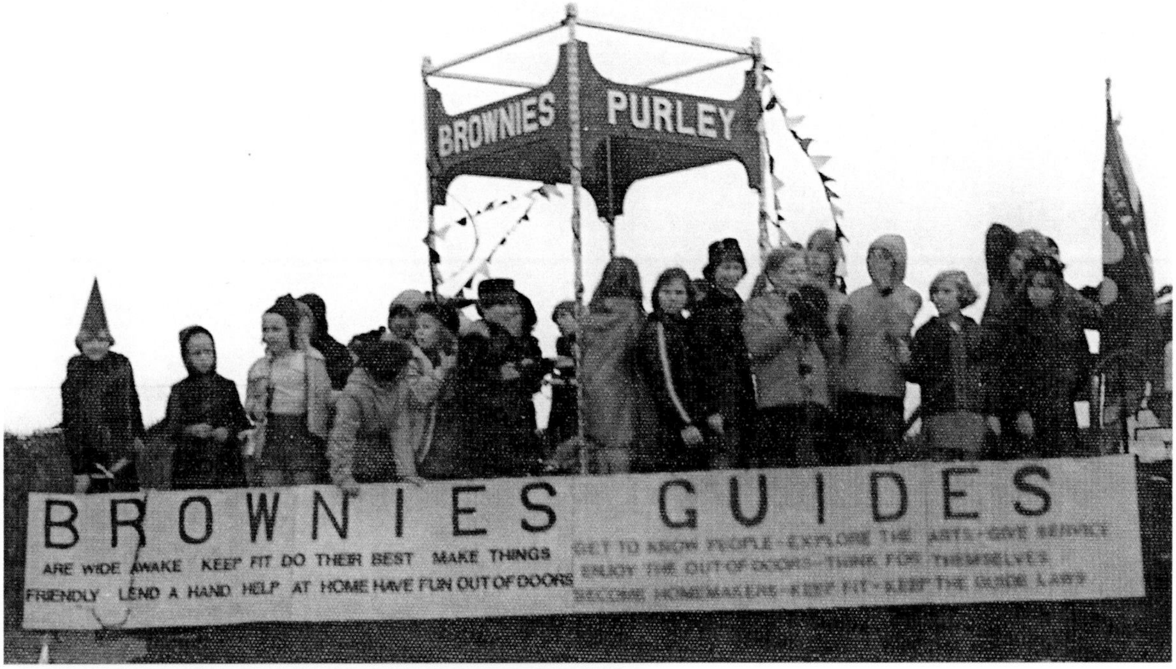

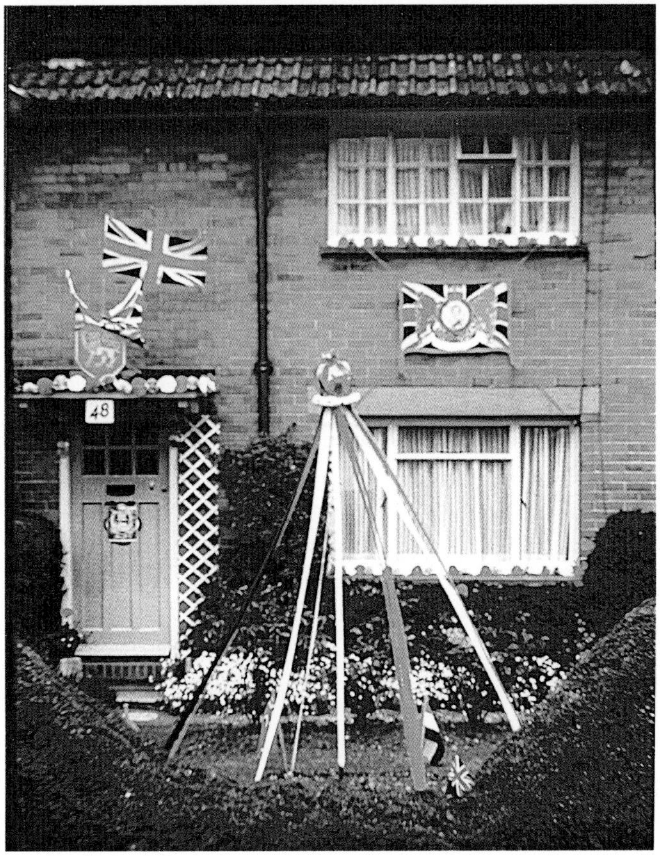

9.38 & 9.39 ***Above and left:*** The Silver Jubilee celebrations in 1977 in Purley included a best dressed house competition, with one contender from Glebe Road seen to the left, and a carnival with a float procession, above. Trenthams provided all the lorries and despite the rain the Brownies and Guides in the photograph above seem to be enjoying the day.

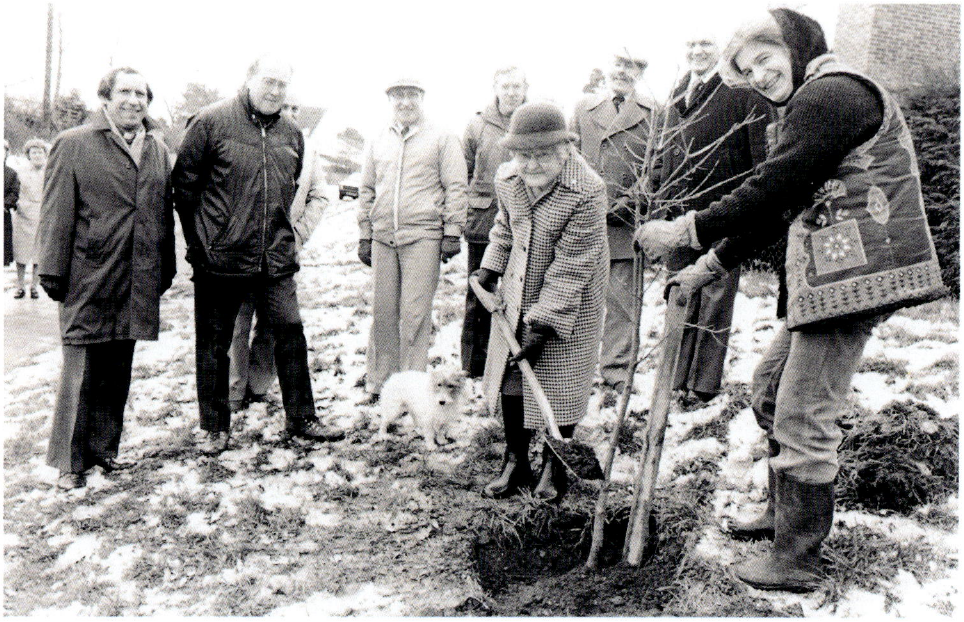

9.40 ***Above:*** Mrs Kit Saunders, assisted by Sybil Pryor, plants an oak tree in 1983 at the bottom of Long Lane in memory of her late husband Fred. She is joined by Revd David Evans, John Chapman, Peter Trentham, ?, Ken Mercer and Reg Marshall.

9.41 ***Below:*** Our final image shows members of the WI committee at their 'bling' party in 2006, their 70th birthday year. From left to right: Lesley Honnor, Margaret Martin, Marilyn Hoare, Bernardine Perry, Shirley Lewis, Marion Peer, Sylvia Conquest, Ann Davis, Edna Bint and Daphne Howard.

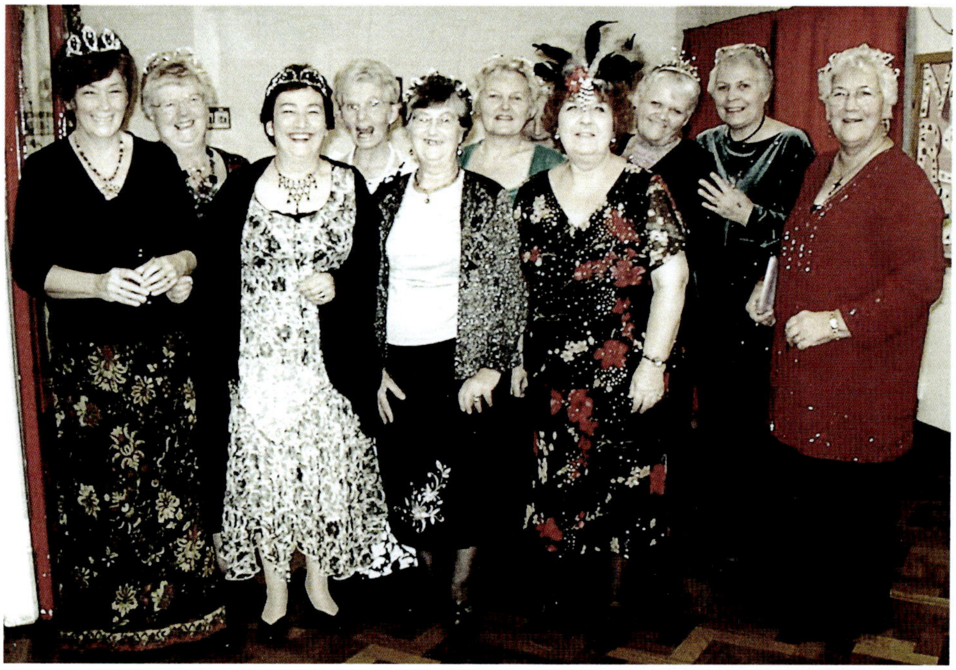

Biographies

Here is a brief guide to some of the people who are mentioned or appear in images in this book.

ALDIN, Cecil Charles Windsor *(1870-1935); artist and illustrator best known for his paintings of dogs and hunting scenes. Appointed Master of Foxhounds for the South Berks Hunt and lived in Belleisle Farm farmhouse, then called Kennelgates, 1915-1931. During World War One he operated a Remount Depot from Purley.*

ALEXANDER, Frederick (Fred) *(b1868); married Lucy. Lived in Purley 1908-1910 where his children attended the Church of England School. Emigrated to America in 1910.*

BADEN-POWELL, Olave St Clair (née Soames) GBE *(1889-1977); lived briefly, at Purley Hall before her marriage to Lieutenant-General Sir Robert Baden-Powell. Became Chief Guide in England in 1918 and the world in 1930. Honoured across the world, she was appointed Grand Dame of the British Empire in 1930 and awarded the Ceres Medal by the UN in 1973.*

BARNES, Thomas *(Born c1838); farmer of Home Farm, Sulham and then Scraces Farm from c1867 through to the early 1880s. Churchwarden of St Mary's Church 1867-1881.*

BARNES, Thomas (Lewis) *(1904-1969); husband of Lynette. Member of the choir of St Mary's Church for twenty two years and churchwarden for five years. Lived in Brading Way.*

BAZELEY, William *(c1834-1915); coachman for Major Storer of Purley Park and lived in the thatched gatehouse on the south side of the Oxford Road. Married Mary House in Purley in 1861 and had ten children..*

BUCKNELL, Arthur (John) Dimond *(Born 1923); son of Arthur William and Emily Bucknell. Farmer of Home Farm, Purley 1953-1983; churchwarden of St Mary's Church 1949-1972; district councillor 1956-1974.*

BUCKNELL, Arthur William *(1882-1953); born Devon and died Purley; married Emily Dimond. Farmer of Home Farm, Purley from 1937 until his death.*

COLLIER, Phillip Osborne	*(1881-1979); Reading-based press and commercial photographer; worked in partnership with Eric Guy from the 1920s through to 1940. Many of Collier's images were sold as picture postcards.*
COOPER, Nelson	*Organist and choirmaster of St Mary's Church 1927-1970 and honorary treasurer 1931-1970. Memorial in St Mary's Church.*
COX, Frederick	*(Born 1842); married Ann. Labourer, cowman and bailiff on Scraces Farm; he lived in Marsh Farm Cottages and then Scraces Farm Cottages until about 1917.*
DAYRELL-REED, Miss	*Headmistress of Purley Church of England School 1915-c1918.*
DEBES, Antoinette (née Müller)	*(c1810-1877); born Germany; wife of Edmund Debes, merchant. Housekeeper and friend of Frederick and Henry Beaufoy Wilder for 45 years; childhood nanny to Frederick Wilder. Buried in Sulham.*
DUDLEY MATTHEWS, Revd John Henry	*Assistant Master of Wellington College 1868-1884; Headmaster of Leeds Grammar School 1884-1902. Rector of Purley 1902-1914; died when his boat capsized in Mapledurham Reach whilst returning to Purley from taking evensong at Mapledurham. Memorial in St Mary's Church.*
EDWARDS, Charles Walter	*(1906-1980); motor and precision engineer of a garage in Purley Rise c1937-1958.*
EDWARDS, Mary Ellen	*Headmistress of Purley Church of England School 1918-1925.*
FULLERTON, George Frederick Downing	*(1857-1916); Gentleman; born Rendcombe, Gloucestershire and died Hampstead, Middlesex. Married 1889 in St Mary's Church to Leila Minna Gertrude Storer. Captain in 4th Battalion Royal Irish Rifles in World War One.*
FULLERTON, Leila Minna Gertrude (née Storer)	*(1862-1918); born London and died Purley Park; only daughter of Anthony Morris and Cicely Barr Storer. Married in 1889 in St Mary's Church, Purley to George Frederick Downing Fullerton and had four children. Inherited Purley Park for life after the death of her mother.*

FULLERTON, Myra Ada Violet Downing	*(Born 1891); second daughter of George & Leila Fullerton. Named as second beneficiary in her grandfather's will to inherit Purley Park.*
GUTCH, Harold	*Nurseryman who lived in The Garden House on Purley Rise (formerly part of the Westfield House estate); sub-postmaster of the Post Office 1955-1977.*
GUY, Eric	*Reading-based professional photographer who specialised in farming and rural scenes. Worked in partnership with Phillip Osborne Collier from the 1920s through to 1940.*
HASEMORE, Eva (née Record)	*Purchased a camping plot with her husband Walter in the 1930s in Colyton Way. Became an active member of the Purley Park River Estate community and was appointed secretary of the Purley Park Property Owners Association when it was formed.*
HASEMORE, Walter	*Husband of Eva. School-keeper and tenor singer.*
HASTINGS, Warren	*(1732-1818); first Governor-General of India from 1773-1785. He was accused of corruption and impeached in 1786 but was acquitted in 1795; he lived at Purley Hall while he was awaiting trial. Made a Privy Councillor in 1814.*
HAWKINS, Revd Harold Frederick	*Gained his licentiate in theology in 1929 at the University of Durham before going on to study at St Chad's College, Durham and Chicester Theological College. Chaplain to the forces (Emergency Commission) 1943-1947 and Honorary Chaplain to the Forces, 1947. Vicar of Nazeing 1950-1961 before becoming Rector of Purley 1961-1969. Retired to Pangbourne*
HODGKIN, Charles Ernest	*(1861-1949); director of Pulsometer Pumps, Oxford Rd, Norcot. Churchwarden of St Mary's Church 1902-1949 and lived in Purley Lodge c1903-1949. Memorial in St Mary's Church. Father of Eliot Hodgkin, artist.*
HOPE, Lieutenant-General Sir James KCB	*(1785-1871); married Christiana Whitling. An officer of the 26th Foot who later commanded the 9th Foot; served with distinction in the Peninsula War. Lived in Purley Lodge in the early 1850s where two of his sons were born.*

HYDE, Ann (née Ayliffe)	*Daughter of Sir George Ayliffe and grand-daughter of the lord of the manor of Purley Magna; in 1632 became the first wife of Edward Hyde, who later became the 1st Earl of Clarendon. Taken ill at Reading with smallpox in 1632 whilst travelling from London to her Wiltshire home and died in the manor house of Purley Magna, the home of her uncle Sir John St John. Buried in Purley and memorial in St Mary's Church.*
HYDE, Edward, 1st Earl of Clarendon	*(1609-1674); studied at Magdalen College, Oxford 1622-6 and was called to the bar in 1633. Became an MP in 1640, an adviser to King Charles I the following year and Lord Chancellor to King Charles II in 1658. He wrote one of the earliest histories of the Civil War. Married twice, his first wife died in Purley and has a memorial in St Mary's Church. His daughter Anne, by his second marriage, was the mother of the future Queens, Mary and Anne.*
ILLSLEY, Jane Elizabeth (Ginny) (née Leath)	*(Born c1904); daughter of Henry and Elizabeth Leath. Worked as an assistant teacher at Purley Church of England School in the early 1920s and married Albert Illsley in 1926.*
KERR, Thomas	*(Born c1871); blacksmith of Whitchurch Hill, Whitchurch in 1901 and Purley Forge c1907-1910.*
KIRTON, Elsie Annie (née Marshall)	*(1898-1991); born in Tilehurst and married Joseph Kirton in 1923. Founder member of Purley Women's Institute. Mother of Doris and Charlie Kirton.*
KIRTON, Joseph William (Jack)	*(1902-1987); born Reading, came to Purley in 1914 and married Elsie Marshall in 1923. Dairy farmer of Yew Tree Farm and lived in Yew Tree Cottage; retired in 1968 at 66.*
LEATH, Henry	*(c1867-1956), born Hope under Dinmore in Herefordshire and married Elizabeth Edwards. Came to Purley c1895 as coachman to Miss Aribella Baker of Purley Lodge until c1902. Continued as gardener for Charles Hodgkin when he moved into Purley Lodge.*
LIEBENROOD, John George	*Merchant from Elrich in Saxony; naturalized by Act of Parliament in 1737. Married the heiress Ann Allen of Purley and built Purley Lodge in the 1750s. Died 1795; memorial in St Mary's Church.*

LISTER, Major Hugh Evelyn Jackson	*(1901-1944); graduate of Cambridge University and Cuddesdon Theological College; ordained in 1922 as an Anglican priest. Active trade union organiser and led strikes in the East End of London in the 1930s. Served with the Welsh Guards in the Second World War and killed in action at Hechtel, Belgium. Lived at the Old Rectory, Purley Village; brother of Elizabeth Pryor.*
MAY, Frederick George (Fred)	*(1912-1999); joined Thames Conservancy in 1934 and was keeper at Northmoor and Clifton Locks before being appointed keeper at Mapledurham in 1946, where he remained until his retirement in 1956. Awarded the Sir Reginald Hanson Challenge Cup for the best kept lock in 1952. Also a skilled caricaturist, contributing to local newspapers and boating magazines. Father of Tony and Peter May.*
MENPES, Mortimer Luddington	*(1855-1938); born Australia and died Pangbourne; war artist and engraver, author, printmaker and illustrator. Married Rosa Mary Grosse in London in 1875. For the last 30 years of his life, he retired to Iris Court, Pangbourne from where he managed Menpes Fruit Farm Ltd (c1910-1940), which included the Carnation Nurseries, on Long Lane, Purley.*
MUNNINGS, Sir Alfred James KCVO, RA	*(1878-1959); artist and known as one of England's finest painters of horses; associated with the Newlyn School of painters. During World War One he worked as a vet for Cecil Aldin at the Remount Depot in Purley before being employed as war artist to the Canadian Cavalry Brigade. President of the Royal Academy of Arts 1944-1949.*
NASH, Arthur	*(Born c1885); carter; came to Scraces Farm Cottages from Mapledurham in 1915 with his wife Agnes and family.*
NASH, Alfred (Alf)	*Son of Arthur and Agnes Nash; worked as a ganger on the Purley stretch of the railway.*
NICHOLLS, Albert (Bert)	*Married Daisy Simmonds; foreman builder who lived in Glebe Road. He brought together and led a group of volunteers who built the Memorial Hall.*
POCOCK, Amy	*(1879-1967); born and died Purley. Daughter of William and Elizabeth Pocock and sub-postmistress of the Post Office 1924-1955 where she also sold sweets.*

POCOCK, William the elder	*(1806-1886); born Compton and died Purley; married Esther. Carpenter and wheelwright; lived in Lichfield Cottage and became sub-postmaster of the Post Office.*
POCOCK, William the younger	*(1838-1924); born Pangbourne and died Purley; married Elizabeth. Carpenter and wheelwright; appointed sub-postmaster in 1887; his daughter Amy succeeded him after his death.*
PRYOR, Elizabeth (née Lister)	*Artist who trained at the Slade School of Fine Art. Elizabeth Pryor's parents bought the Old Rectory in Purley and she lived there for most of her life. Mother of Sybil Pryor.*
RAWLINS, Frederick (Fred)	*Moved to Purley in 1929 from Pangbourne. Married Phyllis Leath in 1936 and lived in Well Cottages before the cottages were demolished and then Hemington.*
RAWLINS, Phyllis (née Leath)	*Granddaughter of Henry Leath who was coachman and gardener to Purley Lodge; married Frederick Rawlins.*
RAWLINS, Ronald William	*(1923-1945); son of James and Mary Rawlins of Long Lane, Purley. Served as a trooper in the Royal Tank Regiment in the Second World War and is buried at the Reichswald Forest War Cemetery in Kleve, Germany.*
REPTON, Humphry	*(1752-1818); English landscape gardener, born in Bury St Edmunds, the successor to Lancelot 'Capability' Brown. He worked on a great number of properties, often presenting his recommendations in red, leather-bound books, with water colour illustrations and flaps that could be lifted to reveal 'before' and 'after' views. Repton's recommendations for Purley Magna were not implemented although a plan in his Red Book for the lay-out of farm buildings was followed at Belleisle as well as a front elevation for the farmhouse.*
ROGERS, James	*(1850-1924); born Whitchurch; tenant of a cottage with four rooms in Purley Village (site is now Cherry Acre and Wisteria). Married Susannah Busby in 1872 and had ten children. Gardener and farm labourer.*
SAUNDERS, Frederick (Fred) BEM	*Purley resident for 30 years and Trenthams employee for 50 years. Awarded the British Empire Medal for his services to the Red Cross. His widow planted an oak tree at the junction of Long Lane and Oxford Road in his memory in 1983.*

SHEPPARD, Edward	*(Born c1851); son of William Sheppard (lock-keeper) and his wife Mary Ann. Fisherman; married Sarah Jaggard. They lived in Corner Cottages in Purley Village.*
SHEPPARD, Sarah (née Jaggard)	*(1847-1945); born Brinkley in Cambridgeshire and died Purley. Arrived in Purley c1866 as housemaid in the Rectory; married Edward Sheppard in 1876 and had four daughters and three sons.*
SHEPPARD, William	*(1804-1889); born Streatley and died Purley; married Mary Ann. Keeper at Mapledurham Lock 1824-1889 and rented fishing rights on the river.*
SHERWOOD, Edith Sophia	*(1854-1900); born Pangbourne and baptised in St Mary's Church, Purley; daughter of Edward and Amelia Sherwood. Missionary with the China Inland Mission who was killed at Kiu-chau, Chekiang during the Boxer Rebellion in July 1900. Memorial in St Mary's Church.*
SHERWOOD, Edward	*(1703-1778); yeoman farmer; married Ann Green in 1730. First member of the Sherwood family to move to Purley around 1732. Churchwarden of St Mary's Church 1732-1763.*
SHERWOOD, Revd Edward Purvis	*(1847-1929); born Purley and died Kenilworth; eldest son of Edward and Amelia Sherwood (née Purvis). He married twice, to Frances James in 1872 and Charlotte Smale in 1909. Managing Director of steelworks in Yorkshire; later ordained into the church and became Rector of Baginton, near Coventry in 1911.*
SKUSE, Revd Ernest Edwin	*Graduated from St Joseph's College, Armidale in 1899, the Australian College of Theology in 1900 and the London College of Divinity in 1905. Incumbent at St Saviour's in Stoke-next-Guildford, Wisley with Pyrford, Monk Sherborne with Pamber and Braywood before becoming Rector of Purley 1931-1956.*
SPONG, Ernest	*Churchwarden of St Mary's Church 1952-1970; former landlord of the Bedford Arms in Reading.*
STORER, Cicely Barr (née Willoughby)	*(1832-1918); sixth daughter of Sir John Pollard Willoughby of Oxfordshire, MP for Leominster. Dedicated the east window in St Mary's Church to her sister in 1873.*

STORER, Anthony Morris the elder, MP	*(1746-1799); MP 1774-1784; collector of antique books and prints. Inherited his father's fortune made from sugar plantations in Jamaica and in 1793 purchased Purley Magna. Commissioned Humphry Repton to design a property 'suitable for a gentleman'; left £15,000 in his will for a mansion house to a design by James Wyatt. Purley Park was built c1800. Belleisle Farm was built about the same time and named after the family's plantations in Jamaica. Memorial in St Mary's Church.*
STORER, Major Anthony Morris the younger, JP	*(1813-1902); born and died in Purley Park. Inherited Purley Park in 1818 following the death of his father Anthony Gilbert Storer. Major in Oxford Militia; married in 1860 to Cicely Barr Willoughby and had one daughter, Leila Minna Gertrude. Lord of the manor of Purley Magna.*
STREET, George Edmund RA	*(1824-1881); architect whose works include Cuddesdon College and the Royal Courts of Justice. Undertook rebuilding of churches all over the country including that of Purley in 1870. Professor of Architecture to the Royal Academy of Arts at the time of his death and also president of the Royal Institute of British Architects. Made a knight of the Legion of Honour in 1878. Buried in Westminster Abbey.*
SYKES, Lady Caroline	*(c1844-1929); wife of Sir Frederic Sykes. Lived in Westfield House 1899-c1915.*
SYKES, Sir Frederic Henry	*(1826-1899); born Basildon Park, died in Brighton and was buried in Purley. Baronet; Captain of HM Regiment of 11th Hussars and subsequently of the Royal Horse Guards. Built Westfield House.*
THEOBALD, Bernard Harold	*Born Oxfordshire, married Gwendolyn and served in the Royal Navy during World War Two. Farmer at Westbury Farm from shortly after the end of the war until 1992 during which time he established Westbury Vineyard. District Councillor 1963-1979.*
TIDBURY, Edith Annie (née Buckland)	*(1888 -1973); born Theale and married Herbert Tidbury (stationer of Pangbourne and sexton in Purley) in 1913. Headmistress of Purley Church of England School 1925-1954.*

TRENTHAM, George Donald
(1904-1983); married Doreen Radcliffe. Chairman of G Percy Trenthams 1941-1983. During his leadership the company built the Ford plant at Dagenham as well as growing to become arguably the largest private construction firm in the UK.

VENNERS, Joseph William Henry
(1883-1964); served in the Royal Flying Corps in World War One before going into partnership in 1919 with E Thomas Jackson, automobile engineer, Pangbourne. Purchased agricultural land off Westbury Lane in 1926 and built Purley Rise Farm farmhouse and a number of other houses in Westbury Lane. Established Purley Rise Poultry Farm with his son Kenneth. Married Margaret Rice.

VENNERS, Kenneth Joseph
Son of Joseph and Margaret Venners; married Monica Smith. Established Purley Rise Poultry Farm with his father. Served with the Pangbourne Home Guard and then the RAF during World War Two. Established Venners Caravans in the 1950s.

WHITE, Archie
(1915-1996); husband of Jessie. Lived in Wintringham Way; technician at Imperial College London.

WILDER, Frederick MA
(1833-1899); of Purley Hall; landowner and JP for Berkshire. Born in Tring, Hertfordshire, he was the son of Revd Henry Watson and Augusta Wilder who were drowned in 1836 when their boat capsized off the Isle of Wight. Married three times; to Sarah Fox Hawes in 1861, to Augusta Dorothea Currie, daughter of Arthur Currie in 1873 and Francis Maria Gregg, daughter of Henry Gregg in 1895. Buried in Sulham.

WILDER, Revd Henry Beaufoy MA
(1834-1908), born in Purley Hall; brother of Frederick above. Rector of Sulham and lived in Sulham Rectory. Keen amateur photographer who took many of the photographs of Purley Hall, its home farm and cottages which appear in this book. Married Augusta Christie in 1858 and had three boys and three girls; buried in Sulham.

WILDER, Sarah Fox (née Hawes)
(1830-1871); second daughter of Benjamin Hawes, KCB Permanent Under-Secretary of State for War and the Colonies. Grand-daughter of Sir Marc Isambard Brunel FRS and niece of Isambard Kingdom Brunel FRS. Became the first wife of Frederick Wilder, above.

WYATT, James RA *(1746-1813); architect whose designs include the Pantheon in Oxford Street, London, Bishop Auckland Castle, County Durham and Purley Park. Appointed Surveyor to Westminster Abbey in 1772, Surveyor of the Ordnance c1782 and Surveyor-General and Comptroller of the Works in 1796. Buried in Westminster Abbey.*

Image Acknowledgements

We wish to thank everyone who has made available to Project Purley the images included within this book and in particular the following individuals and organisations. Unfortunately it has not been possible to trace the owners of all of the photographs and we apologise if we have used any material without permission or due acknowledgement.

Ann Betts: 7.14
Martin Bishop: 9.6
John Chapman: 2.15, 3.19, 4.7, 4.34, 5.33, 5.34, 6.17, 6.20, 6.21, 6.22, 7.9
Trevor Cotton: 4.9
George Critchell: 3.21
Stephen Critchell: 3.28, 3.29
Marion Dabbs: 9.38
Patricia Deane: 3.32
Jean Debney: 3.17
Rita Denman: 2.27, 3.8, 3.24, 4.2, 4.3, 4.5, 4.6, 4.8, 4.14, 4.15, 4.16, 6.18, 6.23, 9.9, 9.11, 9.15
John Edwards: 4.32, 6.5, 6.6, 6.7, 6.8
Peter Fullerton: 2.1, 2.2, 2.3, 2.4, 2.6, 2.7, 2.8, 2.9, 2.10, 2.11, 2.12, 2.13, 2.14, 3.1, 4.4, 5.1, 7.10, 7.11, 7.16, 9.2
© Great Western Society (Didcot): 8.5, 8.6, 8.7, 8.8, 8.17, 8.18, 8.19
Phyllis Hasemore: 7.19, 7.20, 8.3, 8.4, 8.21.
Darrell Hicks: 7.8
Jack Iles: 7.7, 9.5, 9.35
© Images & Voices, Oxfordshire County Council: back cover image
© Imperial War Museum: 2.20 (IWM Image may not be copied without the permission of the Imperial War Museum)
Les Jamieson: 8.20
© Judges Postcards Ltd: 7.1
Shirley Lewis: 9.41
Roger Macdonald: 3.3, 3.4
Les Mitchell: 9.31, 9.32
© Museum of English Rural Life: 2.5, 2.32, 3.2, 3.5, 4.1, 4.11, 4.25, 4.27, 4.30, 4.31, 5.10, 5.11, 5.12, 6.15, 8.13, 8.14, 8.15, 8.16

Ian Nash: 2.21, 2.22, 2.23, 2.24, 2.26, 2.28, 3.6, 3.26, 4.10, 4.12, 4.13, 4.17, 4.18, 4.23, 4.24, 4.28, 5.2, 5.3, 5.4, 5.13, 5.15, 5.16, 5.17, 5.18, 5.19, 5.20, 5.21, 5.22, 5.23, 5.24, 5.25, 5.32, 6.9, 6.10, 6.11, 6.12, 7.17, 9.3, 9.8, 9.17, 9.18. 9.23, 9.24, 9.25, 9.30, 9.33, 9.36
Lynette Nicholson (formerly Barnes): 3.10, 3.11, 3.12, 4.29, 8.22, 9.12, 9.16
Paul Pocock: 3.29.
Sybil Pryor: 3.13, 3.14, 9.27
Courtesy of The Reading Chronicle, holder of the copyright www.readingchronicle.co.uk: 9.40
Courtesy Reading Chronicle collection/Reading Museum (Reading Borough Council). All rights reserved: 6.14, 8.11, 9.21, 9.22, 9.34
Catherine Sampson: 2.18, 3.18, 5.7
Gerald Schofield: 7.18
Richard Sherwood: 2.16, 2.17
Robert Skerritt: 8.9, 8.10, 8.23
Henry Scutt: 2.29, 2.30, 2.31, 2.33, 2.34, 2.35, 4.19, 4.20, 4.21, 4.22, 5.5, 5.6, 5.8, 7.2, 7.3, 9.1
Peter Trentham: 6.19, 9.7
Bernard Venners: 5.9, 5.28, 5.29, 5.30, 7.13, 9.26
Ben Viljoen: 2.25
Women's Institute (Purley): 9.10
Betty Wren: 9.29

We also wish to acknowledge the following historic source for image 7.12: William Cooke, The Thames; or Graphic Illustrations of Seats, Villas, Public Buildings and Picturesque Scenery on the Banks of that Noble River, 1811, Vol I, Plate: Purley Hall (sic) - Mr Storer. Engraving (Cooke after Samuel Owen).

Index

C

G

H

I

J

K

L

M

Q

R

S

T

U

V

W

Y